Ideologies in the Age of Extremes

KEEP IN TOUCH WITH PLUTO PRESS

For special offers, author updates, new title info and more there are plenty of ways to stay in touch with Pluto Press.

Our Website: http://www.plutobooks.com

Our Blog: http://plutopress.wordpress.com

Our Facebook: http://www.facebook.com/PlutoPress

Our Twitter: http://twitter.com/plutopress

PlutoPress
www.plutobooks.com

IDEOLOGIES IN THE AGE OF EXTREMES

Liberalism, Conservatism, Communism, Fascism 1914–91

Willie Thompson

PlutoPress
www.plutobooks.com

First published 2011 by Pluto Press
345 Archway Road, London N6 5AA and
175 Fifth Avenue, New York, NY 10010

www.plutobooks.com

Distributed in the United States of America exclusively by
Palgrave Macmillan, a division of St. Martin's Press LLC,
175 Fifth Avenue, New York, NY 10010

British Library Cataloguing in Publication Data
A catalogue record for this book is available from the British Library

ISBN   978 0 7453 2712 9   Hardback
ISBN   978 0 7453 2711 2   Paperback

Library of Congress Cataloging in Publication Data applied for

10   9   8   7   6   5   4   3   2   1

Designed and produced for Pluto Press by
Chase Publishing Services Ltd, 33 Livonia Road, Sidmouth, EX10 9JB, England
Typeset from disk by Stanford DTP Services, Northampton, England
Printed and bound in the European Union by
CPI Antony Rowe, Chippenham and Eastbourne

To the memory of Douglas Bain
1939–2010
Friend and comrade

Contents

Acknowledgements

The idea for this volume emerged out of a History module that I designed and taught at Northumbria University, Newcastle-upon-Tyne. My thanks are therefore due to my former colleagues and students, and others outside the university with whom I discussed the ideas developed here. In this connection, thanks are especially due to Professor Keith Shaw for the organisational assistance which enabled the volume to be completed.

I am extremely grateful for the encouragement and assistance of David Castle, my editor and perceptive critic, at Pluto Press, as well as Anne Beech, Pluto's Managing Director. Thanks also to Myra Macdonald who read the text and made many valuable improving suggestions. All errors of fact and interpretation are, of course, my own.

Abbreviations

AIB	Ação Integralista Brasileira (Brazilian Integralist Action)
AKEL	Anorthotikó Kómma Ergazómenou Laoú (Progressive Party of Working People)
AKS	Akateeminen Karjala-Seura (Academic Karelia Society)
ANI	Associazione Nazionalista Italiana (Italian National Association)
BBC	British Broadcasting Corporation
BJP	Bharatiya Janata Party (Indian People's Party)
BNP	British National Party
BUF	British Union of Fascists
CCF	Congress for Cultural Freedom
CD	Christian Democracy
CDU	Christian Democratic Union
CIA	Central Intelligence Agency
CIO	Congress of Industrial Organizations
CP	Communist Party
CPC	Communist Party of China
CPCz	Communist Party of Czechoslovakia (Komunistická strana Československa, KSČ)
CPGB	Communist Party of Great Britain
CPI (M–L)	Communist Party of India (Marxist–Leninist)
CPSU(B)	Communist Party of the Soviet Union (Bolsheviks), (Kommunisticheskaya Partiya Sovetskogo Soyuza)
CPUSA	Communist Party USA
DC	Democrazia Christiana (Christian Democracy)
DNVP	Deutschnationale Volkspartei (German National People's Party)
ECCI	Executive Committee of the Communist International
EEC	European Economic Community
ELAS	Ellinikós Laïkós Apeleftherotikós Stratós (Greek People's Liberation Army)
EU	European Union
FBI	Federal Bureau of Investigation
G7	Group of Seven (industrialised nations, including Canada, France, Germany, Italy, Japan, the UK and the USA)
GATT	General Agreement on Tariffs and Trade
GDR	German Democratic Republic
GRECE	Groupement de recherche et d'études pour la civilisation européenne (Research and Study Group for European Civilization)

IKL	Isänmaallinen Kansanliike (Patriotic People's Movement)
IMF	International Monetary Fund
IRA	Irish Republican Army
KGB	Komitet gosudarstvennoy bezopasnosti (Committee for State Security)
KPD	Kommunistische Partei Deutschlands (Communist Party of Germany)
LO-S	Landsorganisationen i Sverige (Swedish Trade Union Confederation)
MP	Member of Parliament
MRP	Mouvement Républicain Populaire
MSI	Movimento Sociale Italiano (Italian Social Movement)
NATO	North Atlantic Treaty Organization
NEP	New Economic Policy
NLF	National Liberation Front
NSDAP	Nationalsozialistische Deutsche Arbeiterpartei (National Socialist German Workers' Party, Nazi Party)
NSM	National Socialist Movement
OAS	Organisation de l'armée secrete (Organisation of the Secret Army)
OPEC	Organization of the Petroleum Exporting Countries
PCE	Partido Communista de España (Communist Party of Spain)
PCF	Parti Communiste Français (French Communist Party)
PEN	Poets, Essayists and Novelists
PNF	Partito Nazionale Fascista (National Fascist Party)
PSI	Partita Socialista Italiano (Socialist Party of Italy)
RSDLP	Russian Social Democratic and Labour Party
SA	Sturmabteilung (Storm or Assault Division)
SAP	socialdemokratiska arbetareparti (Social Democratic Labour Party of Sweden)
SPD	Sozialdemokratische Partei Deutschlands (Social Democratic Party of Germany)
SR	Social Revolutionary
SS	Schutzstaffel (Protection Squadron)
UN	United Nations
USA	United States of America
USSR	Union of Soviet Socialist Republics
WACL	World Anti-Communist League
WTO	World Trade Organization

Introduction
Definitions and argument

This volume is concerned with ideology not in general, but in a specific sense – the four dominant political ideologies of the twentieth century – and at a specific time – not the century as a whole, but what Eric Hobsbawm has called 'the short twentieth century', the 'Age of Extremes', the years between the onset of the First World War and the collapse of the Soviet bloc.

The very concept of ideology, an eighteenth-century coinage, is itself highly ambiguous. When originally used by Destutt de Tracy in the late eighteenth century, it was simply intended to mean a science of ideas; subsequently it acquired very different connotations, both positive and negative.

Neutrally defined, ideology could be regarded as an interconnected system or structure of basic belief applicable to particular social or cultural collectives – one which incorporates conscious beliefs, assumptions and unthinking modes of perception – through which its adherents view the world around them, the interactions and the life processes in which they are engaged. The concept is certainly sometimes employed in that sense, but it must be admitted that this is not the most frequent usage or, as Terry Eagleton expresses it, 'Nobody would claim that their own thinking was ideological, just as nobody would habitually refer to themselves as Fatso. Ideology, like halitosis, is in this sense what the other person has.'[1]

Karl Marx in the nineteenth century used it to mean a false consciousness, generally in the sense of the misperception of human creations for natural realities, 'a solution in the mind to contradictions which cannot be solved in practice';[2] in other words, mystification – yet the twentieth-century state which claimed him as its historical inspiration, the Soviet Union, used the term in a positive sense when applied to its own forms of perception and thinking. 'The falsity of bourgeois ideology is not due to its ideological character but rather to its bourgeois origin.'[3] One of communism's bitterest enemies, the rather spooky organisation Moral Re-Armament, took the mirror-image position, declaring around 1960 that the West must adopt an equivalently powerful ideology (that is, Moral Re-Armament) in order to successfully oppose communism.

If ideology is to be treated as a neutral concept, there is a strong argument that the 'commonsense' of any culture – the taken-for-granted framework of assumptions, habits, metaphysical, social and political beliefs – could be regarded as ideology, a mode of consciousness therefore which is all-pervasive, which none of us can escape, no matter whether we are on the left or right of politics, religious believers or committed secularists, cultural sophisticates, football fanatics or celebrity obsessives – or even if we never give a thought to any of these matters.

However, the notion that ideology is a concept that can be applied to anybody anywhere at anytime in all history is something very different from the meaning which it came to take on in the twentieth century, mostly one of negative connotations – and the particular dimension here is one of politics and, more specifically, of political contestation in an arena where what is at stake is not simply the issue of who will ride on the gravy train, but of challenge to or defence of entire social orders.

> In the most general and benign sense, ideology is organized thought – complements of values, orientations, and predispositions forming ideational perspectives expressed through technologically mediated and interpersonal communication ... *But organized thought is never innocent.* [Emphasis added][4]

Rather, it relates to a will to power.

Such a belief-system, in addition to its political thrust, naturally incorporates economic, social and cultural dimensions. For example (although it is not an invariable rule), political conservatives are on the whole likely to favour stability in social relations and traditional forms of artistic production, while political revolutionaries are likely to affirm social and cultural novelty.

THE SHORT TWENTIETH CENTURY

It is four twentieth-century political ideologies that are our concern here – although they necessarily have earlier ancestries. The four that are addressed all lie on the right–left spectrum and each incorporates – in very different ways – what could also be regarded as ideological outlooks such as varieties of religious belief or its absence, misogyny or feminism and, in particular, nationalism. The latter is certainly a pervasive ideological fact of the twentieth century; in some respects, it can be regarded as the most powerful and pervasive modern ideology of them all – when nationalism comes into collision with any competitor, the outcome is usually one of 'no contest'. In 1914, it instantly swamped international socialism; it has been the standby resource of governments and ruling elites facing a serious challenge, and often, too, a ready weapon of their opponents; Ian Kershaw judges 'integral nationalism' to be the chief culprit of the hyper-violent years between 1914 and 1945.[5] However, my argument will be that those ideologies under consideration here are the key political ones; for example, politicised religion may lie either on the left or the right, motivate either biblical conservatives or proponents of liberation theology, and the same is true of nationalism, the property both of Nazis and the Resistance movements which fought them.

Nationalism is far from being overlooked in this volume. The reason it does not have a separate categorisation is that it permeates all the others, and so is constantly being referred to. Ultra-nationalism was invariably a distinguishing mark, with only one minor exception, of all fascist and quasi-fascist movements. Nationalism had been intrinsic to conservative governments and parties throughout Europe – Bismarck used it to outflank his political rivals in the nineteenth century – and in the UK as well, where it took primarily the form of imperial sentiment. Liberalism, with its commitment to the development of civil society and economic if not political internationalism, was perhaps less addicted to the nationalist drug, but this was only a relative difference and what could be more nationalistic than the predominantly liberal (in economic if not in political or cultural terms) society of the USA? Nor was communism exempt. Not only did nationalism, in the years following 1945, provide the main strength of the communist parties in China and South East Asia, but in the USSR itself Stalin mobilised it to support the war effort between 1941 and 1945 (as did the communist resistance movements in occupied Europe), and afterwards did not scruple to use Great Russian nationalism to underpin his politics. Communist parties in Western Europe during the Cold War appealed to anti-American national sentiment.

Readers will also note that the discussion of left wing ideology in this volume is referred to as communism rather than socialism or Marxism, and that by communism is meant the ideology of the regimes emerging from the Russian revolution and/or claiming attachment to its principles, and the non-ruling parties that were ideologically attached to them. That definition is admittedly contentious, and indeed it has been and continues to be fiercely disputed by a variety of parties, groups and individuals that regarded communism as distorted and slighted by the regimes that claimed to embody it.

However, for better or very possibly for worse it was the definition that dominated the age of extremes and is therefore the one which I am using. Moreover, space does not permit an exploration of the dissident collectives that denied the legitimacy of the franchise on the term claimed by the regimes of 'actually existing socialism', though these are referred to where relevant. Equivalent considerations apply to Marxism.

Readers may also feel some initial surprise that communism's principal rival in the left-wing camp, namely social democracy, does not feature in the list. The argument for this is a controversial one, though not entirely novel. It is that what came to be known as social democracy (the term had a very different meaning prior to 1914) evolved during and immediately following the First World War into a species of liberalism and formed the liberal ideology's left wing, carrying with it until the later years of the century some remnants of its origins and oppositional character, but nevertheless firmly fixed within the liberal tradition. The argument will be developed in what follows.

It goes without saying that political definitions of this sort are inevitably fuzzy and can be compared in this respect to the colours of the visible spectrum – at their edges they merge into one another. The terms 'left wing' and 'right wing' are also contentious, but their continued use despite repeated attempts to discard them demonstrates that they apply to real forms of political relationship and are essential to historical understanding.

In addition to parties and ideologies of the left or right, each of these contains within itself a left and a right wing. In the interwar years the inter-penetration of fascists and right-wing conservatives was notorious yet, for example, the dominant elements within British conservatism could hardly be distinguished from right-wing liberals, nor most British social democrats of the Labour Party from left-wing ones. Within social democracy itself, right and left wings co-existed and quarrelled bitterly.

Nevertheless, I shall argue, there are relevant markers that distinguish adherents of these ideologies from each other. Of the four, communism was the most tightly defined. Until the late 1940s, either you accepted the definition of political reality propounded by the Soviet leadership (although desirable, it was not necessary to adopt Marxist theory) or you were no communist – although in 1948 the Yugoslav and, from the 1960s, the Chinese leadership offered an alternative and rival version of communism.

This volume deals with the intellectual foundations of the ideologies under consideration, but its principal concern is to consider their historical application and operation. Theory is discussed, but it is *praxis* which is emphasised.

The revolt of the masses

The centuries of the modern world have been referred to as 'the age of ideology' and those of the twentieth century were over a hundred years in gestation. The left-wing/right-wing distinction derives from a purely accidental circumstance that occurred during the French Revolution and appeared at first sight to be of no great significance. In the revolutionary Convention of 1792, which initiated the Terror, the more radical deputies sat on the high benches to the left of the chairman, and the more traditionalist ones to the right.

The great French Revolution of 1789–94 was not only the culmination of centuries of popular dissension and upper-class infighting, it also set an agenda. For the first time in history the unwashed masses, Edmund Burke's swinish multitude, not only appeared on the scene of social upheaval – they had done so often enough in the past – but emerged, although briefly, as its driving force, with their spokespeople assuming a leading role.

Most centrally, they claimed political equality. The social reverberations were felt around the world. A hundred centuries of subordination and exploitation were denounced and challenged in the name of liberty, equality and fraternity.[6] Of course these concepts were anything but straightforward. If the democratic constitution adopted in 1793 had ever been applied, it is far from certain that the Jacobin revolutionaries would have won the vote. Accordingly, because these had control of the government, it was not applied. Large elements of the masses, both rural and urban, were appalled by the turn of events, so traditional deference and loyalties combined with material shortages and the demands of the revolutionary regime, both material and ideological, to ignite widespread revolts and uprisings in the name of church and monarch.

Revolutionary ideology did not exist when the upheaval commenced in 1789. The elements from which such an ideology could be fashioned, however, were already in the public domain. In symbolism and rhetoric, the revolutionaries were fond of looking back to the classical world – ancient Greece and Rome, especially the latter. More concretely though, the ideas of seventeenth-century opponents of autocracy such as John Locke, the American revolutionaries of two decades beforehand and, eventually, the writings of Jean Jacques Rousseau were structured into a coherent ideology of liberalism.[7]

LIBERALISM

The strength and appeal of liberalism as a revolutionary ideology has to be appreciated. Ultimately it rests on a foundation of the 'possessive individualism' that emerged in seventeenth-century England as a sophisticated commercial society emerged there with legal and political structures to match. In the words of C. B. Macpherson, 'Society consists of relations of exchange between proprietors. Political society becomes a calculated device for the protection of property and the maintenance of an orderly relation of exchange.'[8]

John Locke is generally regarded as having laid the ideological (or philosophical) foundations of liberalism in the late seventeenth century, and it was in his argument closely entwined with economic considerations. According to Macpherson, 'the aim of mercantile policy and of individual economic enterprise was to Locke the employment of land and money as capital'.[9] However, although economic, political and social liberalism can co-exist (and even be declared by their spokespeople to be interdependent), there is an inherent tension between them.

In societies subjected to unaccountable authority, liberalism as an opposition project has extraordinary ideological power. Logically it repudiates, except under tightly defined circumstances, intrusion on citizens' personal behaviour whether by government, private monopoly or self-appointed moral arbitrators. Liberal ideology therefore holds out many tempting attractions – freedom to live one's own life secure from arbitrary impositions or inflictions by social superiors or compulsory deference to them; free choice of personal lifestyles, of occupation, of sexual partners, of ideological commitment; the possibility of bringing pressure upon unsatisfactory government; and, if one is interested in such things, of entry into the market to enhance one's wealth and status. Not surprisingly then, mass movements demanding far-reaching changes have often enough mobilised under liberal banners. Historically, it has been the opposition ideology of first resort. Liberalism's animating principle is that government is essentially contractual – and in principle that contract can be forcibly annulled if government abuses its authority and violates its terms.

Liberalism was therefore the initial ideology of general emancipation from arbitrary government and hereditary privilege, and continued for many decades to fulfil that role. Liberalism's contradictions as an emancipatory ideology, however, were apparent even during the revolutionary years – even more than with an absolutist monarchy, its implications were to put the propertyless at the mercy of property owners, and amongst the first actions of the Jacobins' predecessors *and* successors was to lock the masses out of the political nation[10] by restricting the franchise to significant property-owners. Much of the contradiction arises from the reality of liberalism's two dimensions – as economic liberalism on the one hand and social liberalism on the other.

Liberalism and democracy

The issue of democracy and the demand for a universal (male) franchise therefore represented the first major ideological rift among the opponents of Europe's *ancien régime*, the issue of course being the question of what the masses might do with the vote once they possessed it. In the early nineteenth century this antagonism was at its most apparent and liberals were seldom, if ever, democrats. However, the political scene promises to be a quieter one if the citizenry at large at least believe that they have ultimate control over the government and are enabled to vote a different party into office – even if that choice is limited to different wings of the property party. Therefore, so long as universal franchise does not threaten property it can be tolerated and even has distinct advantages. Over the course of the nineteenth century, elites learned to control the extension of the franchise so that it never threatened property relations or even systems of elite government, and therefore by 1914 several states, including the major ones of France and Germany, operated a universal male franchise in such a manner that what the rulers regarded as public order was not disturbed.

In the twentieth-century liberalism has tended to have a strong association with democracy, and in nineteenth-century Britain the newly-minted Liberal party was characterised jointly by its embrace of free trade on the one hand and franchise extension on the other. However, the relationship of liberalism and democracy has always been an ambiguous and conflictual one. The issue of democracy in the sense of universal franchise was never as simple as was represented either by its proponents or by its enemies.

Economic liberalism can manage perfectly well without democracy and has often done so, starting with the British Empire and the Dixie states of the USA, and working its way through the twentieth century in formations such as fascist Italy, the apartheid South African regime and other regimes of a dictatorial nature. Moreover, economic liberalism tends to generate monopoly and annul the reality of economic liberty both for workforces and consumers. For giant concentrations of capital, political democracy tends to be an inconvenience because it can interfere with their operations, and while it can be controlled by media manipulation, lobbying and other such techniques, resources still have to be devoted to doing that.

On the other hand, the problems of the democratic concept itself are not inconsiderable. So far as direct democracy is concerned, a lynch mob could be regarded as an example. For representative democracy the point is well made that for it to work at state level a basic level of consensus is needed – the losers must have secure confidence not only that the winners will not cut off their heads or reduce them to penury but that after the due passage of time they will have the opportunity to persuade the voters to change the government. As a rule, that degree of consensus is achievable only in societies with significant all-round levels of material prosperity (although the Indian case is an exception). Otherwise the struggle over resources is likely to generate political segmentation in the form of political collectives or parties which regard their rivals not as opponents to debate with but as enemies to be annihilated. This was the basis of the argument developed against democracy in the interwar years by the German conservative jurist Carl Schmitt as Weimar liberalism appeared to be heading towards social collapse and/or communist takeover via electoral processes. The present-day rulers of China might well use it too if they did not feel obliged to continue with a Marxist rhetoric.

These issues by no means exhaust the range of problems. Even under the most favourable circumstances the sheer complexity of modern government, the existence of party machines, internal or external pressures, intrigues or lobbying, all of which are sanctioned by liberal ideology, may act to frustrate the democratic will. The imperfections cannot be denied. However, the last word is probably Churchill's rather disillusioned observation that representative democracy, the epitome of liberal politics, is the worst possible system of government – apart from all the others.

CONSERVATISM

Prior to 1914, in Europe, the UK and to some extent also in the states of Latin America, all to a greater or lesser degree economically liberal societies, the principal political contender against the liberal ideology was conservatism. The term itself was invented only in the 1830s, but its reality had existed for several decades beforehand. To a significant extent it could be characterised as the politics of nostalgia,[11] and the conservative counterpart to Locke, writing over a century later, was Edmund Burke, most famously in his 1790 *Reflections on the Revolution in France*. It was indeed in the reaction of terrified ruling classes and their followers, such as the English 'church and king' mobs, to the events and promise of the French Revolution – particularly the regicide and the episode of the Jacobin Terror – that the mode of thinking that was to become known as conservatism had its origins.

At bottom, conservatism originated in an ideology of social classes and status groups whose income was derived from landownership and/or the connected traditional institutions such as the church or officer corps, and for whom alteration of the status quo was anathema. As a party name, however, 'Conservative' was devised in the mid-1830s by Robert Peel,[12] following the use of the term 'conservative' by French reactionaries, to signify that his Tory Party would not try to reverse the constitutional innovations made in the aristocratic British constitutional system by its proto-liberal Whig rivals. Instead it would 'conserve' as much as possible of the existing social and as much as feasible of the political structures while being prepared to acknowledge some necessity for minimal reform when scandals became particularly outrageous. Conservatives, too, were happy enough in the main to uphold the sanctity of market relations against objections from the lower orders.[13]

Except in the UK and in Germany (where it was dropped after 1918) the term was not much used as a party label, but the sentiments embodied in it were prevalent among substantial minorities in all of the leading states. Depending on local peculiarities, conservatism might have a distinctively liberal tinge (as in the UK) or an intensely reactionary one (as in France). Its basic principle could be defined as a reverence for traditional hierarchies (preferably validated by divine sanction) and a dislike of economic or social change which might disturb them and lead on to revolutionary horrors. The more intelligent conservatives of all countries, recognising that these changes were unstoppable, followed Peel's prescription and tried to adjust to them politically and to minimise their social impact. Not surprisingly, liberals and conservatives alike hated and dreaded the insurgent labour movement of the turn of the century and frequently formed uneasy coalitions to resist its demands; the great exception – again – being the UK, where both the Liberal and Conservative parties strove to co-opt it, the former with much greater success.

A bird in the hand

Keeping in mind the attraction of liberalism as a political and social emancipatory ideology, it is important not to neglect the appeal, (so far as it is rational, for obscurantist prejudice is very important too) of popular conservatism. Essentially it is based on the 'bird in the hand' principle. If people are living on the margin, significant change to their life circumstances may well be for the worse; even the possibility of a better outcome may not be enough to outweigh the risk of disaster if things go badly. Peasant societies, unless in exceptional circumstances, are as a rule notoriously traditional and conservative both socially and technologically – and they have reason to be, for unsuccessful experimentation there can mean starvation.

The modern world is one of constant and perpetual change, which is why we regard it as the modern world, and far-reaching change whether in hunter-gatherer, peasant or industrial societies usually means bad news for a lot of people – and it is not only material change which is in question. If institutions and practices that provide meaning to life, explain the universe and the individual's place within it, or even simply supply recreation and enjoyment, are uprooted or placed under threat in the name of progress or emancipation, the reaction is likely to be fierce and determined. The same is particularly true if immemorial relations between parents and children or men and women are challenged.

In the European medieval centuries, or many peasant societies into the early twentieth century, landlord oppression precipitated revolt and rural uprisings. As often as not (there were exceptions, for the Christian religion also had a heritage of apocalyptic expectation) these insurrections focused upon the demand for restoration of the 'good old times' (and usually appealed to the monarch over the head of the local oppressor). In other words, they exhibited a conservative frame of mind.

The strategy of modern conservatism has been to link such fears and mentalities with defence of a social structure which retains authority (and property) in the hands of the powers-that-be, and advance a rhetoric that connects elite privilege with concern for the welfare of the common people and promises change, if change there must be, *within* recognised and therefore apparently 'safe' structures. An underlying theme of twentieth-century conservatism has been 'integralism', frequently in connection with the Catholic church, a vision of a society based on mutual obligation between social classes so that the lower orders would fulfil their duties towards god and the church, society and their betters, and these in turn, animated by religion and/or honour, would protect the welfare of their charges against material or cultural disruption. This particular theme is examined in greater detail below.

COMMUNISM/SOCIALISM

The contradictions in liberal ideology even at its most democratic resulted by the middle of the nineteenth century in the appearance in Europe of a new ideology which stigmatised liberalism as the class ideology of the property-owning bourgeoisie and proclaimed itself to be openly class-based while also claiming universality. That was socialism, particularly in its Marxist variant. In the middle of the century Marx and Engels's famous *Communist Manifesto* proclaimed the approaching political rule of the industrial proletariat, with their political vanguard being the communists, whom they distinguished from the socialists of the time, regarded as utopians unaware of class conflict. With the fierce reaction by establishments to the unsuccessful 1848 revolutions 'communist' was too dangerous or provocative a term to use and was replaced with 'social democracy' (that is, democracy was not to be purely political) or, more simply, with the older term, 'socialism'.

Industrialisation throughout Europe in the second half of the nineteenth century, while varying in intensity, everywhere produced an industrial labour movement among whom the socialist ideology was principally based, though it has to be emphasised that significant numbers of industrial workers, even in Germany, where it was most solidly grounded, remained outside that ideology's orbit and many socialists, especially among the leadership of its parties, were not industrial workers.

Throughout continental Europe, with the exception of the Russian Empire where it remained outlawed and underground, the labour movement, though politically oppositional, had been co-opted and culturally incorporated. At the same time it continued to maintain the posture of intransigent political confrontation, with democracy proclaimed as a mere stepping-stone to the ultimate socialist commonwealth. Appearances, however, were deceptive. The individual labour movements in the different countries had grown in size, had acquired property, had established legal political parties, trade unions, retail and manufacturing co-operatives, newspapers and journals, youth organisations, women's organisations, organisations for every manner of social activity – each of which had generated extensive bureaucracies and resources and all of which would be severely jeopardised by any kind of serious revolutionary threat or endeavour.

Naturally their leaders, whether they admitted it or not, were forced to take account of these realities. In Germany, at the beginning of the twentieth century, Eduard Bernstein, the intellectual father of what came to be known as revisionism, wanted them to admit it and accept that Marx's schemata were out of date: the Sozialdemokratische Partei Deutschlands (SPD, German Social Democratic Party) and the labour movement's international organisation, the Socialist International condemned his ideas. The leading theoretician of German socialism, Karl Kautsky, tried to square the circle by declaring that his party, the SPD, was certainly revolutionary – but not revolution-making.

Others recognised and bitterly resisted this drift of events. Apart from the still lively anarchist tradition, continuing strong in southern Europe and the Russian empire, the tendency within the SPD represented most forcefully by Rosa Luxemburg[14] fought vehemently against the quiet sidelining of Marx's revolutionary perspectives. Both factions of Russian Social Democracy, Bolsheviks and Mensheviks, remained committed to uncompromising revolution though they disagreed radically on what that should mean. Minor socialist parties elsewhere such as the Socialist Labor Party in the USA and its namesake in the UK shared similar attitudes. However, in certain countries, and most especially in the Anglo-Saxon world, easily the most formidable revolutionaries of the early century were the syndicalists. They despised orthodox trade unionism and orthodox politics. Their focus was upon industrial workers – they aimed at *industrial* in place of *trade* unionism and the eventual formation of 'one big union' which by means of the general strike would overthrow the bourgeoisie and establish workers' power, exercised by councils of workers, in the workers' state. In the USA, France, the UK and Australia, they established a serious degree of support, either directly or through influence inside existing unions, especially those of the British miners. Their outlook made a significant contribution to twentieth-century communism, which emerged from the crucible of the war.

FASCISM

Another challenger emerging from the war was fascism. The concept and the name were destined to have a far-reaching and infamous future, though very few of the parties and movements which history recognises as belonging to the fascist category actually used that title (the British example was an exception). Representing something dramatically new (the alternative name for the British Union of Fascists was the Modern Movement) – even newer than Leninism, which was a development of Second International socialism – though the prejudices which it mobilised were anything but modern, above all, fascism was the outcome of crisis – the crisis of the war and subsequent social turmoil, of economic collapse and cultural angst. However, it had proto-fascist predecessors and, because few organisations actually used the fascist name, it is notoriously difficult to draw the boundaries between fascist ideology and that of ultra-right-wing conservatism – readers may disagree with some of my placements of particular ideologies and movements in this respect.

THE DELUGE AND AFTER

Prior to 1914 three great political ideologies of the day, which also incorporated social and cultural values, were the only ones of much consequence, although bitter conflict could well exist inside their respective frameworks. The war that erupted in that year was not ideological in any sense. With the exception of Russia, all the European states involved were more or less liberal in their economic order and to a degree in their social structures. In its representative institutions, Germany was in form if not in substance hardly less democratic than the UK. The British and French governments felt no discomfort in allying themselves with the autocratic and ultra-reactionary Tsar.

It has been a frequent trope of twentieth-century historians to call into question many of the popularly recognised turning points in history – to demonstrate that they were much less sudden and much more drawn out than previously assumed, and that possibly not a great deal changed in any case. Not even the most sceptical, however, doubt that the year 1914 really did initiate a new era in world history. Five years later, at least 30 million people had died in the conflict and its violent aftermath; vast social and cultural changes followed in its wake. Europe and Asia echoed to the crash of falling empires, four in all, three of them centuries old; the world's economy was wrenched from its sockets; the overseas empires of the west European powers (apparently at their apogee) were fatally undermined; the dreaded forces of the industrial labour movement, infected with revolutionary fervour, were on the march across the globe – or at least appeared to be. The world of the previous era was gone forever, though of course many parts of it remained standing even if severely battered.

Did it have to be like that? Probably not. Between 1815 and 1914, Europe was afflicted by no general war; those which did occur were brief, confined to few belligerents, and civilian casualties were relatively light. At the outbreak of what was to become the Great War a repeat was expected, and that was very nearly what happened. The Germans came very close to winning the war in the first few weeks, and had they succeeded the history of the remaining century would have been very different.

What made the difference was that neither side could win outright, industrialised military technology not only produced unprecedented casualties running into millions on the front lines but also drew the entire populations of the belligerent powers into the vortex – enforcing their mobilisation to supply the sacrifice of their young men for cannon fodder and their labour for the manufacture of munitions, to cause their economies, their social habits and their expectations to suffer disruption and their civil liberties to be dispensed with to suppress complaint. In short, total war.

In the end the UK and France with the eventual support of American troops emerged as the military winners, but whatever the outcome and whichever side had been the victor, the framework of European society and politics was shattered beyond repair and the experience had generated profound transformations in social mentality and culture. '[T]he First World War broke the liberal order into pieces', is how John Gray puts it. The war profoundly altered and influenced mentalities along with material and social realities. In the circumstances of the time liberal ideology lost its aura as a self-evident interpretation of reality to its adherents (as did traditional conservatism) – what had been the dominant ideologies of pre-war Europe were subjected to forceful challenge.

Ideologies and the years of catastrophe

In little more than 20 years, the Great War became the First World War, the Second, between 1939 (or 1941) and 1945 being one fought with even greater ferocity in Europe and across the globe, with scores of millions of untimely deaths, the majority non-combatants. Following this, the planet lived for four and a half decades with the imminent prospect of nuclear calamity and extermination (not yet entirely vanished).

During the time between the collapse of the nineteenth-century world-order and the emergence of the 'New World Order' (the phrase was briefly and optimistically in circulation) following the final collapse of the USSR and its bloc together with the submission of the other major communist power, China, to market-driven globalisation, world affairs were dominated by political and social movements which were, in historical terms, unusually self-conscious regarding their ideological foundations and character (though they might not like to recognise them as such). These were embodied not only in political parties and their auxiliary collectives but also through cultural formations, intellectual disseminators and – in many cases – states, which had as their purpose the transformation of the world on a universal or at least geopolitical basis. At the same time they were opposed by similar institutions defending the status quo, which were compelled by that challenge to define more clearly their own ideological character. The characterisation by J. Arch Getty of ideologies of this sort is apposite (it is written with particular reference to the Stalinist Terror):

> Like religion, ideologies are 'systems of interacting symbols, as patterns of interworking meanings.' Ideology is, therefore, a kind of template or a 'perspective' or 'orientational necessity' for organizing and shaping a complicated reality. And because ideologies are inherently advocative, they 'transform sentiment into significance and so make it socially available.'[15]

Our concern in the following chapters will be to explore and interpret the ideologies referred to above, which dominated the age of extremes and especially to establish the realities of social action which link them to the circumstances of their time.

I

Age of catastrophe 1914–45

1
Economic and social developments

The guns of international conflict and slaughter finally fell silent in November 1918, but certainly not those of revolution (both social and national), counter-revolution and bilateral national bloodlettings. Sometimes these conflicts were combined – Romanian troops invaded Hungary both to help suppress a communist regime and to seize large territories. The Poles, having already fought the Germans on their western frontier, invaded Soviet Russia aiming to do the same as the Romanians in Hungary; in response, the Soviets counter-invaded Poland with the purpose of spreading the Revolution (and, had the Red Army been successful, would have carried on to Berlin). The Habsburg Empire broke apart – very roughly into its national components; contrariwise, the Serb monarchy established what was in effect a Balkan empire in the guise of a national state. All the new national states contained significant minorities of alien and/or hostile ethnicity.[1]

Social-revolutionary and counter-revolutionary conflicts were if anything even more desperate and bloody than predominantly national ones. The Bolsheviks, having established their power, immediately found themselves faced with civil war and foreign invasion intent on destroying them. Fighting and massacre cost millions of lives, to be followed by famine and even cannibalism, and the Soviets had to solicit foreign charitable assistance. Contrary to every expectation on the part of the Soviet leaders the Revolution failed to spread westwards, although it inspired sufficient emulation to result in ramshackle Soviet regimes seizing power in Bavaria and Hungary. Both were crushed with the utmost savagery, the Hungarian counter-revolutionaries executing, in the words of an American author, everyone they could catch 'who was red or pink or just a little bit too flesh-coloured'.[2] Elsewhere in Germany, including the capital, attempted left-wing uprisings were repressed with much slaughter. Outright civil war raged in newly-independent Finland, with, in proportion to its population, a massive death-roll.

Even the victorious belligerents of Western Europe did not escape the national, political and social upheavals. Guerrilla war, rural and urban, erupted in Ireland, with the loss of three quarters of the island to the revolutionaries, apart from some bitterly resented concessions by them which were subsequently annulled. The mainland was rocked by industrial unrest, army mutiny[3] and police strikes, all of which the government overcame only by a well-devised mixture of manoeuvre and coercion. The country's political map was redrawn and one of its great parties irretrievably wrecked. France, apart from the armed nationalist insurrection, experienced similar developments;

the defeat of a threatening labour movement even being described as an 'industrial Marne'.[4]

It is a striking irony of history that it was at this point that, following the peace settlement of 1919 (intended as much to isolate Soviet Russia as to conclude the war), the formal empires of the victorious Entente powers, Britain and France, were enhanced to the maximum extent they ever reached. This was achieved at the expense of the defeated Central Powers, Germany and Turkey. The former was stripped of all its colonies, which were then divided among the victors – as well as a significant proportion of its metropolitan territory, population and economic potential, these to the gain of Poland, France, Denmark and Belgium. Turkey, now a republic, lost all its Arab imperial provinces and was left only with the relatively ethnically homogenous Anatolian core and corner of the southeast Balkans. Yet it was the same war that had produced these colonial spoils, along with the war's by-product, the Russian Revolution, which nevertheless focused and propelled the growth of the colonial nationalist movements which would eventually destroy the empires and of which the Irish events were a foretaste; while in Europe the redrawn borders stoked up the fury of national resentment on the part of the losers and constituted a longstanding pretext for the threat or actuality of military action.

THE WORLD ECONOMY

Into this maelstrom of blood and disruption exploded an economic crisis the likes of which had not been experienced since the industrialisation process transformed the globe. The European victors had accumulated vast war-related debts; the USA was the universal creditor and it was not disposed to be indulgent. Not only did it insist on repayment, it raised tariff barriers and choked off immigration, thus shutting off the social safety valve which had helped to preserve European stability during the nineteenth century. The victor powers tried to cover their debts by exacting reparations from their late enemies (or, in the Austrian case, what was left of it), thereby driving the latter's economies into total ruin and triggering the notorious hyperflation which destroyed the German currency in 1923 and left a residue of middle-class social bitterness that contributed to the strength of the political ultra-right, represented at this stage principally by the German National People's Party, the Deutschnationale Volkspartei (DNVP).

The economic devastation of Soviet Russia was immeasurably greater than anything encountered in central or western Europe and, in addition, it largely withdrew from the world economy in order to pursue its own course. It also repudiated all of the Tsarist-era debts, with devastating effect on the investors who had financed them (which in France included a substantial swathe of the lower middle classes as well as the wealthy).

An undercurrent in the world economy which might well have prevailed anyway, regardless of the war or its outcome, was a long-term cheapening (or, in market terms, over-production) of primary (agricultural and extractive) products in relation to industrial goods. The outcome was a vicious circle in the exchange relations between the two sectors. Thanks to falling incomes, the primary producers could not expand their consumption of manufactured products and the industrial producers consequently could not expand their sales. For capitalism, growth is everything; stagnation means disaster.

In the course of the 1920s much of the world was gripped in a decade-long recession, with the primary producers the worst hit. Of course this was not uniform in place or time, and there were exceptions. The USA experienced a few years of overheated and precarious stock-market boom. Some industries enjoyed relative success by capturing the markets of less efficient producers – Indian cotton manufacture and Japanese shipbuilding were examples. Germany made a partial recovery from 1924 until 1929 by means of US loans on special terms. In Britain, the older, inefficient export industries of coal, shipbuilding, cotton manufacture, steel making and locomotive manufacture were crippled, with severe unemployment resulting, while newer industries dependent on internal consumer markets, such as chemicals and chemical products, electricity and electrical goods and motor vehicles, did moderately well thanks to rising middle-class real incomes consequent on cheapened foodstuffs and raw materials.

Economic catastrophe

In October 1929, economic disaster toppled over into catastrophe when the Wall Street stock market, overstuffed with dodgy paper assets,[5] crashed spectacularly. The banking system, overhung with unsound loans based on nothing but rapidly evaporating confidence, was the first to feel the impact as their creditors defaulted and bank failures spread across the USA. Before long, the calamity extended to Central Europe where short-term loans offered after the restoration of the German currency were now called in without notice and the collapse of major Austrian and German banks duly followed. Industry and agriculture on a massive scale soon collapsed into bankruptcy. Farmers overloaded with debt[6] found their farms foreclosed as securities; industrial and white-collar unemployment rocketed. In the words of Franz Neumann's classic analysis of the Nazi regime, *Behemoth*,

> Only a small fraction received unemployment insurance and an ever larger proportion received no support at all.
> ...
> [T]here were hundreds of thousands who had never held jobs. Unemployment became a status, and, in a society where success is paramount, a stigma. Peasants revolted in the north where large estate owners cried for financial assistance. Small businessmen and craftsmen faced destruction. House-owners could not collect their rents. Banks crashed and were taken over by the federal government. Even the stronghold of industrial reaction, the United Steel Trust was near collapse and its shares were purchased by the federal government at prices far above the market quotation. The budget situation became precarious. The reactionaries refused to support a

large-scale works programme lest it revive the declining power of the trade unions, whose funds were dwindling and whose membership was declining.[7]

With American and Central European markets in slump and total disarray, primary product prices plummeted around the world; primary producers strove to offset collapsing prices by stepping up production, a counter-productive endeavour, for that only cheapened these products even more. In all the industrial countries, unemployment grew prodigiously. In the UK during the worst year, 1932, it reached a quarter of the workforce and in Germany it was even more severe. Even so, the advantages that the UK enjoyed in the 1920s continued to cushion it against the worst, whereas Germany enjoyed none of those. The Soviet Union, of course, was the only large area of the world's surface completely unaffected by what was going on outside its borders, because it was pursuing a wholly different economic path and, on the face of things, enjoying great success in its industrial drive and growth. That naturally was part of its attraction to many outside its territory who reckoned that such a system might be worth copying, while equally repelling others who dreaded such a prospect.

Rickety recovery

Elsewhere, following three years of utter global economic chaos, a degree of recovery began to show itself; a part of this – although it is impossible to say how great a part – being due to intervention by governments inspired by a range of different motives and coming from different and even hostile ideological directions. The United States saw the institution of the New Deal programmes following Roosevelt's assumption of the presidency in January 1933; in Sweden, Social Democrat-dominated coalitions operated counter-cyclical economic policies; even in the UK a very modest measure of government intervention was tried – for example, the establishment of agricultural marketing boards. Most spectacularly, the German economy was switched from deep slump to rapid growth, based on the destruction of the labour movement both trade union and political, and a drive to war-preparedness with imperial objectives, a drive based on very unsound foundations that might be described as a kind of autarchic militarised Keynesianism. A good part of the Swedish success was due to the markets (especially for iron ore) created in Germany. The Italian and Japanese regimes had already embarked on imperial adventures, destabilising the rickety structure of international relations put in place following the Great War.

By 1939, the recovery everywhere was running out of steam and a new cycle of slump was on the horizon, while the German war-orientated economic 'miracle' was running into insuperable contradictions only resolvable by new acquisitions of cheap land, labour and raw materials. Given the ideological outlook of the Nazi rulers, it was all too apparent where this was leading: German colonisation in Eastern Europe was absolutely central to Hitler's mental framework.[8] Had he not been in power in Germany and compelled his enemies to mobilise their own resources for war, further economic disruption and intense social conflict were highly predictable in Europe and the USA.

WORLD WAR

In the event, however, a different and even more deadly form of conflict was the outcome of the Nazis' imperial ambitions, with the paradoxical result that while the First World War had triggered the ruin of a flourishing and stable global economic system, the Second restored to ultimate prosperity one which was in a state of chronic paralysis.

All the main belligerents resorted to central direction and allocation of resources – raw materials, plant and labour – to support the war effort, even to a degree in the USA. For the Soviet Union of course the principles were the same as those which had been applied for over a decade previously with war production now the priority. The other belligerent which came closest to the command economy model was actually the UK, in spite of the framework of private ownership being maintained, with production, raw materials, consumption and labour being strictly regulated The regulation included the conscription of categories of single young women either to labour or the auxiliary military services.

A war economy certainly solved the unemployment problem in the UK, as had a militarised one in 1930s Germany. The problem was now labour shortage rather than its opposite. War demand also pulled the USA out of depression and threatened slump. Even before the USA entered the war, it had been a vital supplier of foodstuffs and raw materials as well as manufactures to the British war economy – not neglecting to strip British capitalism of its overseas assets in payment.[9] After December 1941, this was greatly extended and, in addition to the USA's own war effort, the British and Soviet allies were being supplied as well through the mechanism of lend-lease – essentially free deliveries paid for by the US government. US industry recovered and thrived, and, of course, it also avoided the severe damage inflicted on the UK and the utter devastation that overtook Central Europe and the USSR. Indeed, the conclusion of the war left the USA even more the universal creditor than it had been in 1919 and the only major state with a flourishing industrial base, as well as enjoying total military dominance over everyone else apart form the severely battered USSR.

The social context

Not since the seventeenth century had Europe, let alone the wider world, experienced anything remotely similar to the social disruption and horror produced by these events – indeed, the Judeocide carried out by the Nazis during the Second World War has no parallel anywhere in history even in the holocausts of Genghis Khan, Timur the Lame or the exterminations of pre-twentieth-century imperialism. Somewhere between 80 million and 100 million people had their lives prematurely terminated between 1914 and 1945 as a direct consequence of political-military actions. The nearest equivalent in proportional, though not absolute, terms was the Black Death of the fourteenth century.

The novel feature, however, was that in the main these catastrophes fell upon societies that were industrialised, highly integrated and with advanced levels of social culture in terms of literacy and education; not societies that were basically agricultural, generally illiterate and loosely integrated. Unprecedented pressures of hunger, distress, fear, insecurity and disillusionment, combined at times with fervent and apocalyptic hope, produced novel forms of perception and thinking, many of them previously unthinkable and unimaginable. Previously unknown and marginal organisations and figures emerged from obscurity to occupy centre stage.

GERMANY

Because Germany was to be the storm centre of the first half of the twentieth century, it is appropriate to begin the examination there. There is some degree of historical argument over how extensive enthusiasm really was for the declaration of war in August 1914, but it seems beyond question that nationalist indoctrination in the schoolroom[10] and barracks (Imperial Germany, like most European states, used peacetime conscription) had produced a general popular sentiment of warm support. The majority of Social Democrats fell into line, portraying it as a defensive war against Russian imperial tyranny. Certainly all the elements of the ruling classes and considerable layers of the middle classes were thirsting for conquest and envisaged enormous territorial gains. Among the elites, plans were drawn up for extensive territorial acquisitions in both western and central Europe and the imposition of German hegemony over the continent – a project evidenced both in the documentary record[11] and in the Brest-Litovsk Treaty they imposed upon defeated Russia in the spring of 1918.

Great success was indeed gained upon the Eastern Front, but the stalemate and slaughter in the west continued relentlessly and the allied blockade combined with the material demands of the war exposed the population to severe shortages and hunger[12] – although nothing so extreme as the century was to see later in other theatres of war. War weariness and discontent built up, expressed in extensive strikes from the early months of 1918 and exploding finally in the revolution of November 1918 that ended the war and overthrew the monarchy.

The Russian precedent was only a year old, and further developments made it apparent that a thoroughgoing revolutionary mood existed among substantial sections of the urban workforce. Nevertheless, events made it equally clear that this mood was not shared even by the overwhelming majority of the proletariat let alone other social classes. That majority continued to adhere to the socialist leaders who had used patriotic rhetoric to support the war from the first day, abandoning the earlier commitments of the International to strive to bring it to an end as speedily as possible (the war was no unexpected cataclysm – it had been foreseen for at least a decade). These leaders, prompted by the military, were reluctantly pushed into responsibility for the state – most of them did not even want to dispense with the monarchy. Their horizons were limited to a fully democratic political system and less restrictive conditions for the labour movement, especially a legally enforceable eight-hour working day and the right to consultation on managerial decisions.

Their hesitation is understandable. The German labour movement, as indicated in the Introduction, had built up enormous assets, all of which would be seriously imperilled by further social upheavals. Moreover, all-out revolution is a very dangerous business for the participants and their families, easily resulting in death or long-term imprisonment, exile and destitution if things go wrong. Even if they go right, revolutions have a nasty habit of devouring their own children, so there was every personal incentive to calm things down, conciliate the classes which had been immediately disadvantaged by events and restore a measure of stability. The *Räte*, the councils set up in imitation of the Russian soviets, were soon marginalised, sidelined and dissolved without much difficulty.

After the conclusion of hostilities, the rank and file of the army largely disintegrated – not to pursue revolutionary courses, but to get home for Christmas. The high command, however, drawn almost exclusively from the landowning classes, remained intact – even if its moving spirit, Ludendorff, fled in panic – and from the most intransigent elements of the frontline officers (again, principally of a landowning background) recruited a corps of trained and well-armed counter-revolutionaries, the Freikorps, which the new Social Democrat government used, along with such disciplined army units as remained, to crush the attempted left-wing revolutions in Berlin, Bavaria and elsewhere.[13] From 1919 onwards, the army, to the extent allowed by the Versailles treaty, was soon reconstituted – small, but perfectly adequate for shooting communists, which it did in the suppression of further revolutionary attempts in 1921 and 1923.

Outside the cities, the peasantry – except, perhaps, the landless labourers on the Junker estates of eastern Prussia – remained solidly reactionary in their social outlook and deeply attached to their Protestant or Catholic conservative religious sentiments. Of all the disadvantages the German revolutionaries faced, this, so much in contrast to Russian conditions, was probably the greatest and it is clear in hindsight that social conditions gave them no chance. The position in the truncated Austrian and Hungarian states was no different, and history in Germany repeated itself in Hungary in even bloodier form, this time taking the form of full-scale civil war. Once again the revolutionary social base, confined largely to Budapest, was wholly inadequate and the communist revolutionaries had no hope of winning, even without the intervention of the Romanian forces against them. Austria at this time avoided actual full-scale armed conflict, but events left behind a legacy of social antagonism exceeded only in Germany.

That was severe enough in the immediate aftermath. The frontline soldiers who felt themselves cheated of victory, were incapable of accepting that the magnificent German army could have been militarily defeated. The officer corps particularly, but plenty of others as well – Hitler, after all, was only a lance corporal – did not take long to embrace the *Dolchenstoss* legend, that victory was within the army's grasp when it had been stabbed in the back by treacherous communists and Jews, the 'November criminals' in Hitler's elegant phrase, which made them boil with hatred against all associated with that abortive revolution. Apart from their 'we wuz robbed' obsession, they also faced, in place of anticipated victory honours and promotion, the material reality of unemployment and hardship – only 100,000 soldiers were permitted by the Allies – and, for the officers, a humiliating loss of caste.

Their sentiments were easily shared by all levels of the German middle classes, who, apart from the brief phase of national solidarity at the war's outbreak, had always detested the labour movement – and worse was to come. Political turbulence including frequent assassinations, violent private armies, re-invasion by the French in 1923 (to enforce reparations), currency collapse followed by semi-recovery and renewed economic collapse, parliamentary deadlock – all led to a polarisation of hatred between right and left such as was seen in no other major country.

Between 1929 and 1933, forces basing themselves on total rejection of the republic advanced rapidly in support. On the right, Hitler's National Socialists were an essentially lower-middle-class phenomenon,[14] although they managed to incorporate a substantial working-class element, especially in their paramilitary wing, the Sturmabteilung (SA), and an upper-class one as well – these men predominated among the second-rank leaders. Their gains were made largely at the expense of the 'respectable' reactionary party, the DNVP, especially when the Nazis won the support of the peasantry suffering large-scale eviction, and for whom the DNVP, committed to market dogma, could do or promise nothing. This gave them in 1930 their parliamentary breakthrough and signalled the beginning of the end for the republic. On the left, the communists, the Kommunistische Partei Deutschlands (KPD), made steady gains at the expense of the Social Democrats, outvoting them in Berlin by 1932, and would have been even more successful but for their own errors. Their growth had a lot to do with the growing unemployment crisis, for the unemployed proved to be the communists' main constituency – the SPD tended to retain the loyalties of those manual workers who held on to their jobs. In the last analysis it was more than anything else fear of the communist success which produced the deal between the social elites and the Nazi leaders which manoeuvred Hitler into power in January 1933.

Having seized the state, the Nazis proceeded to utterly annihilate the labour movement, abolish all other parties (even those of their right-wing allies) and outlaw any kind of political activity apart from their own. Nevertheless Hitler, mindful of November 1918, was at pains to maintain at least a minimal level of consumer satisfaction for all social classes (full employment helped greatly with this) and that policy was even maintained up to the closing stages of the war; while for the educated and upper layers of German society magnificent job opportunities opened up in the ever-expanding state bureaucracy.[15]

OTHER EUROPEAN STATES

No other country in Europe had an experience comparable to the German one, not even the only other indigenous – and indeed the original – fascist regime, namely Italy. What they all faced, in one manner or another and in the context of generalised economic breakdown, was a political, social and cultural challenge from the 'lower orders' to the social elites which had dominated European economy, society and politics until 1914 in spite of all the advances in formal democracy which had taken place in the context of industrial transformation.[16] The challenge was worked out in a variety of developments – much depending on the respective degrees of economic stability and character of the political system. Three examples: the Scandinavian countries, with relatively high living standards and relatively modest social differentiation managed, with the exception of Finland, an unusually (though not entirely) peaceful resolution; the UK (apart from Ireland), a constitutional though conflict-ridden outcome; while in Hungary, Finland, the Irish Free State and Spain, it meant civil war. The others experienced various degrees of violence – moderate in France, despite its revolutionary traditions, intense in Italy, Austria and Romania.

THE SOVIET UNION

Matters were totally different in the former Russian Empire, from 1924 termed the Soviet Union. This was not only because of the enormous losses from the civil war and subsequent famine, estimated to have been as much as five million, but urban society had been torn apart. The two principal cities – and these had been spared the worst of the fighting – St Petersburg/Petrograd/ Leningrad and Moscow had lost from 40 to 60 per cent of their populations through death, military conscription and abandonment by the citizens to take refuge with their rural relatives. Industry had virtually come to a standstill; inflation was rampant. Yet the country was overwhelmingly a peasant one and the peasantry, in spite of massacre, famine, seizure of their goods and product remained, following their centuries-old rhythms and routines – and it was their marginal preference for the Bolsheviks over their enemies which was the principal reason for the former's victory.

At the end of the war, and having then shown their teeth with peasant insurrections, they got their reward: possession of the land (formally it belonged to the state) and an open although regulated market in their product.[17] Social differentiation rapidly followed – a minority of the more successful soon came to control larger acreages than their neighbours, accumulate assets, dominate the villages, employ their less fortunate or less diligent brethren and become the principal mainstay of the country's agriculture. They were known as 'kulaks', a Russian word meaning 'a fist'.

In what was left of the country's industry, 'workers' control' proved a disaster, as the leading Bolshevik A. G. Shlyapnikov complained in March 1918, 'The disorganization and demoralization that prevail in the railway shops defy description .... In a word, the moment the railway employees were granted a minimum wage they ceased to display any minimum degree of efficiency.'

'One man management' was therefore reinstituted – not that there were many capable managers to be found, and those that were naturally had to be rewarded appropriately. Trotsky wanted to put the workforce under military discipline, but this proposal was rejected. Trade unions were, of course, regarded as indispensable in a workers' state, so they were given a high formal status but were in reality more a means of controlling the workforce than representing it. Nevertheless, they had at this stage a certain degree of manoeuvre and their leaders, like Tomsky, if they were energetic and committed, could exercise some influence with management and the Party.

'War Communism' was the term applied to the regime prevailing in Soviet-controlled areas during the Civil War. It gave the Party-controlled government total control over all food surpluses and total direction over all other production and over distribution, with a strict system of rationing. The market was effectively abolished. It was intended by most Bolshevik leaders as an emergency measure since they lived in expectation of revolution in the West which would solve their problems (though they had no clear idea of exactly how they would organise rebuilding of the country supposing the expectation was realised).

There were some in the Party leadership, however, who argued that this form of organisation could be made permanent and thereby, once the material basis was restored, open the door to a full-blown communist society, as 'welcome and timely steps on the road to socialism', in the words of E. H. Carr.[18] What ensured their political defeat was less the quality of their argument than peasant revolts and the mutiny by the Kronsdadt sailors in 1921. The New Economic Policy (NEP) of the same year – no better name could be thought of – was hurriedly put into place instead. It was a form of state capitalism (Lenin himself so described it) whereby agriculture and petty production and trade were handed over to the market, the state reserving to itself ultimate control over foreign trade and banking operations and, naturally, heavy industry – though that had to operate according to market criteria, which could mean unemployment. With some difficulty, the currency was stabilised – enough at least to allow it to function adequately.

If the NEP coped with the immediate economic crisis, the chronic problems confronting the new regime did not go away. These, in their barest essence, sprung from the imbalance in a closed economy[19] between the very weak industrial base and the overwhelmingly predominant agricultural character of the country. How, in these circumstances, to satisfy the demand of the peasantry for manufactured goods and so provide incentives for them to produce sufficient grain and livestock to supply the towns in addition to their own needs?

As with every major dilemma in Soviet Russia, the problem assumed the form of an ideological conflict and in the mid-1920s this came to focus on the alternatives of 'socialism in one country' as against a continuing commitment to world revolution, designated as 'permanent revolution'. For a variety of reasons, the former, with Stalin and Bukharin as its principal spokespersons, won out – but the dilemma remained: if 'socialism in one country' was the project, then how to achieve it?

At first a continuation of the NEP was adopted, with the hope that industrialisation could be developed by means of a slow shift of peasant-generated surpluses into the manufacturing, mining, urbanisation and transport sectors to create a modernised economy. This attempt was not successful, for the peasantry, or rather the kulaks, on whom the state depended for the grain supply, refused to co-operate since the rewards offered were too meagre. In 1928, they effectively instituted a supply strike, demanding the freeing-up of the agricultural market and a better supply of manufactures, only to be achieved by joining the world economy (which might not have been in any case a very happy move given what was about to happen in the United States).

The state's response, with Stalin now the predominant leader and Bukharin sidelined, was to dispossess the peasantry, 'eliminate the kulaks as a class',[20] and turn the rural landscape into one of agricultural factories run either directly by the state or else by 'co-operatives' which were effectively state instruments, a process termed 'collectivisation'. Naturally the peasants resisted desperately, the mass destruction of their livestock representing a frequent mode of protest. The government ruthlessly seized grain surpluses or often the entire stock. Famine ravaged the Ukraine. In some cases, resistance was subdued by armed police formations using machine guns. The impact on Soviet agriculture was catastrophic, the output of grain and other agricultural products plummeted and Soviet agriculture never fully recovered from the trauma, yet the objective was achieved – the state secured control over the grain supply.

Simultaneously, a breakneck programme of industrialisation was launched in the form of the Five Year Plan, state-directed development plans hastily compiled at Stalin's behest and regarded by the experts as wildly unrealistic. The vastly expanded workforce required was recruited from part of the population in the collectivised villages, the displaced individuals now surplus to agricultural requirements. Social conditions in the urbanised areas grew desperate in consequence. With the food supply disrupted, severe rationing prevailed and all social amenities were put under colossal strain as provision of urban transport, housing (especially), medical services and so forth desperately strove to keep up and inevitably failed. Naturally, an extensive black market in goods and services was the consequence. In the workplace itself, hours were long with additional 'voluntary' labour required; where output could be measured, individual quotas were fixed with sanctions if these were not fulfilled; damage to plant or equipment, whether deliberate or accidental, resulted in severe penalties. Such minimal trade union rights as workers still possessed now vanished as the trade unions became, in Stalin's words, mere 'transmission belts' for the state and the Party.

Yet the industrialisation drive, in contrast to collectivisation, was not universally unpopular among those affected by it. The Soviet industrial workforce in previous years had had plenty of reason for grievance. Its members could find themselves unemployed if their enterprise failed by market criteria, consumer goods above the essential minimum were very scarce – and expensive and shoddy in addition. Social amenities were primitive, work discipline was tight. The trade unions, although not yet entirely helpless, were incomparably weaker than their Western counterparts and, moreover, the workers were living in a police state even if it was at that stage an only moderately repressive one. Not surprisingly, many of them openly demanded to know what the Revolution had been for.

Under the Stalin revolution, beginning in 1928, most of these features worsened very substantially, but there was now no unemployment problem; on the contrary, there was instead a serious labour shortage and, provided one had the right class credentials, it was possible to flourish. Surprisingly, perhaps, the regime did not resort to direction of labour and so it was not out of the question to change jobs, and although wages were regulated along with everything else, managers desperate for reliable and hardworking employees were willing to offer underhand inducements. For those who had the talent and the willingness to improve their educational-level highly-skilled manual or administrative and managerial jobs were on plentiful offer. To encourage this process, the regime deliberately widened income differentials and fringe benefits and denounced objectors as petty-bourgeois romantics. In the young communist organisation (*Komsomols*) especially, genuine enthusiasm and sacrificial commitment were also manifested.

Contrary to the official statistics, the first Five-Year-Plan missed most of its intended objectives (particularly in the output of consumer goods), yet again the essential purpose was achieved. The country was industrialised, albeit at the basic level of heavy industry – although needless to say acute social problems, such as alcoholism, prostitution, crime, domestic violence, all of which had been intensified by low income levels and gross overcrowding, continued to flourish unreported.

By the mid-1930s, therefore, the agricultural surplus had been brought under state control and an industrial economy was in place. Stalin even went so far as to promulgate a new constitution (inevitably referred to as the 'Stalin Constitution'), although it was largely drafted by Bukharin, guaranteeing all sorts of civic rights, and to proclaim that the project of 'socialism in one country' was now accomplished. It was at just this time that the Great Terror began and continued for the remainder of the decade. Its most high-profile aspect was the show trials of the Old Bolsheviks, Stalin's former opponents in the Party and also his associates who had offended him or knew too much, as well as the dramatic purge of the military and execution of most of its senior commanders. Much more far-reaching, however, was the arrest of millions of Soviet citizens who, if not executed, went to form the slave labour force of the Gulag.

All of the accused, regardless of whether they appeared in the dock of the highly publicised show trials or else before a local magistrate, where they left no record beyond the official documentation, were coerced into confessing to imaginary crimes of counter-revolutionary treason, spying, sabotage or whatever. The procedures and proprieties had to be observed, however unnecessary to the eventual outcome.

WAR SOCIETY

By the time of the German invasion in 1941, the Terror had begun to ease off, although it was far from discontinued and the Gulag remained well supplied with fresh inputs – necessary (from the regime's viewpoint) to provide a workforce toiling under conditions which would never have been acceptable to free labour. Once the country was under attack and fighting for its existence, though material conditions were harsher still, the scale of the repression (except for groups or nationalities thought to be sympathetic to the enemy – some Caucasian nationalities and the Crimean Tatars) had to be relaxed yet further in order to sustain public morale and achieve the greatest possible level of dedication to victory. Naturally there was widespread public hope and expectation that victory would bring with it better times in all aspects of life.

Two and a half years earlier, the declaration in September 1939 by Britain and France of war against Germany was received by the German public, according to all accounts, with foreboding and apprehension, yet public morale, stimulated by Nazi victories in the first two years of the conflict, appears never to have wavered up to the end, despite the military disasters which subsequently followed, and the destruction and mass casualties resulting from the aerial bombardment of German cities. Compared with Britain or the Soviet Union, the Nazi regime, mindful of what had happened in 1918, and with conquered territories to plunder mercilessly, went to great pains to maintain consumption levels and retain as far as possible the framework of a consumer society within the Reich, and middle-class homes were supplied with domestic slave-labour from among the conquered populations of Eastern Europe. Not until very late in the day was the civilian population, on Goebbels's initiative, mobilised for total war.

The British coalition government of 1940–45 by contrast, building on the foundation of experience gained during the First World War, as well as economic controls noted above, went out of its way to involve the trade unions and the organisational capacities of its workforce in the production drive, by means of production councils. For the general public, a comprehensive system of rationing was instituted for most basic necessities, especially foodstuffs, and many sorts of consumer items either disappeared from the shops or were only occasionally obtainable. The result was that, on average, the population was better fed and healthier than it had ever previously been.

Evidence – not least the outcome of by-elections (for while there existed a truce among the three main parties so that they did not oppose each other in such elections, outsiders could do so) – suggests that there was much more discontent with the government than was publicly admitted at the time. Naturally, for all the belligerent governments control and regulation of information and public discourse took on a high priority. In occupied Europe and the Soviet Union control was as near total as the respective regimes could make it over press, radio and cinema. The British government established a Ministry of Information and the BBC, the only broadcaster easily available, acted in effect as a government agency. It usually refrained from outright lying, controlling its news broadcasting instead by suppression and what would now be termed 'spin'. The government assumed powers to regulate the press, but used them discriminatingly. It banned the Communist Party's daily newspaper – though not the party's other publications – and only fascist groups were outlawed. Although the government had a fierce row with the *Daily Mirror* and actively considered its suppression, in the end it decided against doing so on account of that paper's general popularity.

In varying degrees, all of the European belligerents (and the same was largely true for Japan) experienced a regime of consumer shortages and tight state control over social life – for some an intensification of familiar realities, for others a new experience. The great exception, as ever, was the USA. The war, as noted, had brought the country out of the depression and, as in all sectors of the economy, thrived and generated increasing labour demand. Women – 'Rosie the Riveter' – entered industrial employment on a significant scale to replace men serving in the forces, employers and workforce gained the benefits. Trade unions strengthened their position and leverage, as did the Communist Party USA (CPUSA), but only marginally, while evoking official hostility, and civilian life otherwise continued much as before. It was a portent, and the foundation for what was to come in the following phase of the age of extremes.

2
Liberalism

At the opening of the twentieth century, liberalism was the hegemonic world ideology – or at least that of its ruling sectors, 'spreading right across the political spectrum to encompass nearly the entire political class', as John Gray writes with reference to Britain, but in fact this description applied much more widely. Even the Russian Empire had been obliged to make some concessions, socially if not politically. It is important not to misunderstand: liberalism did not necessarily imply a humanitarian or cuddly outlook. On the contrary, depending upon how it was understood, liberalism left plenty of room for violence, racism, authoritarianism, lightly disguised slavery, even genocide.[1]

Nineteenth-century liberalism sought to combine a doctrine of human emancipation with a central concern for the protection of property and the freedom of exchanging it, and clearly in both of these dimensions it represented an outlook favourable to economic actors – agricultural, industrial, commercial or financial – who relied on the unimpeded operation of market forces to promote their accumulation and profit. Consequently the security of property, the reliability of contract, an impartial judiciary operating a well-defined and even-handed system of civil law, relatively transparent systems of public communication, careers largely open to talent and a general culture of open competition were all either essential or at least highly desirable objectives.

The first, and most vital of these, security of commercial property, implied a political system insulated from interference both from arbitrary governments and also the propertyless masses who might regard such property as less than sacred. Liberal attitudes to freedom and property contradicted each other particularly as far as women were concerned, for the question of inheritance implied tight control over sexual behaviour. It may well be thought essential to keep the masses disenfranchised lest their representatives set about redistributing property by legislative decree or passing laws restricting inheritance controls. Liberalism therefore did not necessarily object to authoritarian government so long as it had a constitutional basis, observed a rule of law, and was therefore rule-governed rather than arbitrary in its authoritarian actions.[2]

Liberalism could therefore define the condition of most European states at the beginning of the twentieth century – and in that sense even early-twentieth-century Japan could be regarded as liberal in essence. It is important to keep in mind the disjunction that could occur between liberalism in the sense of economic arrangements and in that of civil and personal rights. In emergency situations both in the nineteenth and twentieth centuries, when threats from the masses were especially menacing, dictatorship of one sort or another would be found acceptable. Nevertheless a liberal social order remained, so to speak, the default option for a liberal economy. It has the additional advantage that in societies where governmental powers are limited on principle, the market rather than the political authorities can take the blame for social distress or economic breakdown. Yet from the late nineteenth century a trend of 'social liberalism' was emerging, particularly in the UK (in the USA it was known as Populism), which advocated significant state interventions to amend the adverse social effects of uncontrolled market relations.

LIBERALISM TRIUMPHANT AND CHALLENGED

On the face of things, during the last months of 1918 and earlier part of 1919 liberal triumph, effectively under US leadership, appeared to be complete and liberalism in a broad sense to have been historically consolidated despite a rash of communist revolts and labour turbulence in Europe. It was the more autocratic of the belligerent coalitions which had suffered defeat and two of its elements, the empires of Austria–Hungary and Turkey, had dissolved altogether. The German imperial state was overthrown and replaced with an impeccably liberal regime (so it appeared) under the temporary management of the reformed social democrats. Admittedly liberalism had suffered total eclipse in the former Russian Empire, but that was expected to be as temporary as any astronomical eclipse, for in early 1919 the Bolsheviks seemed on the verge of extinction. There was even a short-lived economic surge in 1919 as consumer demand, restricted during the war, ballooned briefly.

Above all, the great liberal exemplar, the USA, now risen to dominate the world economy, for some months became central to world politics as well, and this through the actions of the US President, Woodrow Wilson, a liberal ideologue. Wilson's two central projects, propounded in his 'Fourteen Points' at the beginning of 1918, as a response and challenge to the Soviet Decree on Peace issued at the end of 1917, were to promote policies of national self-determination in Central and Eastern Europe, 'Self-determination is not a mere phrase. It is an imperative principle of action which statesmen will henceforth ignore at their peril... Every territorial settlement involved in this war must be made in the interest and for the benefit of the populations concerned, and not as a part of any mere adjustment or compromise of claims amongst rival States.'[3] His second main objective was to institute an international organisation of member states, 'A general association of nations' to make war a thing of the past – though 'the removal of economic barriers' was also very high up on the list (number three, in fact).

Wilson personally attended the negotiations in Paris which led up to the Versailles Treaty and, although he did not always get his own way and was obliged to accept drastic compromises, so that the eventual treaty would be wildly different from the Fourteen Points and his related declarations, nevertheless, his was still the dominant influence and the Treaty had his stamp. Without his insistence it is unlikely that the League of Nations would ever have come into being. It was not a question of Wilson's personality – his fellow negotiators, the other Allied leaders, had little time for him – but of the power (financial and otherwise) which the United States was in a position to exert.

Liberal expectations unravelled soon enough as economic depression, impoverishment, national persecution and international conflict took over, while the Bolshevik victory removed the former empire, a sixth of the world's land surface, from the liberal order. Although liberal societies at the end of the Great War still had plenty in reserve, notably the economic and institutional strengths of the British Empire and above all the USA, to meet the ideologies old and new which contended with it, for almost the next quarter century it was unquestionably on the defensive.

Certainly it was the politics and social order of liberalism which, explicitly or by implication, were indicted most severely for the catastrophe of the war and its aftermath, both from the left and from the right. The cynical remark of José Ortega y Gasset that liberty was a burden humanity was only too anxious to throw off, was, however, entirely misplaced and revealing of a very selective view of liberty.

Both liberty and liberalism were indeed under attack, liberty from interests who believed that the masses had too much of it, the same as attacked liberalism for the liberty it guaranteed or because or was unable to ensure security for property, the two things being connected in their eyes. But liberalism was also challenged from different political direction because it failed to guarantee meaningful liberty or basic material needs. Politicians, adhering to the values of liberalism in its general sense, in the UK and France (and even to an extent in Germany) had led their nations into the inferno while their publicists and propagandists had drummed the message of no compromise and total victory. The scale of their losses and the aftermath of social turmoil and disillusion occluded eventual victory celebrations in these two countries.

In every major belligerent country, even the USA, the war on the 'home front' was mobilised in a highly authoritarian manner. Not only were resources organised through central control, in addition dissent was briskly suppressed, and media and academic outlets were induced to propagandise on behalf of the war effort and maintain civilian morale. By the end of the war, while in the Allied countries intransigent opponents of the war were locked up and publications suppressed, in the most extreme case German civilians were effectively living under a military dictatorship. Throughout Europe the lesson of authoritarian efficiency was not forgotten.

In Russia, liberalism had proved a dismal failure from any point of view. Following the Tsar's overthrow in March 1917[4] the Russian liberals had had their chance, dominating as they did the early months of the Provisional Government. Wishing to establish, eventually, a constitutional system based on that of Western Europe and heavily influenced by the Entente diplomats in their capital, they proved wholly incapable of coping with the pressing demands of the Russian population. At the behest of the British and French they insisted on continuing participation in the war, which was, from the Russian point of view, clearly lost, and so multiplied human losses with futile military offensives. They restrained the peasantry, both by persuasion and force, from accomplishing their centuries-old ambition of seizing the land they regarded as stolen by the landlords from their ancestors. The government's administration was unable to cope with the disintegrating supply system, especially in urban areas, and shortages were universal.

Disliked and disdained on all sides, the Provisional Government was easily displaced by the Bolsheviks in November. The Russian experiment in liberalism proved to be far from able to cope with the exigencies of war and social disruption, and, if it had not fallen to Lenin's intransigent revolutionary socialists, would certainly have been overwhelmed by right-wing authoritarians.

Versailles and the League of Nations

For four years, Europe, apart from the neutral states, had been steeped in militarism. The structure and functioning of armed forces represent the very antithesis of liberalism. The memory of the war, of the authoritarianism which had prevailed throughout society, in combination with the economic crisis, put the continuation of liberal principles in government at a discount wherever they were not very firmly entrenched. The measures taken towards the political reconstruction of Europe at the war's end did nothing to help.

Despite this, the treaties put in place in the course of 1919, collectively known as the Versailles system – after the Versailles Treaty proper – were supposedly based for the most part upon liberal principles, even if the word was not explicitly used. This is not to exclude the dimension of *Realpolitik*, which played a significant part, but a settlement based purely on that conception would have looked very different from what did actually emerge from the negotiations between the allies (the defeated states were allowed no input into the discussion). As it happened, the liberal principles integral to the settlement fitted in very well and very conveniently with the victors' determination to isolate and weaken as far as possible the distinctly anti-liberal regime ruling Soviet Russia.

The 'Carthaginian' peace which would have been imposed on Germany if French political and military sentiment had had its way was blocked by the USA and British leaders. The country, though drastically weakened and mutilated, was left as an intact, coherent and formally sovereign state (albeit that its sovereignty was limited) with enough of a military establishment remaining to repress internal insurrection. The US president, Woodrow Wilson, was the very embodiment of early-twentieth-century liberalism. Prior to the Armistice, he had insisted on guarantees regarding the 'representative character' of the German government. Being the most influential participant and genuinely believing in national self-determination, he was not prepared to agree to Germany being broken up or even to create 'an Alsace–Lorraine in reverse' by detaching the Rhineland. Nor were the British willing to see Germany too severely damaged – they needed it as a functioning trading partner. Moreover – and this was an argument that resonated even with the French negotiators – chaos in Germany was, so everyone believed, likely to promote the advance of communism in that country.

The main concern of the other treaties in the Versailles system was the territorial rearrangement of Eastern Europe. With few exceptions, such as the compulsory separation of Germany from the new truncated Austria, this merely confirmed what had already occurred 'on the ground'.[5] In the final settlement the principle of nation self-determination, a longstanding liberal principle enthusiastically embraced by President Wilson, often to the dismay of his French and British allies,[6] was to the forefront, though that was overridden when a defeated state had to be appropriately punished. It was further complicated beyond all measure by the actually existing admixture of nationalities everywhere.

Brute realities and armed force therefore largely determined how the boundaries of the new Europe would be fixed; additionally, the new or expanded states formed a most convenient *cordon sanitaire* of anti-communist regimes shutting the USSR off from Europe, and that had been a prime objective of the peacemakers. Nevertheless, the justifications advanced were grounded in liberal ideology, and all of these states, monarchies included, and even Finland and Hungary, which had seen bitter civil wars, were equipped initially with the apparatus of liberal constitutionalism – elections, parliaments, representative government, independent media and so forth.

This, after all, had been 'the war to end wars', to bring to an end aggression, secret treaties and arbitrary power. Those territorial seizures from the defeated powers that were added to the victors' colonial empires were termed 'mandates' rather than colonies and placed formally under the supervision of the League of Nations. This latter institution, written into the Versailles Treaty, was the very epitome of liberal conceptions of international relations; a parliament of sovereign states intended to keep the peace between them, promote international amity and even to punish cross-border aggression. It was disliked by conservatives because it implied limitations on sovereign power and from the other end of the political spectrum Lenin referred to it as the 'thieves' kitchen'. Nevertheless, popular pressure in the UK and France, combined with Wilson's enthusiasm, ensured its establishment, with its headquarters at Geneva in neutral Switzerland.

In relation to the League, one of the lesser-known aspects of the negotiations provides an illuminating insight into the limitations of early-twentieth-century liberalism. When its founding document, the Covenant, was being prepared, it was proposed to include a clause, stating that:

> The equality of nations being a basic principle of the League of Nations, the High Contracting Parties agree to accord, as soon as possible, to all alien nationals of states [which are] members of the League, equal and just treatment in every respect, making no distinction, either in law or fact, on account of their race or nationality.[7]

Ironically, this clause, the extension of a principle relating to religion embodied in the proposed Article 21, was advanced by Baron Makhino, the Japanese plenipotentiary, the representative of what was surely among the most racist cultures on the planet. It was vehemently resisted on openly racist grounds by the Australian representative William Hughes, who regarded it as an attempt by Japan to get around the 'White Australia' policy then in force, and he aimed to keep them out of any of the Pacific islands south of the equator.

As Hugh Purcell notes, 'the White Dominions were almost by definition racist';[8] discriminated against and ill-treated Inuit people, the Australian Aborigines, the Maoris and Africans – not to speak of the situation in the southern USA. Hughes used the telephone to communicate with and stir up a racist American press, suggesting that the proposed clause, even though now modified, would force the Americans to allow Japanese to settle in California. Wilson's adviser, Colonel House, told his leader that to pass the amendment 'would surely raise the race issue throughout the world', Wilson agreed, and when the vote in the Covenant Committee went against him simply refused to accept the result. The British delegate and Deputy chairman, Robert Cecil, one of the League's chief promoters, commented that 'It is better that the Covenant be silent on these questions of right. Silence would avoid much discussion.'[9]

Bad start in the 1920s

The new institutions, both national and international, got off to a thoroughly bad start. The terms of the Versailles Treaty, certainly vicious – especially in their economic features, though overall they might have been even worse – outraged German national sentiment. Particularly detested was the 'War Guilt' clause that their delegates were compelled to accept. It took several years for Germany even to be permitted to join the League. The staggering extent of Allied reparations demands worked havoc with the German economy, leading to its breakdown in 1923.

Widespread boiling indignation provided a convenient resource for ultra-nationalist authoritarian demagogues who made several attempts to overthrow the Republic, once in 1920 coming very near to success; the liberal polity and liberal politicians received the blame for Germany's predicament, along with Jews and perceived 'anti-national' elements on the left. A very large section of the political class, along with their constituents, remained thoroughly alienated from the Republic, and its enemies were to be found not only on the right. The growing communist party, the KPD, was no less antagonistic towards the bourgeois republic created and sustained, as they saw it, by social democratic class traitors.

At least the Weimar Republic, however shakily, survived for over a decade, but, plagued with economic crisis and the heritages of the war, liberalism soon foundered altogether in the new states of Eastern Europe as well as the major and longstanding polity of Italy. For the most part constitutional forms were preserved, for example in Poland during the Pilsudski dictatorship, installed in 1926, and even in the most aggressively right-wing of the successor states, Hungary, but with one exception they degenerated into neutered empty forms fronting irremovable[10] right-wing authoritarian regimes that tolerated low-key opposition only for the sake of appearances. In Poland, Pilsudski dominated over a medley of quarrelling factions with separate party labels, none of which dared to challenge him and allowed him to select his successor. The one exception was the Czechoslovak republic, which managed to preserve democratic standards in spite of severe economic, political and minority nationalist stresses.[11] Even in Western Europe, in the Iberian Peninsula, liberal regimes collapsed or were bloodily destroyed by ultra-conservative and fascist-aligned forces. Similar forces severely threatened France, the exemplar of European liberalism, and the new Irish Free State, precariously liberal in its political system if not its social order, only just managed to preserve these liberal traditions. Only in northwestern Europe – the UK, the Low Countries and Scandinavia (except Finland) – did political liberalism seem secure for the time being.

Beyond Europe, except in the United States, the situation was no better. Leaving aside the imperial colonies (which incorporated virtually the whole of Africa) and China, torn between competing warlords and communist insurgents, at opposite ends of the Pacific, Latin America and Japan displayed, though in very different fashions, the combination of liberal economies and far-from-liberal polities. Since the Meji revolution of the late nineteenth century, the ruling elements of the Japanese elite had set out – successfully – to modernise Japan technologically within a capitalist market framework, while maintaining as much as possible of the inherited feudal values. Constitutional political forms were adopted, but the interpenetrating traditional elites and the military never ceased to be in charge, and the economic crisis of the 1930s saw periods of direct military rule and the launching of imperial adventures against China. These were justified and propagandised through an ideology which, apart from the economic considerations involved, declared the Japanese (excluding those sections of Japanese society themselves discriminated against, the aboriginal Ainu and the outcaste burakumin) to be racially superior beings entitled to the leadership of Eastern Asia.

South America on the face of things looked very different: a congerie of imperfectly modernised states racked by internal and external conflict, the more so when global economic disaster struck. That impression, however, while not inaccurate, was only part of the story – the South American states were well integrated into the global economy of the time, hence the intensity of the crisis when the primary products upon which they depended suffered price collapse. Until the First World War, an informal arrangement between the UK and the USA gave the former commercial hegemony over the southern cone – Buenos Aires was thought of as London on the River Plate – and the latter over the more northerly states.

Nearly all of the states were dominated by bitterly rivalrous factions of traditional landowning, commercial and military elites, with the military intervening frequently to settle these disputes, while populations of peasant cultivators, herders, miners and other primary producers subsisted in direst poverty and religious superstition. Nevertheless liberal constitutional forms were in the main preserved, with elections, political parties, parliaments and presidents, but these represented little more than a top-dressing on deeply conservative elitist and repressive societies.

AMERICAN LIBERALISM AND THE NEW DEAL

The League of Nations never lived up to its promise, even in the comparatively calm decade of the 1920s. A major shortcoming was, of course, that the United States itself was not a member. Although the war and its outcome had secured the hegemony of the United States in the world economy for the remainder of the century and beyond, it was, after a brief burst of enthusiasm, far from universally popular with the American public – Wilson had, after all, been re-elected in 1916 as 'the man who kept us out of the war'. Close involvement in European affairs was obnoxious to substantial sections of the political class and the public; expansionist aims in economic and political terms were directed towards the Americas and across the Pacific, not the Atlantic. Accordingly, as soon as the Republican Party gained control of the Senate, Wilson's foreign policies were repudiated and US participation in the League rejected. The President in any case was incapacitated; Republicans gained the presidency in 1920 and Washington retreated into isolationism.

The version of liberalism that characterised the American polity during the 1920s and secured the election of two further Republican presidents was caught by the stock exchange crash in October 1929, and the rapid transition from boom to bust that followed. The contradictions inherent in American liberalism (leaving aside the terror imposed on the African-American population in the Dixie states) were manifested especially in the sphere of what was regulated and what was not. Not all forms of entrepreneurial enterprise were permitted, for in this decade the manufacture, sale and distribution of alcohol were outlawed.

Public disillusionment with the regime which had presided over the depths of the slump resulted in the election to the presidency of Franklin Roosevelt in November 1932 on the basis of the New Deal platform. To place its ideological content presents some difficulties – it was, after all, distinctively American. The unreconciled free marketers in the United States never ceased to loathe it and regard it as abominably socialist – indeed, verging on communism. The Communists, on the other hand, dismissed it initially as a version of social fascism. It could be viewed either as an American version of social liberalism or the transatlantic variety of social democracy – which does indeed reveal something important about social democracy's character.

Roosevelt

The ideological presuppositions behind the New Deal are well exemplified in the series of radio broadcast 'fireside chats' through which Roosevelt explained his thinking to the American public. On 7 May 1933, he declared, 'The members of Congress realized that the methods of normal times had to be replaced in the emergency by measures which were suited to the serious and pressing requirements of the moment.' However, he was careful to add that the constitutional proprieties and American tradition were being observed:

There was no actual surrender of power, Congress still retained its constitutional authority and no one has the slightest desire to change the balance
of these powers.

...

The only thing that has been happening has been to designate the President
as the agency to carry out certain of the purposes of the Congress. This was
constitutional and in keeping with the past American tradition.

Not only that, he insisted that in acceding to some of the demands of labour
and other interests there was no divergence from traditional American practice:

Well-considered and *conservative* [emphasis added] measures will likewise
be proposed which will attempt to give to the industrial workers of the
country a more fair wage return, prevent cut-throat competition and unduly
long hours for labor, and at the same time to encourage each industry to
prevent over-production .... It is rather a partnership between Government
and farming and industry and transportation.

On 30 September 1934, Roosevelt returned to the theme of state intervention
in a liberal society:

In our efforts for recovery we have avoided on the one hand the theory that
business should and must be taken over into an all-embracing Government.
We have avoided on the other hand the equally untenable theory that it is
an interference with liberty to offer reasonable help when private enterprise
is in need of help. The course we have followed fits the American practice
of Government ....

Liberal credentials are stressed once again on 24 June 1938:

The Seventy-Fifth Congress, elected in November, 1936, on a platform
uncompromisingly liberal .... Be it clearly understood, however, that when
I use the word 'liberal', I mean the believer in progressive principles of
democratic, representative government and not the wild man who, in effect,
leans in the direction of Communism, for that is just as dangerous to us
as Fascism itself.

One issue which is not addressed in the fireside chats is that of race and the
situation of African–Americans whether in the Dixie states or in the north,
for, as one historian has explained:

The race question however, simply was not part of the dominant New Deal
consciousness. When he insisted, years later, that 'there *wasn't* [original
emphasis] any race problem in the 1930s', Thomas G. Corcoran as an
adviser ... had the President's ear. 'When Roosevelt came in 1933', he
explained, 'there were many more things to worry about than civil rights'.

As Rexford G. Tugwell, perhaps the most advanced social thinker of the New Deal period, described Roosevelt's attitude, 'I wouldn't say that he took no interest in the race problem, but he didn't consider it was important politically, never as far as I knew'.[12]

Tugwell admitted that he and his colleagues shared the same attitude.

THE UK

In the UK the great Liberal Party, the political dynamo of the nineteenth century, was wrecked and reduced to impotence, but liberalism itself was never under serious threat as the commonsense of the electorate. What dominated the interwar years with brief intermissions was the more right-wing version of liberalism in the shape of the Conservative Party, which profited from the defection of Irish nationalists from Westminster, from the breakup of the Liberal Party and especially from the red scare, which their publicity strove successfully to convince many voters was embodied, however preposterously, in the Labour Party.

The Conservative Party had objected vehemently to Irish secession from the UK and Liberal efforts to institute devolution, for its leaders and adherents had come to view an undivided United Kingdom as central to British identity,[13] but that issue was solved, at least temporarily. The other Liberal shibboleth they rejected was that of free trade, and in the 1920s allowed their protectionist instincts to come to the fore, instituting a protectionist policy after 1931.

Otherwise their politics were firmly in the traditions of British liberalism (lower case). The remark by the right-wing conservative Ian Crowther, writing in 1982, seems particularly apposite to the interwar Conservatives, 'Many conservatives, innocent presumably of their own tradition … now equate economic liberalism with Toryism and, worse, pontificate upon the problems of our society as though they were soluble by economic remedies alone.'[14] They further assimilated a large section of the surviving Liberal Party in the 1930s, along with the Labour prime minister and several members of his Cabinet.[15]

Liberalism was never seriously threatened in the UK during the interwar years, except possibly from popular revolt in 1919–21 when the onset of depression coincided with exceptional labour militancy and dissention in the state apparatus of army and police. Even then it was not particularly likely and, once conditions had stabilised, the existence of a dependent empire, cheap primary products, rising real incomes for the employed[16] and deep-rooted tradition made the British version of liberalism safe from serious challenge. Even during the slump years following 1929, Communist and Fascist parties remained marginal[17] and the seriously socialist elements in the Labour Party were easily controlled or excluded by its right-wing leadership.

Keynes

Another sphere in which liberalism made significant developments during these two decades was the theoretical, and the outstanding figure in this regard was the British economist J. M. Keynes. It is no accident that Keynes, while a dedicated liberal – and Liberal, he was largely responsible for the Liberal Party's programme of 1928 – was also a passionate (although not wholly uncritical) admirer of Edmund Burke, the reactionary polemicist and consummate hypocrite generally regarded as the founding father of modern conservatism. Keynes was no mere theoretician, for having made a fortune by stock exchange speculation during the 1920s he lost it in the slump – and quickly restored it again.

Keynes was unquestionably a very profound thinker and, although wholly committed to a variety of liberal shibboleths such as free trade, was intensely aware of the contradictions in free market capitalism that were bringing it to its knees during the interwar decades. His analysis, which was developed to maturity in the course of the 1930s, viewed the problem in terms of demand and investment deficiency.

Crudely summarised, it prescribed government intervention to create by extensive borrowing the demand which market forces in the downturn of the trade cycle were incapable of providing. In ethical terms Keynes was a passionate humanitarian, intensely committed to the ideal of a basic material sufficiency all round, but he was no instinctive democrat (hence his admiration for Burke). He could indeed be characterised an unashamed elitist, firmly convinced that the enjoyment of advanced culture was reserved for the minority with the brainpower and resources to appreciate it. Because capitalism was, in his view, the only form of economic system that could ensure that, his aim was to provide the theoretical basis for its preservation, not its overthrow. Nor did he want to eliminate unemployment, being convinced that a moderate reserve of workless people was essential to limit wage demands and hold back inflation.

Keynes's first political intervention came with his excoriating analysis of the Versailles Treaty, *The Economic Consequences of the Peace*, which one commentator has described as a 'full-bore, fangs-bared assault'. Published in 1919 its theme is summed up in its introductory chapter, 'the spokesmen of the French and British peoples have run the risk of completing the ruin which Germany began', and they were sowing 'the decay of the whole civilised life of Europe'. He goes on to demonstrate that the state to which Germany has been reduced makes it impossible for it to fulfil the demands, particularly the economic ones, being imposed upon the country, and as a result 'the industrial future of Europe is black and the prospects of revolution very good'. He refers to the 'serious menace of Spartacism'[18] and notes that 'A victory of Spartacism in Germany might well be the prelude to revolution everywhere: it would renew the forces of Bolshevism in Russia, and precipitate the dreaded union of Germany and Russia.' He quotes the German comment on the Reparations commission pointing out the contradictions in the victors' liberal postures:

German democracy is thus annihilated at the very moment when the German people was about to build it up after a severe struggle – annihilated by the very persons who throughout the war never tired of maintaining that they sought to bring democracy to us ... Germany is no longer a people and a state, but becomes a mere trade concern placed by its creditors in the hands of a receiver, without its being granted so much as the opportunity to prove its willingness to meet its obligations of its own accord.

It has been shown in recent years that in the course of the 1930s Keynes's ideas were making progress within the Treasury,[19] despite the natural resistance of the old guard firmly attached to balanced budgets and the theoretical assault launched against his conceptions by Frederich von Hayek, a very different species of liberal if indeed he could even be regarded as one. Even during the economic crisis of the 1930s Hayek was arguing that unregulated and unobstructed market forces operating in the framework of private property were the only solution. From his liberal standpoint the essential problem was that wages were too high. Nevertheless it is interesting to note that for all their theoretical divergence the two economists were on good terms and respected each other – despite Hayek's remark that Keynes was a 'confessed immoralist'. Keynes at one point wrote to him noting that their ultimate purposes were the same, their disagreements were concerned with the means of getting there.[20]

SOCIAL DEMOCRACY

Liberalism's most serious success, however, during this bleak period was one that went unrecognised, and that was, effectively, to turn social democracy into a variety of liberalism. In understanding this it is necessary to distinguish two forms of social democracy. In the UK, the labour movement, despite sometimes carrying Marx's image on its trade union banners, had nevertheless remained culturally and ideologically attached to its roots in the Liberal Party. In continental Europe by contrast, the social democracies had their roots by and large in the Marxist tradition.

These continental social democratic parties were the product, following the war, of ruptures in the working-class parties. Ostensibly these fractures came as a result of the formation of the Communist International and the conditions which it imposed on any party that joined it; but effectively the division had taken place well before the Comintern's formation. As Ebert, the SPD leader, declared in November 1918 when on the point of forming his government in Berlin:

First, we do not intend to confiscate any bank or savings bank deposits nor any sums in cash or banknotes or other valuable papers deposited in the bank safes. Secondly, we do not intend to cancel any subscriptions to the Ninth War Loan, or any other war loan, or in any other way to impair the legitimacy of those loans.[21]

In addressing the opening session of the Constituent Assembly in February 1919, days after the Freikorps' ferocious destruction of the Spartacists and murder of Luxemburg and Liebknecht,

Only on the broad highway of Parliamentary discussion and decision can
the urgent changes in the economic and social spheres be progressively
achieved without destroying the Reich and its economic position ....
Therefore, we address to the employers the urgent appeal to help with all
their strength the restoration of production ... so must we here in Weimar
complete the change from Imperialism to Idealism, from world power to
spiritual greatness.[22]

In his next address, he more or less apologised for being a Social Democrat:
'I will administer my office not as the leader of a single party, but I belong to
the Socialist Party and cannot forget my origin and training.'[23]

Although it took a long time to recognise, in historical hindsight it is evident
that in 1918 or thereafter European revolution in a recognisably Marxian
sense was an impossible project – in oversimplified terms, the bourgeoisie was
too strong, the proletariat too weak and divided, and Soviet Russia too torn
apart and racked with civil war to offer significant assistance. What was to
become social democracy comprised the section of the labour movement, in
most cases the majority element, which instinctively appreciated this reality,
even if it was not expressed in such terms.

It is important not to oversimplify. The social democratic parties were broad
churches, all of which contained a distinctive range of political attitudes and
projects, and all included significant minorities whose ultimate policy aims
differed very little if at all from those of the communists. Their disagreements
centred not on long-term objectives but on the manner of their accomplishment, particularly the Comintern's dogmatism and authoritarianism.
Nevertheless, even before the fascist eruption following the Slump suggested
the wisdom of unity, there existed tendencies within the social democratic
parties anxious for co-operation with their communist counterparts – which
eventually transpired in France and Spain. The Norwegian Labour party was
even briefly a Comintern member in the early 1920s.

Nevertheless, everywhere in Western Europe the initiative within these
parties was in the hands of the realists, accommodationists, revisionists (or
whatever term might be appropriate) – leaderships who saw no practical
alternative to working for their aims within the framework of capitalist
liberal democracy. They came to regard its preservation as an essential priority
against both left and right, and in the long term turned to embrace its values;
in other words, a development of social liberalism with enhanced emphasis
on collective institutions and initiatives. In the last analysis ideological
commitment is demonstrated less by what its adherents claim or argue than
by what they actually do. In the case of a political formation it is not the
viewpoint of this or that member, but the course of action which is set and
maintained by its leading elements and which is accepted actively or passively
by the rank-and-file.

Politically, social democracy conformed to liberal principles all along the
line – which is not necessarily a condemnation; their spokespeople could have
argued, though they seldom did, that they recognised and valued the conquests

of the bourgeois revolution and aimed to ensure that their working-class constituency got their share of these gains. Social democratic governments never made any attempt to interfere with the processes of political competition or representative democracy, or to rig the voting systems in their own favour, and their parties never argued that they should. The rules of law were strictly observed and no project undertaken to 'expropriate the expropriators', to use the Marxist terminology.

The same could be said about the ideology of the New Deal. It involved a relatively favourable attitude towards the trade union movement, minimum wage legislation, government-organised welfare provision, and loans to otherwise unviable concerns to generate employment and even to public enterprises such as the Tennessee Valley Authority. As noted earlier, the programme was bitterly opposed by the entrenched forces of business and from time to time blocked judicially by a conservative-dominated Supreme Court. Undoubtedly it contradicted the prevalent liberal ideology of the American public in general and was made possible only by the recent manifest and disastrous failure of the previously hegemonic economic system and outlook from 1929 onwards.

LIBERALISM AND THE WAR

Between 1940 and 1945, liberalism, represented by the governments of the USA and the British Empire, was mobilised, military and militant. The banner under which the war was fought was above all that of democracy and national rights – in spite of the existence of the dependent British Empire[24] and repression of the Indian independence movement, as well as the suspension of the normal UK electoral process[25] and degree of state control of the economy, and of citizens' rights entirely abhorrent to liberal ideology and inconceivable under any other circumstances. It could almost be viewed (and von Hayek did so view it) as an authoritarian social democratic regime, for the rule of law continued to operate within the emergency legislative boundaries, and along with the authoritarianism – and threat of repression held in reserve – went collaborative relations with the trade union movement, close attention to public welfare and, despite the Prime Minister's own doubts, promise of more of that to come once victory was secured. Nevertheless, no-one was in any doubt that once the war was successfully concluded the apparatus of liberalism would be restored to government, and likewise to public relationships generally.

In 1939, liberalism had been discredited everywhere except in Britain and some parts of its Empire, a few northern European countries and the United States – none of which could be regarded as impressively dynamic polities; by 1945 it was triumphant throughout Western Europe, largely thanks to intervention by the USA, which enabled liberal hegemony to be restored and the emergent challenge of the left to be beaten off, while in the USA itself the capitalist economy, thanks to the war, was restored to full bloom. Liberalism had recovered its credibility.

3
Conservatism

There is a story that King George III, a conservative icon of his time, once reproved a cleric who had written a defence of Christianity, telling him that surely Christianity needed no defence. The naivety of King George masked a more profound perception – for once conservatism in the sense of attachment to inequality and arbitrary authority requires embodiment in an articulated rather than an implicit and unformulated ideology, half the argument has already been conceded. Much better that existing inequities and iniquities should be taken for granted and these embarrassing questions never raised. The French Revolution and its aftermath compelled its opponents to mount an argued defence of their *Ancien Régime*, but they never liked having to do so. Indeed, English conservatives and Conservatives have traditionally made it a point of honour to despise theory, use 'ideology' as a term of dismissal and stress instead the merits of habit, prejudice and common sense. Presenting rational arguments in favour of irrationality is a contradictory undertaking.

Even before the conclusion of the war, the ideologists of articulated conservatism were faced with a substantial credibility problem. It was a mass war the likes of which had never previously been seen on the European continent. To engage the belligerent populations in the degree and the manner which industrialised warfare required – once it was clear that the outcome would not be swift – the appropriate rhetoric had to be projected and certain promises made of the better times expected to follow from victory. National (and in France even Jacobin) sentiment was of course mobilised on all sides with every resource. It was, on the Allied side, following the collapse of Tsarism and US intervention, a war for democracy, which had formerly been a dirty word among conservatives except in America; it was a war for national self-determination[1] – if anything, an even worse one. It was a war for civilisation, and on the German side for *Kultur*; it was the 'war to end war' and to construct in Britain a land filled with 'homes fit for heroes'.

Following the end of hostilities, the shift in public attitudes was demonstrated in political developments, and conservatives, whether they liked it or not – and they certainly did not – had to adapt to the new realities. In Germany the old constitutional framework which had guaranteed conservative hegemony was swept away along with the monarchy, and a system of formally perfect democracy instituted in its place. The main faction of the pre-war Conservative Party dropped that name and adopted instead the title of Deutschnationale Volkspartei.

43

In the UK the Conservative Party certainly retained its name and indeed recovered the political hegemony it had lost in 1905–06, yet, significantly, it could not do so on its own account but had for the purpose to enter into coalition with the Liberal prime minister David Lloyd George and his faction of supporters. Only in 1922 did the Conservatives feel strong enough to ditch him and reassert their undivided rule. The Empire, which briefly following the 1919 Versailles Treaty had reached its maximum formal extent, remained their fetish and they wanted to strengthen imperial economic ties, while ferociously suppressing national revolts or stirrings of insubordination. Lloyd George's coalition partners forced him to impose upon the Irish rebels, about to be conceded effectual independence, formal adherence to the Empire and denial of the republic they aspired to. This triggered the Irish civil war, doubtless to conservative satisfaction. Before he was shot by the Irish Republican Army (IRA) the most passionate advocate of utmost ferocity to suppress the Irish revolt was the top imperial general, the malignant Sir Henry Wilson, who undoubtedly harboured fascist aspirations. Another commander, General Dyer, was responsible in India for the notorious Amritsar Massacre and subsequent brutalities. On his recall he was feted by the Conservative Party and all British conservatives. The later Home Secretary, the ultra-reactionary William Joynson-Hicks, was undisguised about the authentic Conservative attitudes to the Empire in general and India in particular.

CONSERVATIVE RECOVERY

Throughout Europe, once the post-war situation had stabilised and populations were sufficiently appraised of the horrors of communism in general and the Soviet regime in particular, conservatism recovered many sources of strength. Liberalism and liberal parties could be blamed for the unsatisfactory outcome of the war (where relevant), and for weakness in the face of the communist threat. Whatever the outcome of the war in their particular states, whether victorious, defeated or neutral, the pre-war elites (except in Soviet Russia) if on the defensive politically, retained enormous social strength along with their property and property rights. The situation is well represented by the symbol of the '200 families' of great wealth and status who were popularly believed to determine affairs in France regardless of which parties were in government.

Not surprisingly, a widespread nostalgia existed for the stability of social and international relations as they had existed, or were imagined to have existed, prior to August 1914. Such nostalgia was particularly prevalent in the middle classes, although by no means confined to them. Aspirational opportunities for middle-class advancement which had existed before the war had been wiped out by the conflict and subsequent economic depression. Unemployed and disabled veterans roamed the streets of major cities begging or trying to survive by selling knick-knacks – and not all were from the military rank-and-file. Veterans' organisations assumed militantly reactionary postures.

Especially powerful and frightening was the menace of communism. The Bolsheviks, now in control of the former Tsarist empire, had made no secret of their ardour to spread the revolution across the globe and especially to Western Europe. Indeed, they had proclaimed their intention most vociferously and established the Comintern for exactly that intent; and it was busily assisting the establishment of communist parties in every state or colony where opportunity offered. Reactionary conservatism (other than in Italy at this stage) seemed the most powerful and effective antidote – unlike liberal opponents of the red menace they were not afraid to use the most robust means of repression and not squeamish about generalised massacre, White terror and dictatorship. Indeed, exiled Russian Whites constituted a significant lobby in every West European capital. Moreover, by insisting on using the technical Marxist vocabulary and referring to their regime as socialist rather than communist, the Soviet rulers handed conservatives (and liberals) the additional advantage of being able to smear all other socialists with guilt by association.

The pattern could be seen at work even in a context like the Irish civil war of 1922–23, where the ultra-conservative elements of the national movement brutally established their ascendancy in the Free State despite having just fought as rebels against the British Empire. Formally, the split in the republican ranks leading on to civil war was over the question of whether or not to accept a negotiated Treaty and compromise on the total aims of the revolution – the name of the republic and total separation from the Crown (partition, although not unimportant, was actually a secondary issue). Social issues, however, were very much present in the background.

The anti-Treatyites were drawn mainly from the lower ranks of Irish society, in particular the landless farm labourers; and their armed wing, termed the Irregulars by their enemies, constituted the majority of the old IRA. Conversely, nearly all persons of property and all respectable society were on the side of the new Free State and its authoritarian conservative government: their media as well as the Catholic clergy preached blood-freezing sermons indicting the Irregulars (who were almost 100 per cent devout Catholics, but that made no difference) as murderous social anarchists, comparing them with the Bolsheviks at their worst. Once in control, under democratic guises, a regime of intensely repressive social conformity was imposed.

Across the Atlantic, the results of the Russian Revolution and formation of the Comintern were soon apparent – but not in a fashion to gratify the revolutionaries. American communism, although its proponents tried hard, never really got off the ground at this point and experienced the utmost difficulty even in establishing a stable party.[2] That, however, did not prevent panic reactions from setting in among the US authorities, resulting in the notorious 'Red Scare' of 1920. Communist, anarchist or syndicalist propagandists were harassed, rounded up and imprisoned, even judicially murdered. Any without US citizenship were summarily deported. Legal immigration was closed off. Employers assumed more aggressive postures. The Ku Klux Klan underwent a revival. To the south, the picture was not much more satisfactory – in Mexico, the Caribbean and Latin America communist parties were successfully established, many in the face of intense repression, but none was able to exert a mass appeal, let alone lead a revolution. The southern continent, in spite of its political volatility, remained rigidly conservative, its society dominated by landowning elites and underpinned by an intensely reactionary Catholic Church.

The Papacy

Indeed, as was the case following the French revolutionary and Napoleonic wars, the Catholic Church developed as a major force for conservatism. Its preference for authoritarian and undemocratic regimes was open and overt and in the course of the interwar decades it formed close relationships with those in Italy, Austria, Portugal, Spain, Hungary and Poland. In Austria, the regime of the Christian Socials, as the conservative party designated itself, was actually led until 1929 by a priest, Ignaz Seipel. The Church was in the lead among the conservative forces in France and, as indicated above, Ireland. Had the Free State tipped over into dictatorship, no doubt the hierarchy would have embraced that enthusiastically. In the Weimar Republic it had its own political party, known for some reason as the Centre Party (Deutsche Zentrumspartei, or Zentrum), a bulwark of conservative ideology, although rivalled and overshadowed in that respect by its Protestant counterpart and therefore somewhat less vociferous in reactionary attitudes.

In its own attitudes the Church was following the lines established in the nineteenth century when it had emerged as a vehement opponent of democracy, liberalism and all their associated attributes, summarised in Pius IX's 'Syllabus of Errors'. Since its emergence and establishment during the medieval centuries, the Church had remained an intensely authoritarian institution from top to bottom and continued in that tradition. Indeed, it still looked back with nostalgia to the days when it had given commands to kings and emperors, arranged their appointment and dismissal, as well as telling both its own functionaries and the laity exactly what they should do in both their personal and public lives, and permeating every institution of society with its culture and ethos. The popes of that period, who regarded themselves as the successors of Saint Peter, entrusted with the keys to heaven and hell, and therefore entitled to exercise spiritual – and a great deal of temporal – rule over the entire world, demanded absolute unquestioning and comprehensive obedience, even to the extent of refusing assistance to the falling Byzantine Empire because the Eastern church declined to submit to Rome's authority. At the same time of course, and this was wholly necessary to their survival, the churches provided plenty of spiritual and ceremonial consolation and hope to their flocks to compensate the great majority of them for their absence of material liberties and resources.

The above historical excursus has been necessary because in the twentieth century the Catholic Church had by no means given up on such ambitions, merely put them on the back burner. The Papacy remained a naked and unashamed autocracy without a whisper of pretence at any form of representative structure, although by the late nineteenth century the rising profile of social issues consequent upon industrialisation – and the equally rising profile of the labour movement – had induced it to make pronouncements urging amicable relations between employers and workforces on the basis of decent treatment to the latter; and even to sponsor trade unions – so long as they were under its own influence. It gave endorsement to labour politicians if they were sufficiently moderate, reformist and un-revolutionary, such as the Catholic labour leaders in Glasgow – although in Italy it turned its face away from the Catholic-led Popolari peasant movement when that was resisting Mussolini's rise before 1922.

The Pope up to 1914, Pius X, was unusually hardline, traditionalist and reactionary even by Papal standards, though he abated the Church's boycott of the Italian state (a punishment for seizing the Papal States) sufficiently to allow Catholics to vote in elections provided they voted against socialists. His successor until 1922, Benedict XV, adopted a somewhat more nuanced tone of reaction, and his successor, Pius XI, went further in trying to adapt the church to contemporary realities while giving no ground on fundamentals. It was he who signed the Concordats with Hitler and Mussolini, and reaffirmed the integralist social teachings in the encyclical *Rerum Novarum* of his late-nineteenth-century predecessor Leo XIII.

Similar policies were followed in the 1930s and into the wartime years. The last parliamentary leader of the Centre Party was again a priest, before Hitler closed it down. This did not prevent the Vatican signing a Concordat with the Nazis, as it had similarly done with Mussolini, though in the German case the Papacy got the worst of the bargain. In Slovakia the reactionary (in fact, quasi-fascist) leader was, again, a priest, Monsignor Tiso: from April 1939, under Nazi tutelage when, after occupying Czechoslovakia, they recognised Slovakia as an 'independent' state, he became the premier and continued in that office to the end of the war. During the war and Yugoslavia's occupation Archbishop Stepinac was an inspiration to the Nazi-imitating local regime in Croatia, that of the Ustasi, which startled even the SS (Schutzstaffel, Protection Squadron) by its atrocities.

Pius XI in 1937 published in Germany the encyclical *Mit Brennender Sorge* ('With Burning Anxiety' – it was distributed secretly without pre-announcement and read from pulpits), which condemned the extremity of the Nazis' antisemitic project although its principal concerns were with the state's violation of the 1933 Concordat, hostility to any independent Catholic practice (particularly in education) and encouragement of neo-paganism. The following year, he followed this up with a Syllabus which condemned the valuation of racial ideology over that of religion, while nevertheless referring to 'higher' and 'humbler' races.

The UK

In the United Kingdom the social backbone of conservatism since it had emerged as a recognisable ideology had been the country's landowning classes, both the lesser and the greater.[3] They had, until the First World War, reason for self-congratulation, for they had successfully ridden out the immense economic, social, political and cultural transformations of the nineteenth century. They had retained their dominant role in the personnel of government despite the franchise extensions and the bureaucratisation of administration, and despite the fact that the business of government was now primarily directed towards the support of business. They formed the core of the officer corps. They had survived the collapse of grain prices in the last third of the century. They had successfully made a national fetish out of the expanding Empire, used it to extend their electoral viability and compelled their Liberal parliamentary opponents to fall into line on this issue. In the 1880s, thanks to the dispute over Home Rule in Ireland, they had won over a large section of the remaining Liberal aristocracy. Arthur Balfour, following the landslide Conservative electoral debacle in 1906, asserted with some justice that, whichever party was in office, the Conservatives would continue to direct the destinies of the nation and Empire.

British conservatism, however, was unlike its continental counterpart in important respects. There had been a mutual permeation of ideological assumptions between different sectors of the propertied classes (the public school system did a lot to foster this) and British landlords were in effect agrarian capitalists who, under the free trade system then prevailing had, however reluctantly, to take their chance in the world market. E. H. Carr remarked (in the 1960s) that if you scratched a British conservative you would find an old-fashioned liberal under the skin. Authoritarianism pervaded the culture of the times (the British penal system was among the harshest in Europe, and schools and workhouses were operated on a similar model). Conservatives were no doubt the most vociferous exponents of this culture, but liberals, particularly the Liberal Imperialists, were no softies either – especially when it came to repressing popular discontent.

The war and its aftermath marked a distinct change in landlord fortunes – which did not prevent the Conservative Party dominating the politics of the interwar years as it adapted its social base. A symbolic moment occurred in 1922 when the middle-class Stanley Baldwin was preferred to the ultra-aristocratic Lord Curzon as the incoming premier. The dialectic of history overtook the aristocracy and gentry when their young heirs, greatly over-represented in the lower ranks of the officer corps, suffered disproportionate casualties. Shortage of heirs combined with agricultural depression in the 1920s provoked large-scale land sales,[4] in a great number of cases to sitting tenants, so that the proportion of owner-occupier farms rose greatly and the social strength of the landlords decreased proportionately.

With an unbroken record of depression and slump from 1920 industrialists in general suffered no less severely, though clearly they could not resort to similar solutions. Bankers however did much better and it was towards those that government policy was orientated, in addition to which banks bought up and restructured failing enterprises, or at least as emergency creditors took control and dictated their operation. At the same time the great clearing banks gobbled up their last minor competitors – though despite governmental support and overvalued sterling the investment banks were unable to regain the hegemony lost to the USA.

Nevertheless the most distinctive fact of British politics between 1922 and 1940 was that for all but eleven months in 1924 and between June 1929 and August 1931 the Conservative Party controlled the government (from 1931 in the form of a pseudo-coalition known as the National Government) – and this at a time when the franchise had been extended to all men over 21 and women over 30, and from 1928 women over 21 as well.

The principal boast of British conservatives was that they disdained ideology and theory and dedicated themselves to the pragmatic skills of governing for which, they claimed, conservative politicians possessed an instinctive talent appreciated by the greater part of the governed, who therefore entrusted them with office. They kept the ship of state on course and when issues arose, they drew on national tradition and sought solutions which *worked*. To a degree this was actually true. British – in effect English – conservatism had emerged out of sharp struggles and disputes within the propertied class and its cardinal objective was to protect the distribution of property and authority and preserve as much of the traditional institutions as possible. In the last analysis it was not too particular about how this was accomplished – repression was the instinctive response to any challenge, but reforms were acceptable when other courses looked too dangerous or when particular reforms in state or society might prove advantageous. Some fetishes however were too precious to abandon, except in extremity, even when they conferred little practical benefit. The total unity of the United Kingdom was one such, hence conservatives' desperate intransigence over Irish devolution, or Home Rule as it was then called, even to the extent of threatening civil war. However in the end, in 1921, their leaders agreed to concede even the effective independence of the Free State, although not without severe heart-burnings.

The principle of preserving the social order by employing only the minimum necessary repression can be observed in the career of Stanley Baldwin. His government ensured the defeat of the General Strike in 1926, which was correctly viewed by it as a challenge to established political and propertied relations (even if TUC leaders thought otherwise), using significant violence, but refraining from letting loose the kind of ferocity which had been recently exhibited in Ireland. Following the government's victory he blocked the sort of revenge legislation which his wilder colleagues (including Churchill) were calling for and limited repression to the Trades Disputes Act, which the unions might not like but could live with; and thereby preserved the corporatist relations analysed by Keith Middlemas.[5] This 'moderation' was duly rewarded by the compliance of the trade union leaders, who in 1928 entered the Mond-Turner talks.

Nonetheless the Conservative Party and right-wing media did not fail to paint the Labour Party in the scariest of scarlet and imply that it was scarcely to be distinguished from the Bolsheviks. This proved fruitful. Presenting themselves as the stout defenders of Britain against bloody Bolshevik revolution, the Conservatives captured much of the electoral constituency of the disintegrating Liberal Party (the Labour Party also made gains from the Liberal decline). No less important was the effect of this propaganda upon the Labour Party itself. Its leaders, anxious above all to depict themselves as patriotic British traditionalists, were increasingly pushed in a rightward direction and dissociated their party from all but the mildest reformism; it could be argued that they had no choice. A symbolic moment arrived when their leader, Ramsay MacDonald, though lacking a parliamentary majority, was invited in 1924 to form the government and insisted that, in the traditional fashion, his Cabinet wear knee breeches for presentation to the King.

The 1930s saw the Conservative Party in unchallengeable political control. In 1931 the bloc, which they easily dominated, with MacDonald and his close associates, provided them with an electoral landslide. It enabled them to realise what had become their fetish, the reinstatement of protectionism and the creation of an imperial trading bloc. Although the threat of communist revolution emanating from the USSR was long past and the British CP of little account, their terror of the left never abated and was undoubtedly a significant consideration in conservative attitudes towards continental fascism and Hitler's increasingly aggressive claims and behaviour.

Mosley and his Blackshirts were dismissed as posturing nuisances – though matters might well have been different if the British political system had been less secure. Mussolini, however, was much admired (at least up to his Abyssinian invasion) and there existed a very large segment of conservative opinion committed to close solidarity with the dictators.[6] Even among mainstream conservatives Hitler, though his methods of government might be regarded with some disdain, gained approval for his destruction of communism in Germany (even initially from Churchill) and was undoubtedly viewed as a useful obstacle to the spread of communism in Europe. Had circumstances in the 1930s permitted an immediate German military assault upon the USSR it is hard to imagine British conservatives of that era making great objection. Certainly most of them were prepared to let Hitler have his way with Austria and Czechoslovakia (and make sure the French did not interfere). They also sought Mussolini as an ally for as long as possible and with few exceptions applauded Franco's crusade against democracy in Spain. Whether the 'National', that is, Conservative, government actively encouraged Hitler to turn his forces against the USSR is less certain – there is a lot of suggestive evidence but no definite proof.[7]

Overall British conservative ideology, though it may have lacked some of the scarier features of its continental counterparts, had during the interwar years not yet come to terms with the twentieth century; electoral democracy, partial and restricted though it was, was regarded as an unavoidable nuisance to be reluctantly accepted rather than a development to be welcomed. Although far from extinguished, domestic service was in sharp decline and this reality evoked intense complaint and grumbling from those classes which customarily benefited from it, with never a thought about *why* domestic service might be unpopular. The lower orders, Edmund Burke's 'little platoons', existed in the conservative mind primarily to supply the needs and minister to the whims of their betters.

Sentiments of this type pervaded every dimension of the social and political arena. They were the essence of classic conservatism, the reality behind all the discourse of tradition modulated by judicious reform, of the admittance of new wealth to the charmed circle, of patriotism and monarchy. The mentality which fostered the slave trade, which judged that it was expedient to treat soldiers and sailors as foully as possible so that they wouldn't mind getting killed, to tax the poor harshly so that they would be forced to work, and the rich lightly so that they would invest[8] – all that was still alive and flourishing in the 1920s and 1930s. Fascism, so far as it was distrusted, was distrusted on account of its populist character.

Germany

Germany in the days of the Weimar Republic may have been a paradise of cultural creativity but was at the same time a devil's soup of political and ideological conflict, erupting often enough in naked violence. It was beset by three communist insurrections, two attempts at a right-wing coup, regular assassinations, partial occupation, renewed invasion (briefly), hyperflation, and finally economic slump and hyper-unemployment. In the political arena and on the streets communists, socialists, fascists and conservatives fought it out; governments were always coalitions – wildly unstable and becoming more so as time went on. Yet conservatives, usually hankering for the monarchy and all that it represented, contemptuous of politics and hating democracy – whether or not they were affiliated to any of the conservative parties – were always in control up to the end. They overwhelmingly dominated and set standards in the administration, in the judiciary, in the diplomatic service, in the professions, in the schools and universities, and among the clergy both Catholic and Protestant. Above all they were in charge of the military.

Political-cultural hegemony in the republic was fiercely contested, but it was the conservatives who held the advantage. They could not dominate the Reichstag, but the state institutions they certainly did, as well as possessing a private army of their own, the Stahlhelm. As well as the upper classes, the layers of the *Mittelstand*[9] (apart from its bohemian fringes) were, even apart from its material distresses, firmly attached to conservative ideology. They bitterly resented the loss of the war and the subsequent peace treaties, eagerly swallowed the notorious *Dolchenstoss* myth (the 'stab in the back' legend), longed for the restoration of Germany's lost territories, its authoritarian culture, its status as a great power, its national pride and military force. From 1924 onwards the ultra-conservative old militarist Paul von Hindenburg held the Presidency – on the basis of popular election.

In 1920 a serious attempt was made at a reactionary putsch by the proto-fascist Freikorps private army and a section of the military, fronted by a civil servant, Wolfgang Kapp. It failed only because of a general strike and the disinclination of the army leaders to support it. When the Munich-based Adolf Hitler attempted in 1923 to imitate Mussolini's march on Rome the venture's frontman was the military leader of the First World War, Erich Ludendorff. In both cases the leaders and participants escaped any significant punishment.

An important intellectual strain in Weimar conservatism, acting in some respects as a bridge to fascism, was that of the 'conservative revolutionaries', represented especially by Ernst Jünger. This movement rejected many elements of the old traditionalist order, was fiercely militaristic, celebrated the buzz of armed action, and was based on the notion of the fraternal trench community as a model for social relations. They foresaw 'the beginning of the worker's dominion'[10] – by 'worker' was meant servicemen, ex-servicemen, or at any rate men (specifically men) imbued with the military ethos.

The onset of the slump had the rapid consequence that the conservative grip on the consciousness of traditionalists and nationalists began to weaken, to the profit of Nazis, who started to increase their votes at the expense of the DNVP and other conservative parties. German conservatives, for all their neo-feudal traditions, were nonetheless passionately attached to nineteenth-century economic relations, and so when the slump knocked the bottom out of agricultural prices and indigent peasant farmers began to be foreclosed on in great numbers, the DNVP could do nothing for them. The Nazis by contrast made promises, and were rewarded by a massive switch of the agricultural vote in the Reichstag elections of 1930, making them the second largest party in the chamber and now, along with the communists, also rising electorally, capable of disrupting legislative and governmental business.

Two years earlier the DNVP had acquired a more aggressive and hardline leader in the person of Alfred Hugenberg, businessman, media baron and ultra-right politician – resembling Silvio Berlusconi in these respects, without any of the latter's charm. Thinking to draw the Nazis closer to the conservative mainstream, he had helped Hitler to raise his profile even before 1930 by opening his radio station to him during the debate over the reparations adjustment proposed by the US-sponsored Young Plan. Subsequently, as the DNVP waned electorally Hugenberg acted increasingly as a go-between for Hitler and the conservative right. For three years after the Nazi breakthrough the traditional elites' political representatives strove to find a formula for government stability which would neuter the left and incorporate the Nazis while leaving themselves safely in control. In January 1933, terrified by the continuous rise of the communist vote, they thought they had found it by accepting Hitler's condition that he be appointed Chancellor while seeing to it that nearly all the members of his cabinet were conservatives, including the vice-Chancellor, and subject to dismissal if necessary by the President backed by the army.

They were soon undeceived, for within a few months Hitler had sidelined their cabinet and vice-Chancellor and had abolished their parties. A year later, Hindenburg having died, he got them to accept himself as head of state as well, and so established his personal dictatorship. Yet delighted by the destruction of the left and the removal of tiresome social legislation, satisfied by economic revival, rearmament and restoration of national pride, the traditional elite went along with these developments. Until the beginning of 1937 the Foreign Minister, the Minister of War, the Chiefs of the Army and Navy and the Minister of Economics, were conservatives, not Nazis. The

Economics Minister resigned in September 1937 and early the following year, Hitler easily removed all the others with the exception of Admiral Raeder, who was entirely reliable.

Of the German conservative ideologists who contributed to this development, none was more important than the jurist Carl Schmitt. Any examination of Schmitt's career and writings cannot avoid the conclusion that he was an opportunist scoundrel – but an exceptionally clear-headed one. He well understood the reality that political conflict was civil war by other means, to adapt Clausewitz's famous aphorism, and knew which side he was on – he shared the basic outlook of his affluent and devoutly Catholic business background though he lapsed from the religion. In the words of Perry Anderson, Schmitt translated Thomas Hobbes's conception of the war of all against all in the state of nature to, instead, tight political collectives based on economic, social or cultural principles and interests.

The state was the necessarily independent and neutral sovereign which stood above society, mediated or repressed its conflicts and coordinated its national power, particularly in war. Emerging out of the bloody disorder of late medieval and early modern history, the European absolute state operated an implied contract with civil society – while repressing disturbances to public order, especially in the shape of ideological forces which aimed to take the state over, it otherwise left society to get on with its business. In Schmitt's view this was perfectly compatible with the later development of a legislative assembly provided that the latter acted in the manner of the British parliament ('the cunning of parliament' he called it, a nod toward Hegel's 'cunning of reason') where the legislators learned to subordinate party interests to national ones.

Etatism ('statism') was a powerful tradition in German political thinking, generated in particular by the lustre and success of the Prussian monarchy from the seventeenth to the nineteenth century (Hegel regarded it as the culmination of world history). For Schmitt the ideal state of affairs was the Bismarckian *Kaiserreich* of the late nineteenth century, a monarchical, militarist and bureaucratic state that was responsible to the Reichstag only for the budget, and could sideline the latter if necessary. In Schmitt's view the cardinal features of the state were its responsibility for defining friends and enemies and for deciding when it was necessary to pronounce a 'state of exception' and step outside the boundaries of existing legality, as Bismarck had done in the 1860s when he collected revenues by military force and without parliamentary approval.

Like all intransigent German conservatives Schmitt detested the Weimar regime, especially for its inability to resist the terms of the Versailles Treaty, though perceptively he noted that the exceptional powers the Constitution gave to the President in emergency might have potential. But otherwise it was scarcely worthy to be called a state, for the situation of the nineteenth century was now abolished. 'After the debacle of the First World War, and the victory of Bolshevism in Russia, the old political world of landed rulers and limited electorates, modest budgets and stable currencies, had crumbled away'.[11] The state had become the football of rival parties which were less political entities in the old sense and more the political expression of militant politico-cultural collectives, each encased within its own socio-cultural alternative universe and bitter enemies to each other – a truly Hobbesian state of affairs. Schmitt had established himself in the 1920s as a major theoretical spokesperson on the right; he acted as an adviser to the conservative Chancellor von Papen but rallied to Nazism once Hitler came to power and provided 'legal' justification for the arbitrary extermination of the SA leaders in 1934.

Italy

The role played by conservative elites in Italy in 1920–22 was a remarkable anticipation of what was to happen in Germany in 1932–33. These elites again included the military, the civil authorities and the landowners, and the leaders of banking, industry and commerce. One difference was the existence of a monarchy, with a cerebrally challenged monarch obsessed with military ritual, who proved to be as easily manipulable as Hindenburg. Once again fear of red revolution was a significant factor, only this time it had taken the form not of insurrection but of mass sit-in strikes in the northern industrial centres and peasant unrest offering a serious challenge to the hegemony of landlords at a village level.

While repression of the socialist threat in any form may have been at the top of the Italian conservative agenda, it was by no means the only item. Italy itself was a rather ramshackle polity, poorly integrated both economically and administratively, varying in character from the industrially developed north to the neo-feudal agricultural south. No political party actually called itself conservative; the dominant political formation, a friable coalition of upper-class interests, designated itself as liberal; they were in effect the conservatives of that place and time. Their basic purposes were first to keep the state running in the interest of the elites (until 1913 the franchise was restricted to a minuscule percentage of the male population) which they did by buying off opposition – a technique referred to as *transformisimo* – and second to demonstrate the state's virility by acquiring overseas colonies.

Such stagnant attitudes, and the failure to establish a decent colonial presence, were resented by the more dynamic sectors of the bourgeoisie and their intellectual spokespeople. As early as 1900 proposals had been advanced for what certain later historians, with reference to Mussolini's regime, were to term a 'developmental dictatorship'. These proposals included the abolition of parliamentary government, a powerful incorruptible executive above the law to suppress labour, assert Italian power internationally and to drive forward speedy economic growth and industrialisation. In 1910 Enrico Corradini formed the Associazione Nazionalista Italiana (ANI, Italian National Association) with similar aims and with colonial expansion at the head of the list. The ANI was in due course to be absorbed by the Partito Nazionale Fascista (PNF, National Fascist Party).

In essence, after 1920 Italian capital and Italian elites generally had lost confidence in the ability of the liberal parliamentary regime to keep the masses in their place – as in general had the Liberal parliamentarians themselves.

Mussolini was a useful demagogue who had made clear where his basic intentions lay and he was backed by ferocious strong-arm paramilitaries. In the course of 1921, his followers, with a degree of assistance from the police and military, crushed the peasant intransigence and the following year there was little resistance by the conservatives to the blackmail of his preposterous 'march on Rome' and demand for the office of premier.

As in Germany, the cabinet was at first principally made up of conservative politicians, following which, in a process that took two years to Hitler's few months, these were ejected from office and thereafter found themselves in the political cold. In other respects the traditional elites got what they wanted, although they were stripped of political authority – a civil society after their own heart with political opposition and the labour movement totally crushed, capital given free rein and torrential international bluster from the premier which succeeded in impressing the powers of Europe sufficiently to stop them from offering any serious opposition to his territorial aggressions.

Other European states

Outside fascist Germany and Italy, social democrat Scandinavia and the USSR, conservative elites succeeded in maintaining their political as well as socio-economic and cultural ascendancy. Strong and hegemonic Roman Catholic tradition in certain of these states assisted them enormously. That was true of Ireland, Iberia, Austria, Poland and, to a lesser extent, Hungary; although only in Portugal did they succeed without armed conflict in overcoming the eruption of new social forces. Ireland has already been referred to, but it should be noted that in the 1930s, when the opposition succeeded in capturing office through electoral means and generated a brief anti-Bolshevik panic among the establishment, the new rulers were absorbed without difficulty into the prevailing consensus.

The ideological form that this took can be termed integralism and was essentially the outlook of a static agrarian-based social order, where authoritarian hierarchy was omnipresent. It was based – in theory – on reciprocal though unequal responsibilities and personal loyalty focused upwards, where everyone knew and observed their place and where social integration was reinforced by means of a shared culture backed by a state religion. The Catholic Church, with a central authority crossing international boundaries and an ability to mount in Rome spectacular events like the Jubilee years, gave a natural advantage in this respect. In states such as Romania, Bulgaria and Greece, the role of the eastern Orthodox church (or the Lutheran church in Finland), in achieving similar results within these semi-constitutional states, though significant, was necessarily weaker.

The realities of the twentieth century were not, however, absent from these societies and their polities. No less than the most industrialised countries of the globe they were integrated also in a different sense – into the world market and affected equally if not more so by its fluctuations. They had industrialists and bankers, some of international importance, they had in greater or lesser degree industrial working classes, and in all cases urban concentrations with modern forms of communications and education. Consequently, to medieval forms of integralism was added superheated nationalism as a necessary social cement, not least in the form of a promise that achieving national goals would provide solutions to pressing economic and social problems.[12]

'[W]e shall defend the working man against agitators and demagogues – and speculators too. The abuses of the private ownership of capital, which serves as the pretext for revolutionary agitation, will be vigilantly watched.' These perspectives were represented nowhere better than by the virulently antisemitic, French, ultra-conservative propagandist Charles Maurras, the author of the above lines, who can indeed be regarded as their ideological driver throughout the twentieth century, whose influence continued as an underground stream, so to speak, for decades after his discredit and death, and whose ideas provided an essential bridge between ultra-conservatism and fascism.

His long ideological shadow is all the more peculiar in that he was disowned by the forces on whose behalf he wanted to speak, French monarchism and the Catholic Church (paradoxically he was himself irreligious, but revered the church for its institutional authority). A would-be mass leader, he never attained any political position – one critic remarked that he never brought out anything except his newspaper.

Maurras came to prominence initially at the end of the nineteenth century, in the context of the Dreyfus affair where he employed all his rhetorical skills and established the Action Française political group in the service of the antisemitic frame-up and hoped that it might lead to a monarchist coup executed by the military. In the early twentieth century, he took control of the *Action Française* newspaper, which served thereafter as his principal mouthpiece, and soon became the inspirer of the Camelots du Roy, a gang of monarchist antisemitic thugs, mostly middle-class students, whose purpose was to sell the paper and intimidate political opposition, foreshadowing the tactics of the fascist paramilitaries of the interwar years.

Action Française as a political movement continued into the years of post-war crisis, still advocating monarchical restoration although it was overshadowed by other more activist and dynamic fascist and para-fascist organisations; Maurras's organisation remained 'an upmarket talking shop', in the words of one commentator,[13] and was sneeringly referred to as 'Inaction Française' by its right-wing rivals.

Nevertheless Maurras's intellectual and ideological reach was enormous, and, although he was above all a French ultra-nationalist, it extended far beyond French and even European borders, particularly in Latin America. The Iberian and Austrian dictatorships had very evident Maurrassian overtones, and even Mussolini's notion of the corporate state was a (cynical and meaningless) gesture to nationalist integralism, as was the Nazi notion of *Volksgemeinschaft* (which translates as 'people's community'). Creative writers of the first rank such as Paul Claudel in France and T. S. Eliot in the UK acknowledged their debt to Maurras.

Maurras and his followers were extreme political romantics, although paradoxically he denounced romanticism as an intellectual infection responsible for revolution and all the troubles of the modern age and regarded himself as upholding the 'classical' values of the ancient world represented by its aristocratic authors and hierarchical rulers.[14] His almost caricature arrogance is well exemplified by the passage in the manifesto of 1899, 'Dictator and King':

> Since the undersigned writers are prompted by their knowledge of political necessities which may have escaped the attention of their fellow citizens, and since they act as spokesmen and elders of their race, and in full exercise of the rights and duties conferred upon them by the present deplorable state of affairs.
>
> Since they are fully aware of their obligation to minister and to watch over the common good ....[15]

His abiding passion was his incandescent hatred of democracy and all its associations, and this lay behind the quixotic monarchism which features so prominently in his writings – he was still calling for restoration from his prison cell in 1950, 'For France to have long life, long live the king!' In 1899, he had urged the French pretender to take over as dictator – from his point of view, non-royal dictators, however ideologically sound in other respects, suffered the disadvantage of being obliged to mobilise popular support. He regarded democracy as a foreign import – immediately from Germany and Switzerland, and more distantly from Jerusalem – sustained in France by his particular objects of hatred: Jews, Freemasons, Protestants and foreigners, particularly German ones.

> [T]he principle of equality, essence of the democratic system, handed over power to the most numerous, that is to say the most inferior elements of the nation, to the least vigorous producers, to the most voracious consumers, who do the least work and the most damage .... As for the imaginary benefits equality is expected to bestow, they will cause suffering to everyone ... the natural evil is infinitely multiplied by the dream, the system, the artificial stimulants of democracy.[16]

Pétain, upon taking over at Vichy, sent Maurras a copy of his speeches inscribed, 'To Charles Maurras, the most French of Frenchmen'. The policies and ideological expression of the Vichy regime between 1940 and 1944 were based upon his ideas (although he criticised its antisemitic legislation for being insufficiently severe). Following the Liberation, convicted of collaborationism he escaped the well-deserved guillotine or firing squad, possibly because of his intense anti-Germanism aided by his medical condition – he was profoundly deaf – or possibly because he had friends in high places. He tried to claim that Pétain had been secretly working for an Allied victory, and possibly even believed it – Maurras had a boundless capacity for self-deception.

The states which had been losers in the 1914–18 war had extensive territories to recover; there were more ethnic Hungarians living in adjacent countries (especially Romania) than in Hungary itself. Those that had been winners had their gains to preserve – Romania had all but doubled its population (most of its new citizens being non-Romanians). Poland was a special case – it had been revived from eighteenth-century extinction by the outcome of the war and secured additional territorial gains, containing resentful national minorities, to preserve against the Soviet Union in the east and Germany in the west. Finland, although it enjoyed an unusual degree of autonomy when part of the Tsar's Empire, had secured national independence also as a result of the war, but among the most nationalistic elements of the ruling elites much greater gains were envisaged. Fierce anti-Russian nationalism pervaded the three small Baltic States. Yugoslavia provided another special case, and here especially in the Europe of the interwar years religious difference served as a defining mark of national antagonism. The northern populations and their elites were Catholic in their adherence, particularly in Croatia; their Serbian counterparts, who dominated the new multinational state and reserved for themselves its choicest benefits, were attached to the eastern Orthodox faith.

In the Latin countries, and in Austria and Hungary, it was the integralist ideology which more than any other provided the bridge between conservatism and fascism. Roger Austin, in Martin Blinkhorn's *Fascists and Conservatives*, attributes to integral nationalism, 'violent anti-communism, varying degrees of xenophobia, and a degree of vaguely corporatist solutions to … economic problems. They favoured authoritarian forms of government which would strengthen the powers of the executive over parliament.'[17]

Zionism

Zionism, the project of establishing a Jewish state in Palestine, advanced from the end of the nineteenth century and, stimulated not least by the Dreyfus Affair, was a multi-sided phenomenon (as well as being at the time very much a minority trend among the Jewish public). It included left-wing and right-wing versions – and later even a fascist faction of the Revisionist Zionism founded by Ze'ev Jabotinsky, which openly admired Mussolini. However, taken overall, Zionism has to be assessed as a form of conservatism, as its project was essentially a colonial settler one directed primarily against the Arab inhabitants of Palestine, and its strategy prior to the First World War was to win the support of the Turkish Empire (at that time the ruler of the area), Kaiser Wilhelm II and Tsar Nicholas II, both ardent antisemites. After the outbreak of the War and subsequently its leaders sought the sponsorship of British conservatism and received it, embodied in the Balfour Declaration of 1917.

The USA

The hegemonic ideology strongly entrenched in the USA was that of individualistic liberalism, although displaying some very peculiar features and far from liberal in its social attitudes. The 1920s were, after all, the decade of Prohibition and racism was rampant throughout the white population, not by any means confined to the ex-Confederate states where it assumed an especially pathological character.

The two rival dominant political coalitions (it would be scarcely accurate to call them parties) operated within this context and could only with difficulty be aligned upon a right–left spectrum. The Republicans, however, ferociously anti-labour, were eminently and unmistakably the representatives of big capital, which never hesitated to use lethal violence to prevent union organising; the Democrats tended to attract the poorer sections of white American society, but theirs was also the party of the Southern racists. Perhaps on average the democrats were marginally less committed to unrestrained market values.

The centrepiece of conservative values at the time was isolationism – the minimising of US political involvement in the world outside the Americas and the Pacific. It stood as a rallying slogan in opposition to the project of the Democrat President Wilson. An American world-role was not yet on the conservative agenda; it was a Republican-dominated Congress which blocked the participation of the USA in the League of Nations and rejected ratification of the Versailles Treaty which Wilson had signed. Three Republican presidents were elected during the 1920s, Warren Harding, Calvin Coolidge and Herbert Hoover; the first two uncharismatic nonentities, indeed Dorothy Parker quipped, 'How could they tell?' when one of them died. They were, however, hardline conservatives for whom the government's business was business – and for a time it seemed to work, for in the middle of the decade, with the rest of the world floundering in depression, the USA enjoyed boom conditions.

Herbert Hoover, before his elevation, was known as the 'Great Engineer' and indeed in 1928 was elected on that reputation, but began his administration in the year of the slump. The slump was a turning point. American conservatism identified itself with the insistence that government could do nothing to amend the situation and that the traditional norms of balanced budgets and minimal expenditure must remain in place, come what may. The first reaction of the conservative spokespersons, with Hoover in the lead, was to deny that any long-term slump could be recognised; the second was to maintain that market forces would soon amend the situation and overcome the difficulties – government should do nothing apart from suppressing protest by the sufferers. It was not surprising that even with the restricted franchise prevailing these sentiments were rejected by the electorate in the Presidential election of 1932.

American conservatism fought the mild and limited measures of the New Deal tooth and claw. It was denounced and damned in all the media controlled by press barons and by commentators who thought along similar lines. Not much could be done in Congress as long as the Democrats enjoyed a majority there (although Roosevelt had to temper his programme to suit their conservative wing), but the principal stronghold of conservatism was in the judiciary, particularly its higher reaches, with the Supreme Court striking down every New Deal measure that it could. Administrations in individual conservative-controlled states obstructed as much as they were able.

It was alleged that Roosevelt's enemies even plotted a military coup.[18] They must, if the allegations were justified, have been very inept conspirators though, for the military figurehead they had in mind was General Smedley D. Butler, who was in fact a political radical and had previously denounced the activities of big capital in Latin America as well as the military actions it sponsored in which he had been obliged to participate. The coup attempt, if it was real, never came to anything and the allegations were swept under the carpet. These years nevertheless were not wasted ones for US conservatives. They honed and polished their hatred for every form of politics, economic measure, social action or culture that failed to correspond with their conception of the 'American Way'. Forced on the defensive during the Roosevelt years, the adherents of this ideology possessed a strong and extensive social base and were only waiting their opportunity to counter-attack.

East Asia

Roger Griffin writes that one of the reasons for the elusiveness of Japanese fascism is that it was faced with 'a formidably entrenched radical right'.[19] As Perry Anderson noted,[20] Japan, prior to European penetration in the nineteenth century, provided the nearest parallel elsewhere in the world to feudal Europe, and feudal values continued to dominate Japanese culture, an intensely authoritarian society with an emperor standing halfway between a figurehead and an active political leader. His deliberately invented sacramental status made him appear more in the character of a Bronze Age god-king than any European monarch, feudal, absolute or constitutional.

Early-twentieth-century Japan had the civil and political apparatus of a modern state, trade unions, political parties, cabinet government – and in due course even a communist party – but they were no match for the overwhelmingly hegemonic ultra-conservative forces. The concentrated centre of these forces was in the military, and in the wake of the economic slump they were able to push aside all counterbalancing elements in civil society and dictate the direction of Japan's government, most importantly with the invasion of China in 1931. Further imperial expansion was viewed as the answer to economic crisis. On the eve of Japan's attack on the United States in 1941 and transformation of the European war into a world war, they openly assumed control over the government with a military prime minister and compelled all the legal political parties to amalgamate into an association supporting their project.

That project was underpinned by an ideology which focused Japanese culture and education on the person of the emperor and silenced any questioning of his imaginary supernatural descent. Japan was a deeply racist society, and imperialist ultra-nationalism, practised since the late nineteenth century, fitted in very effectively with this separationist culture. The Japanese public was taught by their elites through every available medium of communication to regard their nation as supremely fitted and destined to lead the peoples of eastern Asia, and therefore entitled to exploit them according to their pleasure. During the 1930s and the war, Japan tended to be included by its enemies among the fascist powers and it was, of course, a member of the Anti-Comintern Pact and eventually part of the Axis. Certainly that was more than a marriage of convenience and Nazism was undoubtedly perceived in a sympathetic light by Japan's rulers, but their own form of ultra-conservatism could not with accuracy be regarded as fascist – although it could be no less vicious.

Since 1911, China had been in the throes of revolution, civil war, foreign interference and collapsed central authority. The 1920s saw the emergence of a military strongman in the person of Chiang Kai-shek, who claimed the heritage of the 1911 anti-monarchic revolution and the Guomindang, the party of its inspirer Sun Yat-sen. The ideological form in which he justified his claim to supreme rulership was one of national reunification and restoration but the content was all too evident – the continuing ascendancy of the traditional ruling classes, particularly the landlords, and the traditional cultural norms of subordination and clientage. With Machiavellian instinct he first allied his pretensions to a national liberation ideology with the nascent Communist Party, which, on Comintern instructions, was incorporated into the Guomindang; then, when it had served its purpose, he turned on it and massacred its activists. The slaughter, however, was not quite comprehensive enough and Chiang continued thereafter to be troubled with armed communist resistance as he established his oppressive, shaky and invincibly corrupt regime characterised by savage taxation, no less savage military conscription and intermittent famine.

SECOND WORLD WAR

In the course of these years European conservatism was severely tainted by its all-too-frequent association with fascism, Nazism and Nazi occupation, and immediately following the Liberation was obliged to maintain a low profile. The Iberian regimes were pariahs, particularly the Spanish, and their fall following the Allied victory was universally expected. De Valera's Irish government and Fianna Fail party, a peculiar mixture of radical nationalist rhetoric and intense socio-economic and cultural conservatism, had, like the Iberian dictatorships but without their odium, succeeded in maintaining neutrality and was in no immediate danger.

British conservatism was severely battered by the memory of the 1930s and the appeasement policies of its then premiers, but had preserved its social base and had the advantage of being the leading element in the wartime Coalition government with its leader being the wartime premier and titan of anti-Nazism. His motives however were far from pure. He had been quite sympathetic to Mussolini in the 1920s, and Churchill was above all an arch-imperialist, declaring that he had not become His Majesty's first minister to preside over the dissolution of the British Empire (although that, to a great degree, was exactly what he did). No doubt even before the war he was disgusted by the Nazis' internal regime, but his overriding objection to it was that it was a threat to the British position in Europe and beyond that to its empire. His underlying sentiments reasserted themselves in 1944 in regard to Greece, when in the aftermath of the German expulsion he provided every assistance to conservative ex-collaborators to re-establish their authority and defeat the communist-led national liberation movement. Fellow-feeling with conservatives and Greek connections with British royalty no doubt played a part, but the principal motivation here was to retain British hegemony in the eastern Mediterranean to protect the Suez Canal and the Indian Empire which Churchill saw continuing into the indefinite future. Still, in spite of its creditable wartime record and that of its leader, British conservatism – or at least its political party – was swamped electorally in 1945, although its ideology, penetrating deeply into the public consciousness, continued to exert enormous power.

Conspiracies against Hitler among the conservative military had existed since 1938 (when they had believed that disastrous war over Czechoslovakia was imminent), but were quiescent during the years of stunning victories, and it was only when the war was manifestly lost by 1944 that they, along with other conservative anti-Nazis, attempted a putsch, which failed most dismally. Even had they managed to kill Hitler, as they very nearly did, it is far from evident that they would have succeeded. Certainly they wanted to end the war, but at the same time to preserve as much as possible of the old Germany, and they even hankered after the borders of at least 1938. That was the last political throw of classic German conservatives and unconditional surrender was to be their lot; nevertheless in the half of Germany which fell under Anglo-American control the social base remained sufficiently intact to enable conservatism's political strength to be re-established on a new foundation in the post-war era.

A process virtually identical in its essence occurred in Italy, with certain differences in detail. For reasons similar to those in Germany, namely an irretrievably lost war, the traditionalist conservatives turned against Mussolini and engineered his overthrow. In contrast to Hitler, who was constitutionally untouchable, Mussolini was nominally responsible to the monarch, who could and did dismiss him – for the same reasons in effect as he had appointed him in the first place, the salvation of the old order. After the war, although many uncongenial changes such as the end of the monarchy had to be accepted, the essential aim was achieved.

In Japan, the changes following defeat were even more drastic. The military were stripped of political, social and cultural power and came close to abolition. The Imperial myth was extinguished and the emperor retained only as a figurehead, though his sacramental cultural aura could not be eliminated. Nonetheless, under indulgent American supervision (the USSR having been barred from any participation in the occupation) conservative political strength was rebuilt and its party, now terming itself the Liberal Democrats, ruled Japan continuously thereafter with entrenched political hegemony.

The Second World War accomplished at indescribable human cost the work left unfinished by the 1848 European revolutions and the revolutions following the First World War. The old order inherited from past centuries was finally shattered not only in Europe but throughout the globe. Yet conservative ideology demonstrated its astonishing adaptability and capacity for survival; it maintained its hold on enormous swathes of the public consciousness everywhere, not only among its direct beneficiaries, and before very long its political manifestations were able to rise from the ashes.

4
Communism

COMMUNIST CONTRADICTIONS

A dictionary of politics in the 1950s noted that communism could be seen either as a variant of socialism or its antithesis. It was a perceptive definition. The term first came into prominence in the late 1840s with the establishment under Marx's influence of the revolutionary Communist League and its famous *Manifesto*. The organisation adopted the term to distinguish itself from the early socialists who were seen as both utopian and lacking in militancy.

By the early twentieth century, as explained in the Introduction to this book, the term had to a great extent dropped out of currency. Even the Russian Marxists, who did not conceal their revolutionary intentions, used 'social democrat' as their label when their underground organisation was established between 1898 and 1903, adopting it in imitation of the older parties of the Socialist International, particularly the mighty German example. Following the debacle of the socialist parties in 1914 and the Russian Revolution, the Third International was founded in 1919 to carry that revolution around the world. It reinstated the old communist name to emphasise its commitment to Marx's undiluted programme of relentless opposition to the bourgeoisie and bourgeois property, and distinguish its parties from those of the social democratic 'traitors'. The alternative name for the Third International was the Communist International, shortened to 'Comintern'.

Several questions have to be addressed in relation to the communist movement. First of all, the reason why, though it had its origins in Russian events, it found such resonance on a global scale.[1] Secondly, why its adherents for the most part willingly accepted the drastic alterations in the character of the movement's ideology which took place during the interwar years and directed their actions accordingly. It should be noted that we are discussing here not individuals who were in one way or another under the direct control of the regime but who were, on the contrary, well outside its state authority.

The answer to both is actually not very mysterious. Members of the communist parties outside of the Soviet Union were fired with the conviction that they were engaged in a difficult and dangerous project of universal and universalist emancipation and that 'history was on their side'. They were quickly schooled into a conception of what such emancipation meant (including vengeance on the agents of persecution – landlords, bosses and state servants – particularly marked where class differences were at their most intense) and viewed the 'workers' state', the USSR, as exemplifying that.

Communist ideology has quite frequently been described as a secular religion. This is highly inaccurate and misleading. Since it rigorously excluded all supernatural conceptions (although religious believers could join it if they wished without dropping their private beliefs), it would be necessary to invent another word for what we've hitherto identified as religion. Nevertheless, there is no question that both as an ideology and a practice it did exhibit some of the characteristics of religious evangelism. These included a canon of 'sacred' texts which were virtually exempt from criticism (but open to almost limitless interpretation), practices of total self-sacrificing dedication among its activists, conviction of rightness (and righteousness) which was at certain times highly exclusionary, refusal to take account of evidence manifest to anybody else and in consequence to 'believe ninety-nine impossible things before breakfast', intense feelings of community and solidarity – and with that went formidable social and moral pressures.

These pathologies of belief were conditioned by several factors. For a start, communists shared the conviction that opponents of the movement always lied, so their assertions could be readily dismissed. George Orwell once wrote that 'certain things are true even though the *Daily Telegraph* says them'. For communists, if the *Daily Telegraph* said them then they could not possibly be. Even more important, the Soviet communists had shown the way, they had carried through the revolution when no-one else had done so, therefore they had to be right. In any case, the USSR was the world's last best hope and therefore its defence against all enemies and critics had to be the central priority, and any shortcomings in the regime were best ignored or denied.

It was a striking irony that a movement which disdained all manner of superstition and chose to make a point of describing itself as 'scientific socialism' could fall into the irrationality of accepting whatever pronouncements emanated from the Comintern (in effect from the Kremlin), however they might contradict the clear evidence of circumstances or even reverse what had been the 'party line' the day before. No less contradictory and irrational, but springing from the same source, was the posthumous 'cult of personality' with which the dead Lenin was surrounded, transferred in due course to the still living Stalin. To be sure, it is important not to exaggerate. All available evidence makes it clear that within the limits set by the International the individual parties were relatively free to work out their own approaches. There were also limits even to Stalin's authority. He had to carry the Party bureaucracy with him and his power rested in the last analysis on his claim to be Lenin's closest and most able disciple even while putting much of the latter's ideas and policies into reverse. Had Stalin, to take a wildly imaginary supposition, decreed that the Soviet Union was henceforth to become a Theosophical theocracy, he could never have got agreement to it from his colleagues.

In short, the secret of the power which enabled the Communist Party of the Soviet Union (Bolsheviks)[2] to exercise its control over communists everywhere is to be found in its leadership of the Russian Revolution and the Soviet state, an event and an institution which aroused such ardent hopes and expectations among revolutionaries and radicals around the globe. The attitude may be summarised as, 'the Bolsheviks have done it, let's copy them!' The theoretical presumptions, the basic political perspectives and the outlines of the organisational style adopted throughout the Comintern derived ultimately from Lenin's theory and practice. These are expounded in a number of key writings which reflected changing outlooks throughout the course of his career.

FOUNDATIONS OF COMMUNISM

Prior to 1914 Lenin was an orthodox Marxist, even if one of an unusually quarrelsome and intransigent temper, and frequently referred for support in his ideas to the work of Karl Kautsky, leading theoretician of the SPD. In terms of Marxist ideology there was little before the Russian revolution of 1905 to distinguish him from the other Marxist revolutionaries in the illegal socialist underground of the Tsarist state, but in terms of political practice there certainly was.

Following an abortive attempt to combine scattered groupings into a comprehensive Russian social democrat party in 1898 (it ended with the arrest of all the delegates), discussions continued in the underground and among the Marxist exiles, including Lenin, in preparation for a renewed effort. In this context he wrote the pamphlet *What is to be Done?*[3] (the title of a renowned revolutionary novel by Nikolai Chernyshevsky), which can be regarded as an ideological cornerstone of what was to become the communist movement.

Lenin commenced by attacking the 'Economists' and 'economism', which did not mean what at first sight it might appear to, but rather refers to the political trend which advocated that the workers' movement in the Empire concentrate upon its trade union and related business and leave the political issues to the bourgeoisie; in Lenin's words, 'let the workers carry on the economic struggle … and let the Marxist intellectuals merge with the liberals for the political "struggle"'. This division he of course vehemently opposed, insisting that the Marxist intellectuals must be an integral part of the workers' movement.

This leads on to the famous (or notorious) argument that the working class, of its own accord, forced to concentrate upon the necessities of life and deprived of educational opportunity, was incapable of rising above a 'trade union consciousness' and that its development towards revolutionary Marxism had to be initiated by educated elements who had been in a position to study and understand Marxist theory – though once that had been achieved working class revolutionaries would be perfectly capable of developing Marxist analysis and taking over the leading role – and Lenin constantly complained about the shortage of workers among his followers.[4] The argument took for granted the concept of a false consciousness – bourgeois or 'workerist' ideology – as a veil which concealed from workers their true interests, requiring to be stripped away by conscious Marxists.

There was more. Lenin proceeds to expound his conception of what a Russian social democratic party ought to be. It was like nothing else previously advanced in Marxist discourse. It must be a tightly disciplined, highly organised body of professional revolutionaries, 'tribunes of the people', able to build a workers' movement with political revolution as its goal, capable of outwitting the secret police and not too fussy about the methods which it used to combat the authorities and their dupes – although the latter point, far from advocating amoralism, was indicative of Lenin's commitment to a situational ethic.

The argument was that, in the conditions of Tsarist repression, the methods appropriate to a bourgeois democracy could not apply. That must be equally, indeed especially, true of the revolutionary party itself – in place of the normal mechanism of public discussion and election to leadership positions standard in societies where the labour movement could operate freely, there must instead be, inside the Empire, implicit trust between leaders and activists and willingness to carry out instructions not subject to the processes of debate – on reading the pamphlet, one is reminded of Resistance movements in occupied Europe.

When Lenin's socialist opponents realised with horror what was being proposed they compared him with Auguste Blanqui, the renowned nineteenth-century professional revolutionary who devoted his life (with a total lack of success) to repeatedly setting up conspiratorial revolutionary organisations. At the same time it is important to remember that he regarded himself very much as an orthodox Marxist and social democrat, and saw the procedures of the SPD as wholly appropriate for the situation of the semi-constitutional German Empire. His prescriptions for a 'party of a new type' were at this stage seen as applicable only to states like Tsarist Russia, not in those where the labour movement was institutionally strong and legal. An accidental (and temporary) majority in one of the votes at the founding congress of 1903 (held abroad)[5] enabled Lenin's faction to claim the misleading name of Bolsheviks or 'majority people', their factional opponents being known as Mensheviks. Bolshevism itself was at this time the very reverse of a monolithic party directed by a single will, as dispute and argument raged freely within it; though in the end it came to mean what Lenin said it did.

Attempts were made, not least by the leaders of the International, to get the rival factions (and the rival Social Revolutionaries, SRs) to work together, but these were never very successful, and in 1908 the Bolsheviks declared their definitive separation – or rather claimed to *be* the Russian Social Democratic and Labour Party (RSDLP). By that time, the abortive 1905 revolution had occurred and Lenin in his pamphlet *The Two Tactics of Social Democracy* had, with reference to it, introduced another theoretical innovation.

Naturally it was expressed through Marxist categories and arose from the dilemma that socialist parties aspired to lead a working-class revolution in a country where the non-agricultural, let alone the specifically industrial, working class represented only a very small minority of the population. This had to be fitted into the classic Marxist scheme, outlined in the *Communist Manifesto* and based essentially on British and (especially) French experience, of bourgeois revolution (supported by the embryonic working class) overthrowing the feudal state, preparing the ground for industrial development, working-class growth and self-organisation, to be succeeded by working-class revolution which aimed at the 'dictatorship of the proletariat' – that is, emergency rule by the (representatives of) the working class, and a socialist regime.

The problem with this model in Russian conditions, even apart from the reality of the country's precariously developed industrial bourgeoisie and working class, was that it raised the immediate questions as to why should the class-conscious workers ally with their immediate oppressors, the capitalists who kept their wages low (and only paid them when they felt inclined to), enforced miserable working conditions and called upon the state to shoot them down if they protested too forcefully; or why should the bourgeoisie form a political bloc with their future supplanters?

Moreover, as E. H. Carr remarks, the bourgeois actors at the second performance are already aware of the earlier resolution of the drama and will strive to avoid outcomes unfavourable to themselves the second time around, usually by means of compromise with the tottering feudal state. Even as far back as 1847, Marx had been aware of this problem in relation to Germany and predicted that a large working-class input would be required to carry through even the democratic revolution.

Lenin had already written off the Russian bourgeoisie as a serious revolutionary force. At the same time he could not, without loss of Marxist consistency as then understood, dismiss the need for a bourgeois initial stage to the future state and society. His solution was the rather clumsy (though not necessarily self-contradictory) theoretical concept of a 'democratic dictatorship of the proletariat and peasantry', which would represent the necessary bourgeois first stage, bypassing the actual political rule of industrial and financial capital and opening the way for a smooth transition to the dictatorship of the proletariat once the latter was sufficiently developed.

Later on, still in the dog days of Bolshevik hopes, an important dispute arose on the nationality question, in which Lenin's opponent was Rosa Luxemburg, whose revolutionary credentials no-one could doubt. At issue was the appropriate position for socialists to adopt towards the ambitions of minority nationalities unwillingly incorporated into various empires. To simplify, Luxemburg and the party she had helped to found in Russian-occupied Poland took the view that national sentiment in whatever form was a manifestation of bourgeois ideology, a distraction from the class struggle, and that workers in oppressed nations should focus their endeavours towards socialist revolution in collaboration with their counterparts in the oppressor nation. Marx, after all, had famously declared that 'The workers have no country!'

Lenin countered with the argument that not only was national struggle inside empires a significant factor in weakening the power of the rulers but that the working class of oppressor nations, if they were to retain credibility with their nationally subjugated counterparts, must be willing, on achieving power, to unconditionally concede to national demands, whether in Ireland or in Poland, up to and including political separation. A sharp line was drawn between the nationalism of oppressed and oppressing nations. One problem, from the Leninist point of view, was to define exactly what a nation was. The definition that emerged included territorial, linguistic, and a degree of economic, homogeneity. Stalin was commissioned to produce the definitive theoretical statement of the Bolshevik position; it was his first significant piece of writing.

WAR AND REVOLUTION

It is well known that Lenin, exiled in Switzerland, was dumbfounded and disbelieving when news arrived that the socialist parties of the International had almost without exception reneged on their commitments and opted instead to support 'their own' governments in the prosecution of the war instead of using its outbreak as the opportunity for revolution, or at least acting jointly to bring it to a swift end. Nationalism, after all, had trumped international solidarity.

Once he had recovered from his shock and distress, Lenin set about developing a theoretical explanation for the class treason of the socialist parties, along with an organisation of revolutionary socialists which might become the core of a new International. The latter began with a meeting at Zimmerwald in Switzerland in 1915, which did indeed affirm a strong anti-war stance, though Lenin was dissatisfied that it did not fully commit itself to 'turning the imperialist war into a civil war' against the belligerent governments. His theoretical model of what lay behind the socialist parties' behaviour appeared in the shape of a pamphlet the following year, *Imperialism: the Highest Stage of Capitalism*, which, because it was intended for legal circulation in Russia, did not spell out his conclusions as explicitly as it might have done.

Lenin detected an intimate link between the development of European imperialism since the nineteenth century and the events of 1914. By imperialism he did not mean simply the land grab in Asia and Africa, which he saw as only one aspect of the phenomenon and not the most important. More centrally he blamed the penetration of monopoly capital, pressed by competition in its homelands into regions of the world where cheap land, labour and raw materials would enhance its profit margins. It was not a struggle for markets but for spheres of investment and division and redivision of the world on that account. By this means, super-profits were accumulated and out of these super-profits the leaders of the labour movement, both trade union and political, in the imperialist countries were bribed into betrayal of their principles and, blinded by the ideology of imperialist nationalism, submitted to the demands of capital and sold out their constituency. Lenin did not believe that the working class as a whole had been thus corrupted, for capitalism, in his view, was incapable by any means of raising living standards sufficiently for that. Only the labour bureaucracy and possibly the upper layers of the 'labour aristocracy' were affected. He concluded that the war demonstrated the utter bankruptcy of capitalism and its regimes and that Europe and other parts of the world were now fully ripe for revolution.

The Soviets

During the 1905 revolution, the soviets had made their first appearance. The word simply means 'councils' and these were ad hoc bodies of workers, elected on ultra-democratic principles, which in the general breakdown of the state had taken on governing and administrative functions in various Russian towns and cities. Initially Lenin had been suspicious of them, regarding them as possible rivals to his party, but had come round to viewing them as the appropriate basis for the dictatorship of the proletariat in place of the conventional parliamentary assembly, now regarded as the archetypal form of bourgeois rule – in his words, soviets would be 'a thousand times more democratic'.

When revolution erupted again in March 1917 (February, Old Style) among a population suffering war disaster combined with administrative and supply breakdown, presided over by a hopelessly corrupt and ineffective government, the soviets were swiftly resurrected. These now included rank and file soldiers and assumed, particularly in Petrograd (formerly St Petersburg but now given a Russian name), a situation of 'dual power' in relation to the Provisional Government created out of the remnants of the Duma, dominated by the Constitutional Democrats (Kadets), the representatives of Russian capital, and accepted by all the political forces in the country – including at first the Bolsheviks inside Russia.

It was this last circumstance which roused Lenin's wrath, for he was certain that the time had arrived to dispose of the weak Provisional Government and capitalist rule in Russia, institute working-class power and inspire similar revolution throughout the continent. Hence the slogan 'All power to the Soviets' – though at this stage these were far from being dominated by the Bolsheviks, even in Petrograd. When he arrived there in April via the famous sealed train, Lenin turned on his colleagues in the capital (including Stalin), denounced the position of 'critical support' they had taken up towards the government and quickly succeeded in pushing through his own conception of what Bolshevik policy should be.

In July, however, the Bolsheviks suffered a major setback when they were accused by the Provisional Government and its supporters in the Petrograd Soviet of fomenting a violent anti-government demonstration in Petrograd. Many were arrested, including Trotsky, for years Lenin's opponent but now reconciled, and Lenin himself was forced into hiding.

THE STATE AND REVOLUTION

While concealed in Finland, Lenin occupied his enforced leisure by writing the booklet later published as *The State and Revolution*. It addresses two themes. The first of these is an analysis of the state as an instrument of class rule; its essence as the organisation of coercive power to maintain the supremacy of whichever class it represents; and this as applying to all states without exception from the most democratic to the most dictatorial. Hence, the arguments proceeds, the revolutionary proletariat, when it seizes power, will require to establish its own state, not taking over the state of the displaced class, but utterly destroying and replacing it.

The other theme is what a proletarian state, 'the dictatorship of the proletariat', will actually look like. Certainly it will have a democratic framework – the democracy of the soviets, whose members will not be full-time parliamentarians, but closely connected to their workplace and subject to immediate recall if they fail to satisfy their constituents. As for the actual functioning of such a society, Lenin is convinced there will be little problem – capitalism has already organised economic life to such a degree that administration will be easy and reduced to simple operations of bookkeeping capable of being undertaken by anyone. As society develops, crime and anti-social behaviour will virtually disappear; citizens will be educated to observe the rules of social life and have no reason for doing otherwise. Naturally, living standards will rise and hitherto unimaginable opportunities open out for everyone. Certainly until the 'higher stage of socialism', communism, is reached with the disappearance of class conflict and a society of abundance, a watchful eye will have to be kept on hostile elements from the old society and force used against them if necessary, but that will be a peripheral matter, except when the latter have serious foreign support.

It can be assumed that the musings in *The State and Revolution* represented Lenin's genuine thoughts on the matter, for he wrote it when an anti-Bolshevik reaction appeared to be in command in Russia and with little prospect of his party taking power in the foreseeable future. The combination of realism, to be seen in his analysis of the state, and the utopianism of the kind of society that he imagined to be within easy reach in developed societies (he had no illusions that Russia was anywhere near that stage) is remarkable. It vividly demonstrates the utter conviction of left-wing socialists that the root of all social problems was the existence of class society and that with its removal the rest would be simple.

Immediately following the takeover of 7 November 1917 (25 October in the Old Style, hence 'October Revolution'), Lenin's first government was a coalition not of all the socialist parties, as his opponents had demanded, but only with the Left SRs. These had broken with their own party and aligned with the Bolsheviks on account of their respective attitudes to the agrarian question – the Bolsheviks demanded immediate seizure of the landlords' properties.

In less than a year the already devastated country had become the scene of a civil war of indescribable ferocity, commencing in February 1918 following the government's forcible dissolution of the newly-elected Constituent Assembly where it was in a minority. With the support of the Entente powers all its opponents from royalists to right-wing Mensheviks entered into uneasy combination, to oppose it by military force. Before long, the Left SRs were also alienated by Lenin's insistence on accepting the German terms dictated at the peace of Brest-Litovsk, which surrendered enormous areas of the former empire. The Bolsheviks, soon in 1919 to be retitled Communists, thereafter ruled alone (at least in the areas under their control) and proceeded bit by bit to outlaw all their political opponents.

Such single-party monopoly, never previously envisaged, became intrinsic to communist ideology. The rationale, or rather excuse, was in the first instance that the opposing parties were acting treasonously. Later the principle was invoked that because parties were the political expressions of antagonistic classes, and class antagonisms had been superseded by a comradely alliance between the working class and peasantry under a Communist Party which represented both, there was no longer any reason for competing parties: 'every party is composed of the most intelligent elements of the class to which it corresponds', according to Bukharin.[6]

In military terms the Bolsheviks won the civil war and established their authority over most of the former empire, but in a more profound sense they may be said to have lost it. It was not only the incredible human and material destruction on top of what was already devastated by the World War; even more importantly, the civil war and what was involved in winning it reinforced immeasurably every tendency in Bolshevik practice towards a military style, authoritarianism, dogmatism, brutal solutions and intolerance of dissent or weakness.

THE INTERNATIONAL

It was in 1919, when the civil war was raging and its outcome hung in the balance, that Lenin and Trotsky instituted the Third (Communist) International, the 'general staff of the world revolution', which had been a priority in Lenin's eyes ever since 1914 and was re-emphasised when he returned to Petrograd in April 1917. In 1919 the event was largely gestural, for very few foreign delegates were able to make their way through the battle-lines – only 35 in all, including Russians – attended. As one commentator noted,

> Despite the resolutions that were passed at the congress, the International has no organizational reality in the period immediately following its foundation: it was effectively only a propaganda action, offering no more than a standard around which international revolutionary forces could rally ideologically. It essentially provided them with a series of political analyses and guidelines, such that they would be prepared to lead the proletarian revolution at the earliest opportunity.[7]

He continues, 'Particular stress was laid on the analysis of ... the situation in which capitalism then found itself; the character of reformism, and the (soviet) forms the proletarian revolution had to assume.'

It was in July the following year, when the war was close to conclusion, that the Comintern's Second Congress opened with around 500 delegates in Petrograd (for symbolic effect – it later moved to Moscow). This Congress fully expounded its purposes and drew up the rules, which give a keen insight into the communist movement's early ideological perspectives and convictions.

Its leaders were no less convinced than they had been in the previous year that capitalism was on its last legs and close to collapse; nevertheless there had been a certain change in focus, for revolution had been bloodily defeated in Germany, Hungary and Finland (it was assumed that these setbacks were merely temporary ones).

The conclusion was drawn that such failures were the consequence not of impossible circumstances and overwhelming odds but of the lack of a communist party modelled on correct Bolshevik principles. In contrast to the expectation a year earlier that spontaneous proletarian insurgency organised in soviets would quickly sweep away bourgeois rule, the conviction now was that it could succeed only if led by a party communist not only in name but fully Leninist in character. According to the Comintern President, Zinoviev, 'Had the working class possessed even a small but united working class party at the time of the Paris Commune, the first heroic uprising of the French proletariat would have been more powerful and thousands of mistakes and weaknesses would have been avoided.'[8]

The role of the Bolshevik example and its principles was emphasised further by the fact that the soviets were on the point of prevailing in the Russian civil war, and by the latest phase of military action; 'the Red Army is, at the present time, one of the main forces in world history', as the Congress statement put it. The new conservative–nationalist Polish regime, denounced by the Congress as 'the stronghold of world capitalist reaction' had, without justification or provocation, gone empire-building in the Ukraine and advanced as far as Kiev. The Red Army counter-attacked, and at the time the Congress met was advancing on Warsaw; the delegates convened in a room dominated by a giant wall-map indicating the progress of the war and it was assumed that once the Poles were beaten the Red Army would advance to the aid of the German revolutionaries. But the Poles won.

THE 21 CONDITIONS

The rules and conditions of membership drawn up by the Second Congress were rigorous and exclusionary – and they were meant to be. The famous – or notorious – '21 Conditions', or Conditions of Admission to the Communist International, made this plain.

A central requirement for all communist parties was a posture of uncompromising hostility towards the Socialist International (revived after the First World War) and the parties associated with it, though communists were also required to agitate within working-class organisations linked to the 'social-traitors' in order to expose the latter and win over their followers to communism:

[I]n the trade unions, the co-operatives – wherever members of the Communist International can gain admittance – it is necessary to brand not only the bourgeoisie but also its helpers, the reformists of every shade, systematically and pitilessly.

All elements adhering to reformism and all 'centrists' (that is, political vacillators between reformism and communism) must be categorically excluded from the parties of the Comintern.

The communist parties themselves must be centralised and disciplined along quasi-military lines (referred to as 'democratic centralism'), for 'In almost every country in Europe and America the class struggle is entering the phase of civil war.' Especially important is the requirement to agitate among the rank-and-file of the state forces, especially police and military, and regardless of whether or not the party had legal status, to combine legal with illegal activity and set up a special underground apparatus for this purpose. Moreover, a 'particularly marked and clear attitude on the question of the colonies and oppressed nations is necessary' in imperialist countries, including anti-imperialist propaganda among the troops. Where parties enjoy legality, they must periodically check out their membership ('purges' or 're-registration') 'to cleanse the Party systematically of the petty-bourgeois elements within it'. If the party is illegalised, it should set up legal 'front' organisations that have no formal connection with the party but are nevertheless controlled by it.

It has been accurately remarked that the 21 Conditions made sense only in a situation where revolutionary outbreak was expected imminently and that it was imperative to remove what were regarded as the central impediments to its success – that is, the bad influence of the social traitors who were holding back the masses from fulfilling their historic destiny – and to prepare a military-style organisation to take advantage of the opportunity as the Bolsheviks had done in 1917. Indeed, the Congress documents declared that 'Civil war is on the order of the day throughout the world. Its banner is the Soviet Power.'

In reality, the 21 Conditions were impossible to fulfil. It was not only that the fundamental presuppositions were wrong and the revolutionary wave had passed while capitalism successfully stabilised – as the Comintern itself, in the person of Trotsky, was obliged to recognise at the Third Congress in July 1921, though denying the need for any fundamental reassessment of Comintern strategy or structures.[9] In addition, it was quite impossible over the long term to maintain the movement at the pitch of ardour and readiness which the 21 Conditions presumed. Moreover, a legal communist party rapidly acquired assets in both material and organisational terms which were immediately imperilled by actions along such lines. In particular, no self-respecting bourgeois government was likely to tolerate for long a party which openly maintained an effective underground organisation aimed at subverting the police and military.

In short, communists, whether in Soviet Russia or worldwide, were extremely reluctant to explicitly discard the formula which had worked so well in 1917–18. Ideology therefore was fitted into this framework, with the result that only modest adjustments could be made to take account of changed circumstances – but these adjustments came piece by piece to transform the whole character of the movement.

ELEMENTS OF (EARLY) COMMUNIST IDEOLOGY

From the 'days of hope', which may be regarded as ending with the institution of the NEP in 1921, there emerged a text which embodied them but which until the late 1920s continued to be used as a primer both in the Soviet Union and abroad (an English edition appeared in 1922). It may therefore be regarded as an accurate reflection of communist ideology during the first decade of the Soviet regime. This was *The ABC of Communism* written in 1919 by Nikolai Bukharin and Yevgeny Preobrazhensky, both to become in due course Stalin's victims.

In form, *The ABC of Communism* was a commentary on the programme adopted by the Eighth Party Congress, held in 1919 soon after the establishment of the International. Its authors described it in their foreword as 'an elementary textbook of communist knowledge'. Early on it declares that,

> The epoch of civil wars was ushered in by the Russian Revolution, itself no more than the herald, the beginning, of a revolution that will be general and world-wide.
>
> ...
>
> We must not infer that the Russian Communist revolution is the most thoroughgoing revolution in the world ... anyone who reasons thus is confusing two things: on the one hand the beginning of the revolution; on the other its character, its degree of thoroughness.
>
> ...
>
> In England the revolution will come later. But there the proletariat, after its victory, will organise communism more swiftly.[10]

This text re-emphasises the requirement for central direction of the revolutionary forces on an international scale and the uncompromising hostility expressed in the Comintern documents of this period towards rival understandings of socialism, particularly those embodied in the Second International. In the words of the party programme,

> To bring about the victory of the world-wide proletarian revolution it is essential that there should be absolute and mutual trust, the most intimate and brotherly alliance, and the *highest cohesion* [emphasis added] of the revolutionary activities of the working class in the more advanced lands.
>
> These conditions cannot be realised without making it a matter of principle to break off relations with and to wage a pitiless struggle against that bourgeois perversion of socialism which is dominant in the leading official social democratic and socialist parties.[11]

In relation to the character of the state before and after the revolution, Bukharin very much follows Lenin's analysis in *The State and Revolution* both in its ultra-realist and its ultra-utopian facets. 'Thus the capitalist state is a union of the master class, formed to safeguard exploitation. The interests of capital and nothing but the interests of capital – here we have the guiding star to which are directed all the activities of this robber band'[12] – including religion, 'Thanks to the intimate relation between capital and the church, the law of God invariably proves to be the law of the possessing classes.'[13] He goes on to deal with the apparent anomaly of social protection or welfare exercised by the bourgeois state – these (such as public health measures) also benefit the capitalists, were adopted under working-class pressure, or else are intended to maintain the supply of cannon fodder for military adventures.

In a communist society, matters will be very different:

> In the communist social order there are neither landlords, nor capitalists, nor wage workers; there are simply people – comrades. If there are no classes there is no class war and there are no class organisations. Consequently the State has ceased to exist. ... the state has become superfluous. There is no-one to be held in restraint [because people will act co-operatively as a matter of habit] and there is no one to impose restraint.
>
> ...
>
> The State, therefore has ceased to exist.
>
> ...
>
> Moreover in these statistical bureaux [for co-ordinating production and so on] one person will work today, another tomorrow. The bureaucracy, the permanent officialdom, will disappear. The State will die out.[14]

In other words, the form of society conceived by anarchists will have come into being. The Bolsheviks, and Marx before them, had been quite explicit that this was their ultimate conception. The anarchists' error was not their vision of the good society, but their refusal to accept that there had to be a transition period during which the state – the proletarian state – had to be strengthened in order to crush the continuing resistance of the defeated oppressing classes and to overcome their social heritage. Consequently, because

> A bourgeois state is directed against the proletariat, whereas a proletarian state is directed against the bourgeoisie ... for a long time yet, the working class will have to fight against all its enemies, and in especial against the relics of the past, such as sloth, slackness, criminality, pride.
>
> ...
>
> Though in the intervening period the existence of the workers' State is indispensable, subsequently ... the proletarian State authority will also pass away.[15]

The 'intervening period' turned out to encompass the entire lifespan of the regime. Of course the perspective was intrinsically utopian, irrespective of whether the expected global revolution had actually occurred – it rested on a presumption of limitless natural resources and disregard of environmental constraints, quite apart from a wholly unreal conception of the malleability of human behaviour. In attacking bourgeois individualism and its perversions, the communists ignored the reality that while human beings are social animals they also have individual consciousnesses, projects and desires. It was on this facet of the human situation that bourgeois liberalism laid stress. The Soviet communists made the mistake of disdaining, partly in theory and largely in practice, the conquests of the bourgeois revolution, even though they had acclaimed it in principle and put up a statue to Robespierre.

To be sure, it was not simply a matter of ideological error – though the communists took ideology very consciously and seriously. They were highly conscious of the great French precedent and determined not to repeat its errors – consequently they fell into even worse ones. But quite apart from that, the messy realities of a shattered economy and social structure, which could only be salvaged by the re-institution and toleration of petty capitalism, pushed them in the direction of extreme authoritarian courses so that the concessions they had been forced to make in the economic and social sphere were not to be translated into political or ideological ones.

At least that was to be the case so far as the Soviet state itself was concerned. Abroad, the pressure of reality forced the government to seek diplomatic relations with foreign governments, even bitterly anti-communist ones such as Kemalist Turkey, and in the German case in 1922, military agreements as well – the two pariah powers were consulting their common interests. So far as the Comintern was concerned, the hopes of immediate international revolution were put on the back burner and the strategy adopted of the 'united front' – this involved working inside social democrat dominated organisations (in the British case including the Labour Party) to break the workers' allegiance to their leaders and win them over to the communist parties. In China this even went so far, on Stalin's insistence, as to subordinate the Communist Party to the bourgeois-nationalist Guomindang led by Chiang Kai-Shek – with catastrophic results.

THE STALIN REVOLUTION

Following Lenin's death in 1924, his writings assumed the status more or less of holy writ and were not open to question. Thereafter the twists and turns in Soviet policy, both domestic and international, were justified with reference to these, with interpretations twisted and turned in an appropriate fashion. Because he had written so voluminously and covered such a wide range of situations, this was not difficult to do.

A foretaste of what was about to occur arrived with the concept of 'Marxism–Leninism', propounded by Lenin's successors (excluding Trotsky) to give the writings and outlook of the now safely-dead leader the cachet of being integrally linked with the founder of 'scientific socialism' and therefore of equivalent authority. According to Stalin, this was 'Marxism in the era of imperialism and the proletarian revolution'. It represented an ideological reinforcement of the unchallenged political hegemony which the Soviet leadership, and Stalin in particular, had already achieved organisationally by banning all opposition parties and closing down disagreement within the Communist Party itself and likewise the Comintern. This they were able to do because of the emphasis on political discipline and the military style which had always been present to some extent in the Bolsheviks' basic conceptions and enormously reinforced by the exigencies of the civil war. The question as to the relationship between Leninism and Stalinism has been much debated, especially whether one led directly to the other.[16] Any unprejudiced examination of the evidence will conclude that this was definitely not the case – a number of different outcomes were possible – yet nevertheless certain features of Leninism, its dogmatism, intransigent emphasis on political discipline, and above all the habit of ascribing disagreement to hostile class influences, helped to grease the skids, as it were.

Indeed Marxism-Leninism, in combination with his unscrupulous organisational skills was among Stalin's principal resources in the desperate internal struggles he waged with and against his colleagues in order to achieve supreme power in the Soviet state, which by 1928–29 had been more or less accomplished. Stalin, along with Bukharin, had been the principal sponsor of 'socialism in a single country', a notion wholly alien to the conceptions of Lenin or any other Bolshevik up to the mid 1920s. As *The ABC of Communism* makes clear, all of them had seen the revolution in Russia – the 'weakest link' in the imperialist chain – as merely the overture to a rapid worldwide revolution and were absolutely convinced that socialism in the former Russian Empire was impossible without similar revolution in the advanced countries. 'Socialism in a single country' nevertheless seemed to fit in better with the realities of the times, however utopian it might prove to be in historical perspective.

Trotsky's outlook, vituperatively and baselessly denounced by Stalin in 1924 – 'Trotsky's "permanent revolution" is a variety of Menshevism' – however unreal it might have been, undoubtedly did represent the genuine Bolshevik tradition, and if the party members had been in a position to give an open and honest verdict he and his supporters might well have won the majority. The importance of the slogan 'socialism in a single country' was less in what it openly stated – 'a bizarre irrelevancy. ... metaphorically speaking, the antagonists did not argue whether it was possible or desirable to erect the edifice they wanted ... the only point was whether it would be possible to cover the edifice with a roof',[17] – as in what it implied, 'the subtle, often imperceptible shifts in the emphasis'. The implication was that the Soviet regime would turn in on itself to an increasing extent. Continuing declarations regarding international revolution, such as the one of Stalin's chapters headed 'The October Revolution as the Beginning of and the Groundwork for the World Revolution',[18] would be made more for form's sake than be indications of serious intention.

Nevertheless it is important not to exaggerate. Apart from its domestic significance, 'socialism in a single country' also had an international resonance which added the final brick, so to speak, to the edifice of communist ideology as it actually existed. From the earliest years their efforts in support and protection of the Soviet state had represented a priority for communist parties, but this became even more emphatic when not only was it viewed as the stronghold of working-class power but the one country on earth where socialism was actually under construction. Defence of the Soviet Union by whatever means was now the supreme priority, overruling all other considerations.

The Comintern by the late 1920s had become the Soviet Politbureau's tool – that is, Stalin's, and he was accustomed to treating it in a similar autocratic manner to his domestic party organisations. It should be kept in mind however that outside the borders of the Soviet Union he had no means of compelling communists to follow his instructions or accept his 'party line' – they did so because of their total absorption of the necessary ideological premises and conviction that the party which had overthrown capitalism and was in the process of building socialism could not possibly be wrong. If they lost that conviction they ceased to be members of their communist parties.

That was exactly what happened to the majority of the original communist leaders outside the reach of Soviet state power, if they escaped being murdered like Rosa Luxemburg by local reactionaries or incarcerated like Antonio Gramsci.[19] Strong-minded individuals of independent temperament as most of them were, they were unwilling to subordinate their judgement and their consciences to commands and ideological pronouncements from a Comintern regime whose incoherencies and contradictions reflected those besetting the Soviet state. Those who survived as party leaders were the ones willing to accept these demands – and the minority who did so did it out of conviction, not because they were puppets or moral weaklings. The surviving Chinese communists, isolated in their remote Yenan military stronghold, adopted the tactic of purporting to accept whatever the Comintern decreed and then ignoring it and going their own way.

The Comintern, though transformed into a tool of Soviet control of communists outside its borders, was by no means an irrelevance – though many of its functionaries were privately declaring in 1928–29 that it was a disorganised and demoralised empty shell. Nevertheless that control could be exerted only through the Comintern, which carried the prestige of its early days and linked the Soviet Union to the rest of the world movement. As Stalin declared to a delegation of dissident American communists, 'There have been numerous cases in the history of the Comintern when its most popular leaders, who had greater authority than you, found themselves isolated as soon as they raised the banner against the Comintern.'[20]

Stalin himself never held any office in the International and very seldom spoke at any of its meetings; he left that to his subordinates. In April 1929 a special issue of the Comintern theoretical journal *The Communist International* celebrated 'Ten Years of Struggle for the World Revolution: Lessons and Prospects',[21] and in it Stalin is not referred to. As it happened this was the month when the one-sided struggle in the Politbureau between Stalin and Bukharin, Rykov and Tomsky over the collectivisation programme reached its climax and Bukharin was removed from the Comintern's presidency (though this was not publicly announced until July). The anonymous editorial of this issue venomously attacks Trotsky and (unnamed) Trotskyists for their refusal to accept the 'socialism in a single country' perspective and characterises them as 'renegade defeatists' – though the journal also carries an advert for John Reed's *Ten Days that Shook the World*, in which Trotsky was acclaimed. Rather surprisingly at this date the publication included an article by the disgraced Zinoviev, probably his last published work. Possibly this was a gesture on Bukharin's part (Zinoviev had been the first Comintern president) as the text must have been set up prior to the April Politbureau meeting. Several of the other contributors were also executed during the forthcoming great purge.

The publication eight years later of a special issue on the twentieth anniversary of the Revolution gives a taste of the way matters had developed in the interim. After preliminaries, which include full-page portraits of Marx, Engels, Lenin and Stalin, it passes on to 'Greetings from the EC of the Communist International to Comrade Stalin', opening with the sentence, 'Infinitely beloved leader, friend and teacher, dear to the hearts of millions of working people!' and concludes the greetings with, '*Long live the leader of the working people throughout the world, Comrade Stalin!*' (original italics). Stalin's name crops up everywhere through the 127 quarto double-column pages of text.

THE TERROR

Even today there remain a number of puzzles surrounding the Great Terror of 1936–38 during which Stalin exterminated almost nearly everyone in reach who had ever opposed him, and in addition countless Comintern functionaries, foreign communists resident in the Soviet Union, the majority of his officer corps, particularly in its higher reaches – and innumerable loyal Stalinists both inside and outside the CPSU. Personal guilt or innocence was irrelevant; Stalin persecuted by categories rather than on an individual basis, and even the wrong ancestry could be suspect.

The safest position to be in was that of a manual worker with proletarian parents and without administrative responsibilities or Party membership – although even so, you had to be careful, for if you mishandled machinery due to accident or inexperience you were liable to be accused of sabotage and join the prisoners in the gulag. Even more peculiarly, these purges occurred not during the crisis of collectivisation and the first Five Year Plan but after it was over.

The destruction of his political enemies both physically – and morally, through their forced abject (and preposterous) confessions and humiliation in the dock – is comprehensible enough; this marked the revenge craved by Stalin's vengeance-fuelled obsessions, and, as Isaac Deutscher noted, the elimination of not merely one but several alternative governments. It was, after all, a time of growing international threat.

What is less clear is the rationale for the searing attack on Soviet society itself at all its levels. Certainly the terror acquired a momentum of its own even apart from the intentions of its originators, citizens denounced others to avoid denunciation against themselves, and an atmosphere of constant terror discouraged any potential oppositionists. Moreover, a reliable supply of slave labour for the gulag had to be maintained. However, there was probably more. No-one could have been more acutely aware than Stalin, not least on account of his own experience, of how readily bureaucracies develop a corporate identity and pass out of the control of their ostensible masters. He was evidently determined to prevent anything like that happening in his own bailiwick, and so resolved to break up in the most brutal fashion any hint of such corporatism before it could develop.

These scandals did not lead to mass defections of members in the democracies where communist parties which could still work openly and a largely free media could expose what was going on. On the contrary, the CPs in France, Britain, Denmark and the USA improved their position.

The reasons for this are not very mysterious. As stressed earlier, communists were well schooled in disbelieving whatever reports detrimental to the Soviet Union might appear in the 'bourgeois' media or be uttered by 'renegade' party members. Also, although the show trials were highly publicised, the vast mass of the persecutions was hidden from view so there was no idea of the scale of the catastrophe. Most importantly, fascism was on the march, the Spanish Civil War was raging and the Soviet state was, apparently, the only reliable barrier to a reactionary triumph. These considerations seemed decisive to communists living in the remaining democracies; those elsewhere had other more immediate concerns.

As for the publicised victims, it might seem incredible that a moment's consideration of the trial transcripts (which were translated and published) would not have shown up their absurdity and complete lack of any evidence apart from unbelievable confessions. The very fact that the accused never tried to defend themselves would have told in the same sense. More incredibly still, the entire leadership of the Revolution and the early Soviet governments apart from Stalin and those safely dead were 'exposed' as traitors and assassins. If this really were the case the survival of the regime would have been inexplicable. Yet the very absurdity of the accusations and the behaviour of the accused were, paradoxically, used as an argument for validation: the whole thing, its apologists argued, could make no sense unless it was really what it was claimed to be. All of that was enough to still most doubts.

NATIONALISM

The nature of outlook that these reactions represented goes a long way towards explaining the willingness of communist party members outside the Soviet Union to accept at Stalin's command (although of course it was not presented in those terms) the dramatic switches in direction required by Soviet policy – in the late 1920s this involved acting on the presumption that all other political forces and *especially* every other variety of socialist constituted an obstacle to the impending revolution and were to be combated mercilessly as 'social fascists'. By the mid 1930s, the overriding belief was that the struggle against fascism was the priority and that 'popular fronts' were to be formed with all anti-fascist forces – socialists, liberals and even fascist-opposing conservatives. It was an equivalent mental set which promoted the demonisation of Trotsky and his followers, and induced communists to accept that these were part of a fascist conspiracy, and so, similarly, to applaud Stalin's purge trials and their bloody outcomes.

Sometimes the accusations related to 'bourgeois nationalism' and conspiracy to dismember the Soviet state on that basis.[22] In fact, the question of nationalism was an undercurrent in Soviet affairs during the 1920s and 1930s. Although Stalin was a Georgian by birth, a heavy emphasis was placed upon Great Russia as the leading national element in the union and members of that nationality tended to be preferred for the highest appointments, especially those concerned with security. In the last year of Lenin's life he had denounced Stalin for his 'Great Russian chauvinism' in respect of the way he behaved in Georgia in his role as Commissar for Nationalities.[23] The Union of Soviet Socialist Republics, instituted in 1924, replaced the looser federation of nationalities which had preceded it. Finland had been permitted voluntarily to secede shortly after the Revolution, but the other Baltic states had separated with German assistance against Moscow's will, while the Ukraine and Georgia (at least) were incorporated regardless of their inhabitants' wishes.

However, during these two decades the regime was not faced with any significant nationalist dissension. This can be partly attributed to repression, but more to the existence of the Communist Party as the nervous system of the regime, its penetration into every institution of civil society and ability to maintain a tight bond between the centre and the national periphery. When the 'Stalin Constitution' (guaranteeing all manner of civil liberties and human rights, and largely drafted by the then disgraced Bukharin) was produced in 1936, the 'right' of secession by any of the constituent Soviet republics was written into it for decency's sake, but needless to say the exercise of that right was a complete dead letter, and anyone who had dared to suggest its application would have been arrested immediately and indicted for bourgeois nationalism (at least). Nevertheless, that paper right served to preserve Lenin's principle of national self-determination, theorised by Stalin himself in his 1913 pamphlet, and the pretence that the USSR was a voluntary union of nationalities mutually inspired by socialist commitment.

The official narrative

In the 1920s, supporters of Trotsky against Stalin/Bukharin battled over whether it was possible to establish socialism in one country. In the 1930s, it was proclaimed that this happy state had actually arrived and that, therefore, the paper alterations to the political system embodied in the Stalin Constitution had become appropriate. Private property had been abolished in the means of production, distribution and exchange; the former bourgeoisie – apart from a few irreconcilable elements being attended to by the political police – had abandoned their bourgeois practices and aspirations and been absorbed as sections of the two non-antagonistic classes, the working class and peasantry. Living standards were high and rising – supposedly.

However, Marx's 'higher stage of socialism', communism, remained in the future – that would involve the 'withering away of the state'; the redundancy of society's instruments of coercion, the abolition of money, the society of abundance. Regrettably, that was impossible in the meantime because there still existed irreconcilable conspirators, hostile foreign powers, and a much higher level of production and consumption yet to be attained. The *History of the CPSU (B): Short Course*,[24] published in 1938 and largely authored by Stalin himself, expressed the official narrative: 'our country, where hostile classes no longer exist and where the moral and political unity of all sections of the population is an incontestable fact'. 'Thus, 90,000,000 persons by their unanimous vote, confirmed the victory of socialism in the USSR'.

WAR

The circumstances of the desperate years between 1941 and 1945, not only in the USSR itself, but wherever communist parties were a meaningful political force, had significant implications for the light in which communist ideology viewed the question of nationality. To some extent this represented a continuation of the Popular Front attitudes, when communist parties had made strenuous efforts to claim the national heritage of their countries, or at least its radical aspects and episodes, as their own. The Chinese communists had entered into an (uneasy) alliance with their Guomindang enemies to fight the invading Japanese; when in the summer of 1939 France celebrated the 150th anniversary of the Revolution, the PCF consciously identified itself with the Jacobins; British communist historians around the same time were developing their party's own interpretation of the country's past.[25] National sentiment was mobilised as an additional force in opposing the growing fascist threat.

All of this was greatly intensified following the German invasion. The peoples of the Soviet Union were fighting for their existence; and patriotism, albeit Soviet patriotism rather than that of specific nationalities, was given even greater emphasis than had been done in the 1930s. Communist resistance movements in occupied countries likewise raised their patriotic profile and stigmatised collaborators not only as fascists or fascist accomplices, but as traitors to the nation as well, and so communists either, as in the UK and the USA, supported their bourgeois governments, or in the case of occupied Western Europe, their bourgeois-led governments-in-exile.

Indeed, this development provided a very convenient justification for decisions reached by Stalin on other grounds. In 1943 the Comintern was dissolved. The Grand Alliance was one of necessity, not sentiment, and always fragile, overshadowed by mutual tensions and suspicions. Disbanding the Comintern was a gesture of goodwill which cost Stalin nothing, or at least very little, removing a source of irritation to his allies and, in Isaac Deutscher's words, representing 'his political contribution to the Grand Alliance'.[26] The ostensible reason was that the individual parties were now sufficiently 'mature' to manage without this framework, and anyway it was impossible for it to function effectively in wartime conditions. Lenin would have been appalled, and the resolution of the ECCI Presidium (a Congress was of course out of the question) added insult to posthumous injury by stating, 'Guided by the judgement of the founders of Marxism–Leninism, communists have never been supporters of the conservation of organisational forms that have outlived themselves.'[27] Nevertheless the parties accepted it obediently along with the excuses, and in the Soviet Union itself the *Internationale*, the international communist anthem, was replaced as the country's own national anthem with one which commenced with the following revealing words: 'An indestructible union of free republics Great Russia has rallied for ever'[28] – so combining a gesture towards Leninist internationalism with Great Russian chauvinism.

5
Fascism

The definition of fascism, as we shall see, is extremely difficult to pin down; the multinational movement that was recognised by that term was extraordinarily diffuse and protean. The origins of the name, however, are straightforward enough, being derived from the political groupings formed by Benito Mussolini during and immediately after the First World War, the official date of origin being 1919. The Italian word *fascio* means a bundle or grouping; the fasces were the bundle of rods surrounding an axe carried by the Roman lictors (ceremonial officials accompanying the consuls) as a badge of authority and this was adopted as the movement's official symbol. Mussolini's initial formations were known as action groups and later combat groups (*fasci*) prior to the institution of the fascist party.

During the 1920s organisations modelled or attempting to be modelled on Mussolini's *fascisti* existed elsewhere in Europe, though only in southern Germany and Romania did they achieve any great significance and even in these countries they were no threat to the existing polity. Italy was viewed as a special case and among the propertied classes throughout Europe, Mussolini was greatly approved of with few reservations. The ultra-conservative Austrian regime became, in effect, an Italian protectorate. In this respect as in so much else, the slump changed everything. Fascism spread literally everywhere throughout Europe. There was not a European country that did not give rise to a fascist organisation of some kind – even distant Iceland – although the majority of them never (at least until the Second World War) had any great strength and some remained ridiculously insignificant.

Fascism during this period was to spread even beyond Europe and in one instance at least there, to achieve considerable popular support. This was the Ação Integralista Brasileira (AIB, Brazilian Integralist Action), with an active membership in the region of 200,000. Its leader was Plínio Salgado, who declared,

> Here will be born the new Law, the new politics of the Revolutionary State with a pre-established moral purpose. It will not only be a Totalitarian State with an all-embracing absolutism, but the Integral State which serves as the arbiter of the relationships between social movements. ... re-establishing equilibrium in the light of social justice.[1]

Not only was fascism geographically diverse – it was ideologically diverse as well – the German fascists found it expedient to include the word 'socialist' in their title and fascist movements often purported to stand for a more authentic form of socialism than their rivals. Best known, however, and most striking in terms of their diversity was the role of antisemitism. For a number of fascist movements, most notoriously the German Nazis, antisemitism was absolutely central, and the same was true for their Austrian, Hungarian and Romanian counterparts. It was somewhat less so, although still highly important, for their French counterparts, while in Italy it did not initially figure at all and there were even a few Jewish members of the fascist party – although this did not mean that Italian fascists were any less racist than Nazis towards non-Europeans.

Attitudes to religion varied widely. In his socialist days Mussolini had been a vehement atheist and anti-clericalist, and traces of this still remained in the initial Fascist programme – but soon disappeared once the possibility of Church support arrived on the agenda. It is wholly mistaken to argue that the Nazis were an anti-religious movement; the great majority of the party members were orthodox believers, either Catholic or Protestant, and even those who weren't were certainly not atheists. Himmler was a crank and an Odinist, seriously trying to revive Norse mythology (Norwegian fascists had similar inclinations). Hitler himself (a choirboy in his childhood) can be conjectured to have ceased to be a Christian at some point in his life, but the words 'God', 'destiny' and 'providence' were never out of his mouth. By contrast, for the Romanian fascists, religion in its eastern Orthodox form was as central as antisemitism, and there was every shade of religious attachment in between, although no fascist movement was professedly atheist.

Class and fascism

What then was the 'fascist minimum'? What characteristics entitle historians or present-day commentators to define a political organisation as authentically fascist? It has to be admitted that there is no easy answer to this and indeed no universally accepted answer, despite the best efforts of many able writers. One characteristic that does appear to be shared by all possible candidates is that of ultra-nationalism – but even here there is an exception (admittedly only one) due to the peculiarities of Irish history. Even so, although ultra-nationalism would certainly dispose any political movement towards a fascist outlook, it need not *necessarily* take on that character in other respects.

The question is best addressed historically rather than purely conceptually. What kinds of people were attracted to the movements that would unanimously be agreed to have had a fascist character, which, even if they eschewed the name, openly declared themselves to share basic values with the Mussolini and/or Hitler movements? What defined them – economically, socially, culturally, generationally (certainly they were overwhelmingly male, even if not exclusively so).[2]

Great controversy has swirled around this discussion,[3] but despite all the argument and necessary qualifications that have to be made, it remains unquestionable that on any convincing definition the core membership of all interwar fascist movements was made up of lower-middle-class individuals, who were likewise disproportionately represented overall. With a few exceptions, the founders and top leaders were also drawn from this social stratum. It has been pointed out that the Nazis, who were probably the most diverse of all fascists, succeeded in appealing to all social classes and, indeed, they were particularly anxious to attract both workers and aristocrats whenever they could, the latter finding easy passage into the high ranks of the party and its affiliated organisations. Nevertheless, it remained stubbornly true that the majority of party members as well as its voters were drawn from middle-class backgrounds. These were, in the German case, either the 'old' or the 'new' *Mittelstand*.

It was precisely such people everywhere who were most threatened by the post-war crisis. Their incomes and economic security were endangered by the effects of the depression upon the general economy (in the German case, their savings were destroyed by hyperflation), their own markets by agribusiness and chain stores or their profits by uppity employees, while their prospects were undermined by the squeeze on white-collar employments (particularly severe for discharged or aspiring officers) and their dignity in the defeated states was endangered by the loss of the war and territorial amputations, or in the Italian case by the scrappy gains of the war effort. Above all they were terrified by the well-publicised unnameable horrors of Marxist revolution, bundling together in imagination all the other sources of social panic and imperilling their status, their livelihoods and very possibly even their lives. In central Europe these threats had actually been experienced and in Italy had seemed very close. The future held out little except grim and fearful prospects.

This did not, of course, mean that all middle-class people, or even a majority of them in European countries, adhered to fascist movements or even (except in Germany during the last crisis of the Weimar Republic) gave them their electoral support – when Mussolini fought his first election and at the height of turmoil, his vote was negligible. What it did mean, however, is that a great many of them, together with a penumbra of other social groups, did adhere in one way or another and thus generated a major historical phenomenon, which, in consequence of the Second World War, set the parameters for the remainder of the century and beyond.

Up until the end of the 1920s, conservative and liberal (including social democratic) administrations appeared adequately equipped, except in the special Italian case, to hold social disruption and revolutionism in check and to isolate the red menace inside Soviet frontiers. After 1929, this ceased to be the case. In Germany the KPD made strong advances both in numbers and electoral support (by 1932, it was polling more votes in Berlin than the SPD) helping to make the parliamentary system unworkable. Later during that decade, communists were part of Popular Front coalitions which secured electoral victory in France and Spain, setting off a social earthquake in both countries. It was when normal guarantees of middle-class 'order' and security appeared to be failing that fascism began to look like an acceptable alternative to those who joined the movements, as well as those who sympathised more passively.

PSEUDO-REVOLUTIONARY POPULIST NATIONALISM

In searching for the central core of fascist ideology, which often can appear as little more than a ragbag of sinister and aggressive prejudices, it is useful to begin with the idea advanced by Roger Griffin that this lies in the concept of what he terms 'palingenesis'.[4] In this context, palingenesis (which literally means 'born again') means the conviction, by no means confined to fascism and common to charismatic religious movements, that a desperate state of affairs must, if the appropriate steps are taken, produce by its own momentum a reversal of circumstances, sweeping away the decadence of the past and present and becoming the gateway leading to a glorious future: 'it defines fascism exclusively in terms of its mobilizing "mythic core"'.[5] Griffin therefore insists (although many, including myself, would vehemently disagree) that fascism was a revolutionary ideology.

> Used generically, fascism is a term for a singularly protean genus of modern politics inspired by the conviction that a process of national rebirth (palingenesis) has become essential to bring to an end a protracted period of social and cultural decadence, and expressing itself ideologically in a revolutionary form of integral nationalism (ultra-nationalism).[6]

Griffin, who has deservedly established himself as a leading authority on fascism and edited a most useful fascist reader, has many acute and sensible points to make, though he very mistakenly disdains the aspect of truth in the Marxist interpretation and dismisses Horkheimer's comment that 'whoever is not prepared to talk about capitalism should also remain silent about fascism'. He writes rather dismissively that 'The anti-conservative dimension of fascism is partly obscured by the extensive collusion with traditional power elites ... which both [Mussolini's] Fascism and Nazism were forced to make on pragmatic grounds.'[7]

Not only Hitler and Mussolini did that. Griffin never explains or tries to explain why fascist movements, however great their rhetorical anti-conservatism, *always* relied on conservative forces to gain support and aim at power – never on those of the left.[8] Fascism might better, if more clumsily, be defined as pseudo-revolutionary populist integralism – remembering that integralism is always an extremist validation of exploiting class power – each of these three terms being essential to what Griffin calls the 'fascist minimum'.

Griffin is perfectly aware, as we shall see, that such a platform (or a palingenetic one if that term is preferred) in itself would not necessarily lead to fascism finding wide acceptance – especially given its revolutionary pretensions – as the solution to the distress unless other concepts are also involved. It is not just a question of palingenesis, but of palingenetic ultra-nationalism. Nationalism, since the nineteenth century and as 1914 had dramatically demonstrated, had bitten deeply into the European popular consciousness, although its most committed purveyors were the literate middle classes.[9] That, together with traditional cultural inheritances, rage at prevailing circumstances and panic at the Marxist threat, provided the bowl in which the fascist ingredients were mixed.

Style and violence

What were these ingredients? It was Mussolini himself who remarked that fascism had come out of the trenches (though he himself had spent only a very brief period there, before the fighting got really serious). One of the most visually striking aspects of fascism in all shapes and sizes was its military style.[10] Fascist organisations, wherever they could, established their private militias – usually garbed in a coloured shirt. Other political parties and formations in particular countries did the same, but for fascists the centrality of these militias was much greater.

Military and paramilitary organisations exist in order to inflict violence and generate fear – that is their purpose. The idea of attacking and violently subduing political and ideological enemies was a deeply gratifying one, an expression of hatred and rage against identified scapegoats, with the additional functional result of gaining 'respect' and securing dominance of the streets and public spaces. Not surprisingly, therefore, ex-servicemen comprised a large proportion of the initial personnel of the original fascist parties, hardened to violence and the rigours of military life, brutalised by their experiences in the trenches, socially adrift and embittered by the outcome of the fighting.

Moreover, there were many juveniles too young to have fought in the war who greatly envied those who had done so, longed to imitate them, felt ashamed of their own non-participation and saw in the paramilitary formations a substitute of sorts, promising excitement, comradeship and adventure. In the modern era, theatricality and visual display have served as an important component of military presence and fascism faithfully copied these too – columns marching in step, banners, music, searchlights, orchestrated symbolic rituals, inspirational speeches. Under Goebbels's direction the Nazis brought these practices to a peak of perfection.

Militarist perspectives were intrinsic to fascism and regarded as a suitable model for social relations generally. Hierarchy, authority, discipline, unquestioning obedience,[11] indifference to hardship, and male bonding were attractive notions not only to ex-soldiers (especially ex-officers) but to authoritarians of all stripes. So, to many others as well, adrift in the turmoil, was the abdication of political responsibility to a revered leader figure. Leader worship and the leader principle, embodied in a charismatic figure, was a natural extension of militarist consciousness.

However, not any form of militarist outlook sufficed. There have been plenty of military dictators who were and are singularly uncharismatic, and in terms of its politics and in its economic principles fascism was scarcely to be distinguished from hardline ultra-authoritarian conservatism. However, where fascism differed decisively was that it was *populist*; it directed or wanted to direct its appeal not only to the elites but to the masses as well and to give its followers the sense of participating ardently in a magnificent adventure of national renewal as part of a nation of exceptional worth and merit. Bread as well as violent circuses formed part of its rhetoric – promising land to the toiling peasants, careers at least somewhat more open to talents, removal of archaic social discrimination, full employment and a fair deal to industrial workers if they accepted the fascist social order and abandoned their socialist allegiances.

There was no single defining characteristic of fascism – however, pseudo-revolutionary, authoritarian, populist ultra-nationalism with militarised connotations covers nearly all. It would be nonsensical to suggest that fascism should not be defined as an ideology, but equally certainly it lacked coherence and was poorly articulated. It was more a series of recurrent themes eliciting a significant popular response under particular conditions of crisis. According to Mussolini himself:

> We Fascists have had the courage to discard all traditional political theories, and we are aristocrats and democrats, revolutionaries and reactionaries, proletarians and anti-proletarians, pacifists and anti-pacifists. It is sufficient to have a single fixed point: the nation. The rest is obvious ... everybody is free to create for himself his own ideology and attempt to carry it out with all possible energy.[12]

With this in mind, we now move to consideration of how this worked out in particular states and nations.

ITALY

For the pioneering initiator of the concept, Italian fascism was even less well articulated than its counterparts – and this applied not only to its ideological features but to its organisational character as well. The founder of the movement, Benito Mussolini, an ex-socialist journalist with a background in the lowest stratum of the lower middle classes (rural smallholders, with a father who was a blacksmith and mother a village schoolteacher), was essentially a bombastic charlatan for whom aggression, irrationality and theatricality were not second nature but first.

Dispute around the issue of nationalist violence was the occasion of Mussolini's break with the Partita Socialista Italiano (PSI, Socialist Party of Italy) and emergence as a nationalist demagogue, for the Italian state had preserved neutrality on the outbreak of the European war. Such non-belligerence greatly outraged a section of nationalist opinion, which campaigned energetically for Italian participation aimed at defeating the historic enemy Austria, seizing the Southern Tyrol and extensive territories on the eastern side of the Adriatic. In the lead was the ANI, founded in 1910 by Enrico Corradini, with the aim of instituting authoritarian government to make Italy a genuinely great power. It had already successfully promoted colonial war in Libya against the decrepit Ottoman Empire. After 1914 Mussolini joined the pro-interventionist bloc and, with the help of French and British subsidies, established a newspaper in Milan to campaign for war and, in addition, recruited a gang of hooligans to defend his printing works against indignant socialists.

War was, in the main, welcomed by the Italian industrial and commercial bourgeoisie concentrated in northern Italy. It meant good profits from military contracts, the hope of extended markets from putative territorial gains and tighter discipline for their workforces, but it was more widely welcomed, too, in a spirit of macho romanticism – a purging of the dross of bourgeois complacency, a glamorous and exciting adventure with a taste of self-sacrifice and noble aspiration. It was welcomed by the modernist artistic movement of the Futurists, bohemians fascinated by machinery, speed and all the technology of the contemporary era, among which, of course, military technology was pre-eminent. It was welcomed even by a number of syndicalists and anarchists who viewed it as a form of creative destruction from which would emerge like a phoenix a better society closer to their aspirations – and even as an endorsement of their personal taste for violence.

Initially, however, the most renowned publicist and personal embodiment of these notions and sentiments was not Mussolini but the Nietzschean poet Gabriele D'Annunzio, who satisfied his ego by flying missions over enemy lines. In the political and social crisis that followed the war and peace treaties, he led a band of followers to seize the port of Fiume on the Adriatic, which Italy claimed against the new Yugoslavia, and established there a dictatorial regime with himself in charge. D'Annunzio, however, suffered from two disadvantages. In the first place he was elderly, and therefore not really a suitable icon for macho posturers, and secondly his Fiume enterprise ended in fiasco and he was forced to flee the city. Mussolini admired D'Annunzio and regarded him as a mentor – or at least purported to – but the latter's discredit now left the stage clear for the emergence of Mussolini and his *fasci di combattimento* as central players on the ultra-right.

1920 was the year of the left-wing surge, with factory occupations and actions by peasants in central Italy to curb the power of their landlords in a variety of ways. In 1921 followed the fascist counterattack, with fascist squads, the *squadristi*, rampaging over both rural and urban areas, assaulting, torturing and from time to time murdering their enemies. They also destroyed trade union, co-operative and PSI premises and presses, establishing an atmosphere of terror every bit as violent as that of Hitler's SA ten years later, and meeting minimal resistance. Interestingly, their principal targets tended to relate to the PSI, which had considerable local authority, rather than the newly established and at the time much less significant communists.

However, Mussolini's role in all this, although highly important was, outside Milan, far from dominant. In many instances, and in the countryside almost always, the gangs were organised and led by local entrepreneurs of violence, the *ras*, hired by landlords and businessmen to destroy their enemies. They recruited their squads largely from ex-servicemen, and these constituted a ready pool of disaffection, for they returned from a not-very-successful war to a population which had been on the whole anti-war, and in places where workers or peasants had gained control of employment contracts, as was often the case, found themselves excluded and frequently insulted.[13]

Mussolini, however, as the leader of a party and paramilitary squad, allied to his talent for publicity and self-advertisement, made a convenient figurehead and most of the *ras* acknowledged him as their leader pro forma while continuing to control their own affairs as they wished. Nevertheless Mussolini had gained the tight allegiance of the most effective *squadristi*, the *arditi*, a corps of specially trained military shock troops, particularly resentful at the 'mutilated victory', and whose oath, salute and black shirt were adopted as fascist trademarks. Once the dictatorship was consolidated a few years later the Duce curbed and suppressed his more intransigent followers, threatening even to shoot them, though not with serious intent.

Fascists and conservatives

All of the populist resources would have proved ineffective without the establishment backing that allowed Mussolini to prevail and force his way into the premiership in 1922. The campaign against the left the previous year was assisted and underpinned by the 'forces of order', especially the police and the military and financially supported by a bloc of landowners, industrialists and bankers. The police and the military provided small arms and road transport vehicles (which were particularly important) and on occasion even artillery. In October 1922 they stood aside during the farcical 'March on Rome', which they could have suppressed without difficulty. Instead they easily persuaded the king to call on Mussolini to form a government, which their political representatives happily entered. The institution of the dictatorship at the beginning of 1925 was not quite so straightforward – the premier's elite friends had grown disillusioned with him following the Matteotti murder scandal and it was the *ras* who pushed him into assuming absolutist powers. However, the monarch could readily have dismissed him and called on the forces of the state to enforce the order. He did not. In the words of Denis Mack Smith,

> Fascism was a party not of ideas and doctrine but of action. [Mussolini's] followers were a gang of truculent and ambitious men who wanted power, and were backed by some intelligent and influential members of society who saw the usefulness of such rowdies in helping to suppress socialism, curtail parliamentary liberties, and if possible make the name of Italy feared abroad.[14]

The word 'totalitarian' was invented by Mussolini and intended as a term of approval, but that was little more than public relations spin; the Duce had little interest in ideological refinements – his concerns were with power and prestige. The regime evolved in a fairly ramshackle mode, in its administration, its economic management and not least its armed forces. It was sustained principally by bluff, censorship and astute publicity. It was a key Fascist slogan to 'Believe, Obey, Fight' but it is doubtful if many ordinary Italian hearts throbbed to that pronouncement or joyfully entered the Fascist auxiliary organisations (with the possible exception of the *dopolavoro*, the Italian equivalent of 'Strength through Joy'). Underneath the suppression of political dissent and the blanket of the controlled media, social relations continued much as they had done prior to 1915 – with one important difference.

That difference was of course the destruction of the organised labour movement. Capital got what it wanted and, unlike its German counterpart in the Third Reich, was little bothered by the state. If Fascist Italy was a 'developmental dictatorship' as A. J. Gregor argues, it was so only in the sense that the state kept the workforce helpless so that capital could develop in any manner it saw fit. The notion developed by Italian Fascists of the 'corporate society' was another piece of meaningless public relations. Capital, labour and the state were supposed to constitute the corporate elements and their representatives to meet together to direct the economy and associated matters for mutual benefit – in reality, the decisions were made by capital backed up by the Fascist state and the interests of labour left nowhere.

GERMANY

Early German fascism, which openly drew part of its inspiration from Mussolini and strove to imitate him, was a movement of outsiders that emerged in a number of centres, but above all Bavaria where political tensions were at their highest and where its capital Munich had passed briefly under communist rule. The striking variation was that, in contrast with Italy, racism was absolutely central to the German version; a circumstance reflecting the fact that German reactionaries felt themselves surrounded and threatened by alien and hostile 'races' – French, Slavs and, above all, Jews to whose corrupting influence and malice they attributed their defeat in the late war.

Adolf Hitler's takeover of the German Workers' Party in 1920, while an event of the utmost importance, did not fundamentally alter its character or outlook as a tiny, lower-middle-class would-be populist formation, aspiring to reverse the Versailles Treaty, restore Germany as a major power dominating over its Slav neighbours, and expel the Jews from public life. Its hatred of parliamentarianism and a few vaguely socialistic additions were used to justify its title.

Racism

The ideological inspiration of the party was a mixture of tropes common in late-nineteenth-century German (including Austrian) culture. Racism in general was given bogus scientific credentials from perversions of evolutionary theory and the writings of Arthur Gobineau, and antisemitism in particular derived from a combination of centuries-old religious prejudice and similar pseudoscience. Towards the end of the century, this was expressed with a patina of scholarship by a number of Germanic writers: Julius Langbehn, Paul de Lagarde and probably of most significance, Gerhard von Schönerer, an Austrian. Their books appeared to have a highly influential impact and had countless imitators in the form of cheap pamphleteers. Antisemitism became extremely prevalent throughout Germanic society – the popular and populist Viennese burgomaster Karl Lueger made a career out of it – although it is necessary to keep the German situation in proportion; antisemitism was probably even worse in France and certainly so in the Russian empire.

In the early twentieth century, organisations devoted to advancing the power and status of the 'master race' made their appearance in Germany; small, secretive and semi-mystical in their notions, they were attractive mainly to cranks and social misfits. The most significant of these was the Thule Society, which adopted the swastika as its emblem – several of its members were close to Hitler in his early leadership of the Nazis. Even more important at the time was a small organisation of workers of German nationality in Bohemia, then part of the Habsburg Empire, who actually called themselves national socialists and existed on a basis of racially motivated hostility to their Czech competitors and to social democracy. Some of these too found their way eventually into Hitler's party.

At the time when Hitler assumed leadership over the Deutsche Arbeiterpartei (DAP, German Workers' Party) and added the words 'national socialist' (possibly a recollection of the National Liberals of the pre-war era) to its title, antisemitic sentiment everywhere and especially in Germany had been greatly reinforced by the appearance of the pamphlet *The Protocols of the Learned Elders of Zion*. This was forged around the turn of the century by a Russian Orthodox mystic (it was originally a section of his text predicting the coming of the Antichrist), basing himself on a satire against the French emperor Napoleon III, and brought to Germany by the Baltic German refugee from the Revolution, Hitler's follower Arthur Rosenberg. It purported to be the record of a secret cabal of Jewish leaders plotting to corrupt and take over the world.

> The people under our guidance have annihilated the aristocracy .... Nowadays, with the destruction of the aristocracy, the people have fallen into the grips of merciless money-grinding scoundrels .... We appear on the scene as alleged saviours of the worker from this oppression when we propose him to enter the ranks of our fighting forces – Socialists, Anarchists Communists – to whom we always give support ... the weapons in our hands are limitless ambition, merciless vengeance, hatreds and malice.[15]

In the Nazi interpretation some Jews had been appointed to take over world capitalism, others to lead socialism and communism. The *Protocols* also include Freemasons as tools of the Jewish conspiracy, 'The most secret political plots will be known to us and will fall under our guiding hands on the very day of their conception.' Reading the document, one gets the impression that the author rather admires the sort of bloodthirsty theocratic absolutism that he fantasises the Jews as conspiring to institute – provided it is instituted instead by reactionaries.

Ideology and the advance on power

Hitler's significance was that his personality and theatrical talents enabled the NSDAP to absorb similarly-minded groupings throughout Germany and the party consequently grew (despite the fiasco of the Munich putsch in 1923) from a minuscule sect into a recognisable, though still minor, political force. By 1928, it was probably at the maximum strength that the circumstances of relative social and economic stability in Germany permitted. Hitler's cult of personality indeed came to be central to the Nazi appeal – as only he himself was capable of reconciling the conflicting trends and ambitions among his followers and focusing them onto a joint purpose under his leadership. 'National Socialism is for agrarian reform and against it, for private property and against it, for idealism and against it.'[16] 'The ideology of National Socialism contains elements of idealism, positivism, pragmatism, vitalism, universalism, institutionalism – in short, elements of every conceivable philosophy. But these diverse elements are not integrated.'[17] When bidding for power in the early 1930s the Nazis, when questioned about their policy, would frequently declare 'Our policy is Hitler!'

That is to anticipate. In one sense Nazi ideology was perfectly focused, but in others seriously incoherent. The major source of tension lay between the elements in the leadership, such as Gregor Strasser, or the Nazi 'martyr' Horst Wessel at the rank-and-file level, who attached some significance to the 'socialist' term in the party's title and 'socialist' elements of its supposedly unalterable programme. These in general tended to be more attracted to the SA than the party proper. On the other hand, the party included those like Hitler himself who viewed decoration of that sort as no more than conveniences in achieving the total power necessary to carry through a programme of racism and expansionism. Hitler did not omit to assure a meeting of moneyed men, whose support he hoped to attract, to disregard any socialistic undertakings as mere window dressing. He went on to redefine socialism in such a way that it could include the traditional German elites if they adjusted themselves to the regime he intended to construct: 'And there has arisen ... blood against formal reason; race against purposeful rationality, honour against profit, unity against individualistic disintegration, martial virtue against bourgeois security, the *Volk* against the individual and the mass.'[18]

Electoral breakthrough came in the Reichstag elections of 1930. In the aftermath of the slump the Nazis extended their electoral strength in the urban areas (as did the communists), but the principal effect was felt in the countryside where the smallholders (who had done quite well out of the hyperflation and taken on extensive new debts) found that the bottom had fallen out of the market for agricultural products and they now faced bankruptcy and foreclosure all over Germany. Neither communism nor social democracy was ever going to attract this social group: they were fiercely nationalistic and their principal political attachment was to the DNVP. The ultra-conservative DNVP, however, was dogmatic in its attachment to economic liberalism and could promise nothing, whereas the Nazis sent activists into the villages and promised that under their government the German farmer, the reservoir of the German racial stock, would never be allowed to go under. Promises of smallholder security were immensely attractive and delivered a landslide. Irreconcilable rural conservatives were appalled, and the landowner Major Ewald von Kleist referred to it as 'rural bolshevism'.[19]

The tensions between the social radicals and the opportunists in the ideological bloc which formed the Nazi movement were to be the source of the only really serious domestic crisis the regime experienced prior to the outbreak of war. As noted, the rank and file of the radicals, who tended to be young men with little to lose and frequently unemployed, gravitated towards the SA. The SA member was more likely to have a working-class background than other party members (and, interestingly, to be marginally less antisemitic) though his parents were also less likely to have been part of the labour movement.[20] They also had a leader in the person of the SA chief, Ernst Röhm, who sympathised with their aspirations – which immediately took the form of becoming Germany's primary military force with consequent promotion, income and prestige.

The SS

Once Hitler was in power they began to look forward to some delivery on their expectations and in the spring and early summer of 1934 to grow increasingly restless. The crisis broke at the end of June and was resolved with the murder of Röhm and his close associates to the satisfaction of the conservatives, especially the army chiefs, in spite of the total illegality of Hitler's actions, and also most ordinary German citizens tired of the organisation's destructive rowdiness. What had formerly been a subordinate section of the SA, the black-uniformed SS which had been used as the instrument of the SA leaders' destruction, now came to the fore. Led by Heinreich Himmler (whom even Hitler regarded as a little mad) it formed an elite within the Nazi state and regarded itself not as a gang of murderous functionaries but as the perfect embodiment of the party's ideology and, under the Führer, the chosen leadership of the *Volk*.

The SS was extremist, even by Nazi standards, in its obsession with racial purity; engaged in bizarre Odinist rituals and deliberately cultivated what its *Reichführer* regarded as the qualities essential to a master race – hyper-elitism, physical strength and courage, blind obedience, pitiless dedication to racial superiority and in pursuit of that aim willingness to commit any atrocity without regret or scruple. They replaced the SA as the concentration camp guards and formed the corps of extermination squads and extermination camp operatives designed to implement the 'final solution' – the total extirpation of Jews in Nazi-occupied Europe, down to the last infant.

Carl Schmitt wrote in the year after the massacre,

> A strong State is the precondition for the strong and autonomous vitality of its constituent parts. The strength of the National Socialist State lies in the fact that it is from top to bottom and in every atom of its existence ruled

and permeated with the concept of leadership. This principle, which made the movement strong, must be carried through systematically both in the administration of the State and in the various spheres of self-government.[21]

This remark, however, showed Schmitt to be still afflicted with old ultra-conservative conceptions and not quite in tune with his new masters, for Nazi ideology, if not always practice, validated the movement and the *Volk* above even the state. According to Arthur Rosenberg,

> The revolution of 30 January 1933 does not constitute the absolutist state under a new name; it places the state in a new relation to the people ... What has taken place in 1933 ... is not the establishment of the state's totality but of the totality of the National Socialist movement. The state is no longer an entity juxtaposed to the people and the movement, it is no longer conceived as a mechanical apparatus or an instrument of domination; the state is a tool of the National Socialist philosophy of life.[22]

Or, in Hitler's own words, the state is not a moral concept or the realisation of an absolute idea, but the servant of the racial people.[23]

OTHER EXAMPLES

Romania

Apart from those of Germany and Italy, there was no fascist movement which succeeded in achieving power without outside intervention on its behalf. Ironically, the one that came nearest to doing so was actually prevented by Hitler from attaining its goal. In Romania the Legion of the Archangel Michael was every bit as viciously antisemitic as the Nazis, and its leader Cornilieu Codrianu once remarked that he could teach Hitler a thing or two about fascism.

Romania, a kingdom with a shaky parliamentary regime, was, like all of Eastern Europe, a largely peasant society but possessed of huge mineral wealth in the shape of oil. Class divisions were extreme and the political class constituted a largely closed oligarchy of landowners, businessmen and professionals. Romanian is a Latin language and Romanian nationalism focused on this as a presumed mark of superiority, elevating Romanians, as supposed descendants of Roman colonists, above the barbarous Slavs and other inferior races inhabiting the Balkans. The state religion was Eastern Orthodox.

Romania counted as a victor power in the First World War, and certainly the state had made enormous gains, virtually doubling its territory and population, a development which generated enormous social, political, cultural and national tensions and superheated ethnic Romanian consciousness. In the 1920s this was manifested especially in the universities, where the Legion had its origins. It was characterised by its intense ideological commitment to Romanian ethnic nationalism and its no less intense commitment to extreme violence and leader-worship. These features enabled it to dominate the student union, but otherwise its impact was relatively marginal before the 1930s.

The slump altered all that. The Legion, though abating nothing of its antisemitism and commitment to extreme violence, including the assassination of enemy politicians and academics, set out to win broader support and succeeded spectacularly. It made a particular appeal to the ethnic Romanian peasantry, playing upon the themes of exploitation, religion and paranoid antisemitism (many peasants were in debt to Jewish moneylenders and, to divert hostility, grasping landlords employed Jews as agents to exact their rents).

> Whoever wants to destroy a people will do it in the following way: destroy the link between heaven and the soil, foment fraternal conflicts and discord …
>
> The worst thing the Jews and politicians have done to us, the greatest danger they have exposed our people to, is not the way they are seizing the riches and possessions of our country, destroying the Romanian middle class, the way they swamp our schools and liberal professions …. The greatest danger they pose to the people is rather that they are undermining us racially …[24]

The Legion organised its intake of new followers into a broader movement termed the Iron Guard. This expanded into a formidable paramilitary force, practically dictating government policy until the royal regime struck back, arresting Codreanu and having him murdered in prison. That hardly slowed its momentum; Codreanu was elevated to martyr status, and under his successor Horia Sima the Iron Guard dominated the regime of Ion Antonescu and was on the brink of taking power when Hitler himself intervened. By this time the European war had broken out, and the Führer had been redistributing the territories of his 'allies'. He had awarded large slices of pre-war Romania to the more favoured Hungarian regime, while Stalin, during the period of the Nazi-Soviet pact had retaken some more which had been seized by Romania after the Russian Revolution. Consequently the royal government was in deep discredit and ready to fall.

Hitler, however, preferred a stable right-wing traditional regime as his ally in this sensitive region with its vital oil, rather than the wilful loose cannon of the Iron Guard, and so pressured Antonescu, a military strongman, to suppress it and establish his own dictatorship. German tanks in Bucharest provided support and the Iron Guard was extinguished with much bloodletting. It is probably fair to suggest that something like the Legion and someone like Codreanu would have appeared in Romania even if neither Hitler nor Mussolini had ever come to power – the Legion was in no way imitative, but almost entirely home-grown, and in the absence of a left-wing alternative and against the background of a feared Soviet Union was able to mobilise the discontent and misery prevalent in the Romanian middle class and peasantry.

Finland

Following the end of Russian sovereignty over Finland in 1918, a savage civil war, simultaneous with that in Russia, erupted between left and right, which the latter won with the aid first of German Imperial troops and subsequently Freikorps units. Rather surprisingly in the circumstances, a democratic regime was established in the aftermath and the Communist Party reappeared.

The authentic form of fascist ideology in Finland, the Akateeminen Karjala-Seura (AKS, Academic Karelia Society), was, even more than the Legion of the Archangel Michael, university-based and had the form of a Masonic cabal rather than a political party. The AKS, however, was not irrelevant; many of the Finnish elite – in the army, business, the civil service, academic life and the legal profession – were members or ex-members.[25] Its primary objective was the expansion of Finnish borders eastwards at the expense of the Soviet Union, and its sentiments were ultra-rightist and authoritarian – it was in no sense populist, which might seem to exclude it from the fascist categorisation, although that did not correspond with its own perspective: 'our youth will be fascistized: it will take up the struggle for a new State and a new society, one from which class hatred has been eradicated'.[26] It also sustained a quirky form of racism: contrary to the attitudes of all other racist fascisms, which emphasised racial purity, the Finnish version instead emphasised admixture – Finns were superior because they were – supposedly – of mixed race (principally Russian and Swedish) and therefore the happy possessors of hybrid vigour.

The AKS therefore was fairly marginal to the populist form of fascism or near-fascism which emerged in the aftermath – inevitably – of the slump, when the small farmers, who were the numerically dominant class in Finland, were put under severe economic pressure with the collapse of agricultural markets. This was the Lapua Movement, named after the village where it originated, a spontaneous politicisation of rural smallholders organised by local demagogues, often Lutheran clergymen. The immediate aim of the Lapua Movement was the outlawing of godless communism:

> Two spirits today are fighting for world supremacy, one of them destructive, the other constructive .... There are only two kinds of people: the righteous and the godless .... Between good and evil, life and death, peace and war, light and darkness, Christ and Satan, white and red, the gospel of the churches and atheism, there is no intermediate form, no third possibility .... He who woos pagan anti-Christianity woos the devil himself.[27]

Mass demonstrations intimidating the Finnish parliament enabled it to achieve the aim. The resentment of materially underprivileged traditionalists was directed at outsiders and nonconformists who could be plausibly presented as a threat, regardless of the fact that the Finnish communist party had no power nor prospect of any. Also in the movement's sights was another minority – the Swedish-speakers who constituted around 10 per cent of the population and tended to be in the higher income brackets. These, however, were no outsiders, but contained members of the elite, including the military strongman Baron Mannerheim.

That was doubtless among the reasons why the Lapua Movement, though strong at its height, failed to establish a permanent presence. It also lost credibility and establishment support when, having forced the Communist Party underground, it turned next upon the innocuous social democrats. This time it failed, and that was the beginning of its decline. Its objectives were essentially negative – it had no positive programme or effective demagogue leader. During the war, under Marshal Mannerheim, Finland was a German ally like Hungary or Romania, though less of a satellite; with defeat came discredit for the right, whether fascist or conservative while communism, which had kept a base of popular support, re-emerged as a leading element in the political structure.

Austria and Hungary

Fascism in both these countries developed considerable strength, partly on account of socio-political similarities but also for very different reasons. As fragments of the Austro–Hungarian empire both were defeated powers and desire for national unification with Germany was a powerful sentiment in Austria. This was forbidden by the Versailles Treaty. Here, too, the left, along with the Jews, were blamed for the loss of the war. Bitter tension existed between industrialised, cosmopolitan Vienna with its strong labour movement (mainly social democrat, the communists were relatively marginal) and large proportion of Jews in professional occupations, and the intensely Catholic smallholders of the rural hinterland, the principal reservoir of reaction.

Revanchism was, if anything, even more intense in Hungary, which had been so mutilated by the Treaty of Trianon that almost as many Hungarians lived outside the state as within it, and the aim of re-establishing a Greater Hungary was a cardinal feature of its ultra-right. Moreover, Hungary, as noted, experienced in 1918–19 a brief episode of communist rule followed by savage repression during which the Whites, after much bloodletting, established Admiral Horthy's dictatorship. In the aftermath a constitutional veneer was adopted and an ineffective social democratic party was permitted to exist: this was wholly without influence outside Budapest.

Such circumstances proved advantageous to Hungary's native fascists, the Arrow Cross, who adopted a populist stance directed at the rural population suffering intensely under the control of rapacious landlords particularly in the circumstances of the great depression. This party fitted safely into the state ideology of anti-communism and Magyarism and so could present itself as upholding authentic Hungarian nationalism while at the same time purporting to speak on behalf of the dispossessed. Like their counterparts in Romania they were viciously antisemitic, but (unlike the Iron Guard) never presented a threat to the reactionary regime. All the same, they had influence – the prime minister from 1932 to 1936, Gyulia Gömbos, was sympathetic, but it took

Nazi occupation in 1944 to raise the Arrow Cross to power. Its leader, Ferenc Szálasi, was not the most realistic of politicians:

> The New Hungary has to be based on my personal prestige. Luckily I am here, because there cannot be a New Hungary without me … everyone who … does not want to recognise me as the only leader, or does not want to accept that I have been chosen by higher divine inspiration to redeem the Hungarian nation, or does not understand me, or loses my confidence, can go. With the help of the secret strength inside me I am going to create the Hungarist State, even if I have to do it on my own.[28]

Austria presented the spectacle of different brands of fascism in conflict. Following the suppression of the Viennese workers' insurrection in 1934, Engelbert Dollfuss and his successor Schuschnigg established a quasi-fascist regime and even tried to import a degree of populism. It was modelled on Mussolini's and the Duce acted as its protector at a time when he remained suspicious of his German imitator and rival. The Austrian national socialists were no more than a branch of the NSDAP, but they nevertheless had significant popular support, especially after the establishment of the Reich. Rivalry with Dollfuss' 'Fatherland Front' was bitter. In July 1934, the Austrian Nazis assassinated Dollfuss and staged a coup, which quickly failed thanks to Mussolini's intervention. Their popularity grew nonetheless and, after Mussolini's protection was withdrawn, their opponents had no chance. Hitler intended initially to set up a puppet Austrian regime rather than annex the country, but nationalism in this instance trumped even the Führer; German troops crossed the border and Hitler was welcomed ecstatically.

Other instances

Movements that are historically accepted as belonging to the fascist typology existed throughout Europe and beyond. Few of them were of great political significance, although Brazil appears to have been an exception; so, locally, were Slovakia and Croatia, where, like Austria, fascist populist ultra-nationalism was combined with ultra-reactionary clericalism. All were formed into different shapes by their historical circumstances. All tried to apply the charismatic leader principle, some more convincingly than others. Ireland was exceptional in that it was the only example that was *not* ultra-nationalist, due to the peculiar history of the Free State where ultra-nationalism had been made the property of the Blueshirts' enemies.[29] Fascist-minded demagogues existed in the USA but, with few exceptions, remained politically insignificant.

During the Second World War, Japan, as a member of the Axis powers, was conventionally described as fascist; but although the monarchy-backed military regime certainly showed many fascist social and ideological features, including racist hyper-nationalism, it remained too conservative to really fit the designation. According to Roger Griffin there was only one significant fascist in Japan at the time (he did have a few followers), but he was unpopular with the rulers, sidelined and silenced.

The Iberian regimes established in the 1920s and 1930s have been similarly labelled, but in actual fact neither actually was (though Spain's regime was if anything worse than Italy's) and their fascist movements were very differently placed. In Portugal a fascist grouping of the utmost insignificance was quickly suppressed by the ultra-conservative clericalist regime. In Spain, by contrast, there was an authentic fascist party with an authentically charismatic leader – the Falange led by José Antonio Primo de Rivera, established during the crisis of the Republic. It was never very large or powerful, but on account of the energy and dedication of its members established a significant presence, at least in Madrid. Its fate was to be co-opted and subordinated by the generals who won the civil war, a process made easier by the fate of its leader, who was shot by the Republicans. After Franco's regime was secured, the Falange was established as the only legal political party, creating the illusion of a fascist state, but it lacked any real influence with the government and on the one occasion when José Antonio's successors tried to assert themselves, they were soon taught their place. José Antonio could then be adopted as a harmless icon.

CONCLUSION

It is disturbing to think that, even negatively, the individual with very likely the greatest single impact on the twentieth century and up to the present was Adolf Hitler. Classical fascism may be utterly discredited and abhorrent to all except irrelevant marginal groups of sociopaths, but the influence of its career lingers on and not only in the disguised neo-fascisms which have established a presence in certain parts of Europe.

Much more important are the fundamental shifts in global geopolitics, global economy and global technology which followed from the outcome of the Second World War. The dominance of the USA in all these spheres may very well have been on the cards in any case, given the nature of its economy, society and culture – it effectively dominated in the international economy even by 1939 – but there can be no doubt that the outcome was made certain and enormously accelerated by what happened between 1941 and 1945. Beyond that, the reality of the Cold War and the danger of it turning hot constituted the fundamental world issue between the end of hostilities and the beginning of the 1990s. The futures of Western Europe, India, China and Japan were shifted into different courses. As for the Soviet Union and its central component, Russia, not to speak of the East European states, their future, whatever it might have been, was certainly very different from what would have been the case if Lance Corporal Hitler had stopped a bullet in the Flanders trenches. Africa, too, was transformed for better or worse in a manner which certainly would not have otherwise occurred, and likewise the Middle East, for without the Second World War Israel would never have existed.

To sum up, it is not too much of an exaggeration to suggest that fascism dead has proved more important even than fascism living.

II

Golden years 1945–73

6
Economic and social conditions

The Second World War had been fought on all sides with the utmost mobilisation of the belligerents' human resources both social and ideological. Without that the war could not have been won, and the consequences were momentous.[1] In the USSR, where survival was at stake and the regime was autocratic, the authorities did not have to promise much except survival and victory, though no doubt the populations, as victory grew increasingly probable, expected a post-war future much improved from the 1920s and 1930s. In the West however, where the rules of formal democracy either continued to apply or would have to be restored after hostilities, a new and better world of peace and prosperity was the almost universal expectation.

It was acknowledged on nearly all sides that the impact of mass unemployment had been a major contributor to the 'twenty years' crisis' through its destabilising effects on society and politics, and victorious Western governments entered the peace with determination to avoid any repetition. The coalition government in the UK had in 1944 produced a White Paper highlighting this as a central objective for the post-war years. In the USA, the war had achieved what the New Deal could not and had lifted the country out of depression. The administration was determined to keep things that way. Domestically a number of measures were put in hand and, because they applied principally to veterans, not even the haters of state benefits could convincingly object. Educational provision was made available on easy terms and loans at low interest provided for the purchase of housing, stimulating investment in a number of directions.

International institutions, in some of which Keynes had played a significant part – the Bretton Woods agreement, the International Monetary Fund, the World Bank, the General Agreement on Tariffs and Trade (GATT) were established to keep trade barriers minimal, to iron out fluctuations in the global economy and to stabilise the world monetary system by the US Treasury's guarantee to purchase and sell gold at a fixed rate. The US negotiators ensured that the institutions were set up in such a manner as to work primarily in the American interest and, because they held the advantage, representing as they did the only large, intact and flourishing economy in the world, none could gainsay them – not even Keynes's negotiating talents could produce a different result.[2]

These developments were intended to ensure as far as possible an open global market for US products and investment, and the open international economy was no less important for the continuance of prosperity than any domestic measure. Japan with its huge population was hugely important, and the USA ensured that it was in sole control of the Occupation, excluding any other power, especially the USSR, and so in a position to remodel the Japanese polity according to its wishes.[3] The 'loss' of China, with its even larger population, was a devastating setback when the communist revolution triumphed in 1949 and was to have profound and negative effects both on American domestic politics and American foreign policy. In the event, the US economy survived this 'loss' perfectly well, but that could not have been foreseen at the time.

Possibly the US administration might have hoped that the USSR, too, would become a more open economy than it had previously been, but they could hardly have entertained that prospect seriously – especially when relations deteriorated and the Kremlin began establishing its bloc in Eastern Europe in early 1947, with economies to be modelled on the USSR's and not open to market penetration. Western Europe was a different matter, for here the USA very much had the upper hand.

It would seem that the original intention was not to keep significant military forces in these countries, but rather to expect that the restoration of free markets combined with the international institutions would enable them to rebuild quickly, become self-sustaining, and establish independent but friendly relations with the USA, enabling a natural and painless process of coca-colonisation to take place. These hopes were frustrated, for the West European economies limped and staggered.[4]

In the UK, lend-lease was cut off immediately once Japan surrendered;[5] the country could get a loan only on very harsh terms and the money was soon exhausted,[6] triggering a financial crisis; a policy of 'austerity' was imposed on the population, keeping consumer goods in very short supply.[7] The UK did, however, have certain important assets. These included an empire whose resources could be drawn upon, and in Malaya a bitter colonial war was fought to retain control of its rubber and tin. Another was that the British industrial economy, although battered and run down, was relatively intact compared with those of its former European or Japanese rivals, so demand for its products was heavy and the government ensured that they were directed to export rather than home consumption. Even so, economic collapse was never far off the horizon, especially after the unprecedented winter of early 1947.

Other European countries were still less fortunate. Apart from those such as the neutrals, or Norway, which possessed natural resources in high demand, no end to impoverishment and immiseration appeared to be in sight, and therefore the communist option, despite the increasing discredit into which Stalin's regime was starting to fall, might seem to grow in attraction. Consequently the USA, having effectively declared the initiation of the Cold War in March 1947, followed this up with the European Recovery Programme, more commonly referred to as the Marshall Plan after the US Secretary of State who promoted it. The dollar aid tap was once more turned on, the crisis averted, recovery set in train, US hegemony in Western Europe asserted, and the countries of the region engrossed in the US-led North Atlantic military alliance.

THE COMMUNIST BLOC

If wartime devastation was severe among the West European belligerents,[8] in the East, with few exceptions, it was indescribable. The Soviet Union itself had lost between 20 and 30 million of its citizens, not counting the disabled casualties. Proportionate losses in Poland were even worse. The retreating Germans razed Warsaw to the ground – scarcely a building was left standing. Millions of refugees, 'displaced persons', sought food and shelter (as was the case in the West though on a lesser scale). It required heroic endeavours by UN relief agencies funded by the USA to avert mass famine.

The USSR government, for the sake of stimulating the popular enthusiasm necessary to win the war, had, in the midst of all the material and human horrors, caused the level of internal repression to be somewhat eased. Once the fighting was over it was fiercely reimposed, partly because iron discipline was needed for the immense tasks of reconstruction that faced the population and partly on account of Stalin's growing paranoia. Ex-service personnel were notified that valorous wartime deeds would count for nothing if they failed now to apply themselves with equal determination to rebuilding their country.

In other words, exacting exploitation of available human resources was the order of the day, and work discipline and the austerity of living conditions were equal to anything that had existed during the 1930s.

The Kremlin, however, had another recourse, since the hope of US aid which Stalin had for a time entertained[9] proved nugatory. This was the seizure, in the form of physical reparations, of intact industrial and agricultural equipment, along with available raw materials from former enemy states – the Soviet zones of Germany and Austria along with the Reich's satellites, Hungary, Romania and Bulgaria. The refusal of the USA to allow the Soviets to take what they demanded from West Germany and Italy was one of the factors exacerbating international tension. Even those states within the Soviet sphere which had been not German allies but victims – Czechoslovakia, Poland, Yugoslavia – were induced to sign trade agreements unfavourable to themselves and conversely favourable to the USSR.

All of these states (the Soviet Occupation Zone of Germany became the German Democratic Republic in 1949) formed the members of the Soviet bloc (including Yugoslavia until 1948). They were effectively single-party regimes (in most, phantom non-communist parties continued, for appearances' sake, to exist under communist tutelage). They were all obliged to adopt the Soviet model of the planned command economy, with emphasis on heavy industry at the expense of consumer provision. Agricultural collectivisation, too, was initiated in most. It was perhaps not to be wondered at that several states of the bloc were shaken by armed revolts or political upheavals in 1953, 1956, 1968, 1970 and 1979, nor that until 1961 there was a mass exodus of GDR citizens from East to West Berlin to enjoy the consumer delights of the 'Free World'.

If the position of the Soviet Union at the end of the war was desperate, that of China was scarcely less dire, having endured nearly forty years of civil war, foreign invasion and occupation before the US-backed Guomindang regime collapsed and Mao's communist armies secured control of the country. Stalin was almost certainly none too pleased, knowing only too well how this outcome would be received in the United States and what it would do to his relations with the Americans. Accordingly he had urged Mao to join in a coalition government with Chiang but the Chinese leader had listened politely and then ignored his advice.

Reconstructing the country was a formidable undertaking. Satisfying peasant demands – for the revolution was as much as anything a gigantic peasant revolt – was a priority, and massive redistribution was put in hand. So was massive retribution, and there was much slaughter of objectionable individuals, especially landlords or persons who might be regarded as such. Capitalists who had not been actively engaged with the enemy, however, were protected in the meantime because their contribution was regarded as essential to economic recovery. Stalin had little option but to publicly acclaim the revolution and to offer military and diplomatic alliance along with economic support, but this was given on hard terms and had to be paid for – a source of resentment to the new regime along with Soviet refusal to consider rectification of the borders imposed by the Tsar in the era of Chinese weakness. As with the USSR, only more so, economic and social reconstruction was going to have to depend primarily on human resources and the simplest of equipment.[10]

DECOLONISATION

The Second World War signalled the beginning of the end for formal European empires. What had happened in East Asia, even if the Japanese were ultimately defeated, was fatal to European prestige. The events of 1941–42 demonstrated that whether British, French, Dutch or American, they could be beaten just like anybody else, and by an Asian power. The populations of the affected areas – Burma, South-East Asia, Malaya, Indonesia and the Philippines – were no longer disposed to tolerate their colonial status and, where independence was resisted, armed revolts erupted.

The peoples of the Indian subcontinent were likewise determined to end the colonial relationship – and because the British could no longer hold it down, and the new Labour government was committed in any case, withdrawal was conceded with relative good grace. Along with India went Ceylon and Burma. However, communal and religious tensions in British India, previously fostered by the colonial power, led to partition and a subsequent bloodbath, weakening the two new states that emerged. By concentrating all their efforts, the British succeeded in militarily defeating the communist-led independence movement in Malaya, but had to concede independence thereafter, while a similar process occurred with the Americans in the Philippines. In Indonesia, formerly the Dutch East Indies, the Dutch were driven out. In South-East Asia at this time, the fighting continued. To the north, the predominantly peasant society of the Korean peninsula was divided between the communist-ruled north and the US-satellite south. Taiwan, the last refuge of Chiang's regime, was still purporting to be the legitimate Chinese government. Protected by the

US navy, his soldiers and bureaucrats treated the local Taiwanese population pretty much as their Japanese predecessors had done when the island was a Japanese colony.

It was the aim of all the new nationalist governments to further economic development and at the same time to secure rising standards in the various dimensions of social life such as education, health and material living standards. In India far-reaching land reforms were projected intending to bring ownership within the reach of all rural dwellers, but accomplishment, if not wholly negligible, was indifferent (Japan, under the Occupation, was actually much more successful). With the communists militarily defeated in Malaya and the Philippines, suppressed in Indonesia, weak in Japan, and with only localised support in India and Burma, all these societies rested on capitalist foundations, but the Indian and Indonesian regimes, by far the largest, declared themselves to be socialist in inspiration and, as the Cold War developed, neutralist as well.

Development to the level of the West or Japan proved to be beyond the reach of any, with one peculiar exception. The British, following their victory over the Malayan insurgents, had created the new state of Malaysia, consisting of Malaya, Singapore and a part of Borneo and passed it to the safely Western-orientated Malayan commercial bourgeoisie. This union was soon disrupted when the ethnic Chinese bourgeoisie who dominated commercial life in Singapore broke away and established a city-state of a single-party, intensely authoritarian temper, which nevertheless attained a high level of material welfare.

THE LONG BOOM

'It was the best of times: it was the worst of times.' These years, Hobsbawm's 'golden age', were the ones that saw unprecedented levels of full employment in the industrialised West and in Japan together with exceptional consumer improvement, and hopes remained alive that what was becoming known as the 'third world' might still follow the same path; while at the same time in the USA, legally enforced racial discrimination was being extinguished and other forms diminished. In the Soviet bloc expectations for a time were also very high and, even when disappointed, some modest if patchy material improvement continued. On the other hand, however, everywhere these were the years of maximum terror at the prospect of maximum annihilation in the event of all-out nuclear conflict – fears that were on at least one occasion very nearly realised.

The consensus of economic and political thinking in the West was that this unusual era of economic stability and growth owed its existence to Keynesian techniques of demand management and financial control on the part of governments, backed up by the international financial institutions. Of course there were hitches and glitches, but these were neither very severe nor very prolonged. Even so, there were signs of erosion as early as the mid

1960s, most evidently in the UK with its overstretched military expenditure and reliance on the strength of the pound sterling.

Certainly it is unlikely that Keynesian instruments, including the international institutions, did not play some part in producing this age of steady economic growth, moderate inflation, expanding consumer choice and social welfare – yet more profound forces were at work and ultimately responsible. This is not to argue that it was all automatic and that specific human choices played no part, that the capitalist world could not have slipped, as many (particularly communists) expected, into deep recession during the late 1940s.

What then were at the roots of a situation which was expected to last forever but in fact coincided in length almost exactly with its nineteenth-century equivalent, described by economic historians as 'the great Victorian boom' between 1850 and 1873? Particular decisions and circumstances have to be taken into account, and the European recovery Programme, popularly termed Marshall Aid, a massive input of scarce dollars under US supervision into the West European economies, was very important – it rescued them from a crisis which would probably have overwhelmed them and that in turn would have drastically curbed the overseas market potential available to the USA. The build-up under US direction of Japan and Germany to functioning industrial economies was a part of the same picture.

More basic still were the deliberate policies of sustaining full employment and, by previous standards, relatively generous public support for those remaining without employment or incapable of working. How far the 'permanent arms economy' with its multiple spin-offs in a militarised West, especially the USA, was crucial to sustaining the boom is disputable,[11] but it certainly was of some significance. More significant still was the long-suppressed consumer demand built up during slump and world war now released to emerge with great force. It was accelerated not only by the spreading availability of the technologically novel products which had initially appeared in the interwar years or even earlier, but by their accelerated development and convenience together with new additions to the range, such as washing machines and home refrigerators in the domestic market, and helicopters and commercial jet aircraft in the transport market. Hardly less important was the growth of the relatively new instrument of credit, which spread universally in the consumer societies – deferred purchase (at a price), or hire purchase.

Taken overall, investment opportunities expanded if not exploded and, naturally, capital was found to take advantage of them. No large pool of domestic reserve labour was to be found in the industrialised nations and, to fill the absence and retard the explosive growth of wages in a tight labour market, they resorted to the import of labour from low-wage economies – Turkey and Yugoslavia in the case of Germany, Algeria for the French low-wage workforce, and the Commonwealth for Britain, mainly from the Caribbean, India and Pakistan.

COMMAND ECONOMIES

During the 1950s, the Soviet economic model of centrally planned command economy appeared to be a very successful one indeed and impressed even the most orthodox economists and politicians in the West. The wartime devastation was restored, even if on a much lower consumer base than was the case in the West (the shoddiness of East European and Soviet consumer goods was proverbial). Then, in 1957, came the technological triumph of the first earth-orbiting artificial satellite,[12] to be followed less than four years later by the first man in space, and in 1963 the first woman.

The publicity effect was sensational, but this was not all. Following Stalin's death in 1953, disputes among his successors centred on the question of moving Soviet industry towards a greater consumer orientation in place of the concentration on heavy industry and armaments that had prevailed hitherto. The eventual winner, Nikita Khrushchev, had originally backed continuing in the old style with the emphasis on producer goods, but once safely installed as First Secretary (and later Premier in addition) he moved towards the opposite viewpoint. Overall Soviet growth rates exceeded the West (or at least purported to) and, at the Twenty-Second CPSU Congress of 1961, Khrushchev extravagantly promised that in 20 years Soviet citizens would enjoy a consumer environment equivalent to that of the USA. These claims, however, in no way corresponded with Soviet realities and the technological triumphs of the space race (soon to be trumped in any case by the Americans) gave a wholly misleading impression.

Yugoslavia, having broken with Moscow in 1948, had reorganised its economic system though continuing with the basic model of the planned economy. In essence, enterprises were given extended independence but in return subjected to greater market pressures in order to raise efficiency – not dissimilar to the Soviet NEP of the 1920s, except that there was a greater degree of workforce participation in management decisions. It also, as indicated above, exported labour to West Germany.

In the countries of the Eastern bloc, developments similar to those in the USSR and prompted from Moscow occurred on a lesser scale, mostly against the resistance of unwilling Stalinist leaders. Conditions, both economic and political, varied significantly from country to country. Czechoslovakia, having largely escaped material destruction during the war, enjoyed, on the whole, superior living standards compared with the other states. Albania (which left the bloc in the early 1960s), with a regime more Stalinist than Stalin, stood at the other end of the scale both in its desperate poverty and the primitiveness of its political system (ironically, its tyrant, Enver Hoxha, was more culturally cultivated than any of the others).[13] In the years of Stalinist paranoia following the Yugoslav defection, suspected dissidents had been weeded out throughout the bloc. In Bulgaria, Hungary, Albania and Czechoslovakia this had meant show trials and executions, but not in the GDR, Poland and Romania, where harsh imprisonment had sufficed.

The uprisings in 1953 in the GDR, 1956 in Poland and especially Hungary challenged the repressive regimes and inordinate managerial demands on the workforces, but not in the main the basic concept of the planned economy. The formerly-imprisoned Cardinal Mindzensky and right-wing groups that emerged during the Hungarian revolution did call for restoration, but these were minority voices. To use an expression from 1968, what was demanded was 'socialism with a human face' – capitalism had yet to recover its credibility. Far-reaching political changes at the top and promise of material improvement satisfied the demands in Poland. The Hungarian insurrection was put down bloodily and followed by numerous executions, but the Soviet-installed government of Janos Kadar proceeded to a consumer-orientated economic programme, the 'New Economic Mechanism', making greater use of market principles, which raised Hungarian living standards to among the highest in the bloc – far inferior, nevertheless, to what was taken for granted in the West.

The Chinese picture was much darker. After nearly a decade of tolerably effective material and social reconstruction, the ruling group, prompted and prodded it seems by Mao, who was dissatisfied with the pace of development, decided to launch, against Soviet advice and warnings, the 'Great Leap Forward', a form of agricultural transformation and breakneck industrialisation quite different from the Soviet example. The aim was to use the most easily available resource, namely the population. Collectivisation in the Soviet fashion was not undertaken, but the villagers were compelled to enter communes and to farm collectively. Worse, the crops to be sown and even the farming techniques to be employed were bureaucratically prescribed from above often on the basis of Mao's own personal prejudices.

The result was a catastrophe if anything even worse than Soviet collectivisation, a famine of incomparable magnitude resulting, according to estimates, in the region of over 40 million deaths. Industrialisation was to be advanced not by the method of emptying the countryside and enhancing the urban population, but by the peasantry itself. At the urging of Communist Party cadres, crudely-constructed steel furnaces were set up all over the countryside and any seemingly useable form of metal, even agricultural implements and domestic utensils, was committed to them. The steel they produced was so inferior as to be useless. The madness continued for years, with none of his colleagues apparently daring to contradict the great leader until at last the scope of the disaster became so manifest that he was eventually sidelined – for a time. Neighbouring North Korea, in contrast to what was to happen in future years, appeared at this time to be an economic success story, recovering from the ravages of the war and developing rapidly.

PROBLEMS OF THE LONG BOOM

Two texts, Daniel Bell's *End of Ideology* and Anthony Crosland's *Future of Socialism* (of which more later), in the USA and in the UK respectively, gave theoretical expression to the sense of confidence and self-satisfaction that this economic miracle produced. The implicit, and sometimes explicit, presumption behind both was that the boom would last indefinitely, rising levels of prosperity would prevail and that any problems appearing from time to time could be dealt with by the apparatus of economic controls developed since 1945.

What was not recognised was that there were systemic problems associated with the boom, which might be exacerbated by some mistaken policy, inflationary acceleration or deflationary dip, but were in fact intrinsic, built into the nature of the boom itself and certain in due course to produce its reversal, however long that might take. From the point of view of business, the basic problem was that the supply of low-wage labour was too small, quite apart from social tensions resulting from its importation into the industrial heartlands. It was insufficient to exert serious deterrent pressure on the generality of self-confident unionised workforces in the metropolises (even in the USA, where capital had the advantage of an internal low-wage pool), particularly when full employment was a central policy of their governments and legal impediments to wage-bargaining were light or non-existent. The arguments of Andrew Glynn and Bob Sutcliffe[14] are now generally accepted – capital was steadily losing out in the eternal battle over the division of the surplus, and recession/depression/slump would sooner or later be the inevitable consequence.

In addition to this basic weakness, subsidiary ones developed over time. The role of the USA in the international economy had expanded enormously in both trade and finance; the dollar was the world's principal reserve currency (though British governments strove to keep sterling as one too – that was a major part of the country's problem). In the 1960s, however, the USA began to run into massive debt, which it was able to sustain only because of its centrality. The principal cause of this was the Vietnam War – it had to be financed by borrowing; the proportionate tax increases that would be required were unthinkable and would have added catastrophically to the headaches that the war's growing unpopularity was already giving to the Johnson and Nixon administrations.

At the same time, the balance established around 1950 was being upset by the re-emergence of Japan and West Germany as major capitalist economic powers, taking off from the rebuilding that the USA had accomplished in these countries during the post-war years. An early sign of this was the destruction in the early 1960s of British motorcycle production due to the import of cheaper and much more efficient Japanese machines, and the challenge in other hi-tech consumer goods was soon to follow, where its impact was felt in Europe and the USA as well. South Korea and Taiwan, politically under US tutelage, were also beginning their economic ascent.

The EEC

The origins of the European Economic Community or Common Market were complex, but essentially driven by the mutual interests of France and West Germany; France wishing to align itself with German economic strength, and Germany with France's international standing – which the latter still possessed despite political weakness and lost colonial wars – thanks to having been a victor power and permanent member of the UN Security Council. The UK, if it had shown any interest at the time, would have been welcome for the same reason. The three Benelux countries of the Netherlands, Belgium and Luxemburg had already by the early 1950s established an economic association and Italy, too, was brought in, not least because the development was viewed as a further impediment to its strong communist party. Accordingly, the Treaty of Rome was signed in 1957.

The central purpose of the Treaty and the new economic framework it established was to rivet the capitalist structure firmly in place in the member states. The free circulation of goods, capital and labour between them was its defining reality, and though public ownership of industrial enterprises was not outlawed any special government favour to these (or indeed any capitalist firms at the expense of EEC competitors) was strictly forbidden.[15] The hope and expectation of economic benefits from the new arrangements was of course also a consideration. For agricultural producers – if not for consumers – these benefits were certainly very real, and that of course had electoral implications.

SECOND-WAVE DECOLONISATION

The military defeat in 1954 of French forces by the communist-led Viet Minh in Indo China did not end the decolonisation struggle in East Asia because the United States intervened to establish a militarily-supported puppet regime in the south of Vietnam and war continued there, as in neighbouring Laos. In the Middle East, formally sovereign regimes had existed since the Second World War and earlier, but under Western diplomatic control. A nationalist attempt (seen as communist-inspired) in oil-rich Iran to attain genuine independence in the early 1950s was frustrated when the Central Intelligence Agency (CIA) re-established the monarchy. In 1958, a comparable monarchy was bloodily overthrown in Iraq and a left-leaning republic established. Government in Syria had moved in a sharply radical direction (again seen as communist inspired) a year earlier. Jordan also made gestures towards independence, though its monarchy survived.

However, in the late 1950s and early 1960s it was Africa that was the focus of decolonisation. The success of Egypt in 1952 of replacing, with a bloodless anti-monarchical revolution, sham independence by the real thing transformed the character both of Middle Eastern and African politics. In 1956, the British government tried to reassert its position with military force in collusion with France and Israel, resulting in humiliation for the Western powers on account of American displeasure at their actions, followed by a corresponding enhancement of Egyptian prestige in spite of its military defeat.

A spate of decolonisation measures soon followed. Independence was transferred without difficulty to the former British West African colonies. Greater difficulty was encountered in East and Central Africa where in some cases aggressively racist settler regimes were locally in control, nevertheless by the middle of the 1960s all were independent and under African government apart from Southern Rhodesia (the present-day Zimbabwe). Care was taken to preserve economic linkages and to leave behind military establishments trained in Britain.

In 1960, de Gaulle conceded paper independence to French tropical-African colonies, all of which, apart from Guinea, remained firmly attached to France. Morocco and Tunisia, where independence had come even earlier, were nationalist but safely pro-Western. Having failed with a final push to subdue the rebels in Algeria, where a particularly savage colonial war had shaken the stability of the Republic and brought de Gaulle to power, he arranged independence there as well, suppressing his own military in order to do so.

The most sinister development at this time occurred in the huge colony of the Belgian Congo straddling the centre of Africa, phenomenally well-supplied in minerals and other primary products and with a no less ethnically and culturally diverse population.[16] Independence in 1960 was proclaimed overnight and hurried through; the Belgian administrators stripped the new state of everything they could remove, down to office typewriters. Remaining Belgian colonists then provoked political and secessionist turmoil and the gruesome murder of the left-leaning Prime Minister, Patrice Lumumba.[17] From the bloody mess which followed over the next few years there emerged, courtesy of the CIA, one of the worst of Africa's kleptocratic tyrants, Mobutu. He had emerged from the colonial-trained military and his example was copied by generals in former British West Africa, provoking in Nigeria, over a secession attempt, a particularly vicious civil war in which the USSR and the UK were united in supporting the federal government (the rival leaders were both military men).

It was a cardinal principle in the independence process that the new states should be formed within the existing colonial boundaries, and there was good reason behind this prescription, for anything else would have resulted in uncontrollable territorial disputes. However, these boundaries often enough defied reason (apart from nineteenth-century diplomatic reason) and moreover they meant that the new Africa was illogically fragmented where it should never have been – or, in the case of the Congo (which Mobutu relabelled Zaire), not fragmented where it would have made more sense to have done so. Add to that the character of many of the regimes which emerged – where governments existed principally in order to suck wealth out of their citizens, usually with the aid of foreign corporations, where corruption and backhanders were an accepted mode of life – and future prospects did not look too promising, justifying all too prophetically the title of a volume published in the 1960s by René Dumont: *Bad Start in Black Africa* (*L'Afrique noire est mal partie*).

DISMANTLING THE DREAM

The West

The pressures building up inside the global economy over the two decades after 1950 would sooner or later have brought the boom to an end, but the explosive charge, as indicated above, was placed by the Vietnam War. By the early 1960s it had become evident that whatever shuffling of the pack and permutations of leadership were carried out in the puppet regime, or however much armament or military advice it received, it could not hope to survive the NLF (National Liberation Front, termed Vietcong in the West) insurgency supported from North Vietnam. By this time, US dignity and prestige were deeply involved in the outcome and no alternative was seen other than the dispatch of huge numbers of American troops. This, maintained over a long period, was ruinously expensive and derailed government finances for nil economic return. In 1970 the Bretton Woods system, the lynchpin of the post-war economic structure, was abandoned – a declaration, in effect, that the USA could no longer sustain the responsibility of holding that framework together.

Meanwhile, the UK was running into increasingly severe economic weather, with currency devaluation and mounting trade union protest at the government's austerity programmes and its unwavering public support for the US war.[18] Competition from Japan and Europe was increasingly felt in global markets and a cultural revolution accompanied with riots and occasional deaths, was in progress throughout the Western world.

Communist states

If less spectacularly, the hopes of the Soviet bloc were also falling away. Trotsky had predicted in the 1930s that, in the absence of a world revolution or at least a political revolution against Stalinism, the regime would be certain to fail because it would never be able to match the productivity of Western capitalism. For a brief space in the late 1950s and early 1960s, that had seemed to be disproved – but in fact his prediction was well grounded. By the end of the 1960s the earlier surge was faltering and consumer indices (except in Hungary) levelling out or rising only very minimally. Poland was plagued with economic crises, generating political ones. Overall growth in the USSR continued but at a much slower rate, technological development was far behind that of the West and the gap was widening, investment went into increasingly obsolescent plants and machinery, and more was spent on maintenance and replacement parts than on new equipment. Khrushchev's extravagant promises were quietly forgotten, discredited along with their author. The economic system, in short, was grossly inefficient and behaved even worse than the West in terms of pollution and plunder of natural resources. It maintained a level of basic welfare provision for its citizens, provided assistance to foreign liberation movements and restrained the adventurism of US governments, but the bright hopes of a decade earlier were comprehensively extinguished.

The citizens of the People's Republic of China were much less fortunate. By the mid 1960s the communist parties of China and the Soviet Union were at bitter odds (see Chapter 9) and all Soviet technical assistance had been withdrawn. Social pressures, especially among a discontented and frustrated younger generation, were building up and tensions were rising within the CPC (Communist Party of China) itself. These were the circumstances which enabled Mao to turn the formal respect and prestige which he was accorded into real power and to restore his place not only as the central political figure in China but to gain elevation to a semi-divine status.

In consequence, the so-called Cultural Revolution was launched in 1966, in which the young were incited by Mao to attack their seniors in the administrative, academic or political hierarchy and accuse them of all manner of political crimes summed up in the phrase 'capitalist roaders'. Most importantly he had the support of the military, without which the enterprise would have been impossible.

The results were devastating; China was thrown into unspeakable turmoil and administration was comprehensively disrupted as gangs of 'Red Guards' roamed the country, molesting and sometimes murdering anyone they targeted for alleged political sins and indicted with preposterous accusations – and occasionally fighting among themselves when they disagreed over interpretations of Maoism. The effect on economic life was disastrous and it was this that finally brought the mayhem to an end, leaving behind a traumatised administrative machine and severe retardation in economic growth.

1973

The Arab-Israeli war of 1967, which was to see Egypt, Syria and Jordan totally defeated by Israel, which at the cease-fire stood on the Suez Canal where it remained for the next six years, was to have the most profound long-term consequences, but it did not immediately impact on the world economy. The Yom Kippur war of 1973, when Egyptian forces crossed the canal aiming to recover the Sinai Peninsula, was very different in this respect: the detonator that set off the economic explosion. It provided the equivalent to 'Black Thursday' in October 1929 on Wall Street. OPEC, dominated by Arab governments, at once pushed up oil prices dramatically and immediately exposed the precariousness of a global economy built on the shaky foundations of the dollar. The sudden rise in the price of a commodity essential to production and countless other purposes, in combination with the overhang of US government debt, tipped the West into a recession from which it never fully recovered.

To be sure, international financial management saw to it that the consequences were not as drastic as those of 1929 and the following three years, but the post-war economic miracle was very definitely at an end.

7
Liberalism on the right

All ideologies present themselves as programmes of emancipation, even the most overtly repressive ones: for these define emancipation as pertaining to the social body and freedom as the mental contentment which results, in their perspective, from willing submission to authority.

Liberalism is exceptional in the emphasis which it places on emancipation as meaning the exemption of individuals from social rules except insofar as these can be justified on pragmatic grounds regarding the preservation of social cohesion – and also of property, which is closely intertwined in liberal thought with the individual personality. Liberal thinking commenced with concern about the security of landed property and proprietors, and gradually extended more broadly. Liberalism's basic conception of the individual is as the proprietor of his/her own person. For this reason it is the most diffuse of ideologies, a circumstance which adds force to the fervent assertions of its spokespersons that it should not be regarded as an ideology in any meaningful sense.

Socially speaking, liberalism, as one might say in a computer-dominated age, represents the default political formation of the capitalist mode of production. Although emergency measures or even dictatorship may be resorted to during its establishment or in times of crisis, the very nature of capitalist functioning favours a constitutional regime based on the rule of law (however skewed and repressive), open circulation of information (however controlled) and elected representation (however restricted). Consequently there are two principal sides to liberalism, or if you prefer, its smiley face and its dismal one. On the one hand it constitutes a socio-cultural theory about property relations, on the other, one about the norms of personal behaviour.

COLD WAR

In the ideological conflict of the Second World War, liberalism emerged as the big winner. Officially, the liberal combatants, the USA and the UK, fought under the banner of democracy – which was ridiculous if one keeps in mind the British Empire or conditions prevailing in Dixie – but it could not be seriously argued that these were not liberal societies and polities. Moreover, during the war both governments and especially the British, to sustain public engagement during the ordeal with its fairly drastic restrictions on democracy, had been obliged to emphasise their democratic credentials, and also in Britain hold out prospects of democratic restoration and significant material improvement once the conflict was over.[1]

For a time, matters looked far from promising for the liberal future. In the immediate aftermath the most apparent outcome was the significant territorial gains by the USSR and its elevation to the rank of superpower. This was shortly followed by the establishment of communist regimes throughout Eastern Europe (Churchill's 'Iron Curtain') which demolished the *cordon sanitaire* of the interwar years and continued with the victory of the communist revolution in China. Appearances were deceptive though. Apart from the social stresses that the nature of these societies involved, their economic foundations were fundamentally unsound and, if the liberal societies could hold their ground for long enough, avoiding economic slump or Third World War, their ultimate victory was certain. Nobody appreciated that at the time.

However, a strategy was adopted, evolving rather than planned. The inspiration came from the USA as did most of the direction, although the Attlee administration's Foreign Office with its puppet Foreign Secretary, Ernest Bevin, made a noticeable contribution. Within US spheres of government, throughout the press and broadcasting media, and consequently widely in American society at large, great hostility towards the USSR – only lightly overlaid by the wartime alliance – was waiting to emerge.

The strategy that unfolded involved a combination of military posture with economic and ideological attack aimed at what rapidly came to be stigmatised as the enemy regimes as well as the supposed internal threat, and accompanied with a drive to win friends and influence governments in the newly decolonised states. The principle was first enunciated in the famous 'Long Telegram' sent by George Kennan from the Moscow embassy in 1945, followed up by the equally famous article in *Foreign Affairs* signed only as 'X', which developed and expanded the arguments in the telegram.[2]

Kennan argued that the USSR was an inherently hostile power, as much because it had inherited the expansionist drive of the pre-revolutionary Russian Empire as on account of its communist ideology. His recipe for dealing with it was 'containment' – the West should adopt an uncompromising though not overtly aggressive posture and deploy its technological, economic, diplomatic and military strength to resist and frustrate any further territorial expansion by the USSR or capture of power by other communist parties, which were assumed to be its surrogates.

Western intentions, according to him, are entirely benign:

> To speak of possibility of intervention against USSR today, after elimination of Germany and Japan and after example of recent war, is sheerest nonsense. If not provoked by forces of intolerance and subversion [the] 'capitalist' world of today is quite capable of living at peace with itself and with Russia.[3]

As for the Soviet leaders,

> In the name of Marxism they sacrificed every single ethical value in their methods and tactics. Today they cannot dispense with it. It is the fig leaf

of their moral and intellectual respectability. Without it they would stand before history, at best, as only the last of that long succession of cruel and wasteful Russian rulers who have relentlessly forced their country on to ever new heights of military power in order to guarantee external security of their internally weak regimes. This is why Soviet purposes must always be solemnly clothed in trappings of Marxism, and why no one should underrate importance of dogma in Soviet affairs ... [but] basically this is only the steady advance of uneasy Russian nationalism, a centuries-old movement in which conceptions of offense and defense are inextricably confused. But in the new guise of international Marxism, with its honeyed promises to a desperate and war torn outside world, it is more dangerous and insidious than ever before .... There is good reason to suspect that this Government is actually a conspiracy within a conspiracy.[4]

The Soviet state is presented as a kind of metaphysical demon able to manipulate at will its perfectly programmed forces and its stooges all throughout the world, 'an apparatus of amazing flexibility and versatility, managed by people whose experience and skill in underground methods are presumably without parallel in history'.

Kennan's prescription in the telegram was essentially for coordinated diplomatic and propagandist activity. In the article, although 'the maximum development of the propaganda and political warfare techniques' was still emphasised, an even more aggressive posture was recommended:

the main element of any United States policy toward the Soviet Union must be a long-term, patient but firm and vigilant containment of Russian expansive tendencies ... Soviet pressure against the free institutions of the Western world is something that can be contained by the adroit and vigilant application of counterforce at a series of constantly shifting geographical and political points, corresponding to the shifts and maneuvers of Soviet policy, but which cannot be charmed or talked out of existence.[5]

Out of that came a recommendation, which was followed by the US administration, to make friends with and secure military bases from the Franco regime – Kennan had previously advocated invading Italy to pre-empt a communist electoral victory.

Later he was to modify his stance, and in his memoirs wrote that, 'I began to ask myself whether... we had not contributed... by the overmilitarization of our policies and statements... to a belief in Moscow that it was war we were after, that we had settled for its inevitability, that it was only a matter of time before we would unleash it'.

Ruptured relations

Relations between the former allies continued to deteriorate. Despite the helpful attitude (decreed by Stalin) of the French and Italian communist parties within their capitalist nations, and Stalin's in relation to British intervention in Greece, it was clear that neither foreign nor domestic communists were to be trusted. The former were denied any participation in the settlement of Italy and Japan, the latter confined to lowly positions in the Popular Front governments of the period. Conversely, it was made clear that the communist parties were determined to dominate (though not yet to monopolise) the Popular Front governments in the Soviet sphere and enforce a tight grip upon their security portfolios.

Truman's renowned speech of March 1947, which historians regard as the effective declaration of the Cold War, essentially followed Kennan's prescription. It was provoked by contingent circumstances with which the Soviet Union had nothing to do – the great blizzard at the beginning of the year and consequent decision by the British government that it could no longer sustain the fight against the Greek communist insurgents (from whom Stalin had distanced himself). Truman, who at the urging of his Secretary of State, General Marshall, had made the Senate's blood curdle by rehearsing the threat posed to the USA itself by communist expansionism, declared that the USA would take over the British responsibility.

He further declared that the USA would provide assistance to any government resisting communist encroachment – whether direct or indirect – in other words, whether the threat came from the USSR itself or local communists. The terminology subsequently used in reference to this speech is, in terms of ideology, highly interesting. It was called the 'Truman Doctrine'. In medieval Europe at the time of the Holy Roman Empire someone once asked who had made the Germans the judges of the world. The American leaders now evidently regarded themselves as divinely authorised to take on that role.

That of course was not the way in which things were seen by liberal ideologues. Their perception is nicely summarised by one of their leading publicists, Daniel Bell:

> And how can we discuss this question [war and peace] ... without discussing the cold war *and the extent to which our policy is shaped by the Russians!* [original emphasis] United States policy since 1946 ... was not a reflex of any *internal* [original emphasis] social divisions or class issues but was *based on an estimate of Russia's intentions* ... [original emphasis]. It was a judgment that Stalinism as an ideological phenomenon and Russia as a geopolitical power were aggressively, militarily and ideologically expansionist and that a policy of containment, including a rapid military build up was necessary ... this underlay Truman's Greco-Turkish policy ... These policies were estimates of national interest and of national survival.[6]

If you could believe that, you had to be a very believing sort of person.

In 1949, the Chinese Revolution was interpreted in the West as an essentially Soviet enterprise using Chinese surrogates as its agents, although in fact nothing could have been further from the truth. Stalin had done his best to persuade Mao to continue the pre-war common front and co-operate with Chiang. In the same year, the USSR astounded and dismayed the West by testing an atomic device years ahead of what was expected, so instituting the concept of a reciprocal balance of terror between the superpowers.

The Western, primarily the American, response was far-reaching. The USA refused to recognise the new regime in Beijing (although the UK did) but provided diplomatic support and military protection to the remnants of Chiang's, now skulking in Taiwan (then called Formosa) and persecuting its indigenous inhabitants. It continued to recognise it as the real China and ensure it retained the Chinese seat at the United Nations. 1949 then saw the establishment of the North Atlantic Treaty Organization, a military alliance of states stretching from the USA and Canada to Greece and Turkey.[7]

It was, of course, aimed against the Soviet bloc, but naturally pretended otherwise, being ostensibly intended for the protection of democracy but exposing its real purpose by including the profoundly undemocratic states of Portugal, Greece and Turkey (Franco's Spain was left out because according it that level of respectability would have been seen as a bit too provocative; bilateral relations with the USA had been established instead).

COLD WAR LIBERALISM

The politics of the early 1950s were overshadowed by the demagogue Joe McCarthy, no liberal on any definition. Even in terms of American red-baiting, McCarthy was an extremist. He had his uses to the political establishment as the McCarthyite assault effectively destroyed the American left – in the administration, academia, the media, the civil rights organisations and the unions, as well as in the CPUSA itself. However, the theoreticians and the organisers of the Cold War strategy, disdaining McCarthy's crudities, followed in general a much subtler approach.

Many of them indeed had their political origins on the left: centrally important ideologists in this area were pre-war US Trotskyists, for apart from Ceylon, Trotskyism had had more impact in the USA than anywhere else in the world. Beginning as communists, disillusionment with Stalinism had caused them to align with Trotsky. Following the War, when Trotskyism was evidently going nowhere, they had concluded that US society, which they were pleased to define as 'democracy', was not so bad after all, or else that the Soviet Union was also capitalist beneath the skin and, being dictatorial as well, the USA represented the lesser evil. To the fore in this project were the group around the journal *Partisan Review* – although others continued to regard themselves as Marxists of a sort, like the editors of the journal *Dissent*.

These transformed themselves into the core theorists and propagandists of Cold War liberalism. A central weapon in their armoury was the concept of totalitarianism. The word had been coined by Mussolini (or his publicist Giovanni Gentile), who used it in a self-congratulatory sense, but it was later picked up by Trotsky, who, in *The Revolution Betrayed*, applied it to Stalin's regime. His ex-disciples now disseminated it in a most effective fashion to bring Nazi and communist societies into the same conceptual category. They were speedily copied by liberal and conservative media of every sort, which fitted in well with the new agenda of the US administration in demonising the ex-ally and emphasising its similarities with the ex-enemy. In the West the USSR had never, except between 1941 and 1945, been regarded as a fully legitimate state like any other, but this had little to do with its abominable record on human rights, for many states with equally terrible or even worse regimes were happily accepted – as was China in the 1970s on realpolitik grounds. It was, rather, its world-revolutionary pretensions and claims on the loyalty of people who were not its own citizens that made it odious to mainstream liberalism.

A clutch of widely disseminated texts published in the late 1940s and early 1950s epitomised the militant liberal anti-communist crusade that was being set in motion. One was a collection of pieces by eminent repentant communists under the title *The God that Failed*, published in 1949 and edited by the British left-wing MP Richard Crossman, after a conversation with the ex-communist Hungarian émigré Arthur Koestler. It went through five impressions in a year. The six authors included Koestler, serial rapist and mystagogue, later McCarthy's pal, and Ignazio Silone, later revealed to have been a snitch for Mussolini's secret services. Koestler was also the author of another of the texts in this group, *Darkness at Noon*, a novel set in the Moscow show trials of the 1930s and which had an enormous impact – though it was the interrogator, Gletkin, rather than the accused Rubashov (a fictional rendering of Bukharin), who had all the best lines.[8] Other volumes of a similar tenor included the *Animal Farm* and *Nineteen Eighty-four* of George Orwell, also a snitch for his secret service, and in the early 1950s Albert Camus's *L'homme révolté* (translated as *The Rebel*).

Alongside the writers and theoreticians must be placed the engineers of consent, the practitioners and publicists engaged in the worldwide propaganda offensive to make liberal ideology prevail throughout what was termed the 'free world' (although the contradictions of this designation were often enough pointed out). Some of that was openly state-sponsored, such as the radio stations Voice of America and Radio Free Europe, but much more of it was covert, and in this the CIA, with which Kennan was closely connected, was of pivotal importance. Besides carrying out various assassinations, coups, and generally assisting torturers and mass murderers around the globe, it covertly financed many projects, including the animated film version of *Animal Farm*.

The CIA developed out of the Second World War spy institution the Office of Strategic Studies, and originally had, if anything, a left-leaning orientation; therefore, it was eminently fit for purpose – 'the most effective place for a non-communist liberal to do battle against the communist menace'[9] – and likely to be the more convincing in broadcasting the virtues of liberalism US-style. In the post-war years, apart from secretly signing up prominent Western politicians, including Hugh Gaitskell, the Labour Party leader, recruiting escaped Nazi war criminals into the anti-communist crusade and overseeing the Western spy agencies, what is most likely to count as its most successful and effective operation was the secret promotion and funding of the

Congress for Cultural Freedom – the funds involved being supplied ultimately by the unsuspecting American taxpayer.

Congress for Cultural Freedom

The Congress for Cultural Freedom (CCF) which had no democratic structures sponsored and financed a string of intellectual journals in several European languages dedicated to promoting the American view of world affairs, although they also discussed other matters. Their flagship English version, *Encounter* – referred to as 'our greatest asset' by chief organiser Michael Josselson – on one notorious occasion included a piece on prostitution, while in another issue it published Nancy Mitford's semi-satirical discussion of English upper-class speech codes. No criticism of the USA, including reference to racial oppression, nor anything favourable to the communist bloc, was permitted to appear in its pages. Big-name writers, including W. H. Auden and left-leaning liberals such as Bertrand Russell, mostly ignorant (as was the general public) of the nature of these journals or that of the CCF, were enticed to contribute, and a formidable intellectual network was created, though little impact could be made on the solidly leftist character of French intellectual culture at that time. There, Sartre was regarded as the most dangerous of enemies, much worse than any overt communist, 'Challenging the intellectual basis for neutralism was one of the principal objectives of American Cold War policy, and it was now assumed as an official "line" of the Congress.'[10] According to Mary McCarthy, 'the Committee ... is principally interested in [fighting] neutralism, which is taking first place as a Menace'.[11] A bitter animus was also directed against Kingsley Martin, the editor of the *New Statesman*, in those days an influential journal of opinion, for his unresponsiveness to Congress blandishments.

The intellectual stars who were at the centre of the project and in on its foundation certainly knew what it was about and who was behind it. They included Sidney Hook, Malcolm Muggeridge, James Burnham, Isaiah Berlin, Raymond Aron, André Malraux, Arthur Koestler, Arthur Schlesinger, Lionel Trilling and his wife Diana, Reinhold Niebuhr, and Philip Rahv (the editor of *Partisan Review*). 'These men were all witting', in Saunders's words.[12] So was the English co-editor of *Encounter*, Stephen Spender, though he later unconvincingly denied it. Spender himself was more of an ornament than a real editor, 'easily conned', and according to Christopher Isherwood, 'an essentially comic character'.[13] The effective editor was its American one, Irving Kristol, later to become an ornament of neoconservatism, whose attitudes were reflected in his statement that 'The elite was us – the "happy few" who had been chosen by History to guide our fellow-creatures towards a secular redemption.'[14]

Populism and God

Of much less intellectual prestige, but with far greater popular reach, was another publication directed from the USA, the monthly *Reader's Digest*. This operated throughout the entire non-communist world, was readable, slickly produced and marketed, and invariably touted American values. Never an issue appeared without at least one item, and frequently more, denouncing the communist bloc and its misdeeds. It is hard to imagine that its impact was not considerable in forming public attitudes around the world.

The *Reader's Digest* was liberal, on the whole, in its anti-communism, avoiding the themes of the more recondite American Republicans like George Dondero, who proclaimed that

All modern art is Communistic ... Cubism aims to destroy by designed disorder. Futurism aims to destroy by the machine myth ... Dadaism aims to destroy by ridicule. Expressionism aims to destroy by aping the primitive and the insane. Abstractionism aims to destroy by the creation of brainstorms ... Surrealism aims to destroy by the denial of reason.[15]

What is notable is not so much the pronouncement but the fact that instead of being universally derided, it was acclaimed by Dondero's Congress allies and the right-wing press. Some even alleged that abstract paintings were really secret maps revealing US military installations. That sort of thing was of course despised by the cultural Cold Warriors of the CCF, whose tastes were very much into modernism.

With less extensive ideological reach than the *Reader's Digest*, but a substantial one nevertheless, was the *Time-Life* publishing empire of Henry Luce, a religious obsessive who declared that 'no nation in history except ancient Israel, was so obviously designed for some special phase of God's purpose'. His publications frequently carried the thoughts of Reinhold Niebuhr, a patron of the CCF praised by Sidney Hook, who applauded his revival of the doctrine of original sin for its political uses and for 'making God an instrument of national policy'.[16]

God, of course, was very much to the fore in American culture, and never more so than in the Cold War 1950s – Kristol himself had become a convert to his ancestral Judaism, declaring that 'The Law was true because it was divine – it was God's Law, a revelation of man's place in the fundamental constitution of existence'[17] – but the deployment of God in the English-speaking world for evangelical Christian purposes mixed with Cold War ideology was developed to a fine art by Billy Graham, who warned that 'Communism is ... master-minded by Satan.' Hollywood, now safely purged of reds, pinks and non-cold-war liberals, was also recruited in the mid 1950s into the worldwide ideological crusade through secret discussions between the military, the CIA and leading Hollywood figures, including John Wayne, to make films subtly and not-so-subtly propagating the American viewpoint in what Frances Stonor Saunders describes as 'a doctrinal campaign'.

Even International PEN (Poets, Essayists and Novelists), an organisation intended to represent the world's writers, was not overlooked, 'But the truth is that the CIA made every effort to turn PEN into a vehicle for American government interests.'[18] According to Andrew Kopkind, 'the CIA supported socialist cold warriors, fascist cold warriors, black and white cold warriors.

The catholicity and flexibility of the CIA operations were major advantages. But it was a sham pluralism and it was utterly corrupting.'[19]

Another ideologist of some influence was the rather loopy Ayn Rand who made even the frantically anti-socialist Ludwig von Mises, Friedrich von Hayek's mentor, look left-wing by comparison. She was the author of indigestibly huge and indescribably badly written 'novels' which were simply tracts in a rickety fictional framework, one being described by a critic as a 'masochist lollipop'. Nonetheless, her sales by the end of the 1980s topped 20 million and she even established a 'philosophical' cult of her own termed 'objectivism'.

BELL AND CROSLAND

With the virtual erasure of the left in the United States during the 1950s,[20] thanks to the McCarthyite purge and reaction from the Soviet admission in 1956 of Stalin's criminality, followed by Soviet suppression of the Hungarian revolution, a phase of unusual political and social conformity together with ideological consensus laid the ground for the impact of Daniel Bell's *End of Ideology*.

Bell's British counterpart was Anthony Crosland, although from 1960 Crosland was a member of the CCF International Council and on the face of things his book's title, *The Future of Socialism* (1956), as well as his argument, could not have been more different. Nevertheless, it provided a striking example and illustration of how thoroughly social democracy had been absorbed into the dominant Western liberal ideology. It was later to be described as 'a blueprint for an Americanized Britain'. Because it chronologically preceded Bell's volume, I will deal with it first.

The Labour Party had lost office in 1951 (though it had the higher popular vote) and its defeat was followed by a bitter internal row between its right wing, led (at least formally) by the former premier, Clement Attlee, and the Labour Party left, symbolised by the charismatic Aneurin Bevan. The right had triumphed, because it was solidly backed by the right-wing leaders of the bigger trade unions, although the Bevanites continued to agitate, and the party entered the era of 'Butskellism'. This term derived from the names of the Conservative Chancellor of the Exchequer and Attlee's successor as Labour Party leader, and referred to the lack of fundamental difference in the policies of the two dominant parties – essentially one of welfare Keynesianism in both cases. Crosland was a member of Gaitskell's shadow cabinet.

During its history, the Labour Party's specific marker had been its commitment to a significant degree of public ownership or, as it was known at the time, nationalisation (though it was never suggested by the dominant bloc within the Party that the entire economy should be publicly owned). The advantage of this was seen as twofold – it would mean a fairer deal for both workers and consumers when private capitalists ceased to dispose of essential sectors of the economy, and it would mean a sufficient measure of public control to regulate the economy as a whole and prevent it from sliding into slump.

Crosland's volume disputed these premises, contending that the nature of ownership scarcely mattered, since Keynesian forms of financial and demand management would in future suffice to keep the economy on an even keel and – because these were also used in the USA – there was no danger of the international economic system running onto the rocks. Moreover capitalists had become socially conscious and responsible and if they were tempted to act otherwise the countervailing powers of government and trade unions were available to keep them in line. 'The traditional capitalist ruthlessness has largely disappeared'[21] and 'Capitalism has been reformed almost out of recognition.'[22] In short, the Attlee government during its years of office had carried through a quiet revolution and similar processes had occurred across the Atlantic – it was now doubtful whether capitalism should any longer be known by that name. Socialists should hereafter concentrate on redressing the remaining cultural inequalities and barriers to opportunity that had been overlooked in the Attlee revolution and learn to love the USA:

> [A]nti-Americanism ... is an almost universal left-wing neurosis springing from a natural resentment at the transfer of world power from London to Washington ... anti-Americanism and anxiety over nuclear weapons are no more the real explanation of militant Leftism than anti-Communism is of American McCarthyism; in both cases these are simply rationalisations of some deep discontent.[23]

For Crosland, left-wing attitudes seem to spring out of personal hang-ups connected to social envy, and it was ever thus. Support in the 1930s for the Popular Front and the Left Book Club is described as 'guilt neurosis'.

It scarcely needs the benefit of historical hindsight to perceive the short-sightedness and complacency expressed in this text, but Crosland was a charming individual as well as writing elegant prose and even demonstrated his wide culture by a gesture of respect to Marx, 'a dedicated genius'. *The Future of Socialism* became the bible of the Labour Party 'revisionists' and its theses were incorporated into the policy document, *Industry and Society*, which was drawn up after further electoral defeat in 1959.

The End of Ideology

Unlike *The Future of Socialism*, *The End of Ideology*, published in 1960 but added to and subtracted from in subsequent editions, was not a political tract but rather an academic study; however, it started from the same basic ideological assumptions. The volume was dedicated to Sidney Hook, ex-communist, ex-Trotskyist, in the process of becoming a right-wing liberal ideologue and FBI informer, and at the time a central motivator of the Congress for Cultural Freedom, with which Bell was also closely connected. At a meeting of the American committee in 1952, Bell refused to support a general condemnation of McCarthyism,[24] although he claimed that his 'own masters' in the study of elites were Dewy and Marx.[25] The text reflects oceanic complacency and a large degree of intellectual snobbery and even racial condescension, 'The Negroes who rebuffed the communists obtained a new dignity.'[26]

Its title (Bell notes that Camus was the first to use the phrase) indicates clearly enough what thesis it was propounding. Ideology in this argument – as he acknowledges in his 1961 introduction – did not include the taken-for-granted common sense of 1950s Western liberalism. It was understood to mean the self-conscious political ideologies – communism, socialism, fascism, and unreconstructed right-wing conservatism – that had dominated the earlier decades of the century.

According to Bell their time was now past, and the conditions that had given rise to the sentiments responsible for ideological expression no longer existed. He displays respect for some of the zealots who had embraced ideological outlooks, provided they had done so with humanity and goodwill, but most had seen the error of their ways and were now reconciled to the realities of welfare capitalism, as was the emerging generation. Those who remained committed to their illusions or continued to be seduced by ideology – right as well as left – were insignificant in number and too marginal to matter.

All the same, 'As a conspiracy rather than a legitimate dissenting group, the Communist movement remains a threat to democratic society',[27] the individual communist 'a hidden soldier in the war against society'.[28] He refers to 'pliable tools of the communist manipulators behind the scenes … upper class matrons and aspiring actresses found in the communist "causes" a cozy non-conformism to replace their passé conventions'.[29] The radical and Marxist-sympathising American academic C. Wright Mills is vehemently attacked for his supposed idea of 'moral equivalence between the blocs' and for developing the notion of a 'power elite' – though on the available evidence, Bell and his circle were not only perfectly aware that such a thing existed but also gloried in belonging to it.

As for McCarthyism, that, too, was a matter of 'status politics'; so were the 'social strains of the last ten years'. That led on to the question of the communist bloc, still very much in existence, apparently thriving, and flaunting its ideological pretensions. Bell, however, very nimbly incorporated that apparent economic success into the fabric of his argument. According to him, as consumer goods multiplied in these states, political and social structures would inevitably relax, culture in the bloc would open up and communist ideology there find its way, in the long run, into the same graveyard as ideology in the West. This was termed 'convergence'. Bell's approach to capitalism reflected Crosland's, 'modified by union power and checked by government control' for 'except as an ideology, no one really wanted "economic liberalism"'.[30] '[F]ew serious conservatives at least in England and on the Continent, believe that the Welfare State is the road to serfdom.'[31] A welcome by-product of convergence would be the relaxation of international tensions and removal of the constant peril of nuclear confrontation and planet-wrecking war.

As time was to demonstrate, the 'end of ideology' was to prove no more than a brief episode in the 'age of extremes', a fantasy and illusion; and if the future of socialism was to be regarded as being anything like that envisaged by Crosland, it was only in the sense in which his opponents stigmatised his conception – that is, not socialism on any account and, as things turned out, not even welfare capitalism. In 1965, Bell along with Irving Kristol founded a journal entitled *The Public Interest* – in Bell's words, 'a journal that sought to transcend ideology through reasoned public debate and disinterested enquiry into public policy' – which was about the very last thing that Kristol was interested in. Kristol soon was to become a leader of the rising neoconservative faction and, in the 1970s, Bell resigned from this journal – but continued to write for it.

Bell and Crosland were certainly theorists, but in a manner that was essentially commentary on their times. Theoretical support at a more general level for liberal ideology was provided by academics of varied dispositions who embraced a variety of viewpoints within that overall framework, ranging from laissez-faire doctrinaires to sympathisers with social democracy.

MISES AND HAYEK

Mises

Of these two, Friedrich von Hayek is much the better known, but Ludwig von Mises was Hayek's guide and mentor. Both in their youth were citizens of the Austro–Hungarian Empire and members of its upper classes, as the *particule* in their names suggests, but from the professional rather than the landowning element. Unusually for someone with that background, Mises was also of Jewish extraction, which did not prevent him from acting as an adviser to the conservative clerical regime of the Austrian priest Ignatz Seipel in the 1920s, or even its Maurrasian successor regime of Engelbert Dollfuss, (sometimes described as clerico-fascist). Surviving the Second World War first in Switzerland and then from 1940 in New York, he was later a close friend of the pretender to the Austrian throne, Otto of Habsburg, and in 1947 a founder-member of the Mont Pèlerin Society, a club, inspired by Hayek, of right-wing liberal movers and shakers (later on a large contingent of Reagan's economic advisers belonged to it).

Mises was one of the most forthright of reactionary liberals, and geniality was not a word in his vocabulary; indeed, it takes a considerable stretch of imagination to see him as a liberal at all, but in the economic sphere that is what he was. His statement of positive belief is a volume entitled *Liberalism*. Indeed, he remains a prime example of the distinction between economic and social liberalism and how they may be altogether divorced. According to Milton Friedman, at the initial meeting of the society, when there was some hint of approval at the notion of progressive income tax, Mises shouted at his colleagues 'You're all a bunch of socialists!' Indeed, Mises wrote on socialism, the full title being *Socialism: An Economic and Social Analysis*. The first German version was published as early as 1932, an English translation appeared in 1936, and an updated edition in 1951.

The rhetoric of this text would be almost amusing if it were not also sinister and Mises a significant influence on the right-wing liberalism which eschewed any notion of social welfare: 'Collectivism is ... the weapon of those who wish to kill mind and thought'.[32] On the other hand, 'predilection for peace ... is the social theory of Liberalism .... That Liberalism aims at the protection of property and that it rejects war are two expressions of one and the same principle'.[33] Any idea that capitalism could be responsible for war is a notion used to deceive the 'unthinking masses'.

Mises is very embittered about the state of the world after the war.

> All present-day political parties are saturated with the leading socialistic ideal ... the socialist idea is nothing but a grandiose rationalization of petty resentments ... destruction is the essence of it ... Marx ... has decked out the resentment of the common man with the nimbus of science.[34]

Even Tolstoy is not spared, being indicted for his anarchistic ('destructionist' in Mises' terms) notions based on biblical models. Labour legislation is a bad thing and he praises the nineteenth-century economist Nassau Senior, who argued that restricting children's working hours would ruin the English cotton industry.[35] Compulsory social insurance is equally bad, and trade unions are the devil's spawn.

'If they did not act as trade unionists, but reduced their demands and changed their locations and occupations according to the requirements of the labour market, they could eventually find work ... unemployment is a problem of wages not of work.'[36] Needless to say, the mass employment of the 1930s is attributed to over-generous wage rates.

The rigours of nineteenth-century English Poor Law are characterised as 'the slight stigma attaching to all who were thus maintained by the community'.

> [A]ccident and health insurance ... promote accidents and illness, hinder recovery and ... intensify and lengthen the functional disorders which follow illness or accident .... No-one any longer denies that traumatic neurosis is a result of social legislation .... Insurance against diseases breeds disease .... Being ill is not a phenomenon independent of conscious will.[37]

Eventually, in his Epilogue, his discourse descends from the preposterous to the clinical. Communications systems are maintained as public utilities only because politicians need them to control public opinion. 'The characteristic mark of this age of dictators, wars and revolutions is its anti-capitalist bias.' 'Every advocate of the welfare state and planning is a potential dictator.' The Nazis 'established a full socialist system', 'What generated dictatorship in Russia and Germany was precisely the fact that the mentality of these nations made suppression of union violence unfeasible under democratic conditions.' '[T]he American New Deal Government embarked upon a thorough-going monopolistic organisation of every branch of American business ....' 'And the Russians yearned for a dictator, for a successor of the terrible Ivan.'

'The German "socialists of the chair" much admired in all foreign countries were the pacemakers of the two World Wars.' 'The intellectuals alone are responsible for the mass slaughters which are the characteristic of our century.'

Mises cannot even bear to acknowledge the Soviet military achievements, and so fantasises,

> Russia was saved by the British ... and American forces. American lend-lease enabled the Russians to follow on the heels of the Germans when scarcity of equipment and the threatened American invasion forced them to withdraw from Russia. They could even occasionally defeat the rearguards of the retreating Nazis.[38]

Hayek

Friedrich von Hayek, though far from emollient, was a somewhat more urbane individual than his mentor and, though never disagreeing with him, occasionally hinted that his tone might be a bit excessive. He expressed disagreement with anti-gay legislation, which in the context of the 1950s in the USA was surprisingly humane, unlike his other prescriptions.

Hayek, who left Austria to take up an appointment at the London School of Economics in 1931 and was Keynes's most persistent critic, is best known for his diatribe in 1944 against the incipient British welfare state, *The Road to Serfdom*. His ideas, however, are expounded at length and most fully in the volume published in 1960 (it incorporated parts of *The Road to Serfdom*), *The Constitution of Liberty*, where he deals with the interpenetration of economics, law, society and politics. Revealingly for such a supposedly comprehensive work, there are no index entries for empire, imperialism or colonialism, and that for 'War' simply says 'see Revolution'.

By the time he wrote this volume, Hayek had, for interesting reasons, become uncomfortable with the word 'liberal' and, in the closing section entitled 'Why I am not a Conservative',[39] explains his reasons, complaining that those who 'cherish freedom' find themselves aligned with change resisters. He is dismayed that American radicals and socialists call themselves 'liberals' and quotes Bernard Crick to the effect that, 'the normal American who calls himself "A Conservative" is in fact a liberal'.[40] 'Whiggism', he writes, 'is historically the correct name for the ideas in which I believe.'[41]

A reader gets the impression that it is with some reluctance that Hayek distances himself from conservatism. He grumbles that conservatism lacks a general theory of society, cannot offer effective resistance to socialism – even shares too many of its conceptions, and that its 'nationalistic bias' 'frequently provides the bridge from conservatism to collectivism'.[42] The British Conservatives in the Churchill Coalition government are attacked for betraying liberalism.

What may be regarded as Hayek's statement of faith is here summarised:

> It is indeed part of the liberal attitude to assume that, especially in the economic field, the self-regulating forces of the market will *somehow*

[emphasis added; one is reminded of Keynes's rejoinder that in the long run we are all dead] bring about the required adjustment to new conditions although no one can foretell how they will do so in a particular instance.[43]

The text of *The Constitution of Liberty* overall is a more temperate, extended and mildly modified rehearsal of the same arguments that Mises advanced. Hayek acknowledges that 'there is undoubtedly a wide field for non-coercive [by coercion he means coercion against capital, not labour] activities of government and that there is a clear need for financing them by taxation',[44] and 'Nobody will deny that economic stability and the prevention of major depressions depends in part on government action.'[45]

Nevertheless, 'It is true that to be free may mean freedom to starve ... the negative of freedom in no way diminishes its value.'[46] He quotes Anatole France's comment that the rich and the poor are equally forbidden to sleep under bridges, and expostulates that 'This famous phrase has been repeated countless times by well-meaning but unthinking people who did not understand that they were undermining the foundations of all impartial justice.'[47] The demand for equality is dismissed as envy, and 'in a free system it is neither desirable not practicable that material rewards should be made generally to correspond to ... merit ....'[48] 'Social justice', he avers, is the concept he most hates, quoting with approval Alfred Marshall that 'I regard all this poverty as a mere passing evil in the progress of man upwards.'[49]

Moreover, 'the whole basis of our free society is gravely threatened by the powers arrogated by the unions',[50] which cannot bring about real wage increases but whose activities nonetheless are 'very harmful' and 'politically extremely dangerous'. Though it would contradict liberal principles to outlaw them (in a free society we must put up with certain evils), they should be rendered ineffective – 'the regular cause of extensive unemployment is real wages that are too high'.[51]

Hayek's approval of democracy (it is probably the best method of achieving certain ends) is grudging, to put it at its mildest, and more reluctant even than Churchill's view that it is the worst possible system of government apart from all the others, for 'it is conceivable that an authoritarian government may act on liberal principles' – which is certainly true, and, 'There can be no doubt that in history unfree majorities have benefited from the existence of free minorities ...'[52] (though no examples are given). His encomium to the US constitution in his eighth chapter naturally excludes any mention of slavery or genocide. Hayek was later to propose a political system in which a senate-type body with a restricted franchise and semi-permanent members would ensure that there could be no tampering with the principles of free market capitalism, while within that framework other sorts of issues could be delegated to a democratic assembly – something not too unlike the present-day European Union.

Hayek was swift to denounce his opponents as utopians, but few visions could be more utopian than his own Panglossian one of a society of limitless technical progress running smoothly on perfect market principles of perfect competition, exempt from wars and civil disturbance, and with workforces always prepared to willingly accept wage reductions whenever the labour market so demanded. It presumed a social order which has never existed, never will exist and could not possibly exist. In the real world, if one had to choose between totalitarianism and a society organised on Hayek's principles, it is far from certain that a majority would be found for the latter – a point with which Hayek would probably not have disagreed, but would have regarded as the triumph of atavism over civilisation.

For him, totalitarianism is the inevitable outcome of any form of government intervention in social affairs beyond the strict limits he lays down in this text and developed later in his writings on law. The Anglo–American tradition of common law, evolving 'spontaneously' and made by judges rather than legislatures, together with the market, are treated as fetishes and regarded in a quasi-mystical fashion. In Hayek's universe, Adam Smith's 'hidden hand' – which translates selfish individual decisions into common good within a competitive society – plays a somewhat equivalent role to that of divine grace in Christine doctrine. Jim Tomlinson, in *Hayek and the Market*,[53] demonstrates that there is a basic incoherence at the root of Hayek's argument. It insists upon invalid 'either/or' concepts (for example, uncontrolled market or totalitarianism; atavism or civilisation), but it ceases to be incoherent when translated from its abstractions into language according to Lenin's aphorism, 'who, whom?', and becomes an apologia on behalf of the wealthy and powerful and a prescription for ensuring that the masses continue to serve them. The market will do that job admirably, nobody can be blamed and social justice will be a meaningless concept.

Although most of Hayek's argument and Pollyanna vision might well consist of, to use his own words, 'a piece of far-fetched and cynical apologetics'; nonetheless, he had an acute and enormously important insight. The market, though not possessing the mystical infallibility with which Mises, Hayek and their disciples invest it, is indeed a most powerful engine driving the economies of the societies in which it operates, and behaves in the short term as a very effective mechanism in bringing inputs and outputs together. (Marx, of course, was not unaware of these properties, but regarded them as historically superseded.) Markets frequently break down, however, often with calamitous consequences, but Hayek did not admit such a possibility; for him it was all the fault of interventionist governments.

Hayek was nevertheless able to demonstrate that a command economy on the Soviet model was incompatible with an advanced consumer society. (Significantly, he never discusses the conditions in which command economies are both effective and essential to survival, the emergency conditions of total war.)

OTHER IDEOLOGUES

Isaiah Berlin

The following ideologues of Cold War liberalism, coming from very different directions, approached their undertaking from the philosophic rather than the economic standpoint. Isaiah Berlin was certainly a very influential thinker, and – as E. H. Carr remarked – 'Even when he talks nonsense he earns our indulgence by talking it in an engaging and attractive way.'[54] His background was Russian, his father being a substantial businessman in the Tsarist era. Following the Revolution the family fled to Latvia, which had become independent, but from there, being subject to antisemitic molestation, moved on to England, Berlin in due course becoming an ornament of academia and the British Establishment A sound anti-communist liberal, he favoured the New Deal and, if less enthusiastically, the welfare state. In the course of the Second World War he worked for a time at the British embassy in Washington; following that he became a leading light of the Congress for Cultural Freedom.

Berlin is most renowned for two short texts, *Historical Inevitability* (which advanced what E. H. Carr was to dismiss as 'the Bad King John' theory of history) and, more importantly, *Two Concepts of Liberty*. This propounded the contrasting notions of 'negative liberty' – freedom *from*, and 'positive liberty' – freedom *to*, a distinction difficult to disentangle, nevertheless eagerly seized upon, for positive liberty was alleged to be the animating principle of revolutionary movements and liable to stray into totalitarian pathways, and negative liberty by contrast was implied to represent the spirit of capitalist democracy – property is barely referred to in this text. 'The point of the exercise', Perry Anderson comments, 'is to discredit a prefabricated notion of "positive freedom" – responsible for modern dictatorship'.[55]

Of course the matter was not presented as crudely as this summary implies, it was hedged around with qualifications, but that is how it was interpreted and disseminated by commentators. Marx was held to be ultimately guilty, though elsewhere Berlin noted (with reference to Burke and Hegel) 'One should never blame people for what their views may one day be thought to lead to.'[56]

Karl Popper

Popper, whose political outlook generally parallels that of Berlin, was a much more considerable thinker if a less urbane one. His insight into scientific method is acute and pertinent – that to be valid, any claim must be advanced in such a manner that in principle it is open to refutation; a self-confirming theory (such as the Freudian) and one for which scepticism about its claims counts as evidence of its truth, is illegitimate.[57]

Popper was born in Vienna in 1902, of Jewish extraction, but his parents had converted to Lutheranism. His father, a barrister, though a 'radical liberal' and a freemason, had received the Habsburg equivalent of a knighthood in view of his social welfare work; Karl was horrified by the abject poverty he encountered, and claims that he was a communist for a few months in 1919. He reneged, according to his own account, because certain unarmed communist and socialist workers were shot by the police when trying to release some communists from the police station. For this he blamed the *workers* involved, and regarded himself as responsible by association.[58]

It is an extraordinary admission, but his comments when he comes to discuss the Austrian situation in the 1920s and 1930s are truly staggering.

Jews, he affirms, were wrong to take advantage of the legal equality they secured after 1919, they

> understandably but not wisely entered politics or journalism .... It seemed quite obvious that with much latent popular anti-Semitism about the best service which a good socialist who happened to be of Jewish origin could render to his party was not to try to play a role in it. Strangely enough, few seemed to think of this obvious rule.[59]

He then goes on to assert that the 'threat of violence' gave the police reasonable excuse in 1927 to massacre social democratic workers and bystanders – their Marxist heritage was the problem – and Dollfuss's bloodbath of social democrats in 1934 is described as the 'final suicide' of their party.

At any rate he was content to live under the Maurrasian Dollfuss/ Schuschnigg regime until 1937, when the rising power of Austrian Nazism led him wisely to emigrate, first to New Zealand, then from 1946 to Britain, where he became a friend of Hayek (though approving in rather tepid fashion the British welfare state). His two key works are *The Poverty of Historicism* (the title is an allusion to Marx's *The Poverty of Philosophy*) and *The Open Society and its Enemies*, the latter published through Hayek's good offices (Popper subsequently dedicated one of his books to Hayek).

'Historicism' is a word of vague and imprecise meaning; generally it was understood in the manner first used by Ranke in the nineteenth century, recommending historians to treat historical eras objectively and not judge them in terms of the historian's own values. In *The Poverty of Historicism*, Popper more or less transformed that meaning, defining 'historicism' as a claim that the purpose of the social sciences is to predict the future course of history, the great sin with which Marxists were supposed to be afflicted – a dubious claim, if not altogether without foundation, but it certainly did not apply to Popper's *bête noire*, Hegel.

In *The Open Society and its Enemies*, which is principally a critique of the alleged enemies, their lineage is constructed, beginning with Plato and running through Hegel and Marx, without any real appreciation of the actual historical circumstances in which these thinkers wrote. The 'open society', never precisely defined, is treated as an abstraction – but not surprisingly, so far as it is characterised, turns out to look very like the advanced western societies of the mid-twentieth century. Added to this is a prohibition on any far-reaching projects of social change, certain to lead, of course, to totalitarianism and the closed society. 'Piecemeal social engineering' (Popper's words) is the recommended approach. His very penetrating philosophy of science supposedly substantiated his poorly informed socio-historical notions and he was soon elevated into an ornament of cold war liberalism.

Raymond Aron

Raymond Aron emerged from very different circumstances. A student friend of Sartre, he joined de Gaulle's Free French in London during the Second World

War and edited its newspaper *France Libre*. Following the Liberation he was among the original editors of Sartre and de Beauvoir's *Temps Modernes*. Soon, however, he broke with that milieu, became a leading light in the CCF and began to defend Pétain and Vichy, despite their viciously antisemitic policies and his own Jewish background, later writing 'In 1941 or 1942 I disapproved of the passion with which the Gaullists, from the outside, denounced the "treason" of Vichy.'[60] On the Second World War, he believes that the Allies' unconditional surrender demand was 'completely unreasonable' and that 'European democracy and freedom and civilisation are the victims even more than Germany, of a victory won in their names.'[61]

His most important text was *The Opium of the Intellectuals* (a reference to Marx's remark on religion being the opium of the people) published in 1955 (English translation 1957). The very first paragraph of his Foreword explaining its origins makes it clear who is being aimed at, 'I had had occasion over the past few years, to write a number of articles directed not so much against the Communists as against those *communisants*, those who do not belong to the party but whose sympathy are with the communist world.' In due course Aron was loaded with honours, academic and otherwise, and according to Edward Shils's gushing foreword to Draus's collection, he was 'listened to attentively' by Robert McNamara and Henry Kissinger.

Albert Camus

Albert Camus had a respectable record as a *résistant* during the Occupation, and during and afterwards was also for a short time a friend and collaborator with Sartre. However, he moved before long towards Cold War liberalism and (at least until he refused to criticise French atrocities in Algeria and against Algerians in Paris) succeeded in presenting himself as a moral icon – a sort of French Orwell. According to John L. Hess, 'For Americans in the 1950s, Camus came on as a dashing figure, a literary genius, an existentialist icon, a champion of our side in the Cold War and a Resistance hero. He rather resembled Humphrey Bogart.'[62]

His most substantial text, which precipitated his final break with Sartre, was *L'homme révolté* (translated as *The Rebel*), published in 1951. It counterposes the revolutionary (bad) with the rebel (good), the former certain to embark upon totalitarian courses. The revolutionary is in the grip of 'Western nihilism' with predictable outcomes of mass murder; whereas rebellion means 'limited culpability' and implies, 'I rebel therefore we exist [and] instead of killing and dying in order to produce the being that we are not, we have to live and let live in order to create what we are.'[63] Camus's objective is to delegitimise revolutionary aims and objectives.

What strikes one about this text is its hyper-abstraction and attribution of the course of modern history to wrong ideas, rather than the press of material circumstances. That, however, may be identified as a recurrent trope in the works of all the ideologues discussed here. Equivalently, liberal society, which has somehow survived despite the perpetual existential threat from the terrible Other, is the product of right ideas. Aron actually quotes a very perceptive comment about himself from Etienne Barre, who writes that he '[deploys] an immense talent in order to explain with irrefutable reasons why things cannot be otherwise than what they are'.[64]

Hypocrisy

The greatest single atrocity of this period was the sadistic slaughter under CIA direction of between 500,000 and 2 million Indonesian leftists in 1965. If any of the champions of liberal democracy discussed here (Camus was dead by then) raised their voices in horror and protest, the fact has up to now escaped public notice. A quote from Camus's own Introduction to *The Rebel* (it is even reproduced in the Penguin blurb) can stand as a marker for their own double standards,

> Slave camps under the flag of freedom, massacres justified by philanthropy or the taste for the superhuman .... On the day when crime puts on the apparel of innocence, through a curious reversal peculiar to our age, it is innocence that is called on to justify itself.

8
Liberalism on the left

Eric Hobsbawm has remarked that what he terms the 'golden age' between 1950 and 1973 came as near as reality permitted to fulfilling, in the industrially advanced West (and to a degree in Japan), the dreams of the socialist pioneers. The barely interrupted economic growth of those years combined with governments committed to the maintenance of full employment and on the whole to social welfare, in the context of a labour market favourable to the employed workforce, promoted an unprecedented advance in material living standards across the board. A cartoon in a British newspaper sums it up. It has Harold Macmillan on the morrow of his 1959 election victory, addressing a circle of his colleagues and saying 'Well, I think we fought a good fight' – his colleagues being a car, a washing machine, a television set and other consumer durables.

At the same time the circumstances of these decades provided, in contrast with the Cold War liberalism discussed earlier, the opportunity for the realisation of projects of radical *social* liberalism; radical in the sense of 'shattering glass ceilings' and extending the scope of *liberté* and *égalité* into areas previously cordoned off from their application. This was liberalism's left face.

SOCIAL LIBERALISM IN EUROPE

In the aftermath of the war and partially in response to the communist challenge, West European states, both victors and defeated such as the UK, the Low Countries, France, the German Federal Republic, Austria and, even to an extent, Italy developed programmes of social liberalism and extended welfare, regardless of their governments' political colour. They could do so thanks to unprecedentedly favourable economic conditions from the 1950s.

But in this respect the Scandinavian countries – Iceland, Norway, Denmark, Sweden and Finland – were in a class of their own, for they, especially Sweden, aided by their natural assets, had been doing that since the pre-war era while remaining liberal capitalist societies. The dominant political orientation was social democratic, though that could mean very different things. Iceland, Norway and Denmark were NATO members and integrated into the US-controlled alliance system. Finland (which had been a Nazi ally with a social democrat as a key minister) and Sweden were neutrals, but of different sorts – simplistically, Sweden was neutral for the West and Finland for the Soviet bloc, and in both countries the communist parties had significant strength, especially in Finland.

Swedish social democracy

Sweden, under the leadership of the socialist party, the SAP, which had been in power since the early 1930s, was the model social democratic polity (though it had its dark side in the compulsory sterilisation of mentally afflicted individuals). Perry Anderson, in one of his early writings, referred to it as 'Mr Crosland's Dreamland',[1] and indeed it is mentioned frequently in *The Future of Socialism*. Anderson characterises it as 'a patent class society, but an exceptionally mild and liveable one'. Malicious reports of intense social anomie and exceptional suicide rates were wholly mythical.

Certainly it was the welfare society *par excellence* with an admirable public culture (even the Swedish Conservatives acclaimed it and had proposed some of the welfare measures), but very definitely a capitalist one. The publicly-owned share of the economy covered only 13 per cent of the total, in contrast to the British 25 per cent. Despite the prevalence of modest-sized enterprises, the labour movement was exceptionally centralised and very happy to work inside capitalist parameters. The individual unions had very little autonomy; wage bargaining was conducted from the union centre, the LO-S (Landsorganisationen i Sverige, Swedish Trade Union Confederation), and unions were required to get its permission before they could take industrial action.

The LO-S was also indifferent and even actively hostile to discussion of industrial democracy or any projects for tackling the dehumanising character of even well-paid repetitive wage-labour in pleasant surroundings. In the view of its leadership, wages and conditions were what the labour movement was about and all else was merely intellectual prattle and self-indulgence. By the early 1960s, Swedish social democracy was ideologically at a loss to define its long-term perspective for Swedish society – it appeared to have achieved all that was feasible, and within a liberal framework that was probably the case.

LIBERALISM AND COLONIAL NATIONALISM

At the outbreak of the Second World War the pattern of European imperial states and colonies established by the early years of the century remained unchanged in essence. The initial Soviet proclamation of September 1939 that this war, like its predecessor, was an imperialist one, though made with totally cynical motives, was not totally without foundation. During the years of the Popular Front, when the Comintern was seeking alliance with all anti-fascist forces and the USSR with the Western democracies, it had toned down criticism of their imperial practices.

One result of this was the disillusionment of the West Indian writer and Comintern activist, George Padmore, who broke with the communist party and went on to become the prophet of Pan-Africanism. An article of his in 1939 is entitled 'The British Empire is the biggest racket that the ingenuity of man has yet conceived', and suggested that Hitler was a mere amateur in comparison with the British imperial experts. This appeared in the anti-

Stalinist *New Leader* (not the sort of thing that journal would have published during its Cold War phase).

The expectation of British and French ruling elites was that once victory was won they would resume their empires. Late in the war even Labour politicians were talking in terms of 'developing' the empire to avert Britain's own looming economic crisis. The Americans were less than enthusiastic about such an outcome, preferring informal to formal empire. In 1945 a Pan-African Congress was held in Manchester. It was chaired by W. E. B. DuBois, the African–American Marxist historian, and attended by individuals among whom were future leaders of some of the new African States. It issued an uncompromising declaration:

> The delegates of the Fifth Pan-African Congress believe in the right of all peoples to govern themselves. We affirm the right of all Colonial peoples to control their own destiny. All Colonies must be free from foreign imperialist control, whether political or economic.... We say to the peoples of the Colonies that they must fight for these ends by all the means at their disposal.

> The object of imperialist powers is to exploit ... Therefore, the struggle for political power by Colonial and subject peoples is the first step towards, and the necessary prerequisite to, complete social, economic and political emancipation.

> The Fifth Pan-African Congress therefore calls on the workers and farmers of the Colonies to organise effectively. Colonial workers must be in the front of the battle against Imperialism ....

> Colonial and Subject Peoples of the World – Unite![2]

By the 1950s it had become apparent that colonialism in the old style had had its day. Asia had been almost entirely decolonised and the French were about to militarily lose their colonial war in South-East Asia; even puppet regimes, such as those in western Asia, had fallen or were threatened with overthrow. The process had started in Africa as well and few doubted that it would eventually reach completion there, despite the ferocious resistance of European settlers and sometimes metropolitan powers.

It was a prime objective of retreating Western powers as they withdrew, and of their American backers, to leave behind regimes that were well disposed to or at least tolerant of private commerce and investment and, if possible, diplomatically aligned with the West. In the former aim they largely succeeded, although the latter proved more difficult.

Certainly in a number of instances the Western powers, with effective manipulation of the independence arrangements, installed as their successors representatives of local elites who were in their debt both literally and figuratively, and thereby preserved their Cold War reach in these areas of the globe. The biggest successes in this regard were Malaysia (with its wealth of rubber and tin), Pakistan, and the Congo (Zaire, with its enormous area, strategic location and huge wealth of all manner of minerals and primary products, especially uranium). However, more frequently the decolonised states preferred a neutral diplomatic stance between the two blocs. This was the case with India, Indonesia and, in Africa, Ghana. They 'rejected the Cold War as an organising principle for international relations', and formed the Non-Aligned Movement. The initiators were Nehru, Nasser, Sukarno, Nkrumah and Tito. At the Bandung Conference of 1955 (which included China), the movement was consolidated and adopted five principles:

- Mutual respect for each other's territorial integrity and sovereignty
- Mutual non-aggression
- Mutual non-interference in domestic affairs
- Equality and mutual benefit
- Peaceful co-existence

However, they did not mean neutrality in the Swiss sense of abstaining from all diplomatic entanglements, not simple neutra*lity* but neutra*lism*. Peter Lyon, a British establishment figure, in his volume *Neutralism* published in 1963, noted that 'By neutrality is meant non-involvement in war, while by neutralism is meant non-involvement in the Cold War' – he meant it critically.

Positive neutralism

These states were indeed anxious to play a significant role on the world stage, both through the UN and otherwise. They referred to their stance as 'positive neutralism' (a position which some in Britain would have liked to see adopted by the UK). They aimed to promote the advance of decolonisation wherever this had still to be achieved and to encourage the reduction of tensions between the two blocs with eventual reconciliation and disarmament. Abstention from the Cold War, however, was not something of which the US government approved; the attitude was 'either you're for us or against us'. At a conference at Ohio State University in 2006 on 'The Global Impact of 1956: Race, Neutralism, National Liberation' in answer to a question on gendered connotations, a participant remarked that 'American officials feminized those leaders that advocated policies that were at odds with US experts. For instance, American policymakers feminized Nehru, especially since he did not drink and eat meat, but [they] spoke of Pakistani leaders in masculine terms.'[3]

Domestically, these neutralist regimes varied widely in their degree of authoritarianism and application of democratic standards. India was, politically speaking, a liberal democracy: however, Nehru's party, the Indian National Congress, always at this period got elected to central power, though this was done without systematic ballot-rigging and regional governments might be controlled by rival parties.[4] Indonesia was a state in extreme tension, and the regime until 1965 rested explicitly on the three pillars: Sukarno the longstanding ruler and his nationalist party, the military, and the powerful Communist Party of Indonesia, the largest outside the communist bloc. In Africa single-party rule was viewed as no disgrace, but was declared by some

African leaders, such as Kwame Nkrumah or the respected Julius Nyrere, to be the optimum method of managing African affairs and the one most compatible with local cultures.

None of these states, neutralist or otherwise, were industrialised, but possessed economies resting on foundations of peasant agriculture (whether cash crops or subsistence) and extractive industries. Indeed they were referred to for some years as 'underdeveloped' until that term came to be considered demeaning and 'developing' was substituted (China also fell into this category). India, however, though it remained basically a peasant economy, had attained substantial industrial growth, not only in textiles but even steel production.

Economically they remained as they had been under colonial rule, market economies more or less open to local and international capital. The notion of socialism was nevertheless very popular and in many cases substantial public sectors were established and attempts made to institute economic planning aimed at eventual industrialisation. However, the wish to fall into neither of the two great camps remained a conditioning factor and no state in the neutralist camp seriously tried to copy either Soviet or Chinese methods. Even where their political regimes were dictatorial their economies were liberal (as in the main were the Third World states in the Western camp).

The ideological rhetoric developed by these regimes can be seen as attempting to reconcile their social aspirations with the realities of their subordinate position in the global capitalist economy. Nkrumah's slogan, displayed on billboards around Ghana, 'We face neither East nor West; We face forward', gave no indication of what 'forward' might mean. Instead, localised 'socialisms' proliferated, at least in rhetoric – Indian socialism, African socialism, Arab socialism, and so forth – which pleased neither the Americans, for whom socialism was a naughty word and who had learned to tolerate European social democracy only with distaste, nor the Soviets, who regarded only their own system as authentically socialist. In spite of that, the latter were far better disposed towards neutralism and made energetic diplomatic efforts to court these states, with the hope of drawing them whenever possible into the Soviet orbit.

In the 1960s positive neutralism unravelled very rapidly. Possibly the first sign came in 1962 with the brief territorial war between India and China on their eastern Himalayan frontier. It meant permanent enmity between the two states and the Chinese sought diplomatic rapprochement with India's longstanding enemy, the Western-aligned military dictatorship of Pakistan. It was also a key stage in the growing enmity between the Chinese and Soviet states, for the USSR had supported its diplomatic ally India in the conflict despite the latter being a capitalist state.

In 1958 a military coup had overthrown the Western-backed monarchy in Iraq, and resulted in a military regime inclined towards the USSR and supported by the Iraqi Communist Party to the extent that it was accused of having moved into the Soviet camp. In 1963 the situation was reversed when with CIA inspiration another military faction, in conjunction with the Ba'ath Party (later to give rise to Saddam Hussein), carried out a bloody putsch, all but exterminating the Iraqi communists and returning Iraq to the Western orbit.

Two years later came the decisive blow to the fragile structure. The injudicious support given by the Communist Party of Indonesia to an attempted coup by leftist elements in the military furnished the pretext for the army, with CIA assistance, to instigate a horrible massacre of communists, with at least 500,000 slaughtered, and the total extirpation of Indonesian communism. The country then became a massively corrupt dictatorship and key buttress of US geopolitical objectives. The Ghanaian leader, Kwame Nkrumah, a major pillar of the neutralist bloc, was likewise displaced by a military takeover the following year and, in 1967, the overwhelming Israeli attack on Egypt (along with Jordan and Syria), though failing to displace the iconic neutralist figure, Nasser, left his military reputation in tatters. An effective neutralist bloc no longer existed; though the name of the Non-Aligned Movement persisted and still does, and conferences continue, it became meaningless – states like US-aligned Pakistan and Indonesia were members.

LIBERALISM AND BLACK LIBERATION IN THE USA

With the fading of direct colonial rule, the principal contradiction in the West's pretensions to liberal forms of government (advertised as democracy) was to be found in the intense racism, which had persisted for nearly a century in the southern states of the USA (matters were only relatively better in the north)[5] and where tyrannical cruelty paraded itself naked and unashamed. Even if the worst excesses had died away since the war, '[slavery] had done its work so well that it left its ex-slaves ... with no vocation but to be Americans'.[6]

In the international struggle to win allies and influence people, especially when these people and their governments were not of European descent, the state of affairs in Dixie was a severe embarrassment to US administrations and one which their enemy did not fail to take advantage of. The balance of US internal politics nevertheless precluded any strong action by the Federal government to rectify matters, until a Supreme Court decision allowed federal troops to be sent to Little Rock, Arkansas, in 1957, to enforce school desegregation.

These were the circumstances in which the Civil Rights movement emerged during the 1950s and reached its climax in the 1960s. We are not concerned, for the purposes of this discussion, to trace a well-known course of events, including the movement's fragmentation, but rather to examine the ideological framework in which it was conducted. There was, of course, only a partial element of central direction, which was provided by Martin Luther King and his colleagues, but in addition there were numerous initiatives from all manner of sources. Finally, out of the civil rights struggle there also emerged in the later 1960s forms of ideological outlook that went far beyond those of the civil rights initiators.

The term 'civil rights' makes clear the sort of ideological banner under which the mainstream struggle was carried on. The term is at the core of advanced liberalism's ideological universe. 'The emergence of the black movement too was an instance ... of the liberal polity.'[7] The protestors were demanding the abolition of discriminatory legislation and social practices and that the provisions of the US constitution should be genuinely applied to all citizens instead of being reserved only for white skins. The point is summarised in a verse from a song about the struggle for school desegregation at Little Rock, Arkansas, in 1957:

Oh listen, Mr. Governor,
And Mr. President, too.
Give me that Constitution
That's what you've got to do.
Give me that Constitution
I ask for nothing more.
Yes, that's what I want to study
In the State of Arkansas.

The importance of this aim should never be disparaged – success would mean the extinction of an eight-decades-long reign of terror. At the heart of King's famous 'I have a dream' speech was his reference to the Constitution:

When the architects of our republic wrote the magnificent words of the Constitution and the Declaration of Independence, they were signing a promissory note to which every American was to fall heir. This note was a promise that all men, yes, black men as well as white men, would be guaranteed the unalienable rights of life, liberty, and the pursuit of happiness.

His first reference to his dream in the speech declares it to be 'a dream deeply rooted in the American dream', and the question of economic, effectively class, discrimination, was not entirely neglected. The march, in August 1963, was after all 'for jobs and freedom', and King noted that 'the Negro lives on a lonely island of poverty in the midst of a vast ocean of material prosperity'. At the same time it was evident that the removal of overt racial discrimination would affect the economic position and life chances of African–Americans in their majority only marginally if at all. 'Either negritude is anti-racist, anti-imperialist, and therefore anti-capitalist – in other words radical, revolutionary and socialist – or it is nothing but a demand for privileged servitude.'[8] 'Racial equality requires respect for racial difference; class equality requires the elimination of class difference.'[9]

Ghetto riots

Discrimination in the North had never been so ferocious as was the case in Dixie, but it was bad enough,[10] and African–Americans there were economically, socially, educationally and in every other respect deprived to an immoderate degree. In the later part of the 1960s, large numbers of their young men in the urban ghettos took steps to improve their economic position and express their outrage by rioting, extensive looting and destruction – between 1964 and 1968 there were 329 riots in 257 cities, according to one source.[11] The phrase 'Burn, baby, burn!' became celebrated across the United States and far beyond.

Out of this turmoil emerged the Black Panther movement and similar bodies which established their profile as serious revolutionaries – Daniel Bell typically refers with racist overtones to Huey Newton 'sitting in a wicker chair holding a rifle in his hand, as an African chief may once have held a spear'.[12] These departed from liberalism by challenging the foundations of the capitalist social and economic order, and its ideological consciousness. Accordingly, they were soon subject to intense repression and several of their leaders were shot by the police. Martin Luther King was also shot, whether by a lone gunman or organised conspiracy, even though he and his movement presented no threat to property or ideology. For that reason it was successful in essence and its degree of eventual ideological incorporation can be indicated by the establishment of a Martin Luther King Day in the US calendar.

LIBERALISM AND FEMINISM

All societies that have left a written record and probably most others as well have been incorrigibly misogynist. The history of women throughout the past ten millennia at least, all over the globe, has been a terrible one. Feminism in its various forms too has had a lengthy history if a much shorter one, and in the late nineteenth and early twentieth century had largely taken a form comparable to the civil rights struggle discussed above – namely a demand for civil equality – which had been expounded by writers such as Mary Wollstonecraft as far back as the 1790s and by the renowned philosopher John Stuart Mill in 1869. In the early twentieth century, campaigners had focused upon the question of voting rights, which in the post-1945 years had been largely attained (except where racial considerations intruded).

The assertion that civic equality was nowhere near sufficient can be regarded as the defining concept of post-1945 feminism. In this sense it marked an advance beyond classic liberalism and drew attention to one of its systemic flaws, but could at the same time be viewed as based upon classic liberal principles of individual equality. The very title of Simone de Beauvoir's *The Second Sex* (*La Deuxième Sexe*) of 1949 summed up this ambiguity – women were classed as secondary beings even when enjoying equal civic rights (though often enough their situation made their enjoyment of these formal rights impossible in practice). 'One is not born a woman, rather one becomes a woman', was the sentence that echoed in the consciousness of its readers – at least those sympathetic to its message. De Beauvoir's summary of her argument in the closing paragraphs expresses the summit of liberal aspiration, 'when we abolish the slavery of half of humanity, together with the whole system of hypocrisy that it implies, then the "division" of humanity will reveal its genuine significance and the human couple will find its true form'[13] (which she specifically links to a quote from Marx with which she follows it).

This volume, widely translated, made an enormous impact throughout Western society and certainly proved to be one of the defining texts of the twentieth century. It provided the foundation and starting point for subsequent argument along similar lines, such as Betty Friedan's *The Feminine Mystique* and Germaine Greer's *The Female Eunuch*, as well as numberless others of a similar nature. In practical terms the full impact of de Beauvoir's volume took some time to make itself felt, but it laid a theoretical groundwork which, in combination with the developments of the 1960s, resulted in the emergence of a politically orientated women's movement in the 1960s and early 1970s. Publication of *The Feminine Mystique* in 1963 was followed three years later by the formation of the American feminist movement, the National Organization for Women, which aimed to bring women 'into the mainstream of American society now' in 'fully equal partnership with men'. In the same decade, the US Marxist *Monthly Review* published an article on the political economy of domestic labour.

Sexual Politics

These developments marked a shift from conventional notions of what constituted politics. They shared a new emphasis on identity politics with the simultaneously emergent gay or black power movements, which demanded liberation and recognition not on the basis of an anonymous individual citizenship but in respect of the kind of people they were – sexually, culturally, ethnically, and so on. These concepts transcended those of classic liberalism – Friedan's background was a Marxist one. At the same time, such perspectives need not necessarily be dissociated altogether from the liberal tradition. Equality and/or assimilation could at least theoretically be conceived to co-exist with the recognition and acceptance of all manner of non-antagonistic differences.

The women's movement, like all those incorporating identity politics, was very fragmented, even in its beginnings, and attempts to give it an institutional framework succeeded only briefly and temporarily, if nevertheless with substantial consequences. The differences within the movement could be presented in various ways, but for the purposes of this discussion, it split along the following fault lines. First were those sections which conceived its lines of advance along an extension of liberal values which would make gender equality a genuine reality in a liberal social context. Second, a rival Marxist approach was propelled by the movement's initial emergence on the left and the dissatisfaction of feminists at the continuance of gender stereotypes within it. This was documented in a British context by Sheila Rowbotham in her autobiography, *Promise of a Dream*.[14] Juliet Mitchell puts the argument forcibly:

Feminism unites women at the level of their total oppression – it is all-inclusive (cf. Black Power and 'totalism'). Its politics match this: it is a total attack. The theory backs this: the first division of labour was the first formation of oppressor and oppressed – the first division of labour was between man and woman. The first domination must be given priority – it must be the first to go.[15]

A third alternative was the perspective of radical separatism, which maintained that women's consciousness was intrinsically different from (and superior to) men's and their sexuality should ideally be lesbian.

> The base of our ideological thought is: Sexism is the root of all other oppressions, and Lesbian and women oppression will not end by smashing capitalism, racism and imperialism ... for every woman who has been raped, physically, economically, psychologically, we take the name of *The Furies*, Goddesses of Vengeance and protectors of women.[16]

Not surprisingly, in liberal, soon to be neoliberal, societies, with Marxist and radical or separist alternatives marginalised, it was the liberal version of women's emancipation which won out.

LIBERALISM AND THE 1960s CULTURAL REVOLUTION

It would be no more than a truism to note that while the post-war wave of economic globalisation has embraced the entire globe, the cultural revolution of the 1960s, centred in the developed countries of Europe and North America, has been a much more patchy affair. Large parts of the world's population – perhaps even the majority – remain relatively unaffected or not affected at all. However, that does not make it any less of a revolution – for revolutions after all, whatever their form, always remain confined to limited areas.

The concept of cultural revolution can also be criticised from a different angle, one which takes the form of Herbert Marcuse's concept of repressive tolerance or repressive individualism. He argues that the liberation sought through the overthrow of repressive moral and cultural norms is no liberation but indeed an illusion, for this too is part of capitalism's strategy to keep the masses from reflecting on capitalism's iniquities and working for its overthrow.[17] *Nineteen Eighty-four* and *Brave New World* may not be too far apart.[18] Terror and hedonism, in this interpretation, represent the two arms of capital's deadly embrace.

Such a critique does have to be taken seriously, although it is open to plenty of objections and will not seem all that convincing to the beneficiaries of the revolution or those unwillingly still enduring the grip of the cultural *ancien régime*. At any rate, the reality of the revolution cannot be doubted. Its brief 'counter-cultural' version was distinguished by ultra-individualism and combined bizarre rejection of both capitalist ambitions and bourgeois rules,

> Compare ... such rites as our hippies improvise for themselves out of potted anthropology and sheer inspiration, and the distinction between good and bad magic should be clear enough. The tribalized youth gather in gay costume on a high hill in a public park to salute the midsummer sun in

its rising and setting. They dance, they sing, they make love as each feels moved, without order or plan ... all have equal access to the event; no-one is misled or manipulated.[19]

Though these particular manifestations proved to be a passing phase, the liberal cultural revolution in general terms has been of deep profundity, the longest-lasting heritage of the 1960s and incomparably more enduring than Mao's 'cultural revolution' of a similar date.

Indications of the force and extent of this revolution – like all revolutions, most enthusiastically embraced and promoted by the young – are provided by a cursory listing of some of the transformations it has brought about, sweeping away literally millennia of repression and enhancing the scope of liberty and equality.

In its heartlands, divorce was made easy, and illegitimacy – birth to unmarried parents – no longer confers disgrace or exists as a legal category. Contraception and contraceptive advice is readily available and, with the notable exception of Ireland, abortion is legal in most economically advanced societies; indeed, in Japan it is a principal contraceptive method. What used to be called 'trial marriage', in the lifetime of many readers a daring and disreputable notion, is now practised routinely and long-term unmarried partnerships have become a wholly unremarkable feature of the social landscape.[20] Gay and lesbian sexuality (the former being strictly illegal in the UK and individual states of the USA, and disdained everywhere, less than 50 years ago) no longer carries an official stigma, and in the UK civil partnership between homosexual couples is now part of the legal system.

Even in the eye of this revolutionary storm there were of course many individuals, women in particular, and young women most of all, who continued to suffer under obscurantist cultural values. Sexism is far from dead, and in the USA and to a lesser extent in the UK, 'single mothers on welfare' continued and continue to be a particular target. Likewise, plenty of informal and vicious homophobic prejudice still exists into the twenty-first century, as is the case with racism, but no figure in the public eye could openly express either without losing credibility – coded language has to be used. The opening up of sexual discourse is perhaps somewhat less remarkable, as the immediately preceding centuries were unusually closed in this respect, but is nevertheless striking considering what was regarded as inexpressible only five decades ago. To be sure, it also resulted in an explosive growth of pornography. The one area where the revolution has been stalled or even reversed is that of narcotic substances, which in the 1960s were very much part of the counter-cultural scene. In this area prohibitionism still holds the advantage, although in the case of cannabis popular attitudes are a great deal more tolerant than judicial ones.

For many of its opponents, of course, the sexual revolution *is* liberalism, or at least its logical consequence and expression of its essence. Indeed, it fits quite readily into the liberal ideological paradigm which repudiates the notion of victimless crime. A consistently liberal position could be argued that in times when sexual behaviour had significant consequences for property (the cardinal liberal concept), it was legitimate to control it closely – particularly in relation to women, but in other respects as well in order to strengthen the family unit so central to capitalist production – but when this had ceased to be the case, that necessity likewise disappeared. At any rate, history demonstrated that neither the sexual revolution, feminism nor black civil rights has been incompatible with liberal regimes and though constantly challenged, their achievements are likely to persist as long as consumer society does.

DIFFERENCES IN MEANING

These two chapters have attempted to demonstrate two things regarding the situation of liberal ideology between the end of the Second World War and the early 1970s when the long boom was on the point of ending and being replaced with a very different economic climate.

Firstly, liberal ideology outside the communist bloc was hegemonic, both in its Western variant practised in the industrial societies of high consumption and in most of the third world societies lying within the Western orbit (despite their different characters) – the partial exceptions are touched on in following chapters. Private property was secure, with judicial systems and state apparatuses which protected it from the unpropertied and regulated its use, its disposal, and relationships among the propertied. Formal legislative authority lay with elected assemblies operating under more or less distorted franchises and, through political parties, more or less oligarchic in character. Circulation of information and expression of opinion were both freely practised and regulated by authority to a greater or lesser degree. In short, this was the 'free world' of Western Cold War rhetoric.

Secondly, within this general framework vast variations and differences of emphasis existed. Social democratic liberalism in Sweden was after all a very different creature from the variety of the ideology current in the United States, let alone in Turkey, Egypt or India (though the Indian government of the time itself had a social democratic orientation).

The differences were not simply a question of dramatic diversity in socio-economic levels and the variations in industrial development which that reflected (although they were certainly related to that sort of thing), but of institutional governmental arrangements, the character of the civil society superstructures which rested on these liberal foundations, and of inherited cultural presumptions. A society would be described as more or less 'liberal' according to the extent to which it embodied the classic features of security of life and property, the rule of law, judicial independence of the executive, freedom of dissent and communication – as well as the character of its cultural norms and the degree to which its citizens could, provided they were not intruding on others' equivalent liberties, choose their lifestyles and go about their business (in both senses) without molestation by the authorities or a disapproving public.

And so it was in this period that liberalism and liberal ideology began to take on the sense in which they tend to be employed in contemporary discourse – namely non-interference in the sphere of personal conduct. 'Liberalism' is consequently deployed in a similar way to the term 'morality' which, unless otherwise stated, is assumed to pertain to sexual conduct (for example, 'moral majority') – vividly demonstrated in the contemporary USA where 'liberal' is evoked in approval or condemnation principally in the struggles around abortion, homosexuality and penal policy.

9
Communism

The years between 1945 and 1975 saw the world communist movement and communist ideology reach the height of its extent, power and influence, and at the same time begin to unravel both in material terms and with regard to its hold on public consciousness.

The geographical spread of its power has already been noted. At the close of hostilities there existed two communist regimes (one of them of little account), by the early 1960s there were 13 (not counting Yugoslavia), covering a third of the global population. A couple more were to be added in the 1970s, apart from a number of favourably-disposed states that were not considered part of the communist camp. However, over the same period the movement became irreversibly split between its two major components, which were on at least one occasion on the brink of armed hostilities. The stresses behind the division were both material and ideological, and these of course were interlinked.

The regimes that designated themselves as socialist – in the Leninist sense – were radically diverse in their levels of economic development, character of social relations and cultural background. Some had emerged from bourgeois democracies overlaid by the experience of World War and/or fascism, others from polities that Marxists would have classed as feudal, or else from colonial status. In line with ideological requirements, the formal nature of their political institutions reflected this diversity, although the essential content was the same in all.

That content can be readily defined. They were all single-party dictatorships oligarchic in essence – which does not necessarily mean that all of them were unpopular – and in the case of the Soviet bloc, subject in the last analysis to decision-making in Moscow. During Stalin's lifetime that was precise and detailed; subsequently a fair measure of autonomy was permitted – provided it was not pushed too far. Common ideology in the main counted for much more than institutional arrangements such as Comecon or the Warsaw Pact, and until the end of the 1950s kept both the European and Asian regimes in relative public harmony (with the exception of the Yugoslav breakaway).

The formal arrangements, however, are important less for their real significance than for the light they throw on the communist ideology of the period. The USSR, being the home of the Revolution and supposed to have abolished capitalism and class antagonism, was regarded as the most advanced. Paradoxically, it was not the most industrially developed, the GDR (East Germany) and Czechoslovakia being economically further ahead. Nevertheless it was supposed to enjoy the optimum political institutions, a single ruling party with no others permitted, and representative assemblies based primarily on workplace assemblies rather than geographical boundaries – all supposed signs of its greater political maturity.

It was a central theoretical postulate that political parties were based upon social classes (in the Marxist definition) and necessarily reflected their interests. There being only workers (white-collar and manual) and peasants in the USSR, two classes of working people, politically united and therefore non-antagonistic, logic required that there be only a single party. In liberated Eastern Europe, however, this level of advance had yet to be achieved. Capitalism as a ruling system had of course been abolished, and exploiting classes of capitalists and landlords no longer ruled, but class divisions persisted and therefore shadow political parties representing peasants and petty capitalists were made to continue in existence, and were integrated in a bloc controlled by the ruling communist party (which had compulsorily absorbed the social democrats). The Soviet-type legislative institutions were not duplicated in these 'People's Democracies';[1] instead, parliamentary assemblies (with membership strictly controlled and without genuine popular choice in elections) formed the institutional framework for appointing the ruling collective. Genuine debate, if any, took place only at the level of the communist party's politbureau.

The formal character of the Chinese People's Republic instituted in 1949 under Mao's leadership more or less followed a similar model, although the term 'people's democracy' was not used. China was even poorer and more economically backward than Eastern Europe and it was recognised that raising its level would require a considerable input from capitalist elements for some time to come. Accordingly, a class of 'people's capitalists' – those not tainted by association with the Guomindang regime – were designated and given considerable economic though not political privileges, for representation at the People's Congress did not amount to anything significant.

In all cases, in accordance with Marxist precepts, it was insisted that the working class was the leading force in the regimes, through its representative, the communist parties, providing political guidance and the active element in their polities – even when the mass of the population and indeed the party membership itself were overwhelmingly peasants or drawn from peasant or intelligentsia backgrounds. Thus was the reality of the regimes established by peasant revolution or Soviet military force made to correspond ideologically with the prescriptions of Marxist theory.

The same was the case in relation to national identity. Once more, the formalities were observed. Leninist theory, attacking imperialism in general and the structure of the Tsarist state in particular, insisted that nationalities must be allowed a free choice of independence if they so wished, and in the Soviet Union itself the pretence was strictly observed that its 14 republics with their component nationalities existed in harmonious voluntary federation. Communist China and Yugoslavia also had federal structures to take into account the mix of nationalities within their borders. Stalin himself in 1913 had written the canonical text on nations and nationalism and his first government position was Commissar for Nationalities, during which, before the Soviet

Federation (predecessor to the USSR) was formed, he had represented the Soviet state at Finland's declaration of independence.

STALIN'S NOTIONS

In the years between 1945 and Stalin's death in 1953, his specific form of Leninist ideology reached its full flowering. Its final form was initially propounded in the pages of the *History of the CPSU(B)*, published in 1938, supervised and partially written by Stalin. This text was studied intensively by communists all around the globe and was, according to Eric Hobsbawm, a pedagogical triumph. It provided the official version of Party history and, through the International, the principles, organisation and ideology that had supposedly made the CPSU so effective were required to be instituted in all the others.

Among those principles was the contention that following the victory of socialist revolution – and even more as the construction of socialism advanced – the class struggle did not abate, but on the contrary intensified, as the remnants of the overthrown social system, seeing their hopes fading, struggled all the more desperately to reassert their former position. This was supposed to justify the tightening of the police regime in the USSR in the 1930s and the post-war years, the purges which occurred during both these periods, and equally the purges in Eastern Europe which followed Tito's defection in 1947.

Stalin's regime in the 1930s, as we have seen, was one which, behind a screen of internationalism, acted in a thoroughly nationalist fashion, emphasising Soviet and even Great Russian interests. Following 1945 and the initiation of the Cold War, with the Soviet leaders feeling again under siege, this trend was greatly emphasised – at times in an absurd and bizarre fashion. Significant aspects of Western science, such as relativity theory, were denounced as 'bourgeois science' in contrast to the 'proletarian science' practised in the USSR such as the biological notions of the charlatan Lysenko, to which foreign communists were obliged to subscribe. (Soviet physicists working on the atomic weapons programme had to use relativity theory on the quiet.) Still more perverse if anything was the ascription of major scientific and technological discoveries (such as radio) not to their universally recognised claimants but to previously unknown Russians.

As early as the 1920s Stalinists had used antisemitism (drawing on its deep reservoir in Russian culture) in an underhand manner (it could not of course be done openly) to attack Trotsky and other Party leaders of Jewish extraction such as Zinoviev and Kamenev who were opposed to Stalin. In the later 1940s and up till 1953 the regime became deeply infected.

Part of the reason was the position of Israel, whose creation the USSR had initially supported hoping it might prove a counterweight to Western influence in the region. Soon it was apparent that the opposite was the case and Stalin, who had always been and was becoming ever more paranoid about anyone who might have been or might potentially be influenced by his enemies,[2] began to more actively persecute widening circles of Soviet citizens with Jewish connections and annihilate the members of organisations which in any way represented a Jewish cultural identity. The Eastern European purge trials tended to focus on party leaders with Jewish backgrounds. All such persons, however loyal they might purport to be, might find a rival focus of identity in a Jewish state. It would have been impermissible for the Soviet Union, which boasted of its abhorrence of racism, to openly profess antisemitism and Kaganovitch, who had Jewish ancestry, was retained in the Politbureau for appearances' sake. Instead, accusations of Zionism and 'cosmopolitanism' were used to justify the persecution.

Nevertheless, although the Comintern had been dissolved in 1943, the Kremlin was still leading an international movement, and moreover there now existed a ring of East European states upon which Stalin had found it necessary to impose communist administrations (probably not his original intention except possibly in Poland). Somehow the paradox of an intensely nationalist USSR/Russia at the head of a bloc of ostensibly sovereign states, and the inspiration and director of parties throughout the globe, had to be resolved.

The primacy of the USSR as the fountainhead of the socialist revolution and the first state to build socialism had to be acknowledged – and was acknowledged – by all other communist parties. In addition, adulation of Stalin reached clinical proportions, particularly in, but not only in, those states subject to the Soviet hegemony. The case of China, however, is the most interesting – it was not subject in this manner, but it was also, since 1949, a communist state and a close ally. Its revolution, although it owed in its final stages something to Soviet supplies, had been independently arrived at. As has been noted, Stalin was far from keen to see that revolution accomplished. He consistently urged Mao to make a deal with Chiang, and his government was one of the last to withdraw recognition from the Guomindang. No doubt he was thinking of the consequences of having another serious leader in the communist movement as well as his relations with the USA.

Once the Chinese revolution was a reality and the PRC established, Stalin had enough sense not to treat Mao in the same way as he had tried to treat Tito, and Mao, who respected him as a great revolutionary, was willing to concede him a formal precedence as long as he kept out of Chinese affairs. After all, the Chinese communists wanted Soviet assistance in helping to rebuild their country and needed Soviet protection from US hostility – though the Kremlin struck hard material bargains in return. An appearance of amity and closeness was therefore preserved, and the Chinese revolution presented in communist propaganda everywhere as the second (in importance as well as time) great socialist revolution of the twentieth century. US propaganda, by contrast, portrayed it as directed and managed from the Kremlin, merely another episode in the global communist conspiracy and China as no different in essence from any East European satellite – presumptions which were at total variance with the actuality.

Stalin's attitude to communist parties in states outside his orbit varied according to their degree of importance. Members of these parties were fond of pointing out that the CPSU had no physical control over how they behaved, so that if they agreed in all respects with whatever the USSR did or believed it could only be out of genuine conviction. In a sense this was true enough, but that was only because CP activists were socialised into habits of rigorous ideological discipline and if they fell seriously out of line they left or were expelled from the party. Their leaders, although accorded a very high status by their membership, would soon enough find themselves in trouble with these same members if they deviated without Soviet permission.

It must have greatly grieved the Soviets that the communist parties in the USA and Britain, the leaders of the enemy camp, remained so small and relatively uninfluential (despite the CPGB having a significant presence in the trade union movement). It was a common trope among the leaders of these two parties that their inability to reach powerful dimensions was due to failure of will rather than objective circumstances. France and Italy were different – by far the most important communist parties in Western Europe – indeed in France the largest political party, with the biggest single vote.

The Cominform

The importance of the French and Italian parties was emphasised when, at the establishment of the Communist Information Bureau in 1947, comprising otherwise the ruling parties in Europe (including the USSR and excepting Albania), they were the only two CPs outside of the USSR and Eastern Europe that became members. The institution was a sign of the tightening of ideological bonds by Moscow in the aftermath of the Truman Doctrine and the Marshall Aid programme. Its central doctrine was that of the 'Two Camps' – that of peace and socialism represented by communist-ruled states, and that of war and imperialism led by the USA.

The French and Italian parties were castigated for ideological sloppiness and for undue liberalism in their political practice (which they had carried out in conformity with Stalin's requirements – at the time), obliged to confess their errors and instructed to mend their ways. They were also given responsibility for acting as the channel between the Cominform and the other European parties – that is, as their ideological overseers.

The Cominform founding conference, through the mouth of the Soviet representative Zhdanov, announced a counteroffensive on all fronts (other than military) against the rival camp, and this was to include a prominent ideological component.

> In their ideological struggle against the USSR the American imperialists ... on this platform of ideological struggle ... [unite] all the enemies of the working class without exception, from the capitalist magnates to the Right Socialist leaders ... would like to have in the USSR the bourgeois parties which are so dear to their hearts, including pseudo-socialistic parties, as an agency of imperialism ....[3]

The conference, held in Belgrade, gave special attention to art and artistic creation, which must be deployed unremittingly in the 'battle of ideas' to present the Soviet Union and the communist movement in a positive light, and do so in the style of the 'socialist realism' that prevailed in the USSR itself – 'realistic, socially-orientated art',[4] with 'positive heroes', simplified conflicts and no stylistic experimentation.

Taking one thing with another, communists in general might well feel that Stalin's last eight years had seen dramatic progress. From the beleaguered communist movement and Soviet Union of the late 1930s, almost overthrown in 1941, its power had expanded from the 'socialist sixth of the world' to comprise a third; communism had become a powerful global force matching the capitalist world, if not on equal terms at least with some degree of comparability. The West, through the Cold War, had succeeded in blocking further advance, but could not reverse what had already occurred. The historical super-confidence that had always been a hallmark of communists' attitudes appeared eminently justified.

DESTALINISATION

The top leadership of the Soviet state, however, were, at least partially, conscious of the shaky foundations on which the achievement rested, even if communists outside the bloc were not. The terror regime that had characterised the dictator's rule was on the brink of becoming unviable. It had been Stalin's technique, by means of recurrent blood purges, to break up and prevent the consolidation of institutional layers that were independent of his political will – whether in the Party or society generally – and at the time he died another one was in the offing. This could not go on: the various bureaucracies which ran the state needed security from arbitrary execution and imprisonment to function effectively, particularly in the changed post-war climate; similarly, the population as a whole needed some minimal relief from the constant pressure to which they were subjected and, if possible, some improvement in basic living conditions.

Almost as soon as Stalin had been embalmed and placed beside Lenin in Red Square, the adulation attending him began to be toned down, the impending purge was cancelled and shortly thereafter his executioner, Lavrentia Beria, and some colleagues were themselves executed; Beria was the last Politbureau member to be shot and these were the last Soviet citizens to be accused for internal political reasons of being foreign agents.

The 20th Congress

For a moment this all seemed very traditional, but in February 1956, at the first Party Congress (the 20th) to be held since Stalin's death, it became evident that a major change was taking place. In the initial sessions, remarks in praise of Stalin were few (though the Chinese fraternal delegates made a point of applauding whenever his name was mentioned) and the veteran Politbureau member Anastasis Mikoyan criticised him mildly. For the delegates, however, the sensation of the event was the speech delivered in a closed session (the fraternal delegates as well as press were excluded) by Nikita Khrushchev, who had emerged as the CPSU First Secretary and principal figure in the government. Though taking care to note Stalin's achievements and deny that they had corrupted the Party or Soviet society in general, he denounced him nevertheless as a tyrant and paranoid mass murderer who had routinely violated 'socialist legality', terrorised his colleagues and sent many good communists to their death. He also damned the 'cult of personality' which Stalin had cultivated around himself. Foreign observers – the 'Secret Speech' soon became public – were quick to point out that Khrushchev dated the 'bad' Stalin from the point where he had begun to persecute Stalinists rather than anti-Stalinists.

Foremost among the tropes employed alike by Khrushchev, Soviet propaganda and foreign communist parties once they had absorbed this new line, was the comparison of Lenin with Stalin. Lenin, by contrast with his successor, had been the perfect leader and everything that Stalin was not – honest about errors and shortcomings, winning his point by argument and not intimidation, considerate, personally modest, loyal to his colleagues. 'Restoration of Leninist standards' became the watchword. Images of Lenin took the place of Stalin's as ubiquitous features of the Soviet and East European landscape.

For foreign communists, leaders and led, the 'Secret Speech' came as an intellectual and moral earthquake (the Polish leader Bierut was said to have sustained a fatal heart attack on hearing of it). Some refused to acknowledge its truth, either privately, or, in the case of the Albanian leader, Enver Hoxha, publicly. There were those, including Maurice Thorez, the French communist leader, who trusted that Khrushchev would be removed from his position and the speech denounced by Soviet authority. The Chinese leaders had their own reasons to be disgruntled with Stalin but thoroughly disapproved of the speech and destalinisation because of its effects on morale and unity – and because they were increasingly resentful at being expected to follow the lead of Stalin's successors. They contented themselves with acknowledging grudgingly that he had had some shortcomings and left it at that.

The problem was that Stalin had not satisfied himself with being acclaimed as an able, outstanding leader and brilliant politician, which might have enabled him to retain his reputation despite Khrushchev's demolition, or at least to suffer less catastrophic damage. But instead he had been presented to his followers as an infallible divine icon at whose shrine they were obliged to worship, surrender their critical faculties, and live their political commitment in pseudo-religious terms. Not unexpectedly, the outcome was barely controllable crisis, at least in Europe, both East and West (and the USA).

The party leaders tried to make the best of it, arguing that the events demonstrated the basic health and moral integrity of the USSR since it had not been afraid to bring its errors into the open and resolve to correct them. Fortunately the foundations of Soviet socialism remained sound and outrages had all been due to Stalin's malpractice and the 'cult of the individual'. It was all very unconvincing. The same year in Poland the repercussions produced incipient revolt averted only by the ability of the Party leadership there to control events and make compromises, and in Hungary actual insurrection, which Soviet tanks crushed with great violence and slaughter.

These events marked a particular point of crisis for Western communists, particularly when combined with the revelations which the revolt exposed about the nature of the 'people's democracy' in that country. Contrary to all material evidence they dismissed the insurrection as a Western-incited conspiracy capitalising on justified public discontent, created by fascist elements that had wormed their way into the security services. Not surprisingly, a very large number of their members remained unconvinced and most of these abandoned their parties.

SCHISM

Perhaps surprisingly, due to subsequent developments the membership losses were largely repaired, but the events of 1956 struck an irrecoverable blow to communist morale. Regardless of the attitude taken up, things would never again be the same. Anyone who felt that Stalin had been unjustly maligned, and that all had been well in the USSR and the communist movement under his stewardship, nevertheless had to come to terms with the fact that it was the Soviet leaders themselves who had denounced him. In that case, how could it be possible to have confidence in them in future? If on the other hand the accusations were accepted as true, and Hungary regarded as a demonstration of everything that was wrong, they had to adjust to the fact that during their lives as communists they had been living a lie. Either way lay disillusion, and that was not altered by the sticking plaster put over the wound by the world communist conference of 1957 which issued the Moscow Declaration, asserting that

> The conference stresses the necessity of resolutely overcoming revisionism and dogmatism in the ranks of the Communist and Workers' parties. ... Dogmatism and sectarianism hinder the development of Marxist-Leninist theory and its creative application in specific conditions, replace study of the specific situation with quotations and pedantry, and lead to the Party's isolation from the masses.[5]

At the same time it was stressed that these 'specific conditions' could sometimes provide the opportunity for socialist revolution by 'peaceful means'.

Three years later, following further Soviet crises and successes – and from late 1959 the disappearance of Chinese contributions from *Problems of Peace and Socialism*, the international communist journal edited in Prague – a further meeting of the 81 parties (the British edition of their statement was titled *36 million Communists say ...*) reaffirmed the 1957 Declaration:

> Revisionism, Right-wing opportunism, which mirrors bourgeois ideology in theory and practice, distorts Marxism–Leninism, robs it of its revolutionary essence, and thereby paralyses the revolutionary will of the working class.

...

Dogmatism and sectarianism in theory and practice can also become the main danger at some stage in the development of the individual parties unless combated unrelentingly ...

All the Marxist-Leninist parties are independent and have equal rights ... and support each other. ... The Communist and Workers' Parties unanimously declare that the Communist Party of the Soviet Union has been, and remains, the universally recognised vanguard of the world Communist movement ...

All 81 parties signed up to this Statement, but by then the bloc was falling apart, though this was as yet to be publicly admitted.

'Peaceful co-existence'

Nevertheless, the new realities were absorbed and the parties one way or another were over time supplied with new recruits who, being youthful, carried none of the baggage of 1956. There was, after all (at least for communists outside the bloc), evidence that the USSR really had come to terms with the dark elements of its past and was embarked on new advances. Economic growth continued impressively (or at least appeared to) and living conditions to improve, allowing Khrushchev in 1961 to make his extravagant promises of consumer abundance.

At the 22nd Party Congress he also floated the concept of the 'state of the whole people', an oxymoron in Marxist–Leninist terms, for it contradicted Lenin's insistence that the existence of the state was necessarily bound to class division, and that only with the advent of full communism and 'withering away' of the state could 'the people' be considered a social unity. Then there were the Soviet technological triumphs, and in China the 'Great Leap Forward' of the late 1950s, which proved to be a disaster resulting in mass famine, but was at the time presented as a triumph.

In international affairs it was not Moscow which was intransigent, it was Washington. This is not necessarily to argue that the Soviet leadership was morally superior to its rival – the Americans, enjoying the advantage, could well afford to reject any proposals which would have lessened that advantage, for example, all-round nuclear disarmament. It was in these circumstances that Khrushchev came to emphasise a concept that had hitherto been marginal to Marxist–Leninist ideology. This was 'peaceful-coexistence'.

Considering the way in which it was to be used in the subsequent ideological polemics, this phrase was, ironically, invented by the Chinese communists and first used in 1954 when China and India settled their mutual relations, and was also used uncontroversially in the 1957 Declaration. In the scope of world affairs and historical development however, Lenin, his colleagues and successors had been convinced that war and violence were intrinsic to the spread of proletarian revolution and an inescapable fact of the transition to world socialism, 'force is the midwife of the new society'. As the centre and stronghold of the world revolution, the Soviet Union would be necessarily involved – treaties and truces were temporary measures. 'Peaceful co-existence' declared the opposite.

Much emphasis was laid on the qualification that this did not mean that the contest between capitalism and socialism was over. Far from it. The social systems would continue to compete energetically, but now the competition would be ideological and by example, and as the superiority of socialism increasingly showed itself, nations would increasingly choose the former. The Cold War could therefore be wound up and the threat of a Third World War, nuclear or otherwise, lifted from the globe. However unrealistic, it was quite an attractive idea and particularly attractive to Western populations, who stood to lose most if the ultimate conflict ever erupted.

The Chinese leaders were far from impressed. At the time they were facing their own problems, but they did not hesitate to make their feelings known, in steadily rising crescendo. Between 1949 and the mid-1950s, they had succeeded in establishing a viable social order and imposing their authoritarian command over China's huge territory and enormous population (including the re-absorption of Tibet, and fighting the USA and its allies to a stalemate in Korea). In 1956, encouraged by Zhou En-Lai, Mao initiated the 'Hundred Flowers' episode which was intended to permit a limited measure of critical comment on the administration with the aim of correcting bureaucratic weaknesses, 'Let a hundred flowers bloom; let a hundred schools of thought contend.' As soon as the criticisms became really pertinent however, this was abruptly terminated and many of the critics persecuted (after which the Great Leap Forward with its disastrous consequences was put in hand).

In 1955 the Soviet leaders Khrushchev and Bulganin had mended the regime's fences with Tito and visited Belgrade in person. This the Chinese chose to interpret, once relations became really strained in the late 1950s, as a right-wing deviation from Marxism-Leninism, or 'revisionism' in the communist vocabulary. The verbal attacks they launched against Yugoslavia were clearly intended to criticise the Soviets at second hand for abandoning the anathema pronounced against Yugoslavia in 1948.

Polemic and counter-polemic

In 1960, on the 90th anniversary of Lenin's birth, the CPC published a pamphlet under the title *Long Live Leninism!*, which, while endorsing 'peaceful co-existence' and making complimentary references to the USSR and Khrushchev, also contained coded comments easily understood by the initiated, criticising the general Soviet approach to international relations:

> We consistently oppose the launching of criminal wars by imperialism … But should the imperialists impose such sacrifices on the peoples of various countries, we believe that … those sacrifices would be repaid. On the debris of a dead imperialism, the victorious people would create very swiftly a civilization thousands of times higher than the capitalist system and a truly beautiful future for themselves.[6]

One of the major Chinese grievances was the Soviet refusal to provide China with nuclear weaponry or the means to manufacture it. The CPC accordingly resolved to do it themselves. The Soviets, in their view, were backward in standing up to imperialist intimidation – which they considered to be the only way to secure world peace. Their signature to the November 1960 Statement represented their final attempt to present a conciliatory image, though by this point they were understandably furious at the Soviets for withdrawing in July of that year all their economic aid, technicians and technical assistance, which had calamitous effects on Chinese industrial construction, intensifying their self-created catastrophe of the Great Leap forward. 'The blow this dealt to China was probably far more cruel than had been, say, the brief and violent impact of Soviet armed intervention in Hungary.'[7]

The ultra-Stalinist Albanian regime, which had, or thought it had, a great deal to fear from a Soviet-Yugoslavia rapprochement, was more forthright, openly condemning Khrushchev and his colleagues (though Albania also signed). As a result it was effectively 'derecognised' by the CPSU as part of the communist community, and initially was used as its surrogate for criticising the Chinese positions. At the 1960 conference its leaders engaged in a bitter and uproarious row with their Soviet counterparts, and effectively fled Moscow before the conference's conclusion, leaving their subordinates to sign the final communiqué. According to the (not particularly reliable) memoirs of Enver Hoxha, the Albanian leader, 'The whole period until the meeting of the parties began was filled with attacks and counter-attacks between us and the revisionists of all ranks.'[8] The Chinese leaders responded by establishing close relations with the Albanian regime and replacing the economic aid that Moscow had withdrawn.

Although the extent of the rupture was concealed for a time, Chinese–Soviet relations, far from improving, continued to deteriorate, and the Chinese CP switched its polemics to attack the Italian communists, who were renowned for their relatively flexible interpretations of Marxism-Leninism and their party's role. Beijing took to issuing a series of pamphlets (in 1963), one of which carried the title *The Differences between Comrade Togliatti and Us*.

The CPC evidently was attempting to win allies among the foreign communist parties as its quarrel with its neighbour escalated, for these attacks though clearly aimed at the USSR by implication were relatively restrained, and the above pamphlet ended with an appeal to the CPI to mend its ways and see the light. The crucial incident which made the breach irreparable occurred in October 1962 (just preceding the Cuban crisis) when the Chinese became involved in military conflict with India over some barren Himalayan rocks on their disputed joint border and the Soviet government leaned towards the viewpoint of its Indian diplomatic ally rather than the stance of its communist comrades.

If the Italian communists were accused of revisionism, the CPSU and Soviet government were accused of worse. Once they had moved on to open attack, the Chinese framed their indictment in ideological terms and denounced actions that were said to follow from ideological deficiencies. Supposed revisionism was the starting point, but the most intolerable behaviour was said to consist of two things. Firstly, the Soviets were said to be cringing before US power, acting according to imperialist demands and thereby reneging on their internationalist duty.

'Peaceful co-existence' in the Soviet style – of 'states with different social systems' – was denounced as a heinous heresy. They were attacked for backing down and withdrawing their nuclear missiles from Cuba, 'a second Munich' (and for putting them there in the first place) and later for signing the test-ban treaty. 'What we have heard from China ... has been less and less the rational argument in the controversy over the means and ends of socialism and more and more the cry of offended and enraged national pride, the cry of the wounded and humiliated.'[9]

The Chinese reiterated the demand that the USSR should be willing to risk nuclear war, which would not be so terrible and would certainly destroy imperialism. However, in Mao's words, imperialism was a 'paper tiger' and would not dare to initiate a conflict if it were dealt with firmly and robustly confronted. The Chinese were not impressed by Khrushchev's reminder that this paper tiger had atomic teeth.

The second principal accusation used the metaphor of an orchestra with the CPSU purporting to be the conductor – trying to force other parties to 'follow the Soviet baton' or suchlike. Indeed the rivals fought a paper war to try to win the parties of the world over to their side of the divide, or, in the Chinese case, to split them if they could not do so. Only the Albanian ruling party lined up with the Chinese (Romania remained neutral), but they also won the allegiance of the Indonesian communists, and succeeded in splitting the Communist Party of India in two between pro-Soviet and pro-Chinese factions. The Eastern Europe regimes (with the partial exception of Romania) of course had no choice in the matter, but the Chinese arguments made very little impact upon West European communists or those located elsewhere. No real splits occurred, only insignificant breakaways to form minuscule sects.

The 'Cultural Revolution'

Matters changed somewhat following the 'Cultural Revolution' initiated by Mao in 1966, though outside China itself this was not of great consequence (the Indonesian communists had been exterminated in the previous year). The impact on Chinese society however was catastrophic. There can be no real doubt that primarily it arose from Mao's determination to regain the power that he had lost to his colleagues, but equally no doubt that the very name given to it reveals ideological considerations as a primary driving force.

The 'Great Proletarian Cultural Revolution' was formally launched in August 1966 at a plenary session of the CPC Central Committee. Its 'Sixteen Points' provide a synopsis of its ostensible purposes and include 'A new Stage in the Socialist Revolution', 'The Main Currents and the Zigzags', 'Put Daring Above everything Else and Boldly Arouse the Masses', 'Let the Masses Educate Themselves in the Movement', 'Firmly Apply the Class Line of the Party', 'Be on Guard against Those Who Brand the Revolutionary

Masses as "Counter-Revolutionaries"', 'Take Firm Hold of the Revolution and Stimulate Production' (this proved to be the deadest of dead letters), 'The Thought of Mao Zedong is the Guide for Action in the Great Proletarian Cultural Revolution'.

The image that persists of the 'Cultural Revolution' is of massed ranks of youthful Red Guards waving Mao's 'Little Red Book', supposed to contain all political wisdom, and screaming its slogans with all the power of their lungs. As the character of the 'Little Red Book' symbolises, the ideology of the 'Cultural Revolution' was one of ultra-simplification. It was also one of ultra-voluntarism. All culture was to be directed towards didactic purposes in a fashion which made the depths of Stalinist social realism appear flexible and sophisticated by contrast. Little was acceptable other than heroic communists under Maoist inspiration slaughtering feudal and imperialist evildoers or undertaking impossible prodigies of socialist achievement. Cultural and ideological remnants of the past were to be utterly uprooted – Confucianism was a particular target.

So, to a large degree were industrial workers, whose material demands were characterised as 'sugar coated bullets', and their persecution resulted in a general strike in Shanghai in early 1967, put down with much bloodshed, and revolt in the industrial complex of Wuhan, where the local garrison rebelled in support of the workers and required a full-scale military assault, lasting a fortnight, to suppress. Heavy fighting also occurred elsewhere, and in one instance rival gangs of Red Guards fought each other with tanks and artillery.[10]

There was more. Mao was concerned that Chinese society might be in danger of repeating the degenerate course which Soviet society was presumed to have followed – bureaucratisation, loss of revolutionary élan, slide into revisionism, subordination to imperialism and eventual capitalist restoration (his party enemies were accused of 'following the capitalist road'). The Soviets were eventually declared to have reached that final destination.

Consequently, roving gangs of Red Guards were mobilised to attack, humiliate, molest and sometimes murder anyone in a position of authority who could on the most far-fetched grounds be suspected of disloyalty to Mao's person or, as was more commonly affirmed, his 'thoughts'. The category of victims included artists, academics, intellectuals, managers and, above all, party functionaries, to the extent that production, urban and rural, was disrupted, administration thrown into chaos and party structures wrecked. Only the People's Liberation Army and the security service were exempt from this form of purge: the former was used to back up the Red Guards where necessary – and eventually, once they had served their purpose, to disband them.

Although carried out in a very different manner, the Cultural Revolution fulfilled a similar function to the Stalinist purges of the 1930s. It both got rid of oppositional or potentially oppositional elements and, equally importantly, broke up and atomised the administrative apparatus (apart from the army), and destroyed the possibility of corporate consciousness forming independent of the ruling group. Not accidentally, as in the 1930s, communists were the principal victims. How mentally competent Mao himself was by this time is open to question – though he was supposed to be leading the Cultural Revolution he scarcely ever spoke in public, and when he did he appeared to be rambling.

International Maoism

The Cultural Revolution was a horror story, yet it was this, rather than the Sino–Soviet dispute, which turned Maoism into a widespread international movement, although composed of rival quarrelling sects and lacking any institutional structures. Beijing never awarded any of the diverse groups its franchise or, it would seem, tried to control them and there was no equivalent to the Third International. The attraction of the Cultural Revolution, seen through an ideological distorting lens, was its apparent spontaneity, the belief that here the masses were on the move, smashing bureaucracy and reasserting the pristine values of the Bolshevik Revolution.

Some quite sophisticated thinkers in the West were taken in or carried away by their own enthusiasm. One such was Rossana Rossanda, the leading figure in the Italian communist dissident group, named after its journal *Il Manifesto*.

> Before [the sociological aspect of the matter] is the idea of securing an all-round development which, by making the whole of society go forward together, destroys at the very roots the social inequality resulting from a certain conception of growth based on according priority to certain sectors and on the division of labour ... 'Politics in command' aims at changing radically ... the state of historical development, the totality of relations between men .... More correctly, it is a refusal to bow to any objectivity but that of the growth of the revolution.[11]

Maoist groupings, sometimes calling themselves parties, appeared in most Western European countries, and even a couple in the East,[12] and some in the USA as well. Maoists were prominent in the *événements* in Paris in 1968 and thereafter, as well achieving a significant presence in the student political milieux of the UK and Germany. Naturally, after China's turn to the right following its accommodation with the USA (which precipitated a quarrel with the Albanian regime), and especially after the fall of Mao's designated successors (which ended the Albanian relationship), Maoism as such quickly faded in the West, though it was to leave behind a significant intellectual heritage.

Orthodox Marxism–Leninism and its rivals in the 1960s

It would be an exaggeration to claim that the Soviet-orientated movement of those years was intellectually sterile, but certainly in an institutional sense it produced nothing of great moment and was mainly concerned with interpreting contemporary realities in the light of party orthodoxy or making adjustments to it when absolutely unavoidable. Exceptions tended to be relatively isolated individuals within its ranks such as Eric Hobsbawm or, most famously, Louis Althusser (though he had some sympathy, apparently, for Maoism).

In 1961, following publication in the USSR, the Foreign Languages Publishing House distributed a text entitled *Fundamentals of Marxism-Leninism*, edited by the old Stalinist apparatchik Otto Kusinen and described as 'a manual'; according to the blurb 'the most complete and authoritative account yet published of the theory and practice of world Communism' as a 'single and integral science'. It covered everything from ancient philosophy to the prospects of extended longevity and certainly represents a handy digest of official theory at the time – Stalin is altogether airbrushed from the picture.

Interestingly the volume acknowledges that it 'cannot be free from shortcomings and defects' and invites readers' criticisms (p.14), and, indeed, outside the USSR party orthodoxy was being stretched, principally by the Italian communists in an endeavour to make the ideology more flexible. Even in Eastern Europe, Moscow was prepared to guide its dependent parties with a looser rein (in the case of Romania very loose, although it bordered the USSR) as long as its own interests were not endangered.

MARXIST REVIVAL

In the 1960s and early 1970s, Marxism experienced an ideological revival in the West – Marxist texts were published in great quantity, often by the most eminent publishing houses; it was much studied and debated in the academic milieu, addressed by commentators in leading newspapers. A lot of this was related to the prison writings of the leading Italian communist Antonio Gramsci, imprisoned under Mussolini from 1927 almost up to his death ten years later. Although an orthodox Leninist, Gramsci rejected the crudities that increasingly passed for social analysis under the Comintern,[13] and explored in historical context and in detail the means through which class power gained 'hegemonic' acceptance at the popular level – no less important than the coercive force at the bourgeois state's disposal. His writings opened up fresh levels of understanding.

Although many Western communist parties were to a degree influenced by and participated in these developments, most of the initiative and the market for Marxist publications came from, on the one hand, individual thinkers such as Herbert Marcuse, Jean-Paul Sartre or Perry Anderson, and on the other, from political groups which had nothing to do with the communist parties. Among these groups were the communists' traditional enemies on the left, the Trotskyites, who, having since Trotsky's assassination in 1940 barely existed on the fringes of the left underwent a striking revival. The Trotskyite movement, such as it was, persecuted to extinction in the communist states, was intensely fragmented between rival centres and rival leaders in the parts of the world where it continued to exist.

Although the different Trotskyite groups mutually excommunicated each other and accused their opponents of all manner of political sins, in actual fact the issues which distinguished them were more ones of political strategy, or even tactics, than of principle or ideology; but in the overheated pressure-cookers of theory that characterised these organisations, what started as minor differences soon escalated into unrestrained denunciation followed by split. A casual reader of their publications would have found it difficult to understand what the antagonisms were about.

All regarded Trotsky as their theoretical inspiration, alongside Lenin the greatest Marxist of the twentieth century in their view. All followed his characterisation of the USSR – and by extension the other communist regimes – as a 'deformed (or degenerate) workers' state' (because despite its political odiousness it continued with socialised property relations), Stalin as the gravedigger of the revolution and 'socialism in one country' as the grave in which it had been interred.

All regarded political (emphatically *not* social) revolutions in these states as necessary to destroy the Stalinist incubus and allow the workers to re-appropriate their revolutionary heritage. Trotskyite parties would have to lead such revolutions. In the 1960s, though never very formidable, they grew substantially and made a considerable impact upon the Western left, as well as producing a number of able theorists. Their resurgence, like the emergence of the Maoists, was a sign of growing disillusionment with official communism as represented by the USSR and the Soviet bloc – this at a time when Marxism and the idea of revolution was increasingly popular with a wider audience. Paradoxically, it was the example of two Soviet-aligned regimes, those of Cuba and North Vietnam, under threat and attack from US imperialism, which had helped to inspire that popularity.

This shift in the ideological climate of the West had inspired in the 1960s the emergence of a school of 'revisionist' historians – not 'revisionist' in the sense in which Marxists used the term, but in relation to the hitherto prevailing Western interpretation of the Cold War. An iconic example was David Horowitz's *Free World Colossus* (also published as *From Yalta to Vietnam*).[14] These reinterpretations suggested that the lead in instigating and pursuing the Cold War was taken not by the USSR but on the contrary by the USA embarked on a project of economic, political and military expansionism.

1968

However, disillusionment with the Soviet bloc and official Marxism–Leninism was greatly deepened by what occurred in Czechoslovakia in August 1968. The 'Prague Spring' earlier in the year had aroused great hope and expectation. The post-Stalinist political structures (more rigid in Czechoslovakia than in neighbouring Hungary and Poland) had been dismantled and, though the Communist Party political monopoly still remained in place, genuine democratisation was in process and appeared to promise more – 'socialism with a human face' in the words of Alexander Dubcek, the Communist Party of Czechoslovakia's (CPCz) general secretary. According to the Action Programme adopted in April,

The Party's goal is not to become a universal 'caretaker' of the society, to bind all organisations and every step taken in life by its directives. Its mission lies primarily in arousing socialist initiative, in showing the ways and actual possibilities of communist perspectives, and in winning over all workers for them through systematic persuasion as well as by the example of communists. ...

The main thing is to reform the whole political system so that it will permit the dynamic development of socialist social relations ... The basic structure of the political system must, at the same time, provide firm guarantees against a return to the old methods of subjectivism and high-handedness from a position of power.[15]

The Warsaw Pact invasion[16] was designed to put a stop to all that – for it would set a bad example. Effective abolition of the censorship, was, according to the Soviets, allowing anti-socialist tendencies to proliferate and rampage. The contrast with Romania is instructive. Although the Romanian regime went its own way diplomatically[17] (and refused to take part in the invasion), it had remained thoroughly Stalinist in character and in no way was likely to provide a pole of attraction for reforming dissidents in Eastern Europe or the Soviet Union itself. In 1971, Brezhnev,[18] the Soviet leader, was to produce the infamous 'Brezhnev Doctrine' (the mirror of the 'Truman Doctrine'), asserting the right of the USSR to intervene in any socialist state where developments appeared to be putting socialism at risk. The excuse in this case was that dark forces from the North Atlantic Treaty Organization (NATO) were undermining it in Czechoslovakia and corrupting the CPCz.

The Czechoslovak events were a fresh reminder that in the countries which have taken the path of socialist construction the internal anti-socialist forces ... may in certain conditions become active and even mount direct counter-revolutionary action in the hope of support ... from imperialism.
...
It was an attempt to strike in this way at the positions of socialism in Europe as a whole and to create favourable conditions for a subsequent onslaught against the socialist world by the most aggressive forms of imperialism.[19]

The invasion did not provoke a mass exodus of members from Western parties, in the manner of Hungary. Firstly, there had been no bloodbath such as in the former case and, secondly, most of these parties, with greater or lesser vigour, officially deplored the invasion, forcefully in the case of Italy and with great reluctance in France. Nevertheless, there was severe demoralisation, reflected in the emergence in the next decade of what came to be known as 'Eurocommunism', the biggest ideological shift among communists since Stalin won out in the USSR. Of course not all disapproved of the Soviet action and there were some who endorsed it enthusiastically. Even among those who did not, probably a majority preferred to leave matters at that and pass on to next business. Ties with the CPSU may have been loosened, but they were never severed as long as the Soviet regime lasted.

Meantime orthodox communism had brought further discredit upon itself among revolutionary-minded youth by the behaviour of the PCF during the *événements* of May 1968. As student riots in Paris were followed by paralysing strikes across the country and the Gaullist Fifth Republic tottered, the Party, though it did not dissociate itself, did all in its power to restrain and channel the militancy into reformist courses and poured scorn on the anarchist, Maoist and Trotskyite student leaders who had ignited the conflagration, accusing them of being ultra-lefts at best, provocateurs at worst. For a time in the aftermath, these groups assumed a high political and media profile, assisted by government attempts to suppress them. Their legacy was to be very important indeed – at least in the cultural sphere – for out of them came many of the exemplars and the main contingent of the missionaries of postmodernism.

By 1973, whatever the continuing institutional strength of the communist regimes, official communist ideology, whether of the Soviet or the Chinese flavour, was in ruins. The Soviet Union and its bloc had forfeited virtually all moral credibility; in Eastern Europe Nicolae Ceauçescu's regime never had any; in Poland the exploitation of antisemitism by Gomulka, the hero of 1956, had failed to prevent his leadership being overthrown in 1970 by economically-provoked popular unrest. In 1972 Mao had embraced the Great Satan both literally and figuratively. If the Cuban and Vietnamese communists continued to enjoy respect at home and abroad, that was essentially because they represented their countries' national independence in the face of foreign threat.

10
Conservatism and fascism

Placing these two ideologies in the same chapter does not mean to imply that the two are identical or even necessarily very close together. They had, however, indulged in a significant degree of mutual accommodation during the pre-war years, and both, though to very different degrees, were in an invidious position following the Allied victory. The impact of openly proclaimed conservatism on public affairs (except in Britain) was very limited and that of fascism quite negligible. They can therefore be dealt with in more summary fashion.

CONSERVATISM

Throughout Europe, as the smoke cleared from the battlefields, conservatism as an ideological position was very much on the back foot. In many if not most parts of formerly occupied Europe, it was seriously tainted by collaboration with the Occupation, and even in the UK where that was not the case, its policies were viewed as being responsible for the miseries of the interwar years.

However, even if the ideology was then at a discount, the interests and classes which had sustained it had by no means vanished from the scene. They might have done so, as happened to their counterparts in Eastern Europe, if the social processes triggered by the Liberation and the Allied victory had been allowed to run their course. What actually happened was that the Anglo–American power intervened to ensure their preservation, assisted in this case by Stalin, who, probably realistically, although his motives were purely selfish, forbade the re-emergent communist parties to push their strength to revolutionary conclusions.

Taking liberated Europe as a whole, although the situation varied very greatly from country to country, such classes consisted of landowners, leading industrialists and bankers, significant sections of the classic lower-middle classes (peasants, craftspeople, shopkeepers, white-collar employees) and, certainly not least, the Catholic Church, which was itself a major landowner with possession of widespread financial interests. They were reinforced by right-wing refugees from Eastern Europe and, very significantly in Germany, the expellees from Poland, with its redrawn frontiers, from western Czechoslovakia and similar pockets elsewhere.

POLITICAL CATHOLICISM

The Pope during the Second World War was Eugenio Pacelli (Pius XII), whose rule during that period remains very controversial. He had been the Apostolic

Nuncio to Germany in the 1930s and apparently on excellent terms with the regime's leaders. A later biography, much attacked and later partially retracted by its author, designated him 'Hitler's Pope'.[1] At any rate, from the time of his papal election in 1939 he was undoubtedly 'Mussolini's Pope' and certainly had no problems with Franco, Salazar, Pétain, Tiso or the unspeakable Ustasi wartime regime in Croatia.

Following 1945, the Vatican had abated nothing of its anti-communism or claim to spiritual absolutism (a Catholic priest in the *Reader's Digest* during the 1950s noted that error had no rights against truth); it also sustained a dislike for democracy, putting up with it as the lesser evil – although it was adaptable enough to accommodate, albeit uneasily, to the communist regime in Poland.

It possessed enormous wealth and an enormous publicity apparatus – countless periodicals everywhere outside the communist bloc, a radio station in the Vatican, not to mention its innumerable centrally-directed clergy – and did not hesitate to make political interventions whenever it could. Very soon parties on the continent were reconstituted to represent conservative interests, though they never used that name and were generally, to gain electoral credibility, obliged to strike attitudes that amounted not merely to liberalism but even social liberalism. The term that was used throughout Western Europe to cover a basically conservative agenda within a social wrapping was 'Christian Democracy' – and by 'Christian' was meant Catholic (even though prior to the war the more conservative elements in the Church had strong reservations about specifically Catholic political parties, fearing they might prove a back door to the Church's democratisation).

Thus in Germany the old Centre Party had, at Pacelli's urging, gone along with the initial Hitler agenda, even if with some reluctance, and dissolved itself at the Führer's command. Its hidden remnants were now reconstituted as the Christian Democratic Union and allied to its Bavarian counterpart, the fervently right-wing Christian Social Union (CSU). Strongly backed by the US occupation authorities while the country remained under Allied supervision, it achieved, with a minor partner, a (perfectly fair) electoral majority within the US-designed Federal Republic covering the western half of Germany secured by the West. It did have some comparatively thin historical credibility to give it ideological legitimacy – its leader, Konrad Adenauer former mayor of Cologne, had been imprisoned briefly by the Nazis (under relatively comfortable conditions) and it could claim that the anti-Hitler conspirators of July 20 1944 had shared its outlook – but always the central plank in its programme was anti-communism. It soon outlawed the re-emerged KPD and refused to recognise the GDR, which it termed 'middle Germany' (eastern Germany being the provinces lost to Poland).

The Italian counterpart, which the Church took a direct hand in establishing, was also called Christian Democracy (Democrazia Christiana, DC). It could trace its ancestry to some rather marginal elements of the forces fighting the German occupation and, further back, the Catholic party of the Popolari, which had opposed Mussolini in the early 1920s until the Vatican told them to stop. It secured its electoral ascendancy by means of its Catholic appeal and especially by anti-communism, for Italy, very unlike Germany, had a powerful and well-respected Communist Party, always threatening to overtake the DC, and the DC had always to rely on coalition partners motivated by the same overriding fear of the red menace. Before long it became invincibly corrupt, gaining votes by means illegitimate as well as regular, developing close links with criminal establishments such as the Sicilian Mafia and Neapolitan Camorra.

In France the Christian Democrat equivalent did not actually use that name, but called themselves the Mouvement Républicain Populaire (MRP) – some of its opponents sarcastically referring to it as the Mouvement des Refoulés Pratiquants (Movement of Repressed Churchgoers).[2] The MRP never made an impact similar to the DC or the CDU, but proved indispensable at the time in attracting enough conservative-minded voters who hesitated to vote for the Gaullists, and so kept the communists out of government even though the Parti Communiste Français (PCF), despite an electoral system designed to disadvantage it, constituted the biggest single party in the assembly and represented the largest bloc of voters.

However, significant changes were to take place in the Church following Pacelli's death and the election in 1958 of Angelo Roncalli (John XXIII). This Pope summoned the Second Vatican Council, 1962–65, which brought about significant changes in a modernising and liberalising direction in Catholic practices and political attitudes, although none of that could alter the institution's essential conservatism and misogyny. Even so, it provoked a fierce reaction among factions of ultra-conservative clergy such as the Society of St Pius X (reactionary even by papal standards, 'imbued with clerical fascism and theocratic antisemitism') led by the Pétainist archbishop Marcel Lefebvre, and eventually disowned by the Vatican, with Lefebvre excommunicated.

The principal concerns of this organisation – which in time succeeded in establishing itself all around the world, not least in French Canada and the USA (although many Catholics there, both laity and clergy, were under attack for excessive liberalism) – were with matters of clerical and ritual observance. It did, though, also have a strong politically reactionary orientation, and its adherents circulated easily between it and politically ultra-conservative and unmistakably fascist organisations, such as Catholic Cité, of which more later. Lefebvre himself applauded Franco, Salazar and Pinochet.

THE USA

Even in 1945 the stronghold of conservatism, ideologically, politically and socially, remained in the USA, and was enormously strengthened by the Cold War despite the fact that the latter was prosecuted under the flag of liberalism. The Cold War soon reignited passionate hatred of communism and the wartime ally was quickly defined as the fount of all evil as its ideological, political and military power spread throughout Eastern Europe and Asia.

McCarthyism

Such was the background to the political/ideological storm that overtook the USA during the late 1940s and early 1950s. It was exemplified by the rise (and eventual fall) of the drunken demagogue Joseph McCarthy, the junior senator from Wisconsin, and the hysteria which he played a leading part in evoking, though clearly the combustible material had to be present in public consciousness before he could set it alight. In the *Penguin Dictionary of Politics* of the 1950s, McCarthyism is defined as hostility to liberalism, as it laid waste the practice of free speech and open debate in the US media and academy while active persecution of real and alleged communists terrorised many others through fear of being associated in any way, real or imaginary, with such ideas.[3] McCarthy himself eventually came unstuck when he overreached himself and began accusing military leaders of harbouring communist tendencies.

It would seem that the sophisticated mandarin George Kennan and the rabid senator could have little in common intellectually, but it was the former who had laid the groundwork, for he had insisted that a key Soviet strategy would be to penetrate and ideologically corrupt organisations with ostensibly liberal aims.

Conservative regroupment

McCarthy was a northern politician, but the reservoir of sentiment favourable to conservative ideology was concentrated in the South. The rigours of segregation were maintained in the southern states of the union and its politicians, the most hard-right in the country, were anything but democrats despite their alignment for historical reasons with the Democrat party. It was Democrat Congressional and Presidential support (albeit opportunist) for desegregation and public welfare in the 1960s that brought about the classic realignment of the south with the Republicans. In 1964 these forces succeeded in achieving a Republican presidential candidate after their own heart, Barry Goldwater, whose autobiography, ghost-written by Brent Bozell, William F. Buckley's brother-in-law, was entitled *The Conscience of a Conservative*.

At least it could be said that Goldwater (or Bozell) left the readers in no doubt about the intended policies, which included race relations, labour relations, education and foreign relations.[4]

On the first of these –

Nothing could so far advance the cause of freedom as for state [that is, not federal] officials throughout the land to assert their rightful claims to lost state power; and for the federal government to withdraw promptly and totally from every jurisdiction which the Constitution reserves to the States.

Social and cultural change, however desirable, should not be effected by the engines of national power. Let us, through persuasion and education, seek to improve institutions we deem defective .... Any other course enthrones tyrants and dooms freedom ... I deny that there *can* be a conflict between States' Rights, properly defined and civil rights, properly defined.

It was a not-very-subtle bid for the Dixie bigot vote.

On labour rights – 'Unions exist, presumably to confer economic advantages on their members, not to perform political services for them. Unions should therefore be forbidden to engage in any kind of political activity.'

On education –

As long as the federal government acknowledges responsibility for education, for example, the amount of federal aid is bound to increase, at the very least, in direct proportion to the cost of supporting the nation's schools. *The only way to curtail spending substantially, is to eliminate the programs on which excess spending is consumed.* [Original emphasis]

On foreign affairs –

If ... our primary objective is victory over Communism, we will, as a matter of course, view such organisations as the UN as a possible *means* [original emphasis] to that end.

...

We should declare the world Communist movement an outlaw in the community of civilized nations. Accordingly, we should withdraw diplomatic recognition from all Communist governments including that of the Soviet Union, thereby serving notice on the world that we regard such governments as neither legitimate nor permanent.

And in general –

an egalitarian society – an objective that does violence both to the charter of the Republic and the laws of Nature. We are all equal in the eyes of God but we are equal *in no other respect.* [Original emphasis] Artificial devices for enforcing equality among unequal men must be rejected.

Goldwater performed disastrously in the presidential election, but proved to be a sign of times to come. One of the speakers at a meeting of Goldwater supporters in the aftermath was a certain Ronald Reagan and, in addition, the mailing lists established in the course of the campaign 'became the foundation of all subsequent organised political activity on the part of American conservatives'.

Religious conservatism

American conservatism came in two varieties, religious and secular, although even the secular had a good element of religious admixture – scarcely any candidate of any politics could hope to be elected to public office without asserting his or her religious conviction. Not accidentally, the Cold War enemy was usually designated as 'Godless communism'.

There were of course numerous liberal (in the American sense) believers and clergymen, but the Protestant Christian right was very 'right' indeed. It asserted aggressively, and as divinely sanctioned, the classic ideological tenets of American conservatism – the intrinsic superiority of the USA and its individualistic values including firearm ownership; the odiousness of public welfare provision and trade unionism; the merit of totally unregulated markets, including and especially those in labour; and, paradoxically (but the paradox was disregarded), the invigilation of private behaviour according to religious criteria. Had they had their way, the USA would have become Margaret Atwood's Republic of Gilead.[5]

In the forefront of Catholic conservatives, a man after Pacelli's own heart (and indeed his personal friend) was the Cardinal Archbishop of New York, Francis Spellman, friend of Republican leaders. He used his office shamelessly to pursue a conservative political agenda and keep the USA internally and externally on a right-wing course, declaring that 'a true American can neither be a communist nor a Communist condoner' and that 'the first loyalty of every American is vigilantly to weed out and counteract Communism and convert American Communists to Americanism'. Spellman was an enthusiastic supporter of Joe McCarthy and thoroughly disapproved of Vatican II, though he had enough sense to decline J. Edgar Hoover's request to denounce Martin Luther King.

The secular conservatives, whatever their private views and references to 'godless communism', operated in their ideological discourse mostly, though by no means entirely, on the secular plane. This was demonstrated by the text with which one of their leading exponents, William F. Buckley, himself a Catholic and cultural philistine, made his name: *God and Man at Yale: The Superstitions of 'Academic Freedom'* (1951) – a somewhat peculiar title for a political manifesto. Being seriously wealthy, which he enhanced further with stock-market fraud (he escaped with a heavy fine), he went on to found and subsidise a journal, the *National Review*, in which conservative values and arguments were tirelessly expounded and which formed a regular stable of writers and helpers of similar disposition including George Lincoln Rockwell, later founder of the American Nazi Party. It would be no distortion to characterise Buckley as the USA's leading conservative ideologue (naturally, he hated Vatican II) rather than the intellectually challenged McCarthy, despite the latter's widespread malign influence. Buckley, who appreciated the senator's 'vivid moral sense', nevertheless admired him, asserting in *McCarthy and his Enemies* (1954) that 'McCarthyism ... is a movement around which men of good will and stern morality can close ranks.'

Buckley came out strongly against the Civil Rights movement, arguing that 'claims of civilization (and of culture and community) superseded those of universal suffrage', writing in the August 1957 editorial of his journal, the central question that emerges ... is whether the White community in the South is entitled to take such measures as are necessary to prevail, politically and culturally, in areas where it does not predominate numerically? The sobering answer is Yes – the White community is so entitled because, for the time being, it is the advanced race.

He was no less opposed to democracy in South Africa, which would threaten 'a return to barbarism'. Later, Buckley, a talented publicist more than an original thinker even in conservative terms, opportunistically reversed his stance, though not neglecting to accuse liberals with their 'utopian egalitarian enticement and incitements' of responsibility for the 1968 ghetto riots.

KIRK AND OAKESHOTT

The other theoretical exponents who are worth considering, though who figure much less in the public eye, were Russell Kirk in the USA (Leo Strauss is discussed in the following section) and Michael Oakeshott in the UK. The former attempted an in-depth defence of conservatism with *The Conservative Mind* in 1953, taking as his starting point not any of the writings of the conservatively-minded Founding Fathers such as Alexander Hamilton, but the writings of Edmund Burke, of whom he was a passionate admirer. He helped Buckley found the *National Review* and himself eventually converted to Catholicism, and was praised by Ronald Reagan in 1981 as having 'inspired a generation'.

His basic attitude is probably best summed up by his summary of the attitudes of an earlier conservative, Henry Adams, with which he is in agreement: 'Human activity reached its point of greatest intensity in the Middle Ages, with the Crusades and the cathedrals; since then its true vitality has been waning rapidly.'[6] He thought that the Liberal government reforms in Britain between 1906 and 1911 constituted 'morbid symptoms of social ennui'.[7]

However, nostalgia for the Middle Ages alone would not have made him an esteemed conservative thinker. Although not very much regarded at the time, his talent was to provide an ideological coherence for a revived conservative project in the US; 'we must be frankly and nobly reactionary', he declared, and 'To the civilized man the rights of property are more important than the right to life'.[8] However he does not like capitalism either – 'The fulfilment of the aspirations of Bentham and Mill ... is communism. Rockefeller and Marx were merely two agents of the same social force.'[9]

The challenge was to discover or invent a convincing reason for authoritarian rule by propertied elites, and this is found in the incapacity and ill will of the masses:

the immorality and selfishness of a populace all too ready to assume that they now have only to obtain their share of an inexhaustible common fund without too much personal exertion [this is a reference to Britain in the late 1940s] ... schooled beyond their proper worldly prospects or indeed beyond their intellectual capacities, lacking property, lacking religious faith, lacking ancestors or expectation of property, seeking to gratify by the exercise of power their loneliness and their nameless hungers.[10]

It reads like a deliberate caricature, but is intended in all seriousness. Leisure, he asserted, was an 'indispensable preparation for leadership'.

Kirk wanted a reassertion of reactionary values and appears to have seriously believed that the masses would welcome this once they appreciated its benefits: '[People] will writhe in the agonies of social ennui until religious consolation, family affections, property and permanence are restored to them.'[11] 'The salvation of civilization is contingent upon the revival of something like the doctrine of original sin.'[12] The 'doctrine of grace' must be central to civilisation. The ruling elite-to-be, with their indispensable leisurely preparation for leadership, are presumably exempted from the burden of original sin or at least feel it more lightly.

The UK and Oakeshott

The UK was something entirely different. Although Evelyn Waugh complained that the problem with British conservatism was that it never put the clock back by a single minute, E. H. Carr wrote of 'a typical English conservative who when scratched turns out to be 75 per cent a liberal',[13] and the Conservative Party, though hammered in the 1945 election, felt no requirement to rename itself – the deadly stigma of Nazi collaboration (or in its case, appeasement) had been adequately washed off by the war and Churchill's role as its wartime leader, but this was not enough to save it from temporary electoral disaster. It rode with the tide of social legislation and in due course returned to power (but on a minority vote), where it continued to apply that legislation and made little effort to dismantle it. Though the representative and defender of property and privilege, it had acquired enough of a reforming tradition in the later nineteenth century to present itself as a socially progressive force.

It maintained good relations with the trade union movement of the 1950s, retained a large working-class electorate and was much assisted by the fact that its Labour opponents shared a great part of its values and ideology, not least a commitment to the British Empire and fierce anti-communism. Indeed, it was the Labour Foreign Secretary, Ernest Bevin (whose immoderation startled even his co-thinkers) who took on the leading role in promoting the establishment of NATO.

One notorious example of this continuity of imperial and anti-communist policy was Labour's precise adherence to the policy established by Churchill of reinstating the royal regime in liberated Greece and crushing the communist-led resistance movement, Ellinikós Laïkós Apeleftherotikós Stratós (ELAS, Greek People's Liberation Army), which opposed it and unquestionably enjoyed majority support. The regime, installed as the result of a lengthy and ferocious civil war, was one of extreme conservatism many of whose leading personnel, especially in the military, had been collaborationists between 1940 and 1944. Here, reaction made plain that its intention was to restore the old order, needing no other justification than to wave the anti-communist flag and purport to be suffering Soviet aggression – the expedient of embracing a calculated measure of social liberalism was not required in this case.

Nor was it in the ideas of Michael Oakeshott, the UK's leading conservative (in the uncompromising sense) thinker of those years. Although a deeper theorist, he had a lot in common with Kirk, who quoted him with approval. In 1932, on the eve of the Nazi takeover, Oakeshott had written, 'Democracy, parliamentary government, progress, discussion, and the plausible ethics of productivity are notions – all of them inseparable from Lockian liberalism – which fail now to arouse even opposition, they are not even absurd and exploded, they are uninteresting.'[14] And in 1940 he was referring to 'clap-trap about government by consent'.[15]

Nevertheless, he joined the army in the Second World War. A footnote in his best-known text *Rationalism in Politics* (1962) gives a revealing insight into his attitudes:

> The army in wartime was a particularly good opportunity of observing the difference between a trained and an educated man: the intelligent civilian has little difficulty in acquiring the technique of military leadership and command, but (in spite of the cribs provided: *Advice to Young Officers*, etc.) he always remained at a disadvantage beside the regular officer, the man educated in the feelings and emotions as well as the practices of his profession.[16]

What Oakeshott termed 'rationalism' in politics, by which he meant any political attempt, even the most modest, at social amelioration, was indeed his *bête noire*. He shared the panic among Conservative traditionalists evoked by the Labour victory in 1945 – when one dowager lady is said to have expostulated, 'But *they* have elected a Labour government and *the country* will never stand for that!' Oakeshott shared her sentiments, even if he expressed them in more sophisticated language, writing in 1947,

> the Labour Party has an *incentive* to become despotic, the *means* to become despotic, and ... it has the *intention* of becoming despotic ... a simple plot to establish, not by force but by subterfuge, a single-party system and the slavery from which it is inseparable.[17]

'Rationalism in politics' for Oakeshott meant any move away from hierarchy, habit and tradition, and he denounced it in the following terms:

> The project of ... open diplomacy ... of a civil service whose members 'have no qualifications other than their personal abilities', of a self-con-sciously planned society, the Beveridge Report, the Education Act of 1944, Federalism, Nationalism, Votes for Women, the Catering Wages Act, the destruction of the Austro-Hungarian Empire ... are alike the progeny of Rationalism.[18]

Oakeshott's attitude to politics was essentially an aesthetic one. 'The controlling imagery is one of literary taste or musical skill'[19] – or better still, a conversation, conducted exclusively by *gentlemen* of refined sensibility. 'Oakeshott was a stranger to argument, which he anyway largely disavowed. His expositions have nothing on it …. What they are is rhetoric – a sustained exercise in the art of seduction, not interlocution.'[20] The metaphor for which Oakeshott is best remembered is that of politics as a ship on an ocean, without destination or any specific purpose, where the officers' only responsibility is to remain on an even keel. The obvious retort is to inquire what passenger would be inclined to board such a ship.

Both Kirk and Oakeshott – like most conservatives from Burke onwards, and including T. S. Eliot for all his modernist poetry – were essentially romantics, inhabiting in their imagination a fantasy world of the past made up of chivalrous knights, elegant ladies, virtuous clergymen, well-apprenticed artisans and dutiful serfs; with famine, plague, massacre, heretic burnings, and relentless toil and lice all airbrushed out. This did not prevent them from having, as times changed, a significant and expanding influence.

CONSERVATIVE REGIMES

Around the world, leaving aside the part still under direct colonial rule, a number of regimes remained in existence that could be most conveniently numbered in the conservative category. They included Japan, whose regime was moulded and put in place by the US occupation authorities, who excluded not merely the USSR, which had declared war only a few weeks before the end, but even the UK, which had not been backward in prosecuting the war. The US-designed Japanese constitution[21] was certainly a liberal one, under the sign of a constitutional monarchy, and indeed the dominant conservative party, well financed by the CIA, called itself the Liberal Democrats. Like its Italian counterpart it had significant criminal connections, but it deviated from the standard model in being very interventionist and directive in furthering the interests of the big capitalist enterprises that dominated the Japanese economy. (It is worth noting that the conservative party in Australia was also called the Liberals.)

Across the South Atlantic the Latin American states, the Caribbean, Central America and South America, were societies of drastic social (and in some cases racial) polarisation. All possessed liberal-style constitutions, but with only a few exceptions these were the merest facades for oligarchic rulers, rigorously exploiting their unfortunate masses (overwhelmingly peasants) for the benefit of landowners, merchants and mine owners. The established parties represented merely competing factions of these same oligarchs, sometimes even agreeing to alternate in power.

These arrangements were justified under the flag of tradition, Christianity and, of course, anti-communism. There were a couple of states where the liberal constitution had a measure of reality – Uruguay and Costa Rica – and a number of outright dictatorships in all three of the regions. Mexico was something of an exception, where there had been for decades single-party rule with only minimal electoral fraud (but much corruption) by a party with genuine revolutionary roots – but apart from nationalisation of the oil industry, its economy and society were certainly conservative in keeping an established elite in power, albeit with a very different rhetoric from the others.

Finally, Turkey, Pakistan, South Korea and the Islamic monarchies from the Levant to Afghanistan must be added to our list, though, such as Mexico, Turkey's situation and historical development were eccentric in comparison to the general run of conservative and ultra-conservative regimes.[22] All alike, however, whatever ideological obfuscation they engaged in, represented government of the elite, by the elite and for the elite, with little (if any) concession to the interests of their citizens.

FASCISM

Fascism in 1945 was at its lowest ebb. With the horrors of the Third Reich exposed, it was eviscerated both politically and ideologically, and the state power which had maintained it from France to the Soviet border had been overthrown and obliterated. Nevertheless, it was by no means dead, neither in Europe nor beyond the continent. Indeed, as early as 1951 fascists from 14 European countries met in Malmö, Sweden, and declared themselves collectively to be a 'European Social Movement'. The first two items in their ten-point manifesto were 'Defence of Western Culture against Communism' and 'Creation of a European Empire'; the tenth, 'The Spiritual Regeneration of Man, Society and the State'.[23]

Regimes

Two European powers, neutral in the Second World War, were commonly described as, and could reasonably be judged to fall into, the fascist category, and one of them, Spain, had been a friendly neutral towards the Axis – its regime expected to fall along with it. Certainly the Franco methods of government had all the characteristics of a fascist political system, and its sole legal party, the Falange, was an explicitly fascist one. However, the reservation is that the Falange was not a ruling party but subordinated to a government not composed of its own leaders. The regime also lacked any trace of the populist dimension that classic fascist parties possessed or aimed at, other than the deployment of anti-communist rhetoric – as was the case with its neighbour.

In Portugal there was no openly fascist element at all, and it had been more genuinely neutral. Although political opposition was outlawed, the infrequently permitted showcase elections a sham and the political system not otherwise unlike that of its neighbour and ally, Spain;[24] it could perhaps be more accurately regarded as an ultra-conservative integralist dictatorship. At any rate the workforce and their dependants, in both the Iberian states, suffered strict repression and exploitation.

In one particular respect Portugal and Spain did differ dramatically – Portugal still possessed a very extensive colonial empire (officially it was decreed to be part of Portugal) – an outcome of the earlier failure of the great powers to decide who should seize which parts of it, while Spain retained scarcely any. Portugal had been the last European state to abolish slavery in its colonies – in a real sense it never had – and the savagery of its colonial administration was a byword even before the establishment of the dictatorship in the 1920s. More than anywhere else, the stability of the regime rested upon the super-exploitation of its colonial territories in Africa and Asia.

By the 1950s the white ascendancy regime in South Africa represented a brand of ultra-conservatism which could reasonably be designated as fascist, its purpose being to keep the black majority in their place as a cheap labour reserve, strictly segregated, with minimal political rights. At the end of the war it was administered by the United Party, the political arm of the English-speaking community, but in 1948 a general election gave victory to the *Afrikaner* electorate, descendants of the original Dutch-speaking settlers, represented by the Nationalist Party, which was based upon a secret society, the *Broderbund*.

This party, having achieved power, kept it for the remainder of the regime by means of electoral gerrymandering and applied its ideology of *apartheid*, which translated as 'aparthood'. Under this, segregation between black and white was to be total – likewise for mixed-race, Indians and Chinese – and without any black political rights whatsoever. For public relations sake, the regime leaders did not formally proclaim an ideology of racial superiority – though that was certainly what they believed and their followers were entirely open about – but of cultural superiority and difference; Africans (whom they referred to as 'Bantu') would allegedly be independent and free in their own territories, supposedly less than a tenth of the country and situated in the least attractive rural areas. Elsewhere they were officially only transients and migrants, strictly controlled and admitted solely for labouring purposes. It was a form of conservatism which could reasonably be regarded as having crossed the boundary of fascism, and indeed many of the regime leaders had, pre-war, been enthusiastic Nazi admirers.

The state was a model example of how an effectively fascist regime could well exist within the framework of a bogus parliamentary democracy. For foreign consumption this was justified on two grounds: firstly the communist menace, and secondly the welfare of the African population. It was alleged that they were being treated appropriately according to their lower level of civilisation, disposition to violence and laziness, and overall in line with their real interests. To the north, in the Rhodesias and Kenya, the white settler-ruled polities, formally under British governance but effectively independent in their internal affairs, aspired to imitate the South African example.

Movements and ideologues

Regardless of how these regimes were classified, they were certainly admired by the remnants of fascist and neo-fascist groupings elsewhere in Europe, whose ideologies were based upon anti-communism above all, to a greater or lesser extent upon nostalgia for past glories, and upon racism; with immigrants of various sorts – Turks, Arabs, Pakistanis or Indians, and African–Caribbeans – taking the place of Jews. They exploited so far as they could the failures of post-war liberalism and the phenomenon of low-level social disorder to advocate authoritarian styles of government.

In Germany, the Federal Republic's continued Allied occupation policy had made any advocacy of Nazism, Nazi continuation parties or display of Nazi symbolism illegal. Attempts to form such parties were however made by ex-Nazi veterans such as Otto Remer, who played an important part in suppressing the 20 July plot against Hitler, but they were closed down. Bavaria had been Hitler's stronghold, and so it was for the Neo-Nazis as well. Eventually a party of this kind did succeed in establishing itself (and still exists) by being careful about the form of its rhetoric, wrapping it up in coded messages, and above all by using the magic word 'democratic' in its title. In the 1960s, as the political situation became more turbulent, it achieved considerable electoral gains and made enough impression to cause considerable alarm both in Germany and outside it.

Neo-fascist Italians grouped themselves together in the Movimento Sociale Italiano (MSI, Italian Social Movement), which was led by Valerio Borghese, a minister in Mussolini's last government, the Italian Social Republic (or Sàlo regime) established by the Germans in the north after Mussolini's fall and rescue by German paratroopers. It had a significant electoral base in the especially corrupt and gangster-ridden south of the country and was able to grow and return deputies to the Italian parliament. Unlike the original fascists it behaved itself – more or less – in terms of public violence, but on its fringes there were elements which openly advocated and indulged in terrorist atrocities, aiming to destabilise the parliamentary regime and open the road for a military-backed fascist takeover.

Julius Evola

In the Italian connection, Julius Evola deserves to be mentioned. This was a Sicilian aristocrat, a Dadaist and a close collaborator with the Fascist regime (and the SS), though not a party member and disliking its populist dimension. He was also into spiritualism, mysticism, occultism, Hermeticism, and all manner of superstitious nonsense, including a 'spiritual' version of antisemitism. Undoubtedly he was somewhat mad. After the war, he became (appropriately enough) something of an ideological reference point for European and not only Italian fascists. According to Franco Ferraresi, 'Evola's thought can be considered one of the most radically and consistently anti-egalitarian, anti-liberal, anti-democratic, and anti-popular systems in the twentieth century.'[25]

Evola's belief was in a 'perennial tradition' of macho aristocratic rule which linked the affairs of the world with transcendental realms and had been degraded by modernity – one of his volumes is called *Revolt against the Modern World.* In his own words, 'We are anti-bourgeois because the bourgeois type, while ranking above the proletarian, yet stands inferior to the soldierly-heroic and spiritual-priestly orders.' He favoured a united Europe – on the lines of his thinking – but not a bourgeois one.

> The European *Imperium* will belong to a higher order than the parts which compose it.
>
> …
>
> So far as 'European culture' is concerned it is in these days the stamping-ground of the pragmatic European, the liberal humanist intellectual …. His 'European culture' is … in reality the clothing of the parvenu, his badge of success. … thus Europe from illuminism to communism has become the breeding ground for the very forces which work to destroy everything which is specifically European …. A united Europe, without a communal spiritual identity and sense of direction would become just one more power bloc.
>
> …
>
> Europe must not be a stage towards the Westernisation of the world but a move against it, in fact a revolt against the modern world in favour of what is nobler, higher, more truly *human.*[26]

The UK

Revived fascism in the UK made scarcely any impact during the period under consideration, but it was energetically active underground, debating its strategy and reformulating its personnel and organisation. An attempt by Oswald Mosley to revive his street politics under the label of the Union Movement was stopped by anti-fascist activists at his rallies. He continued nevertheless into the 1950s, propagandising, advocating a union of white states (especially in Europe and South Africa), and proposing that Africa should be shared between white and black citizens – whites to have the perimeter and blacks the interior, but how large an area that was supposed to comprise for each was left unstated. At the same time, anti-immigrant feeling was being exploited both by Mosley and a racist but supposedly non-political organisation, the White Protection League, with its slogan 'Keep Britain White!'

More impatient spirits formed an openly Nazi organisation called the National Socialist Movement (NSM), a slightly more discreet rival named itself the British Movement. Led by a technical education teacher, Colin Jordan, and assisted by John Tyndall, the NSM indulged in uniformed paramilitary antics and affixed in public toilets stickers decorated with swastikas and the slogan 'Despite the Jewish Lie Machine HITLER WAS RIGHT!' The pantomime was broken up by the police, and Jordan and Tyndall imprisoned, but they continued their fascist activities as soon as they emerged.[27]

Not openly fascist, but part of the same milieu, was the League of Empire Loyalists led by A. K. Chesterton, a drunkard who had been one of Mosley's lieutenants and into the 1960s published a private hate sheet called *Candour*.[28] The League formally existed to resist the dismantling of the British colonial empire and its favourite means of publicising itself was to interrupt Conservative Party conferences with noisy stunts. In 1967, largely due to Chesterton's endeavours (though afterwards he was soon sidelined), the various groupings united in uneasy combination to form the National Front, which went on in the subsequent decade to make a noticeable impact.

The USA

The USA had a ready reservoir on which any incipient fascism could draw, in the shape of the long-standing racist terrorists of the Ku Klux Klan and organisations such as the John Birch Society, founded in 1958 and named after a US missionary allegedly killed by the Chinese communists. They regarded even President Eisenhower as a conscious promoter of the 'communist conspiracy' and alleged that the government was under the 'operational control' of communists. Buckley took a long time to dissociate himself from the John Birchers, although he eventually did so in 1965.

In the 1950s, openly proclaimed fascism was scarcely apparent on the US scene – the economically stable and improving socio-economic conditions for the white majority in the decade were scarcely favourable to it, and the anti-communist paranoia that saturated the American culture of the time was adequately catered for by Cold War liberalism. It was the African–American insurgency of the 1960s that incited the most intransigent elements in the proto-fascist milieu into creating an American Nazi Party, led by George Lincoln Rockwell. They tried to turn around the African–American concept of 'Black Power' and campaigned under the slogan of 'White Power'. They generated a certain amount of publicity, but had no significant impact.

Cité Catholique

What was, however, probably the most important strand of fascism to emerge in these years was not a political party at all but a loose network, with a central focus in an organisation called 'Cité Catholique' (not recognised by the church). It was established as early as 1946 by Charles Maurras's secretary, Jean Ousset, and established links with the Society of St Pius X. Ousset was the author of a text, *Le Marxisme-Léninisme*, which developed the concept of a satanic world conspiracy only to be combated by 'a profound faith, an unlimited obedience to the Holy Father and a thorough knowledge of the Church's doctrines', together with counter-revolutionary warfare and systematic torture, which was justified on theological grounds.

It was through linkage with the Organisation de l'armée secrete (OAS, Organisation of the Secret Army), the fascist-minded section of the French military running the dirty war in Algeria, that the Cité Catholique mixed the poisonous brew of theology and torture that in the 1970s was to afflict the future of Latin America. In the late 1950s and early 1960s, particularly after the destruction of the OAS, a number of its activists ended up in Argentina where they teamed up with the Argentinian military and church hierarchy. Their influence in that setting is discussed in the following chapter.

Estimate

In the 1960s, Bertolt Brecht's satirical anti-Hitler play, *The Resistible Rise of Arturo Ui*, was translated into English and the final line rendered as 'The bitch that bore him is in heat again.' This was something of an exaggeration at that point, and despite the scare created by the German National Democratic Party there was no serious likelihood of a fascist revival in the conditions of the 'long boom' and stable Western political systems – left-wing student protests and even the American urban riots and arson could hardly generate enough panic to propel fascist organisations to the forefront. Despite the Vietnam War, the intensity of the Cold War had abated somewhat and the Soviet bloc was seen as less of a menace than it had been earlier, so the fuel for panic anti-communism was also absent.

Nevertheless, the continuing presence of fascist groupings throughout the West showed that the seeds of this ideology were still in the ground, and changing conditions of economic and political crisis might well give them a renewed opportunity to grow.

III

Crisis 1973–91

11
Economic and social conditions

THE USA AND THE WORLD

The point at which the post-war long boom ended can be dated fairly precisely. It was the autumn of 1973, when in response to the Arab-Israeli Yom Kippur war the OPEC oil producers raised the price of oil by a substantial amount. This proved to be the dislodged pebble that set the landslide in motion. At another time, an oil price hike, even a substantial one, would have been unlikely to have had such dramatic results, but the economic structure of the long boom had been suffering erosion since the middle of the previous decade.

The crisis, however, did not strike out of a clear sky. For 25 years the USA had sustained an apparent balance of payments deficit, although until 1972 its balance in terms of exported goods and services was positive – the 'deficit' arose from the outflow of dollars involved in sustaining the USA's economic, political and military imperium over the 'Free World'. A speech in 1965 by the US Secretary of Commerce made this clear:

> Indeed, while it is most difficult to quantify, it is also impossible to over-estimate the extent to which the efforts and opportunities for American firms abroad depend upon the vast presence and influence and prestige that America holds in the world. It is impossible to over-estimate the extent to which private American ventures overseas benefit from our commitments, tangible and intangible, to furnish economic assistance to those in need and to defend the frontiers of freedom … in fact if we were to contemplate abandoning those frontiers and withholding our assistance … I wonder not whether the opportunities for private American enterprise would wither – I wonder only how long it would take.[1]

Moreover, the US public debt, on account of the Vietnam War, had ballooned, causing market disturbance and a drain on reserves, with the result that an unprecedented haemorrhaging of gold caused Nixon in August 1971 to abandon the gold standard that enabled foreign holders of dollars to redeem them for gold and, alongside that, fixed exchange rates, creating adverse repercussions and uncertainty throughout world markets, and destroying the Bretton Woods system which had been in place since the early post-war years. The latter had acted as a stabiliser in the world economic system, although it had primarily benefited the US, whose position was further strengthened by the invention of the 'euro-dollar' market – short-term deposits in European banks which were denominated in dollars rather than the European currencies.

However, by 1971 the outflow of dollars had caused a build-up of US debt obligations to other countries that had come to be seen as intolerable, and the Nixonian measures caused the *New York Times* to declare that the USA must be 'satisfied that other countries have taken the painful steps needed to restore the US financial position in the world'[2] – a startling revelation of its government's ideological outlook.

Keynesian policies in the West had worked on the whole satisfactorily ever since 1945 in ironing out market cycles, but they have one serious disadvantage, namely that they tend to generate inflation. This is not because of any truth in the crass belief 'public borrowing/spending bad; private borrowing/spending good', but because the combination of strong labour movement with full employment establishes the ground for wage demands which employers have to concede and respond to by raising prices.

The sudden rise in costs to business resulting from costlier oil, though it did not generate a slump on the scale of 1929, plunged the USA and the Western economies generally into deep recession, accompanied – and this was something new – by roaring inflation, for recessions traditionally generated price falls, not the opposite. A gentle measure of inflation is a necessary precondition for growth in a market economy; when it rises above a few per cent, it becomes an indication of trouble ahead.

Monetary inflation has always been a method, whether intentional or accidental, for redistributing income, the losers being those on relatively inflexible incomes or reliant on cash savings. If wages and welfare benefits can be held below the inflation rate by one means or another then income gets redistributed upwards. The circumstances which overtook the world economy in the 1970s and continuing into the 1980s enabled governments, pressured by capital, to curb wage growth, usually by generating unemployment and also by other means in addition; and likewise to enforce severe cuts in welfare levels.

It was at this time that there emerged a cohesive theoretical justification for such a strategy (considered in the following chapter), based primarily upon an economic analysis of what was wrong with Keynesianism and advancing unregulated market solutions accompanied by strict regulation of the labour market to the workforce's disadvantage, as the appropriate answer to the crisis.

Reagan, Thatcher and Western Europe

The election of the Reagan administration in the USA in 1980 and the Thatcher government in the UK supplied the political framework in which such policies could be implemented in these two countries. In the USA the administration embarked upon a programme of welfare curtailment, attack on trade unionism accompanied by business deregulation, setting free capital to behave in an increasingly gangster-like fashion and roam unconstrained across the globe wherever pickings were to be had.

In the UK one of the first financial measures taken by the government was to remove exchange controls, permitting unlimited capital movements into and out of the country. Deregulation of the stock exchange presently followed. Welfare spending was cut most severely, and beggars, sometimes of an extremely youthful age, reappeared on the streets of cities and major towns. The character of the labour market was changed utterly as unemployment was made to escalate by government policy. What had been thought impossible for decades was proved to be possible after all.[3] Tight restrictions were clamped on the activity of trade unions and the government-supported defeat of major strikes, principally that of the miners in 1984–85, was followed by the destruction of the coal industry.

That was not the only industry to be devastated – indeed, the industrial basis of the country as it had existed hitherto was laid waste and the supply of services, particularly financial services, made the backbone of the country's economy. Meantime, profitable public services – telecom, electricity, gas, water, oil and aviation – were removed from public ownership and privatised at knock-down prices. Thus was profitability restored to British capital, though a capital very differently structured from what had been the case ten years beforehand. In carrying through these measures without bringing about social mayhem, the government was assisted enormously by the windfall revenue from the lately discovered oil bonanza in the North Sea.

Although not on the same scale as Britain, the Western European continental states moved in a basically similar direction as the requirements of capital overrode those of the social welfare policies which most had pursued since the 1940s. This is what occurred most demonstratively in France, where, despite the election in 1981 of a left-wing government with communists participating in a minor role, plans for economic expansion and enhanced social benefits had to be reversed at the behest of capitalist interests. Though less dramatically, in Germany the Federal Republic shifted the balance of economic power in favour of capital while Italy increasingly sank into a quagmire of corruption and kleptocratic government, the social democrat Benedetto Craxi being at the centre of these developments.

Even these strongholds of social democracy, the Scandinavian countries were not exempt. All of them were compelled to restrict the growth of their welfare expenditures and loosen up their scale of market regulation, the latter being particularly the case after all of them except Norway joined the European Community, formerly the European Economic Community, soon to become the European Union – whose central remit was to expand the scale of marketisation and discourage public enterprise in its member states.[4] In Sweden, independently of this, the Rudolf Meidner Plan, a scheme to enhance the workforce's stake in company ownership and control was repelled.

> If fully carried out, this experiment would have rendered effective control over profitable firms in Sweden to the worker and public organizations. But the Social Democrats made little effort to educate the public about it or win popular support for it. For eight years Sweden's corporate class railed against it constantly.[5]

In these developments, note must be taken of the role of the international financial institutions, the International Monetary Fund and the World Bank, dominated by the USA and acting effectively as arms of US finance capital. Whenever they supplied funding, as to the UK in 1976, it was on condition of drastic reductions in government expenditure, preferably targeted at welfare services in order to loosen up labour markets, and insisting wherever possible on policies of privatisation and greater scope for private capital. All in all, throughout the West, a growing income gap between the top and bottom of society was manifested, both in strict monetary terms and with even greater disparity once the deterioration of the 'social wage', which happened simultaneously, is taken into account. Throughout Western Europe, though economic growth continued overall, it became slower and jerkier, and these years saw a major rolling back of the social gains of the post-war quarter-century.

In the Iberian countries the dictatorships were both overthrown in the 1970s, in Portugal by revolution, and in Spain by its collapse on the death of the dictator. For some months it looked as though revolution in Portugal would be succeeded by communist power, but this was averted, largely through the efforts of German social democracy providing aid and support to the Portuguese Communist Party's social democrat rivals, the Portuguese socialist party being constituted virtually overnight. In Spain the communist party (Parti Communiste de España, PCE), which looked formidable when democracy was instituted, soon declined and broke up into competing factions. Before long, both states were set on a similar track to that of their European neighbours and both joined the European Economic Community, as did Greece, and the enticing promises which both socialist parties had made to the electorate were forgotten.

THE COMMUNIST STATES

On the face of things these events should have greatly increased the attractiveness of 'actually existing socialism' throughout the globe. In reality the very opposite proved to be the case. To be sure, the Soviet bloc secured a number of diplomatic and foreign-policy successes in the course of the 1970s resulting in an expanded sphere of influence, most notably with the US defeat in Vietnam and the disappearance of its puppet regime, but also in Ethiopia, Angola and ultimately (and fatally) in Afghanistan. In addition the outcome of the Helsinki summit in 1975 was generally satisfactory, with Western recognition of the three-decades-old political settlement in Eastern Europe.[6]

The Soviet Bloc

However, all this was deceptive. The foundations of the command economy structure were rotten, though only a few very perceptive commentators realised this. Generally speaking, although the bright promises of Khrushchev's rhetoric had dulled over, the economies of these states appeared perfectly sound to nearly all observers and set for indefinite continuation. Their social structures certainly looked somewhat more problematic and public dissatisfaction might be expected to express itself one way or another; with the possibility of some creeping liberalisation along Hungarian lines as the old apparatchiks died off and more technocratic ones replaced them, but no total reversal of the social order seemed likely to be on the horizon.

The reality of the centrally planned command economy, whether in the USSR or the 'People's Democracies', was that it was plagued by massive and growing inefficiencies, especially in the consumer industries. Quality control was a major problem. It was inadvisable, in the USSR, to buy a consumer durable made on the eve of a public holiday (they were stamped with their date of manufacture), for the workers were hurrying to make up their bonuses and as likely as not to be inattentive to the way the components were being fitted. It was pointed out that more resources went into the repair of defective machinery of all sorts than into the manufacture of new.[7] It was summed up in the joke, 'we pretend to work: you pretend to pay us'.

From the ordinary citizen's point of view the worst aspects were the shortage of consumer essentials and the endless queuing required to obtain them, a burden falling mostly upon the female citizens. Limitation in variety was another, something which became increasingly evident as Western tourism expanded with the easing of the Cold War and, in the states closest to Western borders, reception of Western television broadcasts increased.

Stifling cultural and intellectual conformity, enforced by the penetration of state supervision into every form of collective activity, even recreational ones, was another source of discontent,[8] as demonstrated by the popular acclaim that had greeted the Prague Spring. In Poland, riots over consumer issues forced the resignations of political leaders – and their replacement with others of a similar character – until in 1980–81 the dramatic emergence of a spontaneously formed and politically-orientated trade union, Solidarity, provoked a Soviet-supported military takeover.

Nevertheless, in spite of these realities (published statistical accounts got thinner as the 1970s progressed, to hide the loss of momentum in economic and welfare growth) a slow process of public welfare improvement was occurring throughout most of the bloc and the 'era of stagnation' in the USSR which Brezhnev's regime was supposed to embody might well be viewed from the future as a lost arcadia.

However, the top leadership in the Kremlin were well aware there were serious problems and from the time of Brezhnev's death in 1982 efforts were made to address them. His successor, Yuri Andropov, a formidable individual, made the centrepiece of his reform programme a campaign against corruption – Brezhnev's own family were soon targeted – but he was already a very sick man and lived only a few years. After a very brief period with a stopgap nonentity, in 1985 the Politburo elected Mikhail Gorbachev, a known reformer, to the leading post. In nominating him, Andrei Gromyko declared that in spite of his amiable appearance he had 'iron teeth'. Nothing could have been further from the truth.

The watchwords of Gorbachev's programme were *glasnost* and *perestroika*. The concern of this chapter is with the latter, which means roughly 'restructuring', and represented an attempt to make the command economy work with some efficiency. Put simplistically, it involved the use of market mechanisms to introduce an element of incentive, such as, for example, allowing co-operative outlets to be set up to amend the deficiencies in state-operated outlets and restaurants.

However it was not purely an economic concept but involved 'a dynamic process of interrelated changes in economy politics and society'.[9] In combination with *glasnost* (openness), however, it proved to be lethal to the regime. It generated discontent among the not insubstantial section of the population who were losers from the process, especially when accompanied with the severe restrictions put on the supply of alcohol in an attempt to deal with endemic problems of drunkenness – it was not banned outright, keeping in mind the consequences of US Prohibition earlier in the century, but it became quite difficult to buy even a bottle of wine. The overall consequence was a steep rise in home distilling with accompanying medical dangers and the diversion of raw materials into this activity.

Even more serious was the disruption generated in the state economy by administrative bureaucrats whose interests were being affected adversely and who took steps to sabotage the programme whenever they could, with resulting chaos and shortages. Political discontent could now express itself and the consequence was social turbulence, an attempted coup against Gorbachev in 1991 by traditionalist hardliners, and the subsequent collapse of the regime and breakup of the Union.

Even earlier their nemesis had overtaken the satellite regimes in Eastern Europe. Whatever their merits might have been, they had no chance of competing in open contest with the glittering consumer spectacle of their Western neighbours and what their publics believed to be true about the USA. Consequently, once Soviet protection was withdrawn – as Gorbachev made clear would be the case – there followed the 'velvet revolutions' of 1989, though not very velvety in Romania, where the overthrow was certainly bloody enough.[10] Hopes that these revolutions might be followed by regimes of 'communism with a human face' on the model of the Prague Spring, or even social democracy in the Scandinavian style were soon shown to be fantasies, and even before the USSR's own collapse unrestrained market regimes were back in the saddle – sometimes under governments dominated by former party apparatchiks abandoning the sinking ship.

China and East Asia

The Chinese People's Republic followed a course that was different, yet in some respects similar, and there the process had begun even earlier. Mao's intended successors, the 'Gang of Four', who aimed to continue his ultra-left policies, were quickly disposed of, and power passed into the hands of Deng Xiaoping, a survivor of the top leaders victimised during the Cultural Revolution.

Ironically, Mao's accusation of 'following the capitalist road' turned out in this case to be entirely justified, for that is exactly what Deng and his colleagues did – for under their guidance China moved more and more in a capitalist direction, beginning with peasant-centred market forces being unleashed in agriculture and subsequently moving into other sectors of the economy. There were discernible similarities to Lenin's NEP, especially in relation to agriculture, but this went enormously further. The import of foreign capital was encouraged energetically and 'special economic zones' were established along the coast (including the entire island of Hainan), and in them capitalist principles and methods ruled supreme. It was very successful.

It was supposed to be a socialist market economy, 'socialism with Chinese characteristics', but there was little socialist about it. Deng might have been quoting Marx, who was scornful of 'barrack socialism', when he declared that 'socialism does not mean shared poverty'– but what this meant in reality was that many would remain poor while others got filthy rich. Naturally this generated social differentiation and impoverishment and, in combination with the inflexible political system – for if there was *perestroika* here there was certainly no *glasnost* – gave rise to the great protests of 1989 that demanded political liberalisation.

With these bloodily and comprehensively crushed, the momentum towards a full-blown capitalist system continued, but in this case the CPC retained tight control over the nature of the process and the social order which sustained it. In a number of crucial respects it acted in the same manner as the ex-communist leaders in the former USSR and Eastern Europe who were able to jump on the new bandwagon, though in this case retaining the name, symbols and structure of the party.

China's communist neighbour, North Korea, followed an entirely different course. In a state where Stalin's cult of personality seemed sober in comparison to that of Kim Il Sung, Stalinist systems of government assumed grotesque, even caricaturish proportions. North Korea had for a time had a relatively flourishing economy following recovery from the comprehensive destruction of the Korean War. All that changed when every available resource was diverted into military defence and the civilian economy was reduced to such straits that the population, kept in a continual state of political mobilisation, was driven to the brink of starvation while every sphere of activity was controlled down to the last particular by government decree and invigilation.

If anyone had been asked to predict which East European regime would put up the strongest resistance to its displacement, the answer would surely have been China's sometime ally, Albania. Under the rule of another ultra-Stalinist, Enver Hoxha, the country had refused to proceed along the path of 'revisionist' destalinisation and maintained until his death the political principles of Hoxha's mentor, complete with purges.

However, there was no attempt at rapid or indeed any kind of industrialisation. The country was kept isolated, and deliberately poor and 'backward' by European standards. Thus was social stability maintained, and under its communist trappings a great deal of traditional culture persisted – religion, in particular. Despite this, while Ceauçescu's Romanian regime collapsed in fierce violence, the Albanian one passed into history with scarcely a murmur (perhaps it might have been different if Hoxha had still been living) and the Albanians were quickly introduced to the delights and shortcomings of capitalist consumerism.

THIRD WORLD CATASTROPHE

In certain restricted parts of the Third World during this period, capitalist economies flourished, thanks to their fortunate insertion in the global market; these were Taiwan, South Korea, Hong Kong (still under British rule), Malaysia and Singapore, and in these territories consumption levels and general standards of living attained almost Japanese or Western levels, although their political systems, with the partial exception of Malaysia, were effectively dictatorships.

Elsewhere it was a recital of misery and horror. In Asia, Indonesia under the right-wing dictatorship which succeeded the military putsch and slaughter of communists in 1965, pirate capitalism based on access to the military rulers despoiled the environment and plundered the populace. Burma and the Philippines were variants of the same except that Burma was not a US ally nor integrated into the world market, and the Philippine state was formally a civilian democracy. However, changes of government there, even potentially revolutionary ones, made no difference. India actually was a civilian democracy (in spite of a dictatorial interlude under Indira Gandhi), but differences in wealth and life chances were extreme, government, both local and national, invincibly corrupt, and superstition rampant.[11]

Further west, the Shi'ite Islamic revolution in Iran was of great consequence both politically and ideologically, but in terms of economic or general social circumstances it made little difference beyond replacing one ruling group with another. Its principal impact on the Iranian population was cultural, resulting in strict enforcement of religious behavioural rules and dress codes, with women principally affected, though in comparison with Saudi Arabia it was liberal in this respect. Its new political system was also more democratic than those of most of its neighbours, though that was not saying a great deal.

The Arab states bordering Iran were also comparatively wealthy, and the small states bordering the Gulf very wealthy indeed mainly thanks to their oil production: a sign of their wealth was that they imported substantial quantities of foreign labour. Socially, politically and culturally they were extremely conservative (especially Saudi Arabia) except for Iraq, which was a right-wing developmental dictatorship with a top-dressing of welfare amenities. Up to the end of this period, as with the other neighbouring states, it was an ally of the USA on whose behalf it conducted a long war with Iran during the 1980s.

Further west, Jordan, Syria and Egypt were impoverished authoritarian regimes, Egypt suffering in addition from excess population growth. Lebanon, on the other hand, was very culturally mixed, with a large (and right-wing) Christian population that had grown comparatively wealthy on commerce and finance until it was ruined in the 1980s by Israeli invasion and civil war. Along the Mediterranean littoral, Libya enjoyed comparative affluence thanks to its small population combined with large oil reserves. Tunisia, though governed in authoritarian fashion, was, like Lebanon, tolerably well-off through commerce and the most culturally relaxed of any Muslim state, later on even going so far as to ban the hijab. Algeria and Morocco were countries of extreme contrasts in wealth, and both effectively dictatorships – one military, the other monarchical.

Sub-Saharan Africa and Latin America

It was, however, in sub-Saharan Africa and Latin America that the effects of the global recession were felt at their most disastrous and with the severest political consequences. Rising social discontent provoked revolution leading on to dictatorship and chaos, as happened in Ethiopia, or else intense military repression ('dirty wars') which occurred in the southern cone of South America (see below). Radical regimes in Angola and Mozambique, liberated from Portuguese control after its 1974 revolution, had their economic infrastructure destroyed by South African surrogates, as happened to the revolutionary regime in Nicaragua at the hands of US surrogates.

Even where the worst was avoided, financial meltdown due to collapsing commodity prices on the world market was succeeded by intervention from the IMF (International Monetary Fund) and World Bank, which insisted as the condition of their loans that the governments in receipt of this aid through Structural Adjustment Programmes open up their internal markets, dismantle social security structures and privatise publicly-owned enterprises and marketing organisations (which were admittedly often enough very inefficient and corrupt).[12] These measures invariably had the effect of constricting public welfare and generating poverty and misery (which, apart from saving government revenue and generating market opportunity, had the useful side effect of creating labour reserves willing to toil for lesser reward than formerly).

The tendency towards, in Mike Davis's characterisation, a 'planet of slums' had been ongoing for decades, as populations displaced or attracted from the countryside of the Third World accumulated on the outskirts of major cities in (depending on the language) shanty towns, favelas or barrios lacking in amenities or public utilities. They drew in families and individuals aiming to secure a livelihood as best they might, or in the distant hope of improving their circumstances. The economic circumstances of the 1970s and 1980s greatly accelerated this trend. This was what urbanisation meant in the circumstances of neoliberalism. The period under consideration here was characterised on a global scale by an immense shift in resources and income from poor to rich.

The years 1973–91 marked a historic shift in the twentieth-century economy and, like the Great Slump and the two World Wars, were to produce the most far-reaching political and ideological consequences. Indeed, it was strongly argued that they marked even more than that – not merely the concluding episode of the 'short twentieth century' but the termination of a phase of world history that had begun with the French Revolution.

12
Liberalism and conservatism coalesce

NEOLIBERALISM AND NEOCONSERVATISM

Among the major political ideologies of the twentieth century, liberalism was the great survivor. It comprehensively defeated and overwhelmed its antagonists, fascism and communism, and absorbed its rival, conservatism. In this respect at least, Fukuyama's thesis[1] could not be considered mistaken.

It is these developments that this chapter will be principally concerned with. They are reflected in its terminology, with the appearance of the concepts of 'neoliberalism' and 'neoconservatism.' The liberal ideology, as expressed in the rhetoric of its spokespersons and statespersons, shifted its orientation from a social liberal one to a conservative one – and pulled social democratic parties and institutions along with it.

The determining factor was the economic crisis beginning in 1973, which gave the opportunity to the paladins of laissez-faire economics, who had not gone away during the reign of the Keynesian consensus which was now in the process of unravelling. In the USA there were further considerations; of which the most important was the youth revolt of the 1960s with its comprehensive attack on traditional American traditions, values and superstitions. That was regarded by horrified traditionalists not only as opening the door to every manner of unsavoury vice but criminality as well, supposedly demonstrated in the ghetto riots and the Weathermen terrorists – and even ultimately responsible for the horrific murders committed by Charles Manson and his associates in 1969. In the words of one later right-wing historian, 'The new militants, were, in fact, revolutionaries. African–American extremists joined white allies in an assault on the most basic institutions of society.'[2]

Entangled with the social and cultural upheaval was vehement opposition to the Vietnam war, voiced both at the grass roots and by a wide range of intellectuals and writers, which went together with the connected theme of questioning accepted Cold War pieties and exposing the extent of US malpractice since 1945. Increasing numbers of citizens were refusing to accept government pronouncements on military affairs and foreign policy as sacrosanct. This bitterly offended traditionalists, who saw it as spitting on the America they loved.[3] Moreover, the success of the African–American civil rights movement in the 1960s removed the most outrageously scandalous reality of American society and the major embarrassment for its traditionalist conservatives, clearing the way for a coalescence on the right.

The tunes of Strauss

The writings and teaching of Leo Strauss (who died in 1973) were highly significant in this process: they were, according to Perry Anderson, 'a systematic political doctrine which has since nurtured the most distinctive and strong-minded school of American conservatism'.[4] In his youth in Germany, Strauss had been an activist in the most right-wing faction of the Zionist movement, Ze'ev Jabotinsky's Revisionists, who admired Mussolini. In May 1933 he wrote to Karl Löwith that Hitler could perhaps be stopped by appealing to the conservatives in his coalition, not on the basis of the Weimar constitution, which Strauss despised, but in terms of Italian fascism, 'fascist, authoritarian, imperial' as an alternative to Nazism. Shortly after, having escaped from Germany with the help of Carl Schmitt, he wrote from Paris to the latter asking for an introduction to Maurras (although later he was also on personal terms with socialists such as R. H. Tawney and Harold Laski). At the end of that decade, he moved to the USA where eventually he occupied a chair at the University of Chicago.

Strauss's field was philosophy and political theory, although –

> he himself therefore rarely spoke out in his own name on issues of political life.
> ...
> He wrote detailed, almost Talmudic interpretative studies, dedicating more space to questions like how often Machiavelli cited the Roman historian Livy than to the substantive discussion of Machiavelli's principles of realpolitik.[5]

He was nevertheless a vehement anti-democrat and celebrant of elites, though not in any crude fashion. An admirer of Plato, he regarded that thinker's elitism as having been misunderstood – for philosophers, he believed, often wrote esoterically to disguise their real beliefs for fear of persecution.

> The Straussian approach to political theory begins from the premise that political philosophers, who are concerned with truth and knowledge rather than mere opinion, have been compelled throughout the history of the canon to disguise their ideas, in order not to be persecuted as subversives. They have therefore ... adopted an 'esoteric' mode of writing, which obliges interpreters to reads between the lines ... Straussians regard themselves as a privileged and exclusive fraternity in their access to the true meaning of political philosophy, taking enormous liberties of interpretation, which stray from the literal text in ways few other scholars would allow themselves.[6]

Strauss utterly rejected that seventeenth-century anti-democrat Thomas Hobbes, much admired by Oakeshott, for Hobbes had regarded all humans (or at least the male portion) as naturally equal and for that very reason requiring to be absolutely subjected to the absolute Sovereign, whereas for

Strauss there was a natural order of inequality which should be reflected in social arrangements. Democracy, he thought, might possibly have its uses if it could be employed to induce the masses to accept their own subordination.

There was, however, an unusual twist to Strauss's conservatism. His own inner beliefs seem to have had similarities to Sartrean existentialism, 'the far more terrible realities of cosmic disorder: the absence of any divine authority, the delusion of any common morality, the transience of the earth and its species – every insight that religion must deny and society cannot survive'.[7] They are 'deadly truths'. Only philosophers could unearth these truths, and only a philosophically competent elite could endure them. For the remainder, what the Athenian aristocratic anti-democrats had termed the *hoi polloi* and Edmund Burke the 'swinish multitude', a security blanket must be provided in the shape of Plato's 'noble lie'. Religion, 'the gods of shuddering awe', or a similar equivalent would do – otherwise society would disintegrate. God might be dead, but he could still find useful employment.

Strauss did not always eschew direct political statements, at least in private. According to Scott Horton, writing in *Harper's Magazine* in July 2009, when Charles Percy (ironically a moderate Republican) was contemplating making a presidential bid in 1964, Strauss advised him as follows:

> There cannot be a *modus vivendi* until Russia abandons Communism, in the sense that it ceases to act on the premises of Communism; for it is utterly uninteresting to us and the rest of the non-Communist world whether the Russians go on paying lip-service to Communism, provided they have become convinced that the Free World is here to stay, and they act on this conviction. To bring about this change of mind, the West must be as tough and, if need be, as brutal as the Communists are to the West. The West must demonstrate to the Communists, by words and deeds which allow no possibility of error, that they must postpone forever the establishment of the world communist society.

And he went on to declare,

> I believe that the following points have not been made, or at least have not been made with sufficient audibility: ... To speak in the only language which Khrushchev understands, Cuba is our Hungary; just as we did not make the slightest move when he solved the problem in his back yard, Hungary, he cannot, and will not make the slightest move if and when we take care of the problem in our back yard, Cuba.[8]

A significant number of Strauss's ex-pupils became the ideologues and functionaries of the right-wing counteroffensive which was prepared in the 1970s, came to power with the Reagan presidency and continued through the 1990s and into the twenty-first century.

THE NEOCONSERVATIVES AND THE IDEOLOGICAL OFFENSIVE

In 2005, Murray Friedman published a volume entitled *The Neoconservative Revolution: Jewish Intellectuals and the Shaping of Public Policy* – a somewhat unfortunate subtitle, for on the one hand it gave a handle to antisemitic populism and on the other provided a ground for later accusations that any criticism of neoconservatism, or even use of the word, was implicitly antisemitic. The book itself is very informative and revealing, though not in the manner intended by its author, who is himself very much (though not wholly uncritically) in the neoconservative camp. He takes as read Soviet aggressive intentions, the 'necessity of bringing down the Soviet Union' and the notion that Washington possesses a divine right to rule the world. He even comes close to hinting that the USSR had something to do with the Iranian revolution.[9] What emerges is that the intellectuals in question were animated less by principle than by their personal hang-ups – or at least that the two things were very much mixed together. They happened to be Jewish, but it could just as easily have been any discriminated minority (though according to Fielder, 'In the transformation of American society after the war, no ethnic group took greater advantage of the new emphasis on egalitarianism than the Jews').

> The postwar years saw the gradual reconciliation of many of the young New York intellectuals with the society from which they had been alienated. One historian has argued that neoconservatism began as a counterprotest against a generation of ungrateful children in the 1960s, although its roots predated that era.
> …
> No doubt the growing success of the Jewish intellectuals and writers hastened their reconciliation with American life.[10]

Irving Kristol once defined a neoconservative as 'a liberal mugged by reality'. On this evidence, mugged by acceptance and money would seem more appropriate.

Initially they were very much on the left, mostly of the Trotskyist variety (so acquiring a bitter hatred of Stalinism) and what Friedman suggests, intentionally or otherwise, is that the source of this viewpoint was their feeling of exclusion from the intellectual and academic establishment. However, the Cold War provided the opportunity to make careers out of their anti-Stalinism, and so they found acceptance and, once having found that, discovered the virtues of American society and its political system. So on the next stage of their intellectual journey they became Cold War liberals, and with changing circumstances duly morphed into neoconservatives. 'Indeed, these disgruntled liberals were convinced that the McGovernites [McGovern was the Democrat candidate in the 1972 presidential election] had hijacked their party and jettisoned liberalism as they had known it' – that is, incorporating extreme Cold War postures.[11]

As a result of the Vietnam defeat, the economic crisis and the Watergate scandal the Cold War liberalism of the post-1945 era was placed on the defensive. A more robust response was called for by determined upholders of the American Way, and veterans such as Irving Kristol and William Buckley resolved their differences and teamed up with a new generation of fervent reactionaries. The new draft of conservatives and Cold Warriors influenced by Strauss – they were mockingly referred to as 'Leocons' – provided a neoliberal amalgam termed neoconservatism. Alongside the military, quasi-military, economic and political offensive against the left-liberal and communist ideological enemies – and all who identified with them – an ideological offensive, partly state-inspired and partly spontaneous, was also underway from the 1970s onwards.

In the US liberal (or, as it increasingly came to be known, neoliberal), economics were its foundation, with undiluted celebration of undiluted deregulated markets.[12] Naturally, care was taken to avoid presenting this in bald terms as a device deliberately intending to shift wealth from low-income groups to the wealthy; instead it was heralded as a necessary mechanism to reward and encourage enterprise, ensure maximum use of capital and provide employment all round.

In popular terms, what was stressed was the alleged 'trickle down' effect whereby growing incomes at the top end of the scale would somehow ensure that those lower down would also rise, if not proportionately then at least steadily. The early nineteenth-century notion that unemployment was always voluntary was revived – work was available if the unemployed would only bestir themselves and, in Norman Tebbit's phrase, 'get on their bikes'. No doubt work always was available – in drug dealing, robbery, prostitution, pornography and suchlike, but these occupations were not what the proponents had in mind.

The heart of the neocon case for a more benign view of capitalism lay less in economics than in its link to personal freedom. Indeed, the market economy, neocons felt, provided the essence of democracy. In 'Capitalism, Socialism and Democracy' Kristol summed up his strong feeling that capitalism was inextricably tied both to human freedom and to broader material well-being. 'Never in human history' he declared, 'has one seen a society of political liberty that has not been based on a free market system – i.e. a system based on private property, where normal economic activity consisted of commercial transactions between consenting adults. Never, never, never. No exceptions'. [History was not Kristol's strong suit][13]

Few if any of the new generation of ideologists, such as Alan Bloom, Paul Wolfowitz, Harry Jaffa and Abram Shulsky, had ever had a Marxist background of any sort, but had emerged from the conservative caucuses and networks that had been established round the Goldwater campaign and did not disappear with its failure. They added to the mix a more raucous emphasis on the necessity of US supremacy throughout world affairs, in everything from military strength to economic dominance to diplomatic reach to ideological penetration – what came to be known in fact as 'full spectrum dominance'.

Their Cold War liberal predecessors helped to get this bandwagon rolling. With their Trotskyist background, or association with the journal *Commentary* ('trusted to tell its readers what was right with American society rather than what was wrong'),[14] they had been disappointed with the outcome of Lyndon Johnson's Great Society project, in which many had participated. They included individuals like Nathan Glazer[15] and the seriously unattractive Norman Podhoretz, who regarded Reagan as a softie, and is notable in that he wrote seriously revealing autobiographies, with their seriously indicative titles, *Making It*, *Breaking Ranks* and *Ex-Friends*. Even Friedman is mildly critical. (Woody Allen was to joke that Podhoretz's *Commentary* and the pseudo-left *Dissent* should combine under the title *Dysentery*). They were joined by renegades from the left such as David Horowitz who in the 1960s had written detailed exposés of US Cold War policies.

Many traditional conservatives, or, as they came to be described, 'paleoconservatives', were less than enthusiastic about these upstart intruders claiming to speak on behalf of US conservatism (Buckley was an important exception). Kirk was scathing: neoconservatives, he fulminated, 'were often clever but seldom wise', deficient in 'the understanding of the human condition, and in the apprehension of the accumulated wisdom of our civilization'. The lesser-known Stephen Tonsor was even less discreet: 'It is splendid when the town whore gets religion and then joins the church. Now and then she makes a good choir director, but when she begins to tell the minister what he ought to say in his Sunday sermons, matters have been carried too far.'[16] Much later, a self-described paleoconservative-libertarian wrote on Irving Kristol's death in September 2009 that,

> In any case, the lasting legacy of Irving Kristol is that he was instrumental in turning the conservative movement away from its radical anti-statism and toward an almost exclusive concentration on the moral imperative of an aggressively interventionist foreign policy. His followers and epigones, who carry on the work in his wake, are the warmongers at the *Weekly Standard* and the Limbaugh-Hannity know-nothing Right, which sees every recognition of the limitations of American power – government power – as a 'betrayal'. This is surely a most unconservative – even anti-conservative – vision, a form of radicalism that resembles nothing so much as Trotskyism-turned-inside-out.[17]

That neoconservative ideology has Trotskyist and Jacobin roots was a frequent trope of the unreconciled 'paleos'. However, it was these traditionalists who were marginalised and had to be content with the neoconservatives' adoption of a few of their bigotries, such as misogyny and homophobia. In the course of the 1980s and early 1990s, the US paleoconservatives rallied around Pat Buchanan, who made an attempt on the presidency but got nowhere. His overt racism and antisemitism (which he tried unconvincingly to deny) did not help. Integralism, represented by such as Kirk, was marginalised in favour of neoliberalism except among the small core of traditionalists, the lunatic right or effectively fascist formations. The USA, with its obsessive individualism, had never been in any case a very favourable environment for integralism.

The Scrutape Letters

Meantime in the UK, a successor to Kirk and Oakeshott had appeared in the shape of Roger Scruton, a barrister whose original field, not accidentally, was aesthetics. His first major venture into conservative ideology came with *The Meaning of Conservatism* in 1980, in the preface of which he emphasised (his own term) that 'This is not a work of philosophy, but of dogmatics.'[18] Two years later, to continue propagating the ideology, he founded *The Salisbury Review*, named after Lord Salisbury, the nineteenth-century British Tory prime minister. It was described by an anonymous *Sunday Times* columnist as 'intellectual terrorism'.

Scruton summarised the essence of his ideology (or dogma) as follows: 'In politics the conservative attitude seeks above all for government and regards no citizen as possessed of a natural right that transcends his obligation to be ruled'[19] – and 'It is through her ideal of authority that the conservative experiences the political world.'[20] 'Conservatism placed duty before right.'[21] 'The Contagion of Democracy' (used as a chapter heading) he describes as a 'disease';[22] yet nevertheless Scruton favoured democracy – in the Soviet bloc – and in fact was active in assisting the oppositional underground there. Polish Solidarity was 'a movement in the direction recommended here' – a less than convincing recommendation. He more or less acknowledges that the purpose of conservatism is to stay in power. 'It must therefore be part of conservative dogma to describe the world not in neutral but in ideological terms', and consequently, 'Like Plato, a conservative may have to advocate a "Noble Lie"',[23] for the masses are too stupid or ignorant to reflect upon affairs of state.

Like all conservatives, Scruton is much attached to the rights of private property, although not in the absolute sense proclaimed by the neoconservative neoliberals. He specifically dissents from Robert Nozick's argument that all taxation is theft; taxation may be legitimate if required by Authority – but not progressive taxation, because that 'jeopardises the ties between the state and its more successful citizens'.

Predictably the relevant chapters of the volume bristle with hatred for trade unions, because they exhibit a potential rivalry to the state, and he even favours unofficial strikes because they *undermine* trade union authority:

It is the absolute duty of the state to have power over its subjects [sic] ... The state has the authority, the responsibility and the despotism of parenthood ... [for otherwise] the government disperses its power among ignorant multitudes. ... [trade union] activities which while legally sanctioned are tantamount to rebellion.

Universal education gives people ideas above their station and while monarchy is the 'most reasonable form' of government, 'there is no better way of ratifying power than through titles of nobility'.[24] (He had earlier acclaimed the hereditary principle.)

For the *canaille,* however,

> It is the possession of that belief [in religion] which enables men to direct their most powerful dissatisfactions away from the ruinous hope of changing things, to a more peaceable hope of being one day redeemed from the need to do so ... seeing such bonds as the expression of Providence, a man will be the more disposed to accept them ... there is a profound, mysterious and beneficial difference between women and men.[25]

Scruton and his 'bizarre collection' of 'assorted misanthropes and cultural pessimists'[26] were hardline conservative traditionalists. He therefore kept his distance from Thatcherite neoliberalism (he was never honoured by her, despite applauding the Falklands War as a selfless enterprise on behalf of 'kith and kin') and could give only 'a qualified endorsement of modern capitalism',[27] though he did not hesitate to dabble in it himself and claim that his privacy had been violated when his mode of doing so was publicised.

These conservative ideas, essentially those of Maurrrasian integralism, had little hope of playing a dominant role in societies experiencing an era of commercial and financial frenzy, culturally dominated by the reactionary populism of Murdoch's media empire. Such an ideology could therefore be used by neoconservatives only very selectively, if at all; nevertheless it was important, for it linked with Strauss's philosophy and reflected one strand of thinking increasingly prevalent among Western elites regarding what they would *like* to do, even while recognising its immediate impracticality.

France

In Europe, too, a new liberalism and a new right emerged, with France as its centre and anti-communism as its focus. Intellectual discourse in French culture has tended to be taken seriously, in a manner not apparent in other European countries, and the new breed of ideologues was able to command a considerable media presence both in print and broadcasting.

This development was greatly assisted when the former Vichyite activist Robert Hersant, imprisoned between 1947 and 1952 for his collaborationist activities, established a press empire covering a fifth of French newspapers. *Le Figaro* and *France-Soir*, falling under Hersant's control in 1975 and 1976 respectively, were used to give these individuals maximum publicity. Their highest-profile figures were André Glucksmann, a former Maoist and pupil of Althusser, and Bernard-Henri Lévy, who shared this background, but also possessed an enormous fortune and no less enormous ego. One commentator characterised him as being 'ambitious and unscrupulous' and having 'picked up on Glucksmann's ideas and turned them into slogans with which to punctuate his baroque and overblown prose'.[28] Lévy is also notorious, despite claiming to be astoundingly well-informed, for astounding factual errors in his pronouncements such as that Himmler stood trial at Nuremberg. 'Lévy's sense of history is, to say the least, vague.'[29]

The group came to be described as 'new philosophers', a designation invented by Lévy and happily embraced by some of them but rejected by others. 'As the Left's dominance of political discourse in France was increasingly shaken, the New Philosophers found a ready audience, not least among editors and television producers'.[30] They all had something in common despite other disagreements, and that was an intense hatred of the Soviet bloc (and of course the PCF) and of Marxism, the former having been acquired in their time as Maoists, the latter after following the disillusioned aftermath of the 1968 *événements* and the utopian hopes which had lasted a little longer. The publication in French of Solzhenitsyn's *Gulag Archipelago* provided a convenient peg on which to hang their political reversal, described by George Ross as 'neo-liberalism with a human face'.

> Since May we'd been living with this absolute certainty that not only was the revolution possible, but that we were in the process of making it. That's what was in the heads of the Maoist activists: that the revolution wasn't to be made, but that it was well and truly being made. So much so that when everything fell apart we found ourselves back with the question of its mere possibility, and as a result the question of activism lost its relevance.[31]

'[T]here first emerged anger that the world was refractory to such visions and then fury at the "straight" left which, in the 1970s, was capitalising on French discontents using traditional political programmes and methods.'[32]

According to Glucksmann, who revived the discredited concept of 'totalitarianism', 'Marxism generates not only scientific paradoxes, but also concentration camps', and from Lévy, 'no socialism without camps, no classless society without its terrorist truth'. The interpretations of the 'new philosophers' were idealist in the philosophic sense: they saw the catastrophes of the modern era as the product of wrong thinking, 'All modern domination is at root metaphysical ... as with reality, history simply does not exist ... there is no world, there is only discourse.'[33] Their prescription was to accept and enjoy the world as it was, with a little humanitarianism thrown in. 'In place of politics they offered ethics, the contemplative judgement of the world based on the choice between good and evil'.[34] However, in place of the Maoist regime which they no longer had as an icon, Glucksmann and Lévy found a substitute in the Israeli one.

In Jim Wolfreys's review of Dominique Lecourt's *The Mediocracy: French Philosophy Since the Mid-1970s* he quotes him as follows:

> The world becomes 'a pitiable tele-spectacle rendering those who allow themselves to be caught up in it hysterical, and consigning those who refuse to go along with the game to a brutal indifference'. The fate of the various and countless victims to appear on screen is presented as a fatality,

while 'a handful of social workers ... confer their blessings on a mass of grateful wretches'. Questions of scale and responsibility are blurred by the portrayal of such situations in terms of good and evil, giving rise to a politics 'pregnant with tyranny'.[35]

Two circumstances peculiar to France helped to accelerate the right-wing trend. One was the presence of two communist ministers, although in lowly positions, in Mitterrand's 1981 government, following a rapid rise in PCF recruitment in the mid-1970s and the bicentenary of the French Revolution in 1989. The first communist ministers in any significant West European government since 1947, particularly when coupled with the abortive radical programme which this government initiated, scared the right and provided the impetus to escalate the ideological offensive. The crimes of communist regimes were displayed as never before, an enterprise which continued unabated after the Soviet bloc collapse.

The bicentenary provided the opportunity for attack from a different angle and, because the event was widely noted throughout Europe, for spreading the ideas widely abroad. In short, the Revolution was portrayed as a bloody mess without meaning or purpose, and this interpretation used to discredit the idea of purposeful, far reaching social change, which in this light could only result in horrific consequences. The Enlightenment was rejected along with Marxism. '[B]y the time of the 1989 *Bicentenaire* ... concepts like class conflict and revolution had completely vanished from Left political and intellectual discourses.'[36] It was, of course, a longstanding trope of right-wing liberalism that the Bourbon monarchy was in the process of reforming itself and that France could have proceeded along a similar path to the UK without the unspeakable revolutionary interruption. This presumption was now revived and disseminated for all it was worth. At the forefront in France was François Furet; and as a populariser in English, Simon Schama, whose volume *Citizens* proved to be a best-seller.

Postmodernism

The bitter disillusion with communism and with revolutionary enterprises showed itself in another intellectual dimension – the notion of postmodernism. This is closely related to (but not identical with) poststructuralism, which is in essence a theory of language and consciousness. What postmodernism dismissed, especially in the persons of Jean-François Lyotard and Michel Foucault, was any notion of historical progress or indeed any capacity to understand the course of historical development over lengthy stretches of time. This cut at the very root of the Marxist conception of historical materialism, the idea of history developing through comprehensible stages towards the improvement – or at least the possibility of improvement – in the human condition.

Although the postmodernist milieu was shared to a degree with the 'new philosophers', it has to be said that the leading postmodern thinkers remained in a sense on the left, even the anarchist left – postmodernism was not a very congenial doctrine to the right – but Fredric Jameson was not wrong in calling it 'the cultural logic of late capitalism', the title of his best-known text. Its leading exponents had often been involved in the *événements* of 1968 and several of them had Maoist, or Maoist-connected backgrounds – as did the founders of the similarly-orientated Indian postmodernist school known as postcolonialism, which was also picked up and imitated in the West.

THE BOYS FROM CHICAGO

The University of Chicago proved to be a powerful motor of right-wing thinking (one ex-graduate characterised it as 'a moral cesspool'). Hayek himself, who had worked there from 1950 to 1962, was still around and his star was on the rise. The problems besetting the world economy in general and the Western industrial ones in particular could plausibly be attributed to the failure of Keynesian prescriptions, which violated the essential principles and rules of free-market operation. Inflation and stagnation were the inevitable consequence. Governments had no business interfering with business (at least in favour of workforce or consumers). Intervention should stop, governments assume a minimal role, trade union power be annulled, public services be privatised and commercial operations deregulated as far as humanly possible.

These nostrums were expounded by think-tanks and well-financed media outlets, particularly in the USA and the UK. Rupert Murdoch's communications empire, with its demonisation of workshy workforces and parasitical welfare scroungers, was especially active in this regard. Its journalists specialised in identifying victims who were then stigmatised as being to blame for all manner of social evils.

With Hayek by this time being elderly, the most prominent and raucous ideologist advancing these prescriptions was Milton Friedman, a professor at the University of Chicago, and his group of dynamic young acolytes that came to be known as the 'Chicago School'. Their obsession, along with the other aspects of neoliberalism mentioned above, was with the money supply and government expenditure, which they regarded as imperative to bring under tight control and restriction.

The Chicago School did not restrict itself to theoretical discussion, but acted wherever opportunity offered to proffer advice to governments of a sympathetic mind, most notoriously during this period in Chile, following the ultra-right coup that overthrew the radical Allende government in 1973. Their recommendation was to drastically lower living standards by wage cuts and abolition of welfare programmes, so as to stabilise the currency and set business on a sound foundation. Whether they also advised on the terror and torture tactics employed to achieve these purposes by the dictatorship is not recorded.

The Chilean example demonstrates well the ground on which neoliberalism and conservatism were to meet. Unregulated markets do not look after themselves; they are certain to generate massive popular discontent and opposition. Hayek was perfectly aware of this and therefore recommended a constitutional structure that would insulate market structures from democratic interference (see Chapter 7).

However, to reach this admirable state or one like it, the popular resistance that it evokes has to be broken, and in most cases the salami-like strategy used by the EU and its predecessor institutions was considered unsuitable. What is required is a 'strong state' that can beat down opposition by force and has the will to do so – either conservative, ultra-conservative or fascist-style regimes, depending on the circumstances, can be employed in this manner.

Reagan and Thatcher

In the USA, the amalgam of liberalism and ultra-conservatism, based above all on unregulated markets, non-unionised labour and intense racist attitudes, had existed for a long time as a regional phenomenon, mostly in the southern states of the former Confederacy. It was mainly during the years covered in this chapter that White voting patterns there shifted from Democrat to Republican. It was as far back as the 1960s that the Republican presidential candidate, Barry Goldwater, had published his ghosted volume. In the UK, Margaret Thatcher during her premiership more than once provoked the remark that she behaved more like a nineteenth-century liberal (or Liberal) than a classic British conservative (or Conservative).

Indeed, in both countries old-style conservatives high in the political hierarchy were sidelined, such as Nelson Rockefeller in the USA or, in the British case, the 'Wets' whom Margaret Thatcher was obliged to admit initially into her cabinets. However, neither Ronald Reagan and the senior Bush, nor Thatcher, were able to complete the job of deregulating their respective economies and dismantling public welfare services. That was left to their Democrat and 'New Labour' successors.

Still, they did their utmost and certainly laid the foundations for the brave new world of unrestrained economic globalisation. Reagan, a reincarnation of Jubilation T. Cornpone, had helped to lever himself into the White House by shifty means – even more sinister (if marginally less blatant) than those employed by the junior Bush in 2000. His agents secretly bribed the Iranian revolutionaries to stall on a solution to the US embassy hostage crisis to discredit the sitting President Jimmy Carter, his opponent in the 1980 election (something unaccountably ignored by Friedman).

Once in office, the rhetoric his speechwriters employed could be summarised as 'America great again' with determination to bury the 'Vietnam syndrome' and assert US status as the superior superpower; this to be achieved abroad by unashamedly aggressive postures. His ambassador to the UN, Jeane Kirkpatrick (in an article astoundingly entitled 'Double standards'), discriminated between 'totalitarian' (that is, anti-US) regimes and 'authoritarian' ones – dictatorial pro-US kleptocracies which, as Friedman tastefully puts it, 'sometimes deviated from this principle [freedom and democracy]'.

Domestically, the neoconservative project was advanced by jettisoning the morally debilitating economics of the Keynesian consensus. The social principles of the Great Society, attacked because it supposedly encouraged welfare dependency, were repudiated (although the gains of the Civil Rights movement were untouchable). Since the 1970s a sustained campaign had been conducted against these programmes, with every error and excess committed in the pursuit of attacking poverty being trumpeted to the skies.[37] It was reminiscent of the ideological campaign conducted by southern racists against the programme of African–American emancipation, following the Civil War.

A start was made on lowering taxation for the super-wealthy, removing curbs on their activities and cutting welfare entitlements. An attitude of unremitting hostility was shown towards the trade union movement and membership discouraged wherever possible. Confrontation was inevitably provoked – in 1981 with the air controllers' strike action; this was faced down and the union defeated.

Margaret Thatcher's government followed an essentially similar course and employed similar rhetorical strategies – the two leaders were close personally as well as ideologically, forming a mutual admiration society.[38] In spite of her three electoral victories, the last two overwhelming, she never achieved a majority of the popular vote, and in Scotland and Wales her party was massively rejected on each occasion. However, she did succeed in achieving a grip on the popular consciousness, whether in adoration (here the assistance of Rupert Murdoch cannot be discounted) or detestation, such as no prime minister since Churchill had experienced.

This phenomenon was referred to as 'Thatcherism', a term coined by Stuart Hall, who foresaw its direction earlier than any other commentator. As he pointed out, she succeeded in developing a coherently articulated interpretation, both ostensible and coded, of the nature of Britain's dilemma, which played to longstanding prejudices rooted in the English cultural psyche, particularly in the country's southern parts. This included dislike and suspicion of foreigners, hatred and contempt for sexual minorities, nostalgia for the days of British imperial supremacy, prejudice against 'bureaucracy' and taxation, linked with prejudice against local government. Thatcherism encouraged instead material and social ambition in an individualistic and marketised mode, which could descend into straightforward bribery, as with the sale of local authority housing and the notorious 'Sid' advertising campaign for the privatisation of public utilities.[39]

By this means she successfully constructed a 'hegemonic bloc' and accomplished things that in the previous four decades the conservative right wing had only dreamed of. Her set-piece battles were with the Argentine military in 1982, the miners' trade union in 1984–85, and thereafter defiant local governments, all of which she won decisively and definitively. She left office in 1990 (having been forced out by her exasperated colleagues who could no longer bear her spiteful, arbitrary and increasingly irrational behaviour) declaring that the greatest achievement of her regime (she herself used that term) was the existence of 'New Labour'.

Military offensive

During these same years, alongside its domestic policies, the Reagan administration mounted a world-embracing assault on its Soviet antagonist, resolved that the time for detente and mutual good fellowship, represented by the Helsinki conference and agreements, had passed. The steady ideological gains the Soviet bloc seemed to be making around the world, despite the evaporation of its ideological credibility, could no longer be tolerated, and US strength must be deployed to halt and, if possible, reverse the trend. There would be no more negotiations without Soviet concessions up front in advance. Reagan famously described the Soviet bloc as the 'Evil Empire'. Jimmy Carter, in the latter years of his presidency, had already begun to move in a hostile direction following the Soviet invasion of Afghanistan in 1979, to support a friendly government there threatened by US- and Pakistani-backed rebel Afghans, and the Soviet-sponsored military coup in Poland the same year, to crush the Solidarity trade union movement. The immediate consequence of these actions was the US-sponsored boycott of the Moscow Olympics in 1980.

Under Reagan (or the people who manipulated him), pressure was enormously increased. A new generation of Cruise missiles, which could fly under the Soviet radar defences, was stationed in forward positions in Europe. This both threatened the USSR and Eastern Europe, and had the additional advantage that Moscow had to commit additional resources to countering them, imposing greater strains on its creaky economy. Moreover, Reagan developed plans for a missile defence shield, popularly referred to as 'Star Wars'. Though wholly unrealistic, it was still threatening.

All around the globe relentless attack, either through surrogates or directly, was mounted against states and movements regarded as friendly to the enemy or failing to see matters in the light that Washington required. Some have been already mentioned. The Central American state of Nicaragua was a particular victim. A socially radical movement, the Sandinistas, had in 1979 overthrown the implacably corrupt and tyrannical dictatorship of the Somoza family and embarked upon a programme of far-reaching reform, accepting assistance from Cuba.

This was interpreted in Washington as unacceptable and the Sandinistas were stigmatised as communists, though they were far from that (the Nicaraguan communists opposed the Sandinistas). Washington was additionally irritated when the Sandinistas declined to follow the usual dictatorial path and confirm the accusation – and so promoted destructive cross-border surrogate attacks from Honduras. US official discourse reached the lunatic lengths of presenting revolutionary Nicaragua as a military threat to the USA – there was even a feature film made on this presumption.

It was in the same year (which has claims to be to the 'Second Cold War' what 1947 was to the first) that the Vietnamese, who had been suffering savage cross-border raids from the neighbouring genocidal Khmer Rouge regime in Cambodia, invaded that country with more than adequate justification, overthrew the Khmer Rouge and – since the remnants of the latter took refuge on the Thailand border and conducted destructive raiding – left behind a military force to support the new Cambodian regime. This was denounced as intolerable aggression and occupation. American pressure induced the UN to continue to seat the Khmer Rouge. All manner of sanctions were decreed against Vietnam, and the surviving Khmer Rouge, in spite of their dreadful reputation, received diplomatic and material support.

Nor was this all. Washington had organised in Indonesia in 1965 the greatest of post-war massacres. Nearly a decade later, when the Portuguese empire collapsed, in part of it, the eastern half of the Indonesian island of Timor, a left-wing government attained power. Henry Kissinger, then US Secretary of State, encouraged the Indonesian military to invade and conduct a genocidal campaign (ultimately unsuccessful) against the East Timorese resistance. It was part of the same pattern as Indonesia, Vietnam and relations with the Khmer Rouge; thus did the God-fearing leader of the Free World exhibit its godly virtue.

If what was being undertaken in South-East Asia was designed to put pressure on and drain the resources of the Vietnamese state, yet more intense efforts were put into Afghanistan, where the US rightly perceived that the Soviet-dependent communist regime was highly vulnerable and that the Afghan guerrillas fighting it were capable of inflicting serious losses on the Red Army. Accordingly enormous assistance was given to them, channelled through Pakistan, and they were supplied with the most advanced weaponry fit for their circumstances. A notion floated in the *Reader's Digest* back in the 1950s, that Islam might one day be mobilised to assist the West in the anti-communist struggle, was eventually taking on reality – as were its unforeseen consequences.

It was wholly appropriate that this phase of international relations should have been given the name of the 'Second Cold War'. Despite all that had taken place in the intervening years since Stalin's death, American government and media were again portraying communism (at least in its Soviet variety) as the unvarying and essential enemy and cranking up the rhetoric to justify the offensives being undertaken.

It was no more than an apparent paradox that towards the end of the 1980s a summit was held in Reykjavik between Reagan and Gorbachev with apparent cordiality all round.[40] The USA had made it plain that a summit meeting would be possible only on the basis of concessions or promise of concessions by Moscow, and at the summit itself further concessions were extracted. Gorbachev, only too conscious of the weakness of his position and the deteriorating Soviet economy and political framework, felt he had no choice.

Naturally, the USA had to promise something in exchange so as not to make the meeting appear totally one-sided, but it received much more than it conceded. In effect, the Soviets offered concessions, the US offered promises which of course it subsequently broke, such as (later under the elder Bush) not extending NATO to the Soviet borders. Had Gorbachev been more historically aware of the US record and US diplomatic habits he might have been less accommodating. However, one of the disadvantages of the Soviet system of single-party monopoly and restriction of debate and information was that its citizens tended to be very badly informed about international realities, even at the highest levels. As Martin McCauley sums it up, 'If Gorbachev's domestic policy failed, his foreign policy was a brilliant success – that is from the West's point of view.'[41]

Iraq

A sidelight on the character of the American state ideology and its international tactics is apparent in its relations with Iraq and Iran. The Iraqi dictator, Saddam Hussein, was throughout the 1980s a sound US ally in spite of his appalling human rights record, for he had all but exterminated the Iraqi communists. His neighbour, the Iranian regime, had not been forgiven for its overthrow of a reliable Western ally in the 1979 revolution, humiliation of the USA and treatment of it as the 'Great Satan'.

Saddam was encouraged to militarily attack Iran on the presumption that this would result in the extinction of its government, and even speedily forgiven when one of his planes mistakenly attacked a US naval vessel, but the enterprise was unsuccessful and resulted in an Iranian counter-invasion and eventual stalemate. Saddam had therefore failed in his commission and become a less useful vassal.

In 1990, to repair his damaged credibility and gain enhanced control over gulf oil output, Saddam seized the neighbouring micro-monarchy of Kuwait with US encouragement or at least lack of discouragement. Immediately he was indicted as an unspeakable monster and tyrant, his previously obscured evil deeds were at once highlighted in the mainstream media and a US-led expeditionary force early in 1991 drove his forces out of Kuwait with great slaughter. It was expected that this would result in his political demise through internal military putsch, but again these hopes were confounded. Shadia Drury later commented, 'It is ironic that American neoconservatives have decided to conquer the world in the name of liberty and democracy, when they have so little regard for either.'[42]

No alternative

'There is no alternative' was a slogan associated particularly with Margaret Thatcher. The inevitability of global marketisation was portrayed as a fact of nature rather than the product of particular decisions made by particular individuals and collectives on particular occasions. The term 'modernisation' was much employed, though in fact what it was referring to was a reversion to the principles of nineteenth-century laissez-faire. Of course it was not really market freedom all round – there was no free market in narcotic drugs for example, nor even a free market in labour across international boundaries, and both the USA and the EU used tariffs and support mechanisms to advantage sectors of their own economies (principally at the expense of Third World producers), the World Trade Organization (WTO) notwithstanding. Moreover, strict regulations were enforced – more in the USA than anywhere else – to protect the interests of corporations and property owners against each other, as the directors of Enron and later Conrad Black were to discover in due course.

What the new times meant in essence was, concurrently with making public utilities and enterprises into private sources of profit, to diminish the levels of public welfare available to those temporarily or long term outside the labour market. For those inside it the effect was to expose them to fiercer competition with reduced collective protection. The terms in which all this was presented drew on rhetorical devices inherited from the past ages of pre-social liberalism that put a positive spin on developments. They would enhance choice, and thereby compel suppliers to be more attentive to their customers. They would stimulate industry and commerce and benefit economic growth. They would compel scroungers, layabouts and slackers to address their behaviour.

Self-help would become the order of the day; it would, again to quote Margaret Thatcher, 'let our children grow tall', a phrase which was made the title of a book of her apothegms.[43] After all, if a B-movie ham actor or an indifferently-talented chemistry student could rise to the pinnacle of their respective states by their own effort, then surely financial security and prosperity was within the reach of everybody if they put their mind to it and practised the Victorian virtues.

Neoconservative neoliberalism was in the driving seat, and social liberalism and social democracy were dragged along behind its chariot. Quite apart from what was happening in the Soviet bloc or China, world politics was being pulled to the right and the ideological climate shifting accordingly. What was being done in Washington and London was indeed accepted as inevitable and necessary. The Democrat party and its spokespeople increasingly moved to accept the presumptions and values of the Republican administration – it corresponded with the public mood; Lyndon Johnson's Great Society was in the process of being dismantled, not to speak of Franklin Roosevelt's New Deal. As growing numbers of the 'underclass' were unable to adjust to the new requirements, growing numbers went into prison, and executions, suspended during the era of radicalisation, were restored.

Following Labour's loss of office in 1979 and at the beginning of Thatcher's administration, the Labour Party had adopted a programme and internal structure more radically left-wing than ever before in its existence. It proved to be a short interlude. In the course of the 1980s, faced with the partial breakaway of its more explicitly liberal elements which went on to align their secession with the Liberal Party, what mainstream opinion regarded as sanity reasserted itself. The radical commitments on the party's agenda were disowned one by one and the transformations brought about by the government accepted explicitly or implicitly.

It was not only the Anglo–Saxon countries which were involved. The social democratic movements throughout Europe were likewise affected, if not altogether to the same extent. The abandonment by Mitterrand's government of its economic and social programme was only the most dramatic example. Probably the mass of social democrats and their electorates from Sweden to Italy accepted the changes without any great enthusiasm, but more in an attitude of resigned helplessness. At any rate social liberalism and social democracy fell into line – ambitious programmes were scrapped and ideology retuned to fit. The problem, especially emphasised after the reintroduction of a capitalist economy in communist China, the East European collapse and the Soviet turmoil, was that there really did appear to be no alternative to the socially unregulated market.

Not that leading American neoconservatives were by any means satisfied. Kristol, so nicely displaying what one historian has termed 'the paranoid style in American politics', was to write in 1993,

There is no 'after the Cold War' for me. So far from having ended, my Cold War has increased in intensity, as sector after sector has been ruthlessly corrupted by the liberal ethos. Now that the other Cold War is over, the real Cold War has begun. We are far less prepared for this Cold War, far more vulnerable to the enemy, than was the case with our victorious war against a global communist threat.[44]

13
Communism

CONSEQUENCES OF 1968

The Warsaw pact invasion of Czechoslovakia in August 1968 did not produce the disruptions and uproar in the world communist movement that had followed from the events of 1956, but it nevertheless marked a definitive stage in the Soviet ideology's loss of credibility. What could not be disguised was that here, in comparison with Hungary twelve years beforehand, there was no insurrection, no threat to withdraw from the Warsaw Pact and not even any plans to abolish the single-party[1] regime. Moscow's official claims that socialism in Czechoslovakia was endangered by West German revanchism, and US imperialism could not be taken seriously except by audiences deliberately kept in ignorance of what was going on or communist traditionalists convinced that the Soviet government could do no wrong.

Clearly, to those who could see and hear, socialism as understood in Moscow and by the ruling elements in the Eastern bloc meant the suppression of honest discussion and debate inside or outside the communist parties, and the retention instead of a rigid straitjacket of Party oversight and direction round the institutions of civil society – even in Romania, which had refused to take part in the invasion. 'The Brezhnev Doctrine', with Moscow's pretension to judge the socialist authenticity of other bloc members, added insult to injury. It also made clear what the Politbureau meant by socialism – the neo-Stalinist system prevailing in the USSR – and revealed the fears now manifested there that developments like the Prague Spring (unlike the diplomatic independence of Romanian Stalinism) would set a bad example that other publics might want to imitate.

The question is raised as to whether 'socialism with a human face' would have been a viable form of political and social organisation, or whether, after the initial holiday atmosphere, internal strains would have caused it to founder and either move back towards a more authoritarian regime or else into a fully capitalist one. Brezhnev was probably right at least in his assertion, if in nothing else, that the Americans would have been unlikely to leave it alone. Perhaps Czechoslovakia could really have become a more socialist version of Sweden, but that seems unlikely.

The Chinese communists condemned the invasion, not for the same reason that the Western parties did, for of course, this being at the height of the 'Cultural Revolution', they thoroughly disapproved of the direction in which the Czechs were heading. Instead they deplored it as a great power act, with the USSR enforcing its will on foreign communist parties. No doubt they were apprehensive that the same logic as had justified the invasion might in due course be applied to themselves. Very possibly it helped to persuade the Chinese leaders that it was necessary to mend fences with their former mortal enemy the USA, the action for which they had previously so bitterly castigated the Soviets.

Nevertheless, by the middle of the 1970s the Soviet bloc (despite the bitter rupture with China, upheavals in Poland and disasters for the communist parties in Indonesia,[2] Iraq, Sudan and Chile) appeared to be very strong indeed – one of the realities which so scared the emergent neoconservatives. In 1975, the NLF and North Vietnamese were on the point of winning the Vietnam War; the Portuguese communists had come very close to gaining power and, despite their failure, had or appeared to have put up an honourable struggle and remained a strong political force. The decrepit Franco regime was tottering to its terminus and bright hopes were held of the communists' future in a post-Franco Spain. Most importantly perhaps from the Kremlin viewpoint, the West was embarked on a project of detente and the Helsinki accords had recognised the post-1945 borders in Eastern Europe.

IDEOLOGICAL SELF-IMAGE

In the same year, the Soviets' Novosti Press Agency issued in many languages a 95-page pamphlet by Boris Leibzon under the title *The Communist Movement Today*, which summarised the official ideological position at that point. In essence, its argument is that the Bolsheviks and the CPSU have been right all along and still continue to be (the Stalin era is skipped over) and that communists remain pristine revolutionaries. Maoists and Trotskyists are routinely attacked for ultra-leftism which presents 'no real danger to the capitalist system', but a lot of the author's polemic is also aimed at the 'revisionists' who have criticised aspects of official Marxism–Leninism, along with communist party structures and practices, as stagnant and mechanistic. The French communist Roger Garaudy and the Austrian Franz Marek are specifically mentioned, the latter accused of arguing that 'revolutionary struggle can be replaced by bourgeois democracy'.

The specifically ideological claims are far-reaching, to say the least.

Thanks to Marxist–Leninist theory, the Party is able to chart a consistent policy course even through the kaleidoscope of the workaday world, and correctly to assess not only fully developed events but those still in the incipient stage.

Moreover the claim on *all* communists everywhere to exhibit *Soviet* loyalty is fiercely reasserted. Leibzon quotes Dimitrov in 1938,

There is not, nor can there be any other, *more certain criterion*, than one's *attitude* towards the Soviet Union, in determining who is the *friend* and who the *enemy* of the cause of the working class and socialism, in determining who is a *supporter* and who an *opponent* of democracy and peace. [Original italics]

Novosti also published for a time *Socialism: Theory and Practice*, a 'monthly digest of theory and political press'. Number 7, also published in 1975, contained an article by M. A. Suslov, the official Politbureau theoretical spokesperson, in which he declared that,

> By its selfless devotion to the people, the Party has won its love, gratitude and confidence; its prestige among the people is boundless ... our Party keeps strengthening the unity of its ranks all the time, which makes it mighty, invincible and capable of solving any problem.

He is prepared to admit that, 'communist construction ... is [not] free of shortcomings, errors, violations of law and discipline, miscalculations, red tape, conservatism, mismanagement, negligence' – all of which can be overcome by Marxism–Leninism correctly practised. In another article, by Ilya Dudinsky, entitled 'Apropos of Contradictions in the Development of the World Socialist System', it is acknowledged that 'a situation of conflict' can arise between socialist countries:

> Contradictions of this kind are the result of a switchover to revisionist nationalist positions. They are fraught with the danger of deformation of the socialist system. The state of affairs inside such a country and its political course may enter into an acute contradiction with the common interests of other socialist countries and the interests of the entire socialist community.

No doubt the author has Czechoslovakia in mind. The Soviet Union is always right.

EUROCOMMUNISM

The Czechoslovak events were not the only motive behind the development in the 1970s of the phenomenon known as Eurocommunism, but they were certainly a major step along that road. As the name implies, this form of communist politics affected the Western European parties. Some, like the Italians, embraced it eagerly, some with moderate enthusiasm, like the British, some, like the French, reluctantly, and others, such as the Portuguese, remained entirely untouched.

Perhaps rather surprisingly, given the outlook of their Iberian neighbours and the similarity of their ultra-right regimes, it was in Spain that the Eurocommunist flag was first openly hoisted. In 1977 a book published by the Spanish communist leader Santiago Carrillo used it in the title, though he put it between quote marks and hyphenated it.

Carrillo denies that he is proposing a reversion to social democrat positions, and continues to justify armed uprising if the ruling classes should reject a democratic verdict against them. 'On the other hand, I am convinced that the dictatorship of the proletariat is not the way to succeed in establishing and consolidating the hegemony of the forces of the working people in the developed countries of developed capitalism.'[3] Socialism should be 'the negation of any totalitarian conception of society'. He rejects as only 'half right' Lenin's assertion that *any* transition from capitalism to communism must necessarily involve proletarian dictatorship, and uses Lenin's remark that such transition will inevitably take a 'diversity of political forms' to insist that these must include ones where proletarian dictatorship is unnecessary.

In essence, what Eurocommunism did was to explicitly abandon the Leninist perspectives, which, in reality, the majority of West European parties had, despite their formal adherence, been doing by implication since the 1940s if not the 1930s. They reconciled themselves to the realities of 'bourgeois democracy' and recognised it as a permanent feature of the socialist society they continued to declare as their aim. Carrillo explicitly criticised Stalinism in the USSR, declaring that the state established under Stalin's regime had 'formal characteristics similar to those of the fascist dictatorships'.[4] It was 'a form of totalitarianism extensively exploited by capitalist propaganda', thus weakening the credibility of Western communists.

Soviet reaction

Naturally, the CPSU was not amused. An article expressing its point of view accused Carrillo of 'disuniting the anti-imperialist forces and splitting and undermining the communist movement', and reminded its readers that a year earlier he had denied that there was such a thing as Eurocommunism. Worse, his ideas would perpetuate the military bloc division of Europe and strengthen 'the aggressive NATO bloc'.[5]

> In the final analysis all these explanations have boiled down to a very simple thing. What they want is that the Communist and Workers' parties in Western Europe should cease to be Communist parties, that they should come out against the scientific communism founded by Marx, Engels and Lenin and – more important still – that they should sever all ties with the Communist and Workers' parties of the socialist countries of Europe and enter into confrontation with them.

'There can be no doubt that Carrillo's interpretation of "Eurocommunism" accords solely with the interests of imperialism, the forces of aggression and reaction', the article declared. Carrillo retorted that 'these gentlemen' believed the communist movement to be a church and themselves the Holy See. He denied that he had advocated Spain joining NATO as the article accused him of doing – although he admitted that the PCE would not oppose the continuation of US air bases in Spain. The following year, the PCE approved Spain's entry into the EEC.

At any rate the Soviet authorities, despite Spanish Eurocommunists' protests to the contrary and CPSU fraternal greeting to their 1978 congress, remained

firmly convinced that Eurocommunism equalled anti-Marxism and anti-Sovi-
etism. Referring to the French Eurocommunist critic of Soviet reality, Jean
Ellenstein, it characterised his politics as 'a vulgar repetition of the inglorious
history of international opportunism dating from the late nineteenth and
early twentieth centuries ... the logic of apostasy'.[6] Ellenstein's language was
too strong even for the formally Eurocommunist PCF and it expelled him in
1980, which no doubt pleased his Soviet critics.

Certainly Eurocommunism was a flexible concept. Those who theorised
it appealed to Gramsci, and, even if they did not use the phrase, the notion
of a 'long march through the institutions'. Put at its starkest, communists
would have to learn to use the capitalist state (and submit themselves to
open elections in a multi-party system) instead of destroying it, as Lenin had
insisted was absolutely essential and differentiated communists from all forms
of pseudo-socialist backsliders, as he regarded them. Naturally this rejection
of Lenin's central postulate was not seen as acceptable by varying proportions
of traditionalists in the Eurocommunist parties, resulting in breakaways, and
in the Spanish case the fragmentation of the party.

TRADITIONALISTS

Outside Western Europe, the CPUSA was definitely not in the Eurocommunist
camp (though the Japanese CP was). Ever since the traditionalists had
reasserted their dominance after the brief 'liberal' interlude in 1956, it had
remained among minor fractions of the communist movement one of the most
firmly neo-Stalinist – and one of the most moribund. It came to life briefly
in the late 1960s when one of its African–American activists, Angela Davis,
became a centre of international attention on account of her persecution by
the state and the threat of a long imprisonment or even execution.

But no revival occurred and when the CPUSA's 1991 convention discussed
whether the collapse of the Soviet Union should mean that the Party reject
Leninism, the Party majority reasserted its classic Marxist–Leninist line,
whereupon the 'social democrat' faction abandoned the Party and renamed
itself the Committees of Correspondence for Democracy and Socialism.

The Latin American parties were hardly more significant, but elsewhere
revolutionary action led by Moscow-orientated communist parties was not
yet extinct. Apart from Vietnam, a communist putsch in April 1979 was
successful in Afghanistan, thanks to deep-rooted support among educated
military officers; it was triggered by the attempt of President Daud to distance
himself from the communists. In an interview with Cuban journalists two
months later, the Deputy Prime Minister, Hafizulla Amin, who was the real
power in the state, claimed that, 'Within the country itself, I see no danger
because the masses strongly supported the revolution', although, 'it's quite
likely that the imperialist circles and their lackeys will want to encourage the
fanatic religious leaders with the help of the feudal lords'.[7]

Before the year was out he had called on Moscow to save the regime from
overthrow by US sponsored and armed Islamists. The Soviets responded,

but they also executed Amin, being convinced that he was more part of the problem than the solution because his brutal methods were alienating popular support. The Afghanistan CP had split into two irreconcilable rival factions, translated as the 'Masses' and the 'Flag' (or 'Banner') who had taken to settling their differences by shoot-outs around the cabinet table. It was scarcely the most effective manner in which to defend a revolution under mortal threat.

If by 1980 revolutionary activists were as likely as not to despise Moscow-style communism, there were plenty of exceptions such as in Cuba, Turkey, South Africa and African states emerging from colonialism, while a Soviet-orientated communist party (which disbanded after the USSR's collapse), was actually established in Saudi Arabia in 1975.

Maoism

Maoism meantime was entering its concluding phase. The reversal of his policies after his death – according to the *People's Daily* in 1978, 'Lin Bao and the Gang of Four were a bunch of fake Marxists and political and theoretical swindlers' – this meant that the source of inspiration for Maoist ideology around the world had disappeared, while the Cubans described the improving Beijing-Washington relations as a 'great betrayal' and a 'loathsome alliance'.

In the split that had partitioned the Communist Party of India, the Maoist-inclined wing had ended as the larger and more important element. They termed themselves the Communist Party of India (Marxist–Leninist) (CPI [M–L]) – the bracketed (Marxist–Leninist) designation being the code which specified Maoist inclinations. Their strength was in West Bengal, where they overwhelmingly dominated regional politics and were constantly re-elected to government – however by then the CPI (M–L) had lost its distinctively Maoist character.

For a time in the early 1970s, the French Maoists achieved the accolade of being considered dangerous enough to be banned by the state: in the later part of the decade they evaporated and their ideologists turned to the right, to postmodernism or to even more bizarre ideological notions. No others in Western Europe were of interest to anyone other than antiquarians of such matters, and the same was largely true of North America. Although lacking in political or social significance, there were several Maoist grouplets in the USA and more especially in Canada. Once disillusioned with their Chinese inspiration, some of them turned for a time instead towards the ultra-Stalinist Albanian regime (there was also one such in the UK) and later disintegrated into complete marginality.

Matters were somewhat different in South America, where one Maoist formation succeeded in making a major impact. This was the Sendero Luminoso (Shining Path) in Peru, whose guerrillas came very close at one point to defeating the government forces and seizing the state. It did indeed imitate Mao's example by enforcing social reform in the areas under its control, but its methods were so savage that it was as much a terror to its adherents as to its enemies (its leader dismissed Che Guevara as 'a playboy'). Eventually, the government overcame it.

The USSR

Probably as much from weariness as for any more principled reason, the tightness of party control over expressions of discontent in the USSR itself was beginning to slacken by the late 1970s. The somewhat injudicious undertaking at the Helsinki Conference to respect rights of free speech, which no doubt the leadership had never expected to be taken seriously in the West, was proving an embarrassment when it came to silencing intellectuals – it was frequently referred to by the Czech dissidents, Charter 77. Open publication could still be barred, but samizdat critiques circulated relatively freely.

Alexandr Solzhenitsyn, though in actuality no more than a harmless reactionary with an intense attachment to patriarchal traditions, was regarded as too much of an irritation to tolerate, but he was expelled rather than being shot, imprisoned lengthily or confined in a mental hospital. Critics like the brothers Zhores and Roy Medvedev, and Boris Kagarlitsky, though subject to harassment, were allowed to continue criticising, even though they compounded their fault by having their critiques published abroad. These critiques were framed within the Leninist discourse – they did not challenge the foundations of the Soviet system. At one time this would have made them doubly suspect, for their actions challenged the Party's monopoly over the interpretation of Marxism and of history – in earlier days the most unforgivable of all deviations.

Intellectually, the official discourse was stifling; the authorised chief ideologist, Mikhail Suslov, was an apparatchik of the most unimaginative sort. In the rest of the Soviet bloc matters were no better. Poland, in spite of its social and political upheavals, had the reputation of being the bloc regime where expression was most free. If that were actually the case it represented a grim comment on what the others must have been like, for the manner in which the regime's linguistic culture handled the public ideology and manipulated language was Orwellian in character. Carl Tighe, in his article 'Partyspeak in Poland',[8] provides many examples; a minor one refers to the use or non-use of initials when naming foreign states. It was considered somewhat derogatory to refer to a state by its initials (such as UK or USA) and consequently, while the German Federal Republic might frequently be referred to by its initial letters (in Polish the NRF), the German Democratic Republic or the Soviet Union never were.

In 1977 the USSR promulgated a new Constitution, or Fundamental Law, the fourth in Soviet history, replacing the Stalin constitution of 1936. In preparation since Khrushchev's time, its preamble, which retained Khrushchev's concept of 'a state of the whole people', asserted that the USSR was 'a society of true democracy, the political system of which ensures effective management of all public affairs', and 'ever more active participation of the working people in public life'. However, Article 6 reiterated the political monopoly of the CPSU, which 'exists for the people and serves the people'.[9]

An internal critic pointed out that

most of the articles in this Constitution were drafted in the form of declarations rather than specific legal norms ... it is just such an absence of the characteristic traits of law, of legal foundations, that transforms this document – potentially of vital importance – into a bombastic and boastful declaration.[10]

The Chinese CP, despite being by then in the post-Maoist phase, dismissed it as, '[codifying] into fundamental law the fascist dictatorship of the bureaucrat-monopoly capitalists and their social-imperialist policies today'.[11]

GORBACHEV AND THE COLLAPSE

The ideological exhaustion of Soviet communism was signalled in the geriatric character of its leadership by the time of Brezhnev's death. (The same was true in essence of their Chinese counterparts, even if those were embarking on a radically new economic programme.) It was underlined by the fact that Brezhnev was also a very sick man and had already been revived from technical death a little earlier. Following Brezhnev's demise, the Politbureau elected a successor, who, though somewhat younger, politically energetic and committed to erasing corruption, worked constantly on the brink of death and his intended reforms were all merely technocratic and administrative. He soon died, and his successor Konstantin Chernenko was near to being a tasteless joke – ageing, mortally ailing and in addition 'a man without qualities'. If the Politbureau had been deliberately searching for a way to waste valuable time as the economic plight grew worse and the Americans stepped up their aggressive postures, they could scarcely have chosen more appropriately.

The eventual appointment in 1985 of Mikhail Gorbachev appeared to promise better. Educated in law and at the age of 55 almost disgracefully young for his office (Lenin had been 47 at the time of the Revolution, Trotsky 40 years old), he certainly had ideas and the potential longevity to see them through. However, bold though these were, ideologically they were a mess, no doubt inevitably given the near-total frustration of Lenin's hopes for world revolution. Gorbachev was a Marxist–Leninist in the post-Stalinist mode, and all his innovations both in the economy and political structure had the effect only of worsening the chronic crisis.

Naturally the appeal was to Lenin and the programme was presented as a development of his ideas, but one of the effects was actually to undermine Lenin's credibility, for the *glasnost* innovations enabled public discussions to take place on Lenin's role and record, and these discussions became increasingly critical. More sinisterly, it permitted the open revival of some of the worst ideological features of pre-revolutionary Russia, above all antisemitism. In the end of course it also destroyed the regime.

Glasnost proved to be a very double-edged development. In principle it was not opposed to Lenin's ideas of how a society should *ultimately* function, but certainly was not recommended for a situation of turmoil and disruption.

Perestroika, as pointed out earlier, had no great success, being resisted and sabotaged by the apparatchiks who were adversely affected by its implementation. Ideologically, it was either un-Leninist or else a confession of failure of the Soviet economic system to date, for it represented the introduction of market disciplines into the economy in an attempt to repair its defects. For Lenin that kind of thing was acceptable only as a temporary emergency measure, to be accompanied by the tightening up of repression inside and outside the Party, certainly something to be discarded as soon as it had served its purpose.

It is scarcely surprising that the interests in the USSR which were adversely affected by the innovations should resist them determinedly and see them as an abandonment of everything that the socialist state represented. When the consequence was social and cultural turmoil, and the eruption of independence demands in the peripheral republics, they naturally regarded their critique as confirmed.

The women's movement in the USSR

The official Soviet ideology was one of complete gender equality and it frequently boasted of how the Revolution had freed Soviet women, especially in the Asian republics, from centuries-old servitude. This, though, did not preclude a theoretical acceptance of preferred gender roles – the workforces of the schoolteaching and medical professions, for example, were overwhelmingly female. Nor was homosexuality acceptable, and male homosexuality remained a criminal offence.

In practice the proclaimed gender equality was a fiction, and a deep vein of misogyny ran through Russian and other Soviet culture. Issues such as rape, prostitution, abortion and sexual relations generally were tabooed from public discussion. Condoms were manufactured, but crudely – they were referred to as 'galoshes' and understandably unpopular. Overall, in 1985 women made up 51 per cent of the workforce, but all the higher positions in politics and administration, apart from token exceptions, were monopolised by men. The number of women who ever served on the Soviet Politbureau could be counted on the fingers of one hand. The structure was particularly unjust, as women were expected almost universally to take complete responsibility for household and child-rearing tasks in addition to their paid employment. As Martin McCauley remarks, queuing in the inefficient distribution system consumed billions of man-hours, 'or rather, woman-hours'.

The introduction of *perestroika* was not wholly favourable to what was already the seriously unjust situation of Soviet women. The introduction of market reforms meant that they were exposed to increasing risk of unemployment. With the abandonment of quotas for female representation in the soviets – local, republican and all-Union – the number and percentage of female delegates collapsed dramatically. With *glasnost*, however, the scope for expressing grievances and raising issues was greatly enhanced and, despite opposition, the borders of what was permitted were constantly being pushed outwards.

Dissatisfaction found expression even in the official Soviet Women's Committee. In 1987 Valentina Tereshkova, its outgoing chair, declared that 'we do not have profound, fundamental and theoretical research into the position of women in Soviet society'.[12] (Though Mary Buckley, who reports the remark, does not mention this, Valentina Tereshkova was also in 1963 the first woman to fly in space.)

Buckley also notes that an autonomous women's movement was slow to develop in the Soviet Union:

> While popular fronts were quick to form, attracted large memberships and made bold, even violent demands, women's groups established themselves slowly, were small in size and refrained from making forceful interventions in politics. Indeed, some female academics, who for years had examined women's subordination in the workforce and in the home, and who were personally committed to changes in gender roles, in interviews as late as 1989 reiterated the view that 'it is premature to form a women's movement. Society is not ready for this'.[13]

It was only in 1990 that an attempt was made to combine numerous small women's groups into a broader movement. One of the originators, Olga Lipovskya, edited in Leningrad a cyclostyled journal *Zhenskoe Chtenie*, which concentrated on translating extracts from Western feminist writings. One humorous piece was entitled 'Why cucumbers are preferable to men', and contained explanations such as:

> It is not difficult to get to know cucumbers
> With a cucumber you never discover dirty socks in your washing
> A cucumber never gives you a birthday present paid for with your money
> A cucumber won't reduce you to tears.

Nevertheless, Buckley concludes, 'Hard hitting radical feminism which isolates men as its main target ... is largely unknown in the USSR.'[14] Indeed, in Lithuania the nationalist *Sajudis* women's movement appears to have wanted to *intensify* gender roles. Women could not be 'complete' in the Soviet Union, one activist asserted, because the importance of home and family was downplayed. The clear message, Buckley writes, was that 'we want women to become women and men to become men. We are not a feminist movement.'[15] Creches and kindergartens were dismissed as oppressive Russian cultural impositions which caused children to suffer 'atrophied brains'. According to Buckley, 'women in *Sajudis* claim widespread support for their vision of Lithuanian independence ... which celebrates *Kinder*, *Kirche* and *Kucher*'.[16]

Overall collapse

In his penetrating analysis of Soviet history,[17] Martin McCauley identifies a problem that had its roots in the Stalin era and throughout the state's subsequent history had grown implacably worse. It can indeed be seen as a confirmation of Marx's dictum that socio-political structures mirror those prevailing in the economy (crudely, base and superstructure). The centralised command economy directed by a monopoly party could work only under the most specialised conditions – that is, those of the initial Five Year Plans followed by total war. Even under those it could still not function effectively unless there was a considerable devolution of authority downstream, as it were, both geographically and institutionally, to subordinate production and political managers. In both respects power, if not formal authority, tended to drain from the centre to the periphery.

Stalin, sharply aware of the problem, had tried to rectify it by repeated purges and so prevent the apparatchiks developing a corporate identity by keeping them in a state of perpetual terror, but not even he could succeed altogether. A key reform of the post-Stalin period was to lift the terror and give the bureaucrats personal and occupational security, which naturally accelerated the process, as did the shift towards greater consumer satisfaction which implied growing complexity in the economy and 'human management'. There were echoes of medieval feudalism, where the sacred monarch and his court could only rule with the consent and co-operation of the territorial barons.[18] 'The network of interest groups was so dense and regionalism so powerful that Moscow could not impose its will.'[19]

> Marxism–Leninism as an ideology proved quite incapable of reacting creatively to the changing environment. It is surprising that the ideology, which was an obligatory subject for all students, remained a wooden subject devoid of intellectual content .... The party filled up with careerists. ... [A]bout 80 per cent of party members in 1991 ... [but] even in ideology there was no overall co-ordination.
>
> The party did not recognise that the growing level of culture among the population meant that the party's word carried less and less credence ... Ironically the federal Soviet State, designed by Lenin to overcome nationalism and regionalism, fostered it. Had the USSR been as rich as America or Saudi Arabia, then the State might have held together. However, economic decline, the inevitable result of the bureaucratic market, sealed its fate.[20]

Even the term 'command economy' is somewhat misleading, for the complexity of a would-be consumer economy not founded on market principles was so formidable that the actuality was somewhat more like a horde of mini-command economies (sometimes reaching down to plant level) with chaotic relations between them. For example, bicycle chains manufacture was concentrated in Latvia, and if the management there proved obstructive no working bicycles could be provided.

It is clear that the military were also unhappy for two principal reasons. In the first place, the programme of cutting military expenditure both affected them personally and offended their patriotic feelings as constituting a danger to Soviet military preparedness. Similarly, the government's willingness to give up defensive positions by withdrawing from Eastern Europe, retargeting missiles and withdrawing protection from the bloc states, not to speak of the humiliating abandonment of Afghanistan, represented a policy of enormous concession to the enemy with no corresponding quid pro quo. Western commentators did speculate about the possibility of a military putsch to reverse the Gorbachev process, but the tradition of military subordination to the civil authority was too deeply ingrained to make that a realistic prospect.

Collapse

By 1991, with the Baltic republics in practically open revolt, a shooting war in progress between the Armenian and Azerbaijani republics and Boris Yeltsin having established a commanding position and presence as the popularly elected first President of the Russian Federation, the attempted coup in August by hardline traditionalists came as little surprise to observers. The conspirators were not without reason to hope that they would be supported – growing disorder, criminality and international humiliation were beginning to alarm many ordinary citizens as well as the vested interests of the *nomenklatura*, with whom Gorbachev was most unpopular. They seemed to expect that merely by proclaiming their purpose they would gain the acquiescence of the population, and that Gorbachev, on holiday and imprisoned in his Black Sea dacha, would crumple before their demands.

However no more inept band of plotters could possibly be imagined. They had taken no precautionary steps to assure support where it mattered – such as the barracks – to organise informal armed forces at their command, to seize control of communication centres or to neutralise their most dangerous enemies. They do not even appear to have read Marx's own sensible advice on how to seize power, beginning with, 'Above all, never play with revolution'; play with revolution is exactly what they did.

When it became clear that Gorbachev would not play ball and militant, though as yet non-violent, opposition erupted on Moscow streets (other parts of the country seem to have remained quiescent) and the military looked the other way these would-be revolutionaries (or counter-revolutionaries depending on one's viewpoint) lost their nerve and caved in: the revolt of the living dead was rapidly over – it was claimed that some of them were even drunk at the time. The winners did not even bother to punish them severely.

Yeltsin was the acclaimed hero of the hour and wholly overshadowed the rescued and returning Gorbachev. When the former (wholly illegally) declared the suppression of the Communist Party and sequestration of its assets, the fact that it had become an empty shell was brutally exposed. A surge of popular fury swept the CPSU into oblivion, demolished its organisation, seized its property, defaced its symbols and annihilated its pretensions to popular legitimacy. The party as such remained passive during the attempted putsch, made no coherent response as events developed, and was incapable of even finding a quorum for its Central Committee. Certainly no class-conscious masses rushed to its defence in the wake of Yeltsin's decree. In the end it collapsed almost as easily and comprehensively as the Tsarist regime in 1917. The later-reconstituted Russian 'Communist Party', ultra-nationalist and verging on fascism, had nothing in common with its predecessor apart from the name.

The year before, the last vestige of international communism, the journal *World Marxist Review* (in Russia its title was *Problems of Peace and Socialism*), published in Prague but under the control of the CPSU, closed down and its premises were acquired by the Catholic Church.

EASTERN ASIA

The developments in China following Mao's death and the imprisonment of his intended successors highlighted the contradictory character of the regime's development. Superficially, that could be seen as an imaginary scenario of how things might have gone in the 1920s Soviet Union if Bukharin rather than Stalin had prevailed and the economic hegemony of the NEP had been enhanced rather than crushed by collectivisation and the Five Year Plan. However this would be seriously misleading. The Bolshevik leaders, whatever they might be doing in reality and whatever the popular attractions of 'socialism in a single country', remained locked in an internationalist mindset; they were obliged to take into account the existence of the Comintern, however they might subordinate and abuse it, and the Soviet regime's discourse was saturated with international concepts. Somewhere in the depths of his consciousness, Stalin himself probably believed in them – at any rate, for reasons of policy, if he was to convincingly present himself as Lenin's successor, he could not afford to abandon internationalism.

The Chinese leaders, by contrast, had, with the ending of the Cultural Revolution or even earlier, abandoned internationalist pretensions and fallen back on their state's exclusivist and imperial heritage, transmogrified in the twentieth-century context into an intense nationalism. Even while Mao was alive it had mended fences with its supposedly mortal enemy, representative of everything most hateful about world imperialism. Indeed, it had even entered into informal alliance with the USA – Stalin, in signing the Nazi–Soviet pact, did not go so far as to take Hitler (or his representative Ribbentrop) on a tour of Russia's beauty spots. Therefore, when the encouragement of first rural, then industrial and service sector capitalism, produced dramatically encouraging results, there was no great ideological barrier to hastening further and faster down the capitalist road, and even to smashing the state-supported 'iron rice bowl' of basic nutritional and welfare provision.

Inevitably, all this produced growing income differentiation and concurrent social tensions – and as usual the discontent was articulated by those social elements most able and motivated to do so: the educated youth. These realities were at the root of the demonstrations that erupted in 1989 demanding democratisation of the regime, most famously in Tiananmen Square. In essence they were agitating for an open system in which opposing interests could argue freely against each other and struggle for influence outside the confines of a police state.

Accounts suggest that the Party leadership debated long and hard between concessions and repression, and finally, drawing on their traditions and no doubt conscious of the growing disturbance in Soviet affairs, resolved on savage military repression. After that there was no doubt that the reversion to undiluted capitalism would remain under the control of a ferociously authoritarian state[21] using nationalism as its ideological prop. It retained the symbols and procedures of the CPC, but discarded all elements of its previous ideological character.

Vietnam, Cambodia and North Korea

Communism's last great victory came just short of 60 years after the October Revolution. In 1975 the forces of the NLF and the North Vietnamese military, having forced a US withdrawal two years earlier, took Saigon, toppled the regime which the Americans had left behind them and reunited the country. Vietnam, despite, or rather because of, its proximity to China, was in the Soviet camp during the ideological dispute. China was a centuries-old traditional enemy of Vietnam, to which it had laid claim as part of its imperial domain. The Vietnamese through the centuries had been obliged to fight to retain their independence. Nevertheless correct relations were maintained during the course of the war, though the Chinese government may have impeded Soviet military supplies.

The Khmer Rouge regime in Cambodia, renamed Kampuchea, which had come to power in the same year was entirely a product of the war, during which the country had been devastated by US bombing and was ultra-Maoist in character. Its atrocities against its own people far surpassed those of Stalin in everything but scale, and even those of Mao himself, though of course the ideological presentation was rather different. In a rare interview that the Khmer Rouge leader, Pol Pot, gave to a group of rather ingratiating Yugoslav journalists in 1979 (the massacres naturally went unmentioned), he smoothly claimed that all the regime's policies were determined by popular demand. Immediate urgent practical concerns, he asserted, were responsible for the emptying of the cities, the abolition of schools, money and trading networks, and as for their revolutionary neighbour, 'It is unacceptable for us to become a slave of the Vietnamese ... it is unacceptable to our people and our army.'[22]

Ultra-nationalist and indeed racist, the regime began, probably under Chinese inspiration, a pogrom against Vietnamese living in the border areas, claimed Vietnamese territory and started cross-border raids. When the Vietnamese responded by invading and overthrowing the Khmer Rouge, the Chinese found pretexts to militarily attack Vietnam, or as they put it, 'teach them a lesson'. The People's Liberation Army recruits, however, were no match for the experienced Vietnamese military, who quickly repelled the assault.

The episode sent a shiver through what was left of the communist movement in the West. The Khmer Rouge could be written off as a rogue element and the Sino–Soviet ideological dispute was bad enough, but here now were two authenticated socialist states in military conflict with each other. How could such a thing be? Nationalism in communist parties was supposed to be no more than an expression of cultural pride and anti-imperialist sentiment – it should never inform international policy, above all between fraternal communist regimes (one pretext of the Soviet attack on Carrillo was his suggestion that the USSR might have great-power interests).

It might therefore be regarded as all the more surprising, in view of this conflict, that in the 1980s and thereafter Vietnam followed a similar route to China, dismantling its communist economic structures, replacing them with market-orientated ones and opening up its economy to foreign penetration. The attractions of market-driven economic growth were just too strong to be resisted, especially once the USSR was no longer in a position to offer support. North Korea followed a different route, with fairly drastic consequences for its population, with a regime that might almost have been modelled on Orwell's *Nineteen Eighty-four*, even if it did not rival the psychopathic actions of the Khmer Rouge. No doubt that had a lot to do with the severe military threat maintained by the USA on its borders (everything about the country was orientated towards defence) and the personality of its megalomaniac maximum leader, Kim Il Sung. It made Chinese authoritarianism seem relaxed and liberal by comparison.

CONCLUSIONS

So ended what one commentator has chosen to describe as 'the illusion of the century'. What most of its obituarists, however, fail to do is identify the reasons why so many millions found that illusion attractive and answering to their human needs.

The popular canard of identifying communism as a form of religion has been put the wrong way round. It is much more appropriate to view certain elements in the monotheistic religions (the comparison hardly works for the others) as a primitive anticipation in non-scientific eras of the possibilities inherent in social life and production if only malign social structures (misconstrued as individual depravity) were to be removed.[23] It is therefore hardly astonishing, when such possibilities really do appear on the agenda, that the adherents of a coherent outlook directed towards achieving them should display zeal and commitment equivalent to their religious predecessors.

Utopianism is a closely related strand, and without doubt Marxism, and communism possibly even more so, possessed a strongly utopian strand, for all Marx's own warnings against utopianism and his and Engels's particular care to dissociate themselves from what they termed 'utopian socialism'.[24] It was hardly avoidable; William Morris, who regarded himself as a Marxist, wrote a utopian novel. Much of the publishing output from Soviet publishers, whenever it reflected on future prospects, was clearly utopian in character.

For communists in developed economies, their purpose was to 'break the fetters of capital' and allow the possibilities of modern science and technology directed towards the public good to blossom; for their counterparts in the largely peasant Third World, it was somewhat different. Here, along with liberation from foreign domination when that was relevant, the politics of vengeance was very much to the fore – vengeance on landlords, tax collectors, usurers and army recruiters. Marcel Liebman, in discussing this issue and writing from a Leninist perspective, provides an account of some of the horrors these parasites visited upon hapless peasant households.[25] Communist leaders in these areas of course had longer-term perspectives as well; for them, communism among its other assets constituted a development strategy for catching up with the West.

Certainly communism has to be judged not solely in terms of its aspirations and perspectives, its achievements, or the horrors which it in turn inflicted once in control of the state, but also in terms of the enormous social energies which it released and channelled. What these accomplished during the first four decades of its existence was truly stupendous, and even afterwards was in some cases and places no mean achievement.

The very existence of communist states, even when elsewhere communist parties were weak or negligible, was itself highly significant. Without the Russian Revolution and subsequent survival of the Soviet state it is highly likely that most of the former colonial world would still consist of colonies and China would remain a dominated semi-colony or even a fragmented collection of principalities. Moreover the threat of communist appeal to West European populations during the Cold War checked the predatory instincts of capital and ensured that trade union strength was tolerated, and adequate welfare systems (now in the process of dismantlement) were financed and put in place to neutralise that appeal.

Yet the ideology was profoundly flawed. Nonetheless, it is a mistake to attribute the failure entirely to the inherent imperfections of the ideology rather than to material realities and pressures – a more sophisticated version of the pronouncements by US apologists that all the problems of the Cuban economy are down to its state-controlled character and none to the US blockade.

Can we therefore assume that matters would have been substantially different if the USSR, the Soviet bloc and world communism in general had not been subjected to relentless attack and threat by its international enemies, and compelled to devote enormous resources to its defence? In detail perhaps, but in essence probably not, assuming that some kind of functioning market economy had continued in the remainder of the world. In any such case, the possibility of long-term peaceful co-existence was itself utopian. There was no chance of the October Revolution triggering a similar world or even European revolution. That was Lenin's fundamental error (though, to be fair, he could not reasonably have foreseen it) and as he himself emphasised, if capitalism survived, it would remain adamantly hostile.

Nevertheless, not even that was the main problem. The problem was the ideological assumption, insisted on particularly by Lenin in his *State and Revolution*, that capitalism had created an economic administrative system that could be easily taken over – in weeks or months even! – then socially organised and applied to humane social purposes. In reality, none of the revolutionaries had at that point the faintest idea of how a socially owned and operated economy could work – the only people who had given it any thought were the British Guild Socialists and the British Fabians, not real socialists but crypto-liberals as Lenin correctly recognised. The eventual solution adopted to the dilemma, the command economy, was unviable in the long term and, even without the pressures noted above, would have eventually have proved to be so. That was the central weakness, to which communist ideology as understood in the twentieth century had no answers, nor could have any.

14
Fascism

Fascist ideology of various sorts sustained a substantial underground existence after 1945 alongside a rather less substantial public presence. The more unfavourable economic climate and the greater political instability which set in during the years after 1973 provided fresh opportunities, as they had done for neoconservatives. The new combination of circumstances, though in no way so desperate as those of the interwar decades, did present some resemblances to the earlier period. Economic uncertainty, inflationary pressures and rising militancy among workforces – which in Britain even overthrew a government – coalesced with cultural angst inherited from the previous decade and the emergence of new threatening collectives such as minority nationalism, militant women and gays. Communism appeared to be making (though misleadingly as it turned out) steady international progress, and orthodox governments and parties to be quite unable to address these issues effectively.

Alarm of this sort promoted a rise in the profile of the World Anti-Communist League (WACL), an organisation which formally would have disavowed fascism but was nonetheless riddled with fascist activists and with evident fascist tendencies. It had its origins in the 1960s, being promoted by the Chiang Kai-shek and the billionaire Korean cult-leader Sun Myung Moon, characterised by one source as 'the L. Ron Hubbard of the East'. The WACL was described by a defector as 'largely a collection of Nazis, Fascists, antisemites, sellers of forgeries, vicious racialists, and corrupt self-seekers'. The president of its US branch was the vehemently ultra-right retired general John Singlaub, dismissed for insubordination in the 1970s by Jimmy Carter.

None of the groupings, old or new, so far as I can determine, actually used the fascist name. A few, mostly confined to the United States, continued with 'Nazi' or 'National Socialist' titles; these were groupuscules that were content to remain tiny and cultivate their fantasies without any expectation of wider impact.

Although antisemitism remained and remains very much on the fascist agenda, its loss of respectability, the relatively small numbers of Jews remaining in Europe and the terrible memories of the Nazi extermination campaign, meant that in Europe –and even in the USA, where there was a large Jewish population[1] – it could no longer provide a populist focus. As hate figures, Jews were replaced by immigrants, of which there were large numbers both in Europe and the USA – Turkish and Yugoslav 'guest workers' (*Gastarbeiter*) in Germany; Algerians in France; West Indians, Pakistanis and Indians in Britain; Indonesians in the Netherlands; and Latinos in the USA.

However, informal racism was one thing, channelling it into conscious fascist activity was another. What the economic depression of the 1970s did was to enable fascists to link together more effectively issues of racism and material discontent. The depression generated a new constituency not traditional to fascism, one of disaffected unemployed working-class youth (who, on account of their unemployment, were out of touch with the labour movement, its traditions and its official anti-racism) ready-made to absorb the fascist celebration of violent domination.

EUROPE

Europe, where fascist traditions remained strong in certain quarters and had shown themselves active even in the 1960s, was the main stem of fascist regrowth. Indeed, in 1973 three regimes were in place that were popularly regarded as fascist in inspiration, although that designation is ambiguous and they had little to do with what went on elsewhere in Europe. The Spanish regime, which continued to base its legitimacy on the boast that it had saved Spain from communism and freemasonry, was by the early 1970s tottering towards its close.

It was understood – no formal pronouncement was ever made – that on Franco's death the monarchy would probably be restored, but no hint was given that the character of the regime would be altered, and Franco had appointed a strongman, Admiral Luis Carrera Blanco as his successor to rule the future monarch and ensure that its essence was maintained. At least that was the plan until in 1973 the Basque separatist guerrillas succeeded in blowing Blanco up and the scheme fell apart, Franco himself by then being in an advanced state of senility. The Falange was dismissed from history with less trouble even than the CPSU was to be in 1991. An attempted coup by the old guard a few years later proved to be a comic-opera affair and easily suppressed. Portugal's fake democracy had been overthrown rather more spectacularly in the year before Franco's death and the ultra-right disappeared as a meaningful factor in Iberian affairs for the foreseeable future.

The Greek colonels' coup of 1967 could be interpreted as an ultra-right conservative episode with its roots in the anti-communist civil war of the 1940s, undertaken to prevent the election of a radical left government, naturally accused of communist intentions (similar plans were ready in the files for Italy), rather than a specifically fascist enterprise, and certainly no significant fascist organisation was involved. Nevertheless, there was a definite fascist strain associated with the coup – not so much in mainland Greece as on the closely-linked, Greek-speaking Republic of Cyprus, where a well-entrenched and popular communist party, AKEL (Anorthotikó Kómma Ergazómenou Laoú, Progressive Party of Working People), supported the government of Archbishop Makarios. Cyprus's detachment from the British Empire had been attained in the 1950s largely by the guerrilla efforts of the right-wing nationalist Enosis movement, whose objective had been unification with Greece – Britain had insisted on independence instead, both to save face and to satisfy the Turkish-speaking minority passionately opposed to such union.

Unequivocally fascist elements in the island inspired by the Greek junta, approved by Henry Kissinger fearing 'a Cuba in the Mediterranean', and led by the journalist Nikos Samson, carried out a putsch in 1974 against Makarios aiming to achieve the desired reunification. Within days, however, the whole thing came apart when the Turkish government invaded Northern Cyprus, where the Turkish minority was concentrated, and proclaimed a separate state there. The coup collapsed; so did the now discredited colonels' regime in Greece, and the Greek right sanitised itself.

Italy

Italy during these years contained the largest reservoir of fascist activity on the continent. Pre-eminently, the MSI, as noted, served as a direct attempt to reconstitute Mussolini's party. It lacked respectability, however, and pursued its existence on the fringes of political life – the fascist heritage was too strong to be forgotten during these years, and there was no reason to imagine that the MSI would ever amount to anything.

At the same time there were elements of a much more aggressive variety operating underground, some of which might or might not have had secret links with the MSI. Their objective was nothing less than by means of terrorist tactics – such as exploding a deadly bomb in Bologna railway station[2] – 'the strategy of tension', to destabilise the state and prepare the way for a fascist takeover assisted by similarly-minded elements in the military and security services. Such projects were not as bizarre as might appear at first sight; for plans of that nature really did exist and were related to a secret organisation called Gladio (which also had connections with Cité Catholique) set up by the Western powers in a large number of European countries, but Italy above all, during the Cold War to prevent by means of military coup any communist takeover, democratic or otherwise, and if that failed to oppose it with terrorist measures.

> You had to attack civilians, the people, women, children, innocent people, unknown people far removed from any political game. The reason was quite simple: to force ... the public to turn to the state to ask for greater security.[3]

According to the Pentagon document, *Field Manual FM 30-31B*, as quoted in the above source, 'US army intelligence must have the means of launching special operations which will convince Host Country Governments and public opinion of the reality of the insurgent danger ... special operations must remain strictly secret.'[4] Naturally, it did not take very long for adventurous fascists to become well integrated into these underground networks.

Particularly associated with the Italian fascist outliers was 'Third Positionism', supposedly seeking a 'third position' between communism and classical fascism. The proceedings of an Italian neo-fascist conference in 1981 were published under the title 'Beyond Right and Left'. Roger Griffin in *Fascism* is at pains to emphasise that this was also an international trend and prints material from British and German expressions. The Italian extract which he uses aspires to 'rediscover the mythic and sacred roots of European civilization', and seeks out,

> *mythic figures* which throughout the centuries in which society and culture formed an organic whole operated subliminally as the *atemporal archetypes* of European civilization ... opening up access to the sources of the Sacred in its expressions which are most appropriate to binding together practically a supernational community through the rediscovery of the sacredness of the world and the liturgy of existence.[5]

Decipherment of what was actually going on in Italy was much complicated by the ostensibly left-wing terrorists of the 1970s, the Red Brigades. Certainly these commenced as a splinter from the Communist Party by elements dissatisfied by its cautious and non-revolutionary politics. They proved to be the most effective of all terrorists in European democracies, assassinating various individuals in high office and finally kidnapping and murdering a prime minister. Not unnaturally they were soon suspected, not least by the communists, of being no more than a front for the ultra-right or at least being covertly aided by the security services. The truth or otherwise of this allegation remains unclear, but the balance of probability is that it was not, and that their outlook was more akin to the anarchists of the late nineteenth century.

At the same time, an intellectual sanitation of fascism and denigration of the wartime Resistance (with which the communists were particularly identified) was occurring. Central to this was the historian Renzo De Felice and his school. De Felice was the author of a gigantic multi-volume biography of Mussolini, still unfinished at the time of De Felice's death, written with every appearance of scholarly erudition (though in very convoluted style) and tending – though De Felice was not a member of any of the fascist organisations – to rehabilitate the Duce and his regime.

Germany

In Germany the NDP had, by the 1970s, faded into relative insignificance, and although organisations of SS veterans, ultra-right organisations of expellees from the eastern borderlands and other potential centres of fascism still continued to proliferate, no fascist grouping attained a significant profile during those years. Not only the memory of the Reich but the generally right-wing disposition of German politics served to narrow the space for such movements. The German counterparts of the Red Brigades, the Red Army Fraction (or Bader-Meinhof group), though carrying out spectacular assassinations, had virtually no wider base of support and never came near to destabilising the state.

France

It was quite a different story in France, where Vichy traditions lived on, while disillusion with the outcome of the 1968 *événements*, the socialist–communist alliance of the late 1970s and the appointment of communist ministers in

Mitterrand's government of 1981, generated a growing fascist and fascistoid milieu, both organisational and intellectual.

We have already noted the prevalence of ex-Maoists among the exemplars of the postmodern sensibility. However, it has to be acknowledged that in their formal politics most of these remained on the left and few diverged to the right let alone the ultra-right (if any did they ceased to be postmodernists): there was nothing comparable with the Italian anarchists and syndicalists[6] who rallied to Mussolini. The emergence of a substantial fascist party, the Front National, had other sources – economic discontent due to the global crisis, apprehension at the memory of 1968, fear of a resurgent left, and those whose social roots reached into the Vichy regime and the pre-war ultra-right and remained unreconciled to the democratic republican tradition.

A further factor lay in overcoming the difficulty which had impeded interwar French fascism's effectiveness – the lack of a single charismatic leader figure and consequent division of the movement between several rival minor contenders. Now such a personality did appear, Jean-Marie le Pen: a crude and brawling one-eyed ex-paratrooper who had served in the Algerian 'dirty war' and succeeded in imposing himself on and pulling together an inherently fissiparous movement.

The *Front National*, founded in 1972 from the parliamentary movement established by an existing fascist organisation, *Ordre Nouveau*, its initial leaders drawn from the offscourings of Vichy and the OAS, propagated an ideology of 'essential Frenchness'. It adopted Joan of Arc as its icon, and made its focus anti-immigrant propaganda. In the mid 1960s it began to achieve electoral success and, particularly with the decline of the PCF, established itself as a permanent presence in French politics.

Separately but simultaneously an intellectual movement was developing, less blatantly fascist in character, but tending in a similar direction (it is easy to confuse with the 'New Philosophers', but the two trends are quite separate). This version of the ultra-right (self-described as a 'think-tank') which attained a considerable media presence was known by the acronym GRECE (Groupement de recherche et d'études pour la civilisation européenne, Research and Study Group for European Civilisation), which is likewise the French word for Greece, and also used a Celtic cross as its logo. Its essential theme was the superiority of Europe and European civilization over all other cultures. If not explicitly, its arguments and implications were racist in character.

According to its principal spokesperson, Alain de Benoist, described by Griffin as 'by far the most prestigious ideologue' of the European New Right (and Benoist is certainly intelligent), 'We want to substitute faith for law, mythos for logos ... will for pure reason, the image for the concept, and home for exile.'[7]

Benoist rehearses a common fascist trope when he writes that,

Despite their mutual hostility, liberalism and Marxism basically belong to the same universe and are both the heirs of Enlightenment thought ... In almost all respects, liberalism has only realized more effectively certain objectives it shares with Marxism: the eradication of collective identities and traditional cultures, the disenchantment of the world, and the universalization of the system of production.[8]

He circumvents the accusation of racism by distinguishing between 'universalist anti-racism' (that is, real anti-racism – bad) and the 'differentialist anti-racism (that is, racism – good) that he himself adheres to. According to de Benoist, all cultures and ethnicities are valid in their own fashion but not equally valid, and should for their own benefit practise relations of apartheid among themselves. The relevant section is actually headed 'Against Racism; For the Right to Difference'. Feminism and democracy are dealt with in much the same manner as racism – by shifting definitions, humpty-dumpty style, so that he can claim to endorse both while actually attacking them.[9]

GRECE's major influences include Nietzsche and Evola and so it naturally despised Judeo-Christian culture as one fit only for slaves and weaklings. Benoist is into paganism (or the contemporary notion thereof, he does not appear to have advocated the animal sacrifice which was intrinsic to classical paganism). There are sections of international fascism which take this sort of thing seriously and like Evola have moved into the yet more bizarre ideological realms of occultism, or even further – particularly the neo-Nazi rock bands which have been a feature of international fascist fringe, particularly in Britain

A recent statement by the Black Order, supposedly a new alliance of nazi [sic] satanists, [aiming at] the political and religious awakening of Europe … lays heavy emphasis on the cultural struggle and offers this analysis: 'One of the most important factors in the battle for the soul of Europe is that of music. The metal, skin and industrial genres all playing significant roles.'[10]

The idea that fascism could be adopted as a political ideology by fundamentalist Protestants, fundamentalist Catholics and Satanists all together is a truly intriguing thought. The attitude of the New Right, as distinct from the political activists, was that a cultural counter-revolution would be necessary before a political movement of this type could have hope of success. As Griffin puts it, 'the theme of "right-wing Gramscianism" [was] the idea that "metapolitical" cultural transformation is the precondition for political transfromation'.[11] In some cases the debt to Gramsci's methodology, though not his politics, was explicit. Griffin quotes Pierre Krebs, a German counterpart of de Benoist, who writes that,

An Italian Marxist, Antonio Gramsci was the first to understand that the state is not confined to a political apparatus … in other words each political apparatus is reinforced by a civil consensus, the psychological support of the masses … In order to exist at all, political power is thus dependent on a cultural power diffused within the masses.[12]

The UK

In the UK, or more precisely in England,[13] fascism, in the 1970s, again became newsworthy. The issues paralleled those in France – economic distress, immigration, and a militant and temporarily successful labour movement. The organisation which embodied the fascist reaction, much less successful than its French counterpart, had the same name – the National Front. It originated in 1967 from a combination of explicitly neo-Nazi sources – Colin Jordan's National Socialist Movement (he was personally discredited by then) and other racist and fascist-connected organisations and individuals. It was initially fronted by the founder of the League of Empire Loyalists and former Mosley aide, A. K. Chesterton, whose main activity at that time was the production of the previously mentioned hate-sheet newsletter *Candour*. Chesterton remained as leader only briefly before being replaced by John Tyndall, formerly Colin Jordan's lieutenant.

The National Front attracted followers and generated much publicity, particularly around the violent behaviour of these supporters, but achieved little significant success, other than to provide the matrix from which the later more effective BNP (British National Party) was to emerge. Tyndall himself proved a singularly uncharismatic leader, but, through expertise in factional manoeuvre and control of funds, kept himself in the leadership position or else split the organisation and set up his own rival fascist grouping. Vicious factional struggles were the order of the day, and owing to this weakness, militant opposition from the left and the attraction of its less committed followers to the more right-wing form of conservatism which came to prevail under Margaret Thatcher, it faded to a great extent during the 1980s.

LATIN AMERICA AND THE FRENCH CONNECTION

Perhaps the most successful fascist collective, or more accurately, network of the post-1973 era, was wholly traditionalist and is also one of the least known in the Anglophone world. La Cité Catholique ('Cité' in this context meaning 'citadel'), as discussed in Chapter 10, had Maurrasian and Vichy roots and was established as early as 1946, an offshoot of Action Française. Its founder was Jean Ousset; in the words of Horacio Verbitsky, 'La Cité Catholique brought a doctrine of counter- revolutionary warfare and torture, justified as part of Thomist dogmatism.' That doctrine, though Griffin does not discuss the organisation, was clearly of a fascist character and certainly embodied a form of palingenisis. Cité Catholique, though not formally affiliated, later developed close links with Marcel Lefebvre's Society of St Pius X.

Much of what is known of this organisation's role is thanks to the work of Horacio Verbitsky, an award-winning Argentinean journalist who could be regarded as the Simon Wiesenthal of the South American 'dirty war'.

In his book *Le Marxisme-léninisme*, Ousset states that this enemy [communism] can only be successfully combated by a 'profound faith, an unlimited obedience to the Holy Father, and a thorough knowledge of the Church's doctrines'.

Charles Lacheroy, a member of La Cité Catholique, was the first person to reflect on the ideological and technical reasons behind the defeat of the French colonial army in Indochina in 1954. Another member, Roger Trinquier, theorised on the use of torture in *Modern Warfare*, a bible for its followers.

Another of Ousset's recruits was the chief French expert in psychological warfare – Colonel Jean Gardes. Between them they developed a new concept, that of subversion. This conceived a protean, quintessential enemy who, rather than being defined by his actions, was seen as a force trying to subvert Christian order, natural law, or the Creator's plan. For this reason, Ousset states that 'the revolutionary apparatus is ideological before it is political, and political before it is military'. This explains the wide range of enemies he sought to define.[14]

As a result, Cité Catholique became entrenched among sections of the reactionary military in Algeria and the Secret Army Organisation (Organisation de l'armée secrète, OAS) that they had established in the last years of the war to try to retain French control and murder de Gaulle when the latter made clear his intention of conceding independence. Even before that, as early as 1958, Ousset was extending Cité Catholique to other countries, particularly Argentina, and following the collapse of the OAS several of its members ended up in the organisation via a rat-run through Madrid. They included the OAS chaplain, Georges Grasset. One member of the organisation described Grasset as 'a true soldier-monk, a virulent anti-communist, who became the spiritual guide of the OAS'.[15]

Under the sponsorship of the Cardinal-Archbishop of Buenos Aires, Antonio Caggiano and his secretary Bishop Emilio Grasselli, together with elements of the Argentine military, especially in the navy, they began to teach the latter their torture techniques and the ideology to accompany it, all of which these happily passed on to their counterparts in the Southern Cone – Chile, Uruguay and Paraguay. Caggiano wrote, in a foreword to the Spanish translation of Ousset's book,

> Marxism, [he wrote], 'is born of the negation of Christ and his Church, put into practice by the Revolution'. He affirms that Ousset's book is a training tool for the 'fight to the death' to which 'all the peoples of the western world, America and those in Asia who are still resisting, are in grave, imminent danger of falling victim'.[16]

When a formal course was inaugurated in the Higher Military College, instructors included OAS refugees and priests chosen by Caggiano.

At the start of the course, the director of the Higher Military College explained that it would be dealing with a new kind of warfare 'which we could call 'internal warfare', to be fought 'without concern for the means, or scruples, or ethical principles'.

This warfare knew no boundaries. Among the enemies were demagoguery, immorality, vices of all kinds, and low passions, all of which were employed 'through the dialectic of communist action' in order to create 'confusion and contradictions'.[17]

This was in the 1960s. Its fruits were gathered in the next decade, when 'Operation Condor' was put into effect. 'Operation Condor' was the 'anti-subversive' programme which covered nearly every state in South America, was fully backed up by the CIA and the State Department under Henry Kissinger, and extended even into Europe through the channel of Italian fascists and secret state agencies in France and Spain as well as Italy.

Torture and murder were its weapons of choice, with at least 60,000 murders, although the exact number is unknown. Victims included not merely citizens of the junta-ruled states, but foreigners as well, both those involved in left-wing activities – including progressive clergy and even two nuns – and others not. Most prominent victims were the exiled loyal Chilean general Carlos Prats, and the exiled former foreign minister Orlando Letelier, who was assassinated in Washington, DC. The Cuban ambassadors in both Mexico and Argentina were targeted, though unsuccessfully, but two Cuban diplomats in Buenos Aires were kidnapped, tortured and murdered. Even a US senator and later New York mayor, Edward Koch, was threatened with assassination for trying to cut off US aid to Uruguayan murder squads. It was a rerun of events in Indonesia in 1965, though ultimately less successful.

The politics of Latin America were amazingly diverse and complex, but the states composing it had certain features in common. Dramatic polarisation in wealth was the most evident, with tiny proportions of enormously wealthy people, varying sizes and affluence of middle classes and enormous populations of desperately impoverished living in rural indigence or the expanding fetid slums encircling the major cities. All relied on primary production, vegetable or mineral, and all to a greater or lesser extent were, with the exception of Cuba, vassals of the USA.

During the 1960s there were few explicitly fascist movements of any account in Latin America, for the very influential Peronists of Argentina, although often categorised as such, were not really so. Argentina had been among the favourite refuges for Nazi war criminals, and especially among these exiles Nazi movements did exist but they were small and unimportant.

In reality, there was small need for fascist organisations to control an insurgent working class, dispose of communists and preserve the inequitable social order, for generally the military, or more accurately the officer elite, frequently trained in or by America,[18] fulfilled the ultra-right role under the slogans of family, fatherland, religion – and anti-communism. Such was the case in Colombia, Venezuela, Brazil, Uruguay, Chile and Argentina – in the latter two, the 1973 Chilean military coup and a split in the Argentinean Peronist movement gave the right-wing and the generals their opportunity to implement in Operation Condor the techniques they had been taught under the inspiration of Cité Catholique. In Argentina, the dirty war was the dirtiest of all until the generals were brought down by their inability to resist Margaret Thatcher's re-invasion of the Falklands in 1982.

THE USA

Not surprisingly, the fascist phenomenon in the USA, given a new lease of life by the crises of the 1970s, was (and is) an amazingly diverse and divergent complexity, covering all points on the religious and irreligious spectrum, including even prison gangs; a quote from the journal *Searchlight* (though used in a different context) sums it up well: 'a global network that is infested with religious antisemites, Holocaust deniers, Old School fascists, white nationalists, faith-based Third Positionists and anti-democratic clerics'.[19] A brief outline, which is all that is possible here, is bound to be cursory and inadequate. Anyone whose nerves are sufficiently strong can explore it easily enough through the Internet.

Despite fascism's prolific character in the USA, the character of the Reagan government from 1981 and its successes in relation to the USSR were sufficient to satisfy most right-wing tastes, but there were, of course, irreconcilables. The successors to the US Nazi Party continued to exist, as did the John Birch Society and a bunch of equally or even more marginal organisations. Among these were the survivalists, paranoids who were convinced that the USA was on the point of being overrun by the forces of evil. They therefore set up hideouts in wilderness areas from which they engaged in practising survival skills and weapons training with the aim of conducting guerrilla attacks on the occupiers once the time came.

Following the success of the civil rights movement, a very large reservoir of white supremacist bitterness remained in US culture, particularly in the Dixie states, and this readily fed into fascist, neo-fascist and Nazi organisations. One name in particular stands out, that of Willis Carto, as something of a godfather to post-1945 American fascism. The invaluable Anti Defamation League has described him as

> one of the most influential American anti-Semitic propagandists of the past 50 years. Since emerging as a right-wing organizer in San Francisco in the early 1950s, he has been associated with nearly every significant far-right movement in the country, from neo-Nazism to militias, segregationism to Holocaust denial. Known for his reclusiveness, he has founded and overseen from behind the scenes an intricate network of bigotry ... most notably, Liberty Lobby.[20]

Carto, a rabid antisemite, was influenced by the writings and person of Francis Parker Yockey, whose tome *Imperium: The Philosophy of History and Politics* (1948) has affinities with Arthur Rosenberg's *Der Mythus des 20. Jahrhunderts* and was dedicated to 'The Hero Of World War II' – that is, Hitler. Carto himself wrote that,

> Hitler's defeat was the defeat of Europe. And of America. How could we have been so blind? ... If Satan himself, with all of his super-human genius and diabolical ingenuity at his command, had tried to create a permanent disintegration and force for the destruction of the nations, he could have done no better than to invent the Jews.

Liberty Lobby, founded as far back as 1958, undoubtedly became influential in the 1970s, Carto keeping himself out of the spotlight and trying to pretend that it was a mainstream right-wing conservative lobby. By the early 1970s it had around a dozen supporters in Congress, a radio talkshow and, in that decade, brought out a very successful tabloid, *The Spotlight*, which in 1980 had a weekly circulation of around 300,000. Carto was the actual founder, in 1979, of the notorious Holocaust-denial Institute for Historical Review.

In 1978 there was produced a novel entitled The *Turner Diaries*, a psychopathic fantasy in which a Nazi-style movement takes over the USA by terrorist methods, exterminates African–Americans, Jews, Hispanics and 'race traitors', and, once in control of the government, destroys all 'non-Aryans' throughout the globe. It became, along with the slogan 'white power', the treasured cultural property of the entire fascist spectrum in the USA. The author was William Luther Pierce, a former associate of George Lincoln Rockwell, who went on to establish the National Alliance, which, though small, was said to be the best disciplined and the most prolific in publicity of all these organisations.

Had the US fascists been able to combine their forces they would have represented a significant political force. However, they suffered from the inherent fissiparous character of all fascist movements, with countless rival führers. Carto himself was notoriously quarrelsome and managed to get himself displaced from almost all his projects. An additional difficulty, one which was peculiar to the United States, was the ingrained individualism and hatred of national government endemic to the American right – one of the groups, the Sovereign Citizen Movement, was opposed on principle to any government or collectivity whatsoever.

The most successful possibly was the Conservative Citizens Council, a supremacist and segregationist organisation derived from the White Citizens Councils of the 1950s and 1960s, and with all the usual ultra-right baggage targeting welfare recipients, feminists, homosexuals, gun control and suchlike. This represented the 'respectable' face of American fascism and succeeded in attracting recognition and support from various right-wing politicians, including nationally elected representatives, mostly in the South.

Conspiracy theories of dark forces plotting to destroy America and the American dream were meat and drink to the US fascistoid ultra-right. Usually this was supposed to work through sinister agencies, such as the Bilderberg Group or the Trilateral Commission, Freemasonry (even the Skull and Bones

Yale University fraternity), and topped out by the Soviet Union or United Nations according to time and taste; all designing to subject America to the evil New World Order, believed by the most paranoid to be run by Jews and already in existence.

> There is a worldwide conspiracy being orchestrated by an extremely powerful and influential group of *genetically-related individuals* (at least at the highest echelons) which include many of the world's wealthiest people, top political leaders, and corporate elite, as well as members of the so-called Black Nobility of Europe (dominated by the British Crown) whose goal is to create a One World (fascist) [sic] Government, stripped of nationalistic and regional boundaries, that is obedient to their agenda. Their intention is to effect complete and total control over every human being on the planet and to dramatically reduce the world's population by 5.5 billion people.[21]

The author of this gem, one Ken Adachi, was duly accused by a rival conspiracy theorist of being himself an agent of the New World Order.

THE USSR AND ASIA

The last place where a fascist presence might have been expected was the USSR, yet in the final years of its existence, as the economic and social framework unravelled, one did develop. There were reports of Moscow teenagers in cinemas who, when footage of the war was shown, cheered the Nazi tanks. The antisemitism of the Tsarist years had, of course, never died out and had erupted from time to time during Stalin's regime – it was present as a persistent undercurrent. From 1989 onwards, it found expression.

This happened through the medium of the *Pamyat* organisation. The word means 'memory' and it had originally been instituted to care for war memorials. However it soon fell into virulently antisemitic hands and set about trying to 'purge' cultural institutions such as the Writers' Union, breaking up meetings, assaulting Jewish writers and throwing them out of the building. It was able to get away with this kind of behaviour because of the general breakdown in state authority, and by being protected by individuals in high places, most especially the KGB (Komitet gosudarstvennoy bezopasnosti; Committee for State Security) apparatus.

Post-1973 fascism, as can be seen from the above, was concentrated in parts of the globe inhabited by European populations or controlled by those of European descent. However, it was by no means confined to those. The rise of the nationalist-conservative BJP (Bharatiya Janata Party, Indian People's Party) and its exclusory 'Hindutva' ideology in India has been proposed as the emergence of fascism on the subcontinent, and around it and linked to it there formed a penumbra of organisations which are difficult to describe as anything other than fascist in character.[22] They shared of course the BJP's ultra-nationalist ideology but revealed their fascist disposition in their formation of paramilitary squads with regimented drilling, martial arts training and violent attacks on opponents, together with the incitement of pogroms against Muslims by Hindu mobs. They were, to suggest a historical analogy, the Freikorps of the Indian right.

Nor had fascism – or its Japanese equivalent – died in that country. The domination of the right, and of Japanese politics, by the Liberal Democrat party did not leave a great deal of space available for right extremist politics. Fascist-minded collectives therefore took the form of associations and pressure groups rather than rival parties. They sought two objectives in particular, first of all the removal of constitutional restrictions on Japanese military activity and the turning of the Japanese Defence Force (a formidable enough apparatus in its own right) into a regular army, navy and air force capable of extending a military presence throughout the Pacific – and the acquisition by Japan of nuclear weaponry.

Their second principal objective was to sanitise Japan's military record during its imperialist campaign in China from 1931 and the Pacific war, to deny the atrocities committed during those episodes and to purge school textbooks which dared to refer to such matters. They were, in addition, ultra-royalists, wishing to restore the Emperor to his previous divine status and under him to de-democratise and remilitarise society. In short, they were nostalgics wanting to recreate the great days of the imperial past and appealing to the racist and supremacist tendencies that still persisted in Japanese culture.

ASSESSMENT

Fascism had, during the twentieth century, been a diffuse form of politics, and at the end of the twentieth century it remained so. It had been from its inception an ideology generated by crisis and its post-1973 incarnations were no different – it was the renewed impact of crisis that had revived a relatively moribund form of politics. There were therefore substantial differences between the various fascist movements under consideration here, though they agreed on more than they disagreed. However, among these sources of disagreement were the egos of the various leaders and would-be leaders, and so the individual parties and groupings were riven with disputes, especially in the attempts to establish international linkages.

The common features of fascism had indeed not changed much since the 1920s. Anti-communism still remained a dominant theme and fascists were most unwilling to recognise the decrepitude of the communist system by the late 1980s, and indeed in some cases the fact that the Soviet bloc and Soviet Union had really collapsed in 1989 and 1991 – it was assumed to be a trick.

Added to this was a contempt for democratic norms that was not merely present in their ideology, but unconcealed and unashamed; democracy was rejected per se as a mode of public decision making: the *Führerprinzip* lived on. Finally, the latter-day fascists continued to adhere to the interwar fascist heritage, for although this was often played down for respectability's sake, and even questioned from time to time by some of the groups' own adherents who regarded it as outdated, in reality it never died.

15
Aftermath

The USSR was finally wound up in December 1991 and communist principles abandoned in nearly all of the states which had previously adhered to them. In the same year the outlines of the 'New World Order' showed themselves with the military attack on Iraq by the USA and several of its vassal powers, punishing Saddam's regime for the kind of breach of international law that they found convenient to overlook in other circumstances. Iraq, after all, was not the only state in the Middle East that attacked its neighbours and seized their territory, possessed or aspired to possess weapons of mass destruction, disregarded UN resolutions and cruelly oppressed the minorities under its rule.

The economic roller coaster had by no means halted. This was demonstrated by the crisis of the European Exchange Rate Mechanism in 1992, which destroyed the credibility of the newly elected Conservative government; the near-collapse of the East Asian stock markets later in the decade; and, finally, the sub-prime lending crisis in the USA and the UK in 2007 occasioning the worldwide financial meltdown of the following year.

Nevertheless, in the early 1990s, within the global economy a situation had been reached of unstable equilibrium (or stable instability) with growing polarisation of wealth on a world scale, curtailment of welfare provision, a much harsher climate and shrinking employment prospects for workforces everywhere. A growing trend in the developed world was to substitute easier credit and growing debt as a compensation for slow-growing incomes among the working population – which was to prove a major contributor to the calamitous developments of 2008.

In a capitalist environment (and the entire world – with insignificant exceptions – was now exactly that), the opportunities for marketisation, particularly in China, provided a formidable engine of global growth; growth accelerated after 1992 and the recession could then be declared to have ended. In one sense, globalisation could have been said to have existed since the sixteenth century[1] and been steadily expanding its scope ever since, but in the 1990s it entered a novel phase, with an unprecedented fluidity in the transmission of capital, assets, material goods and even, although to a lesser degree, labour.

Global politics and ideology mirrored these trends. The USA no longer had any serious world competitors. The most that other countries could aspire to was to protect their own social order, political systems or culture (though even that was difficult enough and available only to the strongest). Conservatively-inflected liberalism truly had triumphed. Neoliberal economic policies were perforce adopted in one variety or another by governments all around the world, and if they showed themselves reluctant they got plenty of prodding from the international economic agencies. Public attitudes too played their part – for except in the most destitute parts of the globe, liberalised economics looked like the gateway to the consumer paradise and were immoderately hyped as such by the globalised media.

THE END OF HISTORY

Right at the beginning of the New World Order, in 1992, Francis Fukuyama sought to celebrate the triumph of liberal capitalism with his volume *The End of History and the Last Man*, sometimes regarded as contemporary in form as well as content by being treated as a postmodernist text, though this is inaccurate. He had already sketched his thesis as early as 1989 in the right-wing journal *The National Interest*, and was closely associated with right-wing think-tanks and neoconservative groups (since when he appears to have modified his views in a more *realpolitik* direction and renounced neoconservatism).

Fukuyama's argument, basing itself on a Hegelian analysis, was basically that history had reached its culmination in a politics of liberal democracy, understood in the American sense, and an economics of liberal capitalism. 'At the end of history there are no serious ideological competitors left to liberal democracy.'[2] This was what universal society had been struggling towards for untold generations, for the most part unconsciously and only latterly with conscious intention. Now happily it had triumphed. Those parts of the world that did not yet enjoy its blessings would do so before long, for nothing better could possibly be contemplated.

To be sure, his volume contained a fair measure of superficiality – he imagines, for example, that the concept of totalitarianism was invented to characterise Hitler and Stalin (Mussolini does not appear in his index), and that the Bolsheviks 'sought to create a society based on complete human equality'.[3] There is complacency too, with the crimes and massacres of the Western powers being quickly skated over. His grasp of economic and even political history is fragile, to put it kindly, and he argues that the principal driving force in history is *thymos*, the demand for recognition of one's personality and/or superiority.

However, the book is not altogether a triumphalist exercise and there are some intelligent perceptions, especially regarding *thymos*, even if its role in human affairs is much exaggerated. He is, as any Hegelian should be, conscious of the contradictions and dialectical stresses in the happy state of affairs the world has reached. He is aware, as the title's reference to the 'Last Man' (a Nietzschian phrase) suggests, of the anomie and lack of purpose that might overtake an unchallenged affluent liberal capitalist society, although he puts rather excessive weight on some of the mad prophet's wilder pronouncements. Fukuyama is also quite sharply conscious of the environmental threat, which he refers to on several occasions and describes as 'a central issue', but rather overconfident that it can be coped with by means of technical fixes.

Nevertheless, the title was not so silly as it sounds today, for in 1992 there really did not appear to be any serious ideological challenger to liberal capitalism. If by the mid 1990s neoliberal economics had not yet homogenised all 6 billion of the world's population into interchangeable labouring and consuming units, it certainly appeared to be well on the way to doing so, having achieved its greatest triumph of all in the former Soviet bloc.

POST-COMMUNISM

It would certainly be a mistake to conclude that the overthrown system was wholly and universally rejected by the populations that had lived under it, and perhaps one of the more surprising aspects of the 1990s was how well the displaced parties survived – the Bulgarians, for example, were so inconsiderate as to re-elect an unreconstructed communist party in an open election, and so were made to hold another election to amend the error.[4] However, there can be no doubt that even if the publics of the USSR and the Eastern European states regretted losing certain aspects of their former regimes, overwhelmingly they had no wish to see the return of the material austerity, state intrusion and party monopoly of public discourse which had characterised them.

In consequence, the former communist parties of Eastern Europe all changed their names – as did the majority of their counterparts in the West if they did not actually dissolve themselves – the 'communist' title was perceived to be a liability. They went further than that, entirely repudiating the past, both in its political and economic aspects, accepting liberal democracy and market supremacy as well.

For in all except a few favoured areas such as the Czech Republic (Czechoslovakia had soon split in two), the result of the transition to free market fundamentalism was a general lowering of material living standards for the majority of the population and the accumulation of enormous wealth by the new rich able to profit from the installation of gangster capitalism, many of these former members of the *nomenklatura*.

The process was at its most extreme in the former USSR itself, not least because there were much larger assets there to plunder. In circumstances like these it was not surprising that the Communist Party, having re-emerged from its brief period of suppression, continued to attract popular support. Indeed, despite the restrictions under which it laboured, it rose electorally to become the second party in the state after whichever party Yeltsin and his chosen successor Putin cobbled together to give themselves an electoral base. The successor communist party (the Communist Party of the Russian Federation) retained the name and even used some of the same language but was in every other respect completely unlike its predecessor. Principally, though, it did not ignore social issues, it appealed to the sense of national outrage among the Great Russians at what had been done to them.[5]

Under the CPSU, whatever its shortcomings, the USSR had been a great power, incorporating the western borderlands and Caucasus, dominating Eastern Europe. Its leaders, whatever else one might think of them, had made its enemies fear and respect it, and radical movements all over the world look to it with hope and approval. Now, territories that for centuries had been part of the Russian empire had made themselves independent around its perimeter; it was despised and kicked around by its former adversaries and living standards had worsened catastrophically. In the presidential elections of 1996 the communist leader Zyuganov came very close to defeating the West's man, Boris Yeltsin and would probably have done so but for electoral rigging. His party's subsequent decline is probably not unrelated to the fact that the regime under Putin proceeded to steal quite a significant portion of its nationalist ideological clothes.

Although the citizens of the former USSR were the most dramatic victims of the neoliberal economic blizzard, they were far from being the only ones, as everywhere around the globe the project was implemented of pushing back the overall cost of labour-power (which did not preclude some gains for favourably placed sections of the labour force) and attacking both money income and the social wage. Whatever the meaning of communism's collapse or abandonment might have been for the populations under its rule, it was certainly bad news for those outside it, for the disappearance of a substantial competitor meant the removal of any restraint on the predatory instincts of capital, which now found itself more favourably placed than at any time since 1914.

From the debris of the Western communist movement a couple of parties, the Portuguese and the French, survived as significant though minor forces within their countries, others either transformed their character (most successfully in the now reunited Germany) or else declined into nostalgic insignificance. Elsewhere, communists in South Africa and India remained politically significant while having to accommodate to the neoliberal reality.

POLITICAL AND IDEOLOGICAL CONSEQUENCES IN A UNIPOLAR WORLD

In the globalised market all capitals were theoretically equal, but some were most definitely more equal than others, and the most equal were those which had a strong state behind them and supporting them. The strongest state of all was the United States of America, which did not at all feel obliged to abide by the same economic standards that it urged upon others. It continued to protect its own producers from competition in all manner of ways and to find means of supporting them with subsidies. Globalisation was far from a state-neutral process equally affecting all parts of the world; it was driven from a particular centre, the USA, which was its main beneficiary. Globalisation in its late-twentieth/early twenty-first-century form played the same role for the USA as an earlier version of free trade had done for the UK in the nineteenth century.

The Project for a New American Century was established by the right-wing elites in the course of the 1990s – its co-founder was William Kristol, son of the veteran Cold War fundamentalist Irving – declaring that 'American leadership is both good for America and good for the world'. As the name suggests, its proclaimed objective was world hegemony, or as they phrased it, 'full spectrum dominance' – in military power, economic strength, diplomatic control and cultural superiority, not to mention positions in the administration for the think tank's acolytes. One of the signatories of the founding document was Jeb Bush, the Florida ballot-rigger of 2000.

The Project and the US ultra-right in general did not neglect to consider the rising star in the east, China, where, with capitalism given its head within the framework of a powerful and authoritarian government capable of quickly crushing any labour or other dissent, economic growth was spectacular and became increasingly so. It was a powerful and nuclear-armed state, clearly not to be trifled with. More significantly still, it had made the USA financially dependent upon it, for it had bought up a large percentage of the accelerating US public debt (and a much smaller but still significant share of US private assets), so that if all of that was to be released simultaneously onto the market the results would be catastrophic. In short, the Chinese were by the early twenty-first century in a position to bankrupt the US state if they ever felt it necessary to do so. From the point of view of the neoliberal neoconservatives, China had ceased to be an ideological threat, but had come very much to constitute a national one and an obstacle to US world supremacy. The wars in the Middle East and the diplomatic manoeuvrings in central Asia can be seen as preliminary moves in preparation for the ultimate conflict with China – and they were openly discussed as such.

Identity politics

The New World Order of the 1990s and the twenty-first century, having wiped out the existing landmarks of opposition to globalised capitalism and US power, generated new ones in their place. It also released forms of ideology that were not directly opposed to the New World Order, but which had been constrained by the bipolar world of the age of extremes.

By far the most formidable of these was militant nationalism, a form of identity politics whose strength had varied greatly in the course of the previous two centuries but which had remained significant at all times. During the Cold War decades both sides had made every effort to exploit it to their advantage. As the international communist movement had begun to unravel, long before the collapse or transformation of its individual parts, the force of nationalism had begun to make itself felt.

As far back as the 1940s, the breakaway Yugoslav regime had appealed to its public on a national basis no less than over questions of communist ideology to support it against Soviet domination; in the following decade the same was true of the dissident Poles and the rebelling Hungarians. Without its nationalist credentials, Castro's regime could probably not have held out in Cuba. The Chinese revolution had been almost as much a national as a communist one, directed first against the Japanese and subsequently against the USA – the same being true for Vietnam. In the 1960s, Chinese nationalist rhetoric was turned against the USSR; the North Korean regime appealed to national sentiment in constructing their garrison state of ultra-barrack socialism.

In the 1970s it got much worse: the Khmer Rouge were psychopathic nationalists as well as psychopathic killers. Any hint of un-Khmer attitudes, let alone activities, incurred an automatic death sentence, and it was their intense anti-Vietnamese behaviour rather than their genocidal proclivities that provoked the latter's invasion in 1979. From the 1990s, nationalist ideology became the central reference point everywhere except in the parts of the world where another form of identity politics combined with it and came to overshadow it.

During that decade, the full extent of nationalism's sinister force was first felt in Yugoslavia as the communist regime melted away.[6] Yugoslavian nationalism soon proved to be a mythical construction as the country fell apart into its separate national components – irreconcilable divisions of economic development, historical tradition and resurgent ethno-religious divisions (though not of language) took over, and the greater part of the country collapsed into bloody chaos.

The state was an artificial creation resulting from the outcome of the First World War; its original name was The Kingdom of the Serbs, Croats and Slovenes, and it was in fact a Greater Serbia constructed to fulfil the ambitions of the Serbian monarchy. The Yugoslav communists had tried to reform the state and satisfy constituent national aspirations by means of a rather complex federal system. After 1989 a combination of general political uncertainty, social disintegration and economic breakdown led to coalescence around national identities – which in addition became identified with differing religious attachments, and each of the national components[7] voted to secede from the federation and strike out as independent states. Slovenia in the north and Macedonia in the south departed without too much trouble – it was the remainder of the former country which became a bear-pit of violence and atrocity.[8] The principal ideological driver of the catastrophe was Serbian nationalism; the outcome eventual foreign intervention, which resulted in Bosnia, where the fighting had been most bitter, being turned into a UN (effectively a US) protectorate.

A close parallel to the Bosnian events then developed in Kosovo, which actually was a part of Serbia – however, given the mixed nature of nationalities in the Balkans and the historic territorial divisions of the twentieth century, it was overwhelmingly populated by Albanian speakers and during the Tito years had, in recognition of this, been accorded a degree of autonomy. The eventual result was the same, military intervention, this time directly by the US, and the establishment of a UN/US protectorate – along with a massive US base on the Macedonian border.

Religion

In the case of Yugoslavia, the definition of nationalities in religious terms was largely artificial – those who were really serious about religious belief, whether Catholic, Orthodox or Muslim, were very much a minority; the terms served largely as cultural and hence ethnic markers. Nevertheless, the global resurgence of religious ideology, a phenomenon of the late twentieth century, growing stronger with every decade, has been one of the most startling of contemporary developments. It had always been a presence in American politics, despite the paradoxical strict separation prescribed in the Constitution, and expanded in importance steadily from the 1970s after the unprecedented Watergate scandal as well as in reaction to the quasi-revolutionary developments of the 1960s. Jimmy Carter, elected in 1976, was anxious to stress his religious credentials as a born-again Christian, but it was Ronald Reagan's team who succeeded in mobilising white American Christianity, overwhelmingly a right-wing phenomenon, behind their candidate and establishing a highly successful conservative bloc. No serious presidential candidate could afford to offend it too drastically.

Eric Hobsbawm in *Age of Extremes* has identified 1979 as a major turning point, with the religious/political revolution in Iran and its impact upon the Muslim world. It was in the same year that the religiously-inspired resistance to the Soviet occupation in Afghanistan made its presence felt. In the 1990s that religiously-inspired resistance triumphed, but was then in turn displaced by the ultra-orthodox Taliban.

With the social and political failure of secular governments throughout the Muslim world, fundamentalist orthodoxy made progress; governments, even secular Turkey, permitted it greater elbow room. In Lebanon, religiously-inspired militias made up the principal combatants in the country's civil war; politicised religion provoked an even more vicious civil war in Algeria, which the secular government contrived to win, but at enormous cost – and, of course, following the US-led invasion and occupation of Iraq, amid abominable destruction, rival religious militias seized control of the country's civil infrastructure outside the Kurdish provinces.

Religiously-defined nationalism, this time Buddhist and Hindu, drove the continuing civil war in Sri Lanka, and religion is central to the right-wing nationalism constituting the main rival to the Congress Party in India. Judaism, too, is not an absent ingredient in this holy cauldron of politicised religion, for the behaviour of the Israeli state, with an increasingly religious identity, constitutes the central problem of Middle Eastern politics and in turn influences world affairs on account of its symbiotic relation with the US state and the strength of Jewish religious sentiment in that country.

Commentators have expressed surprise at this dramatic revival of religious attachment in an era of globalised modernism and pointed to it as a refutation of the secularisation thesis, but in reality it is not so very astonishing. In a world which in one way or another remains a scary place for most of its citizens and where secular hopes, primarily represented by socialism, have run into the sand, superstition in one form or another remains a likely substitute.

In addition, there are very rich and powerful individuals and organisations in the USA, Rome, Saudi Arabia, and Pakistan working industriously to promote their own brand of religious bigotry. So far, their institutional impact has been felt mostly outside Europe, which to date has remained relatively immune, even in the Balkans (the mujahadin who offered their services to the Bosnians were not welcomed). The Orthodox church has been reinstated in

Russia, and the unspeakable last royal couple elevated to sainthood (Rasputin unaccountably has been omitted), but there is no evidence that it exerts a significant influence on politics or government decisions.

Terrorism

Terrorism, 'the weapon of the weak', has been widely resorted to since the nineteenth century by persecuted minorities finding no other outlet for their outrage and frustration, and has experienced a significant revival in the late twentieth century. Occasionally it proves successful, if widely supported and if the political conditions are right, as was the case for the Zionists in the late 1940s, and to a limited degree in the Northern Ireland context after 1970. The tactic of the suicide bomber was pioneered by the Tamil Tigers in Sri Lanka where, as believers in reincarnation, presumably death in such a manner was seen as improving the bomber's life-prospects next time round.

It was subsequently adopted by Muslim intransigents who expected it to provide the gateway to a glorious afterlife. It also proved very handy to the terrorists' enemies, who, dismissing the outrage occasioned by their own actions, found in it an admirable excuse to stigmatise as 'terrorist' or cognate with terrorism all manner of opposition practices, even non-violent ones,[9] and escalate repressive measures in a fashion previously unthinkable.[10]

Fascism

As a form of identity politics, fascism also experienced a recrudescence after 1991. Like fundamentalist religion, it found its raw ingredients in material discontent that could be processed into ideological consciousness. Since the end of the Second World War, anti-immigrant prejudice had formed one of its most consistent themes. In Europe, borders were opening wider thanks to the expanding EU, and even as they were formally closing against non-EU citizens, refugees from the world's multiplying trouble spots were pushing them open again.

A rhetoric of exclusion and scapegoating against immigrants of all sorts re-energised fascist parties and groupings. In Italy, the Netherlands and Austria they succeeded in entering the government, though in the Italian case in somewhat explosive combination since one group, the Mussolini tradition-alists, was based primarily in the south of the country and the other, the newly-established Northern League, wanted a separate northern state taking away all the more economically-developed provinces.

However, in none of these three cases were they able to transform government office into dictatorship and in the Dutch instance, with their charismatic leader Pym Fortuin assassinated, their success soon resulted in their disintegration. The other strong fascist movement (all of them disavowed the fascist label; the Italian MSI, which could not deny its ancestry, claimed to have renounced it) was Le Pen's Front National. Well entrenched, it defeated the Socialists in the first round of the 2000 presidential election though easily beaten in the run-off.

Minor fascist movements such as the BNP also improved their electoral standing throughout Europe, and there was plenty of unorganised fascist sympathy among alienated hooligan street gangs. This was particularly true of the former East Germany, where unification had brought few material rewards for low-income groups and where the murder of individual immigrant victims was their speciality. All the ex-communist East European countries produced a fascist resurgence in some degree. There, the Roma minority was the favourite scapegoat, and in Romania the Iron Guard remained a significant nostalgic memory for certain elements, a few of whom have even tried to reconstitute it. In Russia, while the fascist political party, the 'Liberal Democrats', faded, Pamyat continued to flourish, though it lost some momentum after the death of its leader; and in the USA, Nazi and neo-Nazi organisations continue to proliferate, many of them, inevitably, tied in with religion.

Anti-globalisation

During the 1990s and the early years of the twenty-first century, the anti-globalisation movement made a considerable impact. It mobilised large numbers of supporters internationally and mounted impressive demonstrations at meetings of organisations promoting globalisation such as the IMF, G7 and WTO. Its critique of globalisation, focusing on its deleterious effects and the fate of its victims, was expounded through the writings of its spokespeople and at its conferences such as the World Social Forum. Its arguments were both penetrating and pertinent, but the movement's amorphous nature and lack of any structure, while being a strength in some respects, was in others a significant weakness. On the one hand this discouraged factionalism and theological-type quarrels, but on the other it meant that it could achieve little beyond the demonstrations, which, producing few concrete results, inevitably gave rise to exhaustion if not disillusionment. Also it did not have any striking or convincing alternative to the system that it was attacking – its critique was a negative one.

Of late, popularly-supported regimes have emerged in Latin America which have taken a stance against the impact of globalisation and done so in a manner which has much of the traditional left character about it. This has occurred in Venezuela, Ecuador and Bolivia, embodied in charismatic leaders – to the intense dismay of both local and international capital, which have done their best to overthrow them, though at the time of writing still unsuccessfully. Paradoxically, the social programme carried through in Venezuela has been made possible only by the global market, for it is financed by the oil wealth resulting from the reality that Venezuela is a major supplier to the USA of that commodity.

Green issues

The threat to the environment of unconstrained and unremitting economic growth was perceived many decades ago,[11] and by the 1980s was of significant concern, but only since the 1990s has it become a central issue for all forms of politics. For liberalism it presents a particular problem, because that is intimately bound up with capitalism, which requires continuous and sustained growth – the faster the better – to survive: steady-state economy is of no use to it. Communist states, too, put their emphasis on industrial expansion and had a thoroughly wretched record in relation to environmental issues, but in principle the command economy did not require indefinite expansion and could in theory have been held in a steady state. How a surviving Soviet bloc might have handled environmental issues after 1991 was never put to the test, but it is unlikely that it would have proved much better than the Chinese, whose rush into capitalist consumerism has degraded the country's environment most severely and threatens to contribute massively to global warming.

Forced, though very reluctantly, by incontrovertible evidence, most governments, even recently the USA, have been obliged to acknowledge the existence of the problem but their attitude has invariably been to try to get away with the minimum possible intervention and propose totally inadequate measures, not to speak of the witlessly complacent climate change deniers. Consequently the crisis has accelerated towards impending catastrophe and in response – and linked to the anti-globalisation agenda – green movements have appeared everywhere throughout the world.

Some of these, and among the most prominent, were single-issue pressure groups such as Friends of the Earth and Greenpeace, but even early on green parties were established as political movements. In the mid-1970s the Ecology Party was set up in the UK, subsequently evolving into the moderately successful Green Party.[12] A much more spectacular development occurred in West Germany with the foundation of Die Grünen, which established substantial parliamentary representation and even coalition office in regional and national governments, and, though declined from its earlier prominence, at the time of writing continues to be a force in German politics.

Appropriately, the Green focus was directed towards the environmental crisis, but the movement, and especially its party political component could not avoid being on the left, as it was the economic system of which liberalism and neoliberalism were the political embodiment that generated the crisis in the first place. The Greens' problem was to find a balance between their green agenda and a position that was capable of attracting support in consumer societies or societies aspiring to reach that status. In the German case this was manifested in the division between 'realos' and 'fundis', the names indicating adherence to policies of pragmatism on the one hand, or on the other uncompromising demands for drastic measures which would inevitably damage immediate consumer interests.[13]

It was inevitable that their enemies would accuse Greens of being anti-science, anti-modernisation and anti-technology. Some indeed were like that and would have looked forward to reversion to subsistence agriculture in the style of the Amish without the religious component. More extreme still, among the animal rights movement, proponents of 'deep ecology', such as the American version of Earth First!, welcome the extinction of the human species. '[T]he spiritual and visceral recognition of the intrinsic, sacred value of every living thing' is, according to one of their websites, a key principle. Whether this is supposed to include lice or plague microbes is not specified. However, the principal thrust of the mainstream green movements has been to propose means by which the benefits of modernisation can be preserved while at the same time minimising its deadly effects – a difficult enterprise indeed.

CONCLUSION

All consciously articulated ideologies, political and otherwise, in some sense bring with them an emancipatory promise. Even those which demand the most rigorous subordination promise that through willingly embracing that subordination the believer will experience subjective emancipation; the phrase in the Catholic liturgy, 'whose service is perfect freedom', makes the point. The four considered in this volume offer similar hopes.

For liberalism this is expressed in terms of individual freedom and autonomy, to be achieved through the removal of arbitrary restrictions not justified on rational grounds on what an individual can do or become. In addition, it involves security of person and goods via the rule of law, and a constitutional right in some degree to question authority. This provides scope for great variation in practice; from a laissez-faire regime of restricted franchise and unconstrained capital freedom with no social provision, where the weakest go to the wall, to a social democratic welfare state of equal citizenship underpinned by significant social ownership.

The conservative promise of emancipation treats the liberal version of individual freedom and autonomy as an illusion, and advances instead a corporate alternative. In this ideological perspective individuals are inherently unequal, not merely in the obvious biological senses, but in their capacity, their status and their permitted degree of aspiration. Nevertheless, anyone can find fulfilment by accepting the role in the hierarchy to which they are assigned (there may be more or less room for movement within it) and everyone has the right to respectfully address their superiors to remind them of *their* obligations. Above all, conservatives promise that acceptance of this ideology will protect both individuals and institutions such as family or religion from being cast adrift by social earthquakes. The age of extremes has shown that a large degree of interpenetration is possible between liberalism and conservatism, or even that they can morph into each other.

The communist ideology was also the inheritor of the liberal democratic tradition (though its ideologues often enough forgot this) and its promise was also of individual emancipation, in the sense of autonomy and aspiration – but not by liberal means. Instead this was to be achieved through collective revolutionary endeavour, the centrally important collective currently being the industrial working class, which would give the lead to other exploited classes. Ultimately a classless society would be achieved in the society of abundance, made possible by advancing technology.

Fascism's emancipatory promise was cruder than the others, though in the right circumstances none the less effective for that. What it promised was exemplary vengeance upon scapegoats held to be responsible for popular distress, 'to purify the world through the annihilation of some category of human beings imagined as agents of corruption and incarnations of evil', in Norman Cohn's words. This would be followed by individual fulfilment through the immersion of self in a national collective led by a charismatic leader whose charisma demonstrated his (always his) fitness for the office. This would in turn be accompanied by material benefit and career opportunities for (male) society in general, and loyal followers in particular, even at the expense of traditional elites. The twentieth century showed that fascism could accommodate easily enough to certain varieties of conservatism and that, as occasion demanded, the two could readily combine.

The world of the present is one of intense ideological competition and confusion within a framework of dominant neoliberalism. The only safe conclusion which it is possible to make about the future is that it will differ from expectations – although at least it is difficult to imagine how massive environmental crisis can be averted. Even so, the eventual results of that probability are no more predictable than anything else.

One point worthy of note is how persistent is the heritage of the defeated ideology. To be sure, elements who continue to assert that the presumptions and practices of Marxism–Leninism (whether in Soviet or Maoist style) were spotless, that accounts of the horrors perpetrated by its regimes are lies or grievous exaggerations, and that its demise was due to malevolent traitors, are small and marginal, but they do exist.[14] Less crude forms of nostalgia are still quite prevalent.

However, in the mainstream it is the victors who appear unable to let this issue rest. Following the appearance in 1997 of *The Black Book of Communism* (subject to much incisive critique as well as mutual recriminations between its several authors), comprehensive denunciations continue to pour from mainstream presses and other media. Lenin once noted that the bourgeois ideologists declare Marxism to be refuted for the hundredth time – but still go on to refute it for the hundred and first. This is a spectre which still continues to haunt the world.

At the same time it is clear that communism will never return in its previous form. Nor will fascism. This is not to say that a significant fascist revival is impossible – indeed it is rather more likely than a communist one since fascists are able to exploit sources of atavist irrationality unavailable to Marxists. However, should such an eventuality occur, it will not be like classical fascism but instead a sanitised and 'respectable' version – for public memory of the Third Reich is too lively to allow unashamed neo-Nazis the mass support needed to give them credibility.

In the West (which also includes much of the East and South), liberal ideology rules everywhere and has almost totally assimilated conservatism except in the USA. Even there, present-day conservatives are not so different from nineteenth-century liberals in their attitudes to social living and public affairs. China of course is different, and it is important to remember that it contains a quarter of the world's population. Currently it remains a bureaucratic dictatorship (preserving, for whatever reason, communist symbols and forms), but with the expansion of its capitalist economic base the likelihood is that it too will shift towards some form of liberal ideology (parallels with Taiwan and South Korea may be instructive) though possibly as different from western liberalism as Maoist communism was from the Soviet variety.

It is a recurring trope among liberal scholars that communism was a version of apocalyptic religion, promising the extinction of the intolerable present, punishment of evildoers and the establishment of a new heaven and earth.[15] It would perhaps be more accurate to view the latter as primitive anticipations and poetic longings by oppressed groups, classes and nations of the kind of society that is only made possible by developed science and advanced technology, and which communist ideology aimed to bring about.

Nor is liberalism free of its millenarian aspects, which are also particularly rampant among American conservatives and Islamic fundamentalists in a debased religious form. Francis Fukuyama, poised between liberalism and conservatism, indeed thought that the millennium had arrived, although to be fair, he was conscious of some of the problems which might accompany that happy state. Historical experience has shown that crisis and disaster do not extinguish such hopes; if anything they intensify them. Oscar Wilde once remarked that a world map without utopia on it somewhere was of no value. We can reasonably expect that maps of the sort approved by Wilde (and representing time rather than space) will continue to be utilised.

Notes

INTRODUCTION

1. Terry Eagleton, *Ideology: An Introduction*, Verso, 1991, p.2.
2. Jorge Larrain, *The Concept of Ideology*, Hutchinson, 1979, p.46.
3. Ibid., p.15.
4. James Lull, *Media, Communication, Culture*, Polity, 1995, pp.6–7.
5. The other two guilty ideologies, he argues, are colonialism and socialism. Ian Kershaw, 'War and Political Violence in Twentieth-Century Europe', *Contemporary European History*, 2005; 14: pp.107–23.
6. Or in the words of Richard Rumbold, about to be executed for his part in the unsuccessful 1685 revolt against James II, 'no man comes into the world with a saddle on his back, neither any booted and spurred to ride him'. Originally from a collection of State Trials published in 1816; available from http://www.bartleby.com/268/3/15.html (last accessed July 2010).
7. According to John Gray the term was used first in a political sense by the Spanish party the Liberales in 1812. John Gray, *Liberalism*, 1986, University of Minnesota Press, p.ix.
8. C. B. Macpherson, *The Political Theory of Possessive Individualism: Hobbes to Locke*, Oxford University Press, 1961.
9. Ibid., p.205.
10. Their counterparts in the USA attempted the same, and the provision in the constitution for the election of the President by an electoral college rather than directly by popular vote produced a counter-democratic result as late as 2000.
11. See Albert O. Hirschman, *The Rhetoric of Reaction: Perversity, Futility, Jeopardy*, The Belknap Press of Harvard University Press, 1991.
12. Who, it should be noted, came from a manufacturing background, not a landowning one.
13. Burke, for example, denounced attempts by workers to use traditional legal means to prevent wage reductions.
14. For Rosa Luxemburg, see the renowned biography by Peter Nettl, *Rosa Luxemburg*, Oxford University Press, 1966.
15. J. Arch Getty and Oleg V. Naumov, *The Road to Terror: Stalin and the Self-Destruction of the Bolsheviks, 1932–1939*, Yale University Press, 1999.

CHAPTER 1

1. The Sudeten minority in Czechoslovakia became the most notorious example. Portugal was the only country in Europe without any national minority.
2. Howard K. Smith, *The State of Europe*, Knopf, 1949.
3. The mutinies occurred in French depots, the grievance being the slow speed of demobilisation.
4. From the battle at which the German advance was stopped in 1914.
5. There are clear parallels with what occurred in 2007 and 2008. In the 1920s, it was known as 'pyramid selling'.
6. The farmers had benefited from the hyperflation of 1923; it had enabled them to wipe out their debts. Subsequently, they had continued to borrow.
7. Franz Neumann, *Behemoth*, Victor Gollancz Ltd, 1942, p.35.
8. See Ian Kershaw, *Hitler 1889–1936* and *Hitler 1936–1945*, both Allen Lane History series, Penguin, 1998 and 2000, respectively.
9. See Robert Skidelsky, *John Maynard Keynes*, vol. III, *Fighting for Britain 1937–1946*, Macmillan, 2000, ch.4.

10. The schoolroom was certainly an important element in Hitler's political outlook.
11. See Fritz Fischer, *Germany's Aims in the First World War*, W. W. Norton & Co., 1967.
12. Children were dying from malnutrition and the blockade was continued into 1919 until the Germans signed the Versailles Treaty.
13. The Freikorps was dissolved after the failed Kapp Putsch of 1920.
14. Stein Larsen, Brent Hagtvet, Jan Myklebust (eds), *Who Were the Fascists: Social Roots of European Fascism*, Universitetsforlaget, Bergen, Oslo and Tromsø, 1980.
15. Ibid.
16. See Arno J. Mayer, *The Furies: Violence and Terror in the French and Russian Revolutions*, Princeton: Princeton University Press, 2001.
17. See Alec Nove, *An Economic History of the USSR 1917–1991*, Penguin, 1993; E. H. Carr, *The Russian Revolution from Lenin to Stalin 1917–1929*, Macmillan, 1979.
18. E. H. Carr, 'Editor's Introduction' to N. I. Bukharin and E. Preobrazhensky, *The ABC of Communism*, Penguin, 1969, p.23.
19. It was not totally closed, but foreign trade was severely limited both by choice and western hostility
20. Which did not mean that they were to be extirpated down to the last infant like Jews under Nazi control, but instead they, with any non-kulaks who resisted the collectivisation programme, were deported to inhospitable areas beyond the Urals and left to cope as best they might. Naturally, the death toll was enormous.

CHAPTER 2

1. See Mike Davis, *Late Victorian Holocausts: El Nino Famines and the Making of the Third World*, Verso, 2001.
2. Endless examples could be quoted – one would be the enclosure of the English commons in the eighteenth century.
3. Address to Congress, 11 February 1918.
4. February, by the Julian calendar then used in Russia.
5. In some cases, such as the Baltic States and the Polish eastern frontier, this was settled without reference to Versailles.
6. The British government, for example, had never wanted to break up the Austro–Hungarian Empire.
7. Quoted in Hugh Purcell, 'Paris Peace Discord', *History Today*, 2009; 59: p.39.
8. Ibid.
9. Hugh Purcell, 'Paris Peace Discord', p.40.
10. This irremovability did not exclude shuffling of existing personnel.
11. However, there was certainly a degree of discrimination by the Czech majority against ethnic Germans in the west and Slovaks in the east.
12. Nancy Joan Weiss, *Farewell to the Party of Lincoln: Black Politics in the Age of FDR*, Princeton University Press, 1983, pp.35–6.
13. Similar attitudes were also present across the main political divide. A large defection from the Liberal Party in the 1880s over Irish Home Rule had created the Conservative and Unionist Party and brought with it a significant injection of liberal ideology into the party.
14. Ian Crowther, 'Eric Voeglin', in R. Scruton (ed.), *Conservative Thinkers: Essays from The Salisbury Review*, London and Lexington, 1989, p.261.
15. But not Philip Snowden, Chancellor of the Exchequer, who resigned over the abandonment of free trade.
16. Overall output actually increased during the interwar period despite the collapse of traditional industry.
17. A few communist MPs, notably Saklavalta, were elected in the 1920s in association with the Labour Party, which was permitted at the time; one in the 1930s for the Communist Party, and no fascists in either decade.
18. The *Spartakusbund*, led by Rosa Luxemburg and Karl Liebknecht, was the left-wing breakaway from the SPD and the core of the future KPD.

19. See Roger Middleton, *Towards the Managed Economy: Keynes, the Treasury and the Fiscal Policy Debate of the 1930s*, Methuen, 1985.
20. Robert Skidelsky, *John Maynard Keynes*, vol. II, *The Economist as Saviour 1920–1937*, Macmillan, 1992, p.458.
21. www.firstworldwar.com/source/abdication_ebert.htm (last updated 22 August 2009; last accessed July 2010).
22. www.firstworldwar.com/source/germanassembly_ebert1.htm (last updated 22 August 2009; last accessed July 2010).
23. Ibid.
24. These were the territories governed directly from London, unlike the effectively independent Dominions.
25. A general election had been due in 1940, but none was held during the war.

CHAPTER 3

1. Only for 'civilised' nations of course, and not even all of these.
2. See James R. Barrett, *William Z. Foster and the Tragedy of American Radicalism*, University of Illinois Press, 1999, ch.6.
3. See David Canadine, *The Decline and Fall of the British Aristocracy*, Yale University Press, 1990.
4. Examples are mentioned in C. L. Mowat, *Britain Between the Wars*, Methuen, 1959, p.203.
5. See Keith Middlemas, *Politics in Industrial Society*, Andre Deutsch, 1979.
6. See Richard Griffiths, *Fellow Travellers of the Right: British Enthusiasts for Nazi Germany 1933–39*, Constable, 1980.
7. See Clement Leibovitz and Alvin Finkel, *In our Time: The Chamberlain-Hitler Collusion*, Monthly Review Press, 1997.
8. This was being openly argued at the beginning of the nineteenth century.
9. The old *Mittelstand* were essentially the trading, handicraft and peasant middle classes. The 'new *Mittlestand*' were the white-collar workers.
10. Roger Griffin, *Fascism*, Oxford University Press, 1995, p.111.
11. Perry Anderson, *Spectrum: From Right to Left in the World of Ideas*, Verso, 2005, p.25.
12. Oswald Spengler, in *Prussiandom and Socialism*, 1920, specifically identified socialism with Prussian integralism.
13. Peter Davies and Derek Lynch, *The Routledge Companion to Fascism and the Far Right*, Routledge, 2002, p.249.
14. See, for example, the incoherent preface to *Romanticism and Revolution*, 1922, printed in J. S. McClelland (ed.), *The French Right: from de Maistre to Maurras*, Harper & Row, 1970, pp.239–63.
15. McClelland, *The French Right*, p.226.
16. Ibid., pp.254–90.
17. Roger Austin, 'The conservative right and far right in France: the search for power 1934–44', in Martin Blinkhorn, *Fascists and Conservatives*, Unwin Hyman, 1990, p.179.
18. Jules Archer, *The Plot to Seize the White House*, Hawthorn Books, 1973. Online text available at: http://www.chris-floyd.com/plot/The_Plot_to_Sieze_the_White_House_by_Jules_Archer/ (last accessed July 2010).
19. Griffin, *Fascism*, p.238.
20. See Perry Anderson, *Lineages of the Absolutist State*, Verso, 1974.

CHAPTER 4

1. Right-wing commentators have tended to follow in the tracks of Burke and de Maistre in relation to the French Revolution – it was all a horrible conspiracy; indeed, 'communist conspiracy' was a staple of US McCarthyite rhetoric.
2. It had a number of slightly varying names at different times.

3. The full title was *What is to be Done: Burning Questions of our Movement.*
4. Nevertheless, every one of the Bolshevik top leadership (and most of the second-rank ones as well) was an intellectual of bourgeois background. Ironically, among the former, Stalin, if partially, came nearest to a working-class origin.
5. Referred to as Second Congress.
6. E. H. Carr (ed.), N. Bukharin and E. Preobrazhensky, *The ABC of Communism*, Penguin, 1969, p.62.
7. Bertil Hessil, 'Introduction', in Alix Holt and Barbara Holland (trans. and ed.), *Theses, Resolutions and Manifestos of the First Four Congresses of the Third International*, Ink Links, 1980, p.xvi.
8. Ibid., p.68.
9. Ibid., pp.181–203.
10. Bukharin and Preobrazhensky, *The ABC of Communism*, pp.176–7.
11. Ibid., pp.433–4.
12. Ibid., p.82.
13. Ibid., p.280. One section title is 'Why Religion and Communism are Incompatible'.
14. Ibid., p.118.
15. Ibid., pp.118–19.
16. Ironically, both Stalinists (they still exist) and anti-communists are, for opposite reasons, in passionate agreement upon this question.
17. Isaac Deutscher, *Stalin*, Oxford University Press, 1961, p.288.
18. J. Stalin, *Leninism*, Lawrence & Wishart, 1940, p.113.
19. Seven members of the Executive Committee of the Communist International (ECCI) elected at the 1928 Sixth Congress had been expelled from their communist parties by 1930.
20. Quoted in Kevin Macdermott and Jeremy Agnew, *The Comintern*, Macmillan, 1996, p.88.
21. Vol. VI, Nos 9–10 (English edition).
22. For the principal victims, however, the accusation was usually that they were plotting to hand over parts of Soviet territory to Hitler in return for his assistance in overthrowing the regime.
23. See Moshe Lewin, *Lenin's Last Struggle*, Faber, 1969; and *The Soviet Century*, Verso, 2005, chs 1–2.
24. Central Committee. Communist Party of the Soviet Union (TsK KPSS), *History of the Communist Party of the Soviet Union (Bolsheviks): Short Course*, Foreign Languages Publishing House, 1939.
25. See A. L. Morton, *A People's History of England*, Gollancz, 1938.
26. Deutscher, *Stalin,* p.475.
27. McDermott and Agnew, *The Comintern*, p.249.
28. Deutscher, *Stalin*, p.491.

CHAPTER 5

1. Plínio Salgado, *Let us Wake Up the Nation*, quoted in Roger Griffin (ed.), *Fascism*, Oxford University Press, 1995, p.237.
2. However, Hitler prior to seizing power had a substantial female vote, Mosley's British Union of Fascists (BUF) had a female section. The British Fascisti of 1923 was founded by a woman, Rotha Lintorn Orman.
3. See, for example, Aristotle E. Kallis (ed.), *The Fascism Reader*, Routledge, 2003.
4. Roger Griffin, *The Nature of Fascism*, Routledge, 1993, pp.32–6, et seq. See also R. Griffin, (ed.), *International Fascism: Theories, Causes and the New Consensus*, Arnold, 1998 and Michael Mann, *Fascists*, Cambridge University Press, 2004.
5. Ibid., p.13.
6. Ibid., p.35–6.
7. Ibid.

8. See Martin Blinkhorn (ed.), *Fascists and Conservatives: The Radical Right and the Establishment in Twentieth-Century Europe*, Unwin Hyman, 1990.

9. See Benedict Anderson, *Imagined Communities: Reflections on the Origin and Spread of Nationalism*, Verso, 1983.

10. Communists, it has to be admitted, sometimes shared that particular characteristic.

11. Referred to in the German military as 'corpse-like obedience'.

12. Franz Neumann, *Behemoth*, Victor Gollancz, 1942, p.378.

13. See Joseph Baglieri, 'Italian Fascism and the Crisis of Liberal Hegemony: 1901–1922', in Stein Larsen, Brent Hagtvet, Jan Myklebust (eds), *Who Were the Fascists: Social Roots of European Fascism*, Universitetsforlaget, Bergen, Oslo and Tromsø, 1980, p.328.

14. Denis Mack Smith, *Mussolini's Roman Empire*, Harmondsworth, 1977, p.1.

15. These quotes are taken from an English translation (reprint) published in 1936 by the Britons Publishing Society. The translator, Victor Mardsen, was a journalist on the ultra-conservative *Morning Post* and a friend of the Prince of Wales. The anonymous Introduction of 1922 writes that 'under his [Kerensky's] successors the possession of a copy by anyone in Sovietland was a crime sufficient to ensure the owner's being shot in sight. The fact is in itself sufficient proof of the genuineness of the *Protocols*.'

16. Neumann, *Behemoth*, p.357.

17. Ibid., p.377.

18. Ibid., p.379.

19. Not to be confused with his relative, the Field Marshal of the same name.

20. See Peter H. Merkl, 'The Nazis of the Abel Collection: Why they Joined the NSDAP', in Larsen et al., *Who Were the Fascists*, pp.268–82.

21. Carl Schmitt, in Griffin, *Fascism*, pp.138–9.

22. Franz Neumann, *Behemoth*, p.57–8.

23. Ibid.

24. Codreanu, quoted in Griffin, *Fascism*, p.221.

25. See F. L. Carsten, *The Rise of Fascism*, Batsford, 1980, pp.160–9.

26. Griffin, *The Nature of Fascism*, p.214. The quote is from a speech made by a Lutheran clergyman, Elias Simojoki, leading member of the AKS and its successor the Isänmaallinen Kansanliike (IKL, Patriotic People's Movement).

27. Editorial in *The Lapua Daily Order*, the movement's newspaper, in Griffin, ibid., p.213.

28. Speeches in 1942. Griffin, ibid., p.225.

29. It is worth noting, however, that the Blueshirts were the part-ancestors of the current Fine Gael party.

CHAPTER 6

1. See Correlli Barnet, *The Audit of War, The Illusion and Reality of Britain as a Great Nation*, Macmillan, 1986, for a highly disputed interpretation of British circumstances.

2. Robert Skidelsky, *John Maynard Keynes*, vol. III, *Fighting for Britain 1937–1946*, Macmillan, 2000, ch.12.

3. The same was true for Italy.

4. For an overview see Carlo M. Cipolla (ed.), *The Fontana Economic History of Europe: Contemporary Economies 1*, Collins, 1976; Alan S. Milward, *The Reconstruction Of Western Europe 1945–51*, Routledge, 1987 (which is sceptical of the importance usually attached to Marshall Aid) and David W. Ellwood, *Rebuilding Europe: Western Europe, America, and Postwar Reconstruction*, Longman, 1992.

5. US lend-lease ships were even turned back midway across the Atlantic.

6. Paid off in 2006.

7. Bread, which had been unrationed (though of poor quality) during the war, was rationed in 1946.

8. There was famine in the Low Countries.

9. To sustain this hope, Stalin ordered the Western communist parties to subordinate themselves and refrained at first (except in Poland) from imposing communist regimes on the liberated countries of Eastern Europe.
10. A glossy, foreign-language publication was titled *China Reconstructs*. Unsurprisingly it presented a very prettified picture.
11. See Michael Kidron, *Western Capitalism Since the War*, Penguin, 1970.
12. Which could also carry nuclear weapons.
13. See Enver Hoxha (edited and introduced by Jon Halliday), *The Artful Albanian: The Memoirs of Enver Hoxha*, Chatto, 1986.
14. Andrew Glynn, with Bob Sutcliffe, *British Capitalism, Workers and the Profit Squeeze*, Penguin, 1972.
15. Although de Gaulle secured an exemption for agriculture – rural France was his electoral base.
16. The country, under the name of the Congo Free State, had been acquired in the 1880s by the murderous Belgian king, Leopold II as his personal estate.
17. See Conor Cruise O'Brien, *To Katanga and Back*, Simon & Schuster, 1962.
18. Although it avoided sending troops.

CHAPTER 7

1. Of which the William Beveridge-chaired social security report (Report of the Inter-Departmental Committee on Social Insurance and Allied Services) of 1942, the full employment white paper and Butler Education Act of 1944 were indicators.
2. See Daniel Yergin, *Shattered Peace: The Origins of the Cold War and the National Security State*, Penguin, 1980.
3. The Long Telegram, from The Charge in the Soviet Union (Kennan) to the Secretary of State, Moscow, 22 February 1946 – 9 pm. Received 22 February 1946 – 3:52 pm. 511. Answer to Department's telegram 284, 3 February 1946.
4. Ibid.
5. Ibid.
6. Daniel Bell, *The End of Ideology: On the Exhaustion of Political Ideas in the Fifties*, Harvard University Press, 1988, pp.72–3.
7. West Germany was admitted later.
8. A point also noted by the British Labour politician John Strachey.
9. William Colby, quoted in Frances Stonor Saunders' *Who Paid the Piper? The CIA and the Cultural Cold War*, Granta, p.42.
10. Saunders, ibid., p.89.
11. Ibid., p.199.
12. Ibid., p.131.
13. Ibid., p.111.
14. Quoted in Saunders, *Who Paid the Piper?*, p.249.
15. Ibid., p.253.
16. Ibid., p.281.
17. Murray Friedman, *The Neoconservative Revolution: Jewish Intellectuals and the Shaping of Public Policy*, Cambridge University Press, 2005, p.33.
18. Ibid., p.362.
19. Andrew Kopkind, 'CIA: The Great Corrupter', *New Statesman*, 24 February 1967, quoted in Saunders, p.409.
20. Surviving elements, such as the CP, the Trotskyist Socialist Workers Party and the journal *Monthly Review*, were very marginal to the culture.
21. Anthony Crosland, *The Future of Socialism*, Jonathan Cape, 1956, p.37.
22. Ibid, p.517.
23. Ibid, p.195.
24. Saunders, *Who Paid the Piper?*, p.199.

25. Bell, *The End of Ideology*, p.48.
26. Ibid., p.305.
27. Ibid., p.123.
28. Ibid., p.303.
29. Ibid., p.296.
30. Ibid., pp.109, 80. The CIO (Congress of Industrial Organizations) appears in the index, but not the CIA.
31. Ibid., p.402. See below for the significance of 'the road to serfdom'.
32. Ludwig von Mises, *Socialism: An Economic and Social Analysis*, Jonathan Cape, 1951, p.64.
33. Ibid., p.70.
34. Ibid., pp.457–67.
35. Ibid., pp.470–5.
36. Ibid., p.485.
37. Ibid., pp.476–7.
38. Ibid., p.556.
39. F. A. von Hayek, *The Constitution of Liberty*, Routledge and Kegan Paul, 1960, p.397ff.
40. Ibid., p.529, n.2.
41. Ibid., p.409.
42. Ibid., p.405.
43. Ibid., p.400.
44. Ibid., p.257.
45. Ibid., p.264.
46. Ibid., pp.18–19.
47. Ibid., p.235.
48. Ibid., p.94.
49. Ibid., p.509, n.1.
50. Ibid., p.269.
51. Ibid., p.280.
52. Ibid., p.32.
53. Jim Tomlinson, *Hayek and the Market*, Pluto, 1990.
54. E. H. Carr, *What is History?*, Palgrave, 2001, p.85.
55. Perry Anderson, *English Questions*, Verso, 1992, p.71.
56. Ramin Jahanbegloo, *Conversations with Isaiah Berlin*, Peter Halban, 1992, p.71.
57. This rule, though a bedrock of scientific method, is open to possible abuse. See David Stove, *Popper and After: Four Modern Irrationalists*, Pergamon, 1982.
58. Karl Popper, *Unended Quest: An Intellectual Autobiography*, Fontana, 1976, p.33.
59. Ibid., p.107.
60. Francizek Draus (ed.), *History, Truth, Liberty: Selected Writings of Raymond Aron*, University of Chicago Press, 1985.
61. Ibid., p.74.
62. *Monthly Review*, December 1998.
63. Albert Camus, *The Rebel*, Penguin, 1962, p.218.
64. Draus, *History, Truth, Liberty*, p.129.

CHAPTER 8

1. Perry Anderson, 'Sweden, Mr Crosland's Dreamland', *New Left Review*, no. 7, January–February 1961, pp.4–12, (continued in *NLR*, no. 9). See also Donald Sassoon, *One Hundred Years of Socialism: The West European Left in the Twentieth Century*, I. B. Tauris, 1996, pp.157–8.
2. George Padmore (ed.), *History of the Pan-African Congress*, 1947, reprinted in Hakim Adi and Marika Sherwood, *The 1945 Manchester Pan-African Congress Revisited*, New Beacon Books, 1995.

3. https://kb.osu.edu/dspace/bitstream/1811/29990/1/1956%20Conference%20Proceedings. pdf
4. Although the centre acted to arbitrarily depose a communist government in Kerala.
5. African–Americans in the South had the option only of moving 'from a smaller ghetto to a larger ghetto', in the words of Martin Luther King.
6. Herminio Martins (review of Kenneth M. Stampp, *The Peculiar Institution*), *New Left Review*, no. 25, May–June 1964.
7. Daniel Bell, *The End of Ideology*, p.426. This appears in the 1988 edition of the book. He notes 'the expansion of civil rights' without reference to the nature of the process or acknowledgement of its neglect in the first edition.
8. Carl Oglesby, from the compilation he edited, *The New Left Reader*, Grove Press, 1969, p.208.
9. Walter Benn Michaels, 'What Matters', *London Review of Books*, vol. 31, no. 16, 27 August 2009, p.12.
10. Desmond King and Stephen Tuck, 'De-Centering the South: America's Nationwide White Supremacist Order after Reconstruction', *Past & Present*, no. 194, February 2007, pp.213–53.
11. Murray Friedman, *The Neoconservative Revolution*, Cambridge University Press, 2005, p.100.
12. Bell, *The End of Ideology*, p.427.
13. Simone de Beauvoir, *The Second Sex*, Pan Books, 1988.
14. Sheila Rowbotham, *Promise of a Dream: Remembering the Sixties*, Allen Lane, 2000.
15. Juliet Mitchell, *Woman's Estate*, Penguin, 1971, p.87.
16. Quoted in Barbara S. Tischler, 'The Refiner's Fire: Anti-War Activism and Emerging Feminism in the Late 1960s', in Gerard J. DeGroot (ed.), *Student Protest: the Sixties and After*, Longman, 1998, p.199. See also Daphne Patai, *Heterophobia: Sexual Harassment and the Future of Feminism*, Rowman & Littlefield, 1998.
17. Herbert Marcuse, *One-Dimensional Man: Studies in the Ideology of Advanced Industrial Society*, Beacon Press, 1964.
18. Varda Burstyn, 'The New Imperial Order Foretold' in *Socialist Register*, 2005, pp.1–22.
19. Theodore Roszak, *The Making of a Counter Culture: Reflections on the Technocratic Society and Its Youthful Opposition*, Faber, 1971, p.149.
20. It is worth noting that these two forms of cohabitation were never actually illegal in the UK, but before the 1960s public sentiment had made them unthinkable for all except the bohemian fringe.

CHAPTER 9

1. Although Bulgaria in 1945 actually proposed to join the USSR.
2. International brigaders, for example, and foreign communists living in the USSR.
3. From Robert V. Daniels (ed.), *A Documentary History of Communism*, vol. 2, *Communism and the World*, I. B. Tauris, 1985, p.147.
4. Zhdanov, quoted in *Modern Quarterly*, 2/2, Spring, 1947, p.104.
5. Daniels, *A Documentary History of Communism*, p.250.
6. Extracted in G. F. Hudson et al, *The Sino-Soviet Dispute*, *The China Quarterly*, 1961, pp.93–4.
7. Isaac Deutscher, *The Unfinished Revolution: Russia 1917–1967*, OUP, 1967, p.92.
8. Enver Hoxha (edited by Jon Halliday), *The Artful Albanian: Memoirs of Enver Hoxha*, Chatto & Windus, 1986, p.232.
9. Deutscher, *The Unfinished Revolution*, p.93.
10. Adam Westoby, *The Evolution of Communism*, Polity, 1989, p.258.
11. Reprinted in *Socialist Register*, 1971, pp.67–71. The editors of *New Left Review* for a time maintained a favourable attitude, as did Sartre.
12. In Hungary and Yugoslavia.

13. The Italian communists had previously concealed his writings to avoid their Stalinist condemnation.
14. Horowitz subsequently became an adherent of neoconservatism, and has published such titles as *Why I'm Not a Liberal*, *The Feminist Assault on the Military*, *Noam Chomsky's Jihad Against America*, *Liberal Racism* and *How the Left Undermined America's Security*.
15. Daniels, *A Documentary History of Communism*, p.329.
16. It included a German contingent – not a very tactful act.
17. Earlier in the year, Ceauçescu had been warmly welcomed on a state visit to Czechoslovakia.
18. Enver Hoxha commented of Brezhnev, 'let us give him his due: he is a comedian only in his eyebrows, while his work is tragic from start to finish'.
19. *24th Congress of the Communist Party of the Soviet Union March 30–April 9, 1971: Documents*, Moscow, 1971.

CHAPTER 10

1. John Cornwell, *Hitler's Pope: The Secret History of Pius XII*, Penguin, 2000.
2. Quoted in Julian Jackson, 'Homosexuality, Permissiveness and Morality in France and Britain', in Marcus Collins, *The Permissive Society and its Enemies*, Rivers Oram, 2007, pp.81–2.
3. See David Caute, *The Great Fear: The Anti-Communist Purge Under Truman and Eisenhower*, Secker & Warburg, 1978.
4. All quotes here are taken from www.freerepublic.com/focus/f-news/1205133/posts (last accessed July 2010), a website favourable to Goldwater.
5. *The Handmaid's Tale* is a feminist dystopian novel that envisages an America ruled by religious fundamentalism.
6. Russell Kirk, *The Conservative Mind from Burke to Eliot*, Faber and Faber (amended edition), 1954, p.317.
7. Ibid., p.345.
8. Ibid., p.380.
9. Ibid., p.386.
10. Ibid. pp.401, 407.
11. Ibid. p.442.
12. Ibid., p.366.
13. E. H. Carr, *What is History?*, Macmillan, 1961, p.32.
14. From an essay on John Locke in the *Cambridge Review*, quoted in Perry Anderson, *Spectrum: From Right to Left in the World of Ideas*, Verso, 2007, p.6.
15. Ibid., p.7.
16. From *Rationalism in Politics*, excerpted in Jerry Z. Muller, *Conservatism: An Anthology of Social and Political Thought from David Hume to the Present*, Princeton University Press, 1997, p.310.
17. Anderson, *Spectrum*, p.10.
18. Muller, *Conservatism*, p.297.
19. Anderson, *Spectrum*, p.21.
20. Ibid., p.27.
21. Japan recovered its formal sovereignty in 1952.
22. See Perry Anderson, 'Turkey', in *The New Old World*, Verso, 2009, pp.392–472.
23. Roger Griffin (ed.), *Fascism*, Oxford University Press, 1995, p.342.
24. General Humberto Delgado, who had the effrontery to seriously challenge Salazar's stooge candidate for President in 1958, was murdered for his pains.
25. Franco Ferraresi, 'The Radical Right in Postwar Italy', *Politics & Society*, 1988, vol. 16, no. 1, p.84.
26. Julius Evola, 'The True Europe's Revolt against the Modern World', in Roger Griffin, *Fascism*, pp.343–4.
27. Jordan was discredited when arrested for shoplifting women's underwear.
28. He denounced Eichmann's trial as Jewish malevolence.

CHAPTER 11

1. H. L. Robinson, 'The Downfall of the Dollar', *Socialist Register*, 1973, p.405.
2. Ibid., p.418.
3. The dramatic rise in unemployment could not be hidden even though large-scale statistical manipulation was practised.
4. Community rules did not prohibit public ownership, but placed it under severe restrictions.
5. Gary Dorrien, Transcript of lecture delivered at Union Theological Seminary, New York, 25 March 2009. Available at: http://www.tikkun.org/article.php/may_jun_09_dorrien (last accessed July 2010).
6. However, the Soviets also agreed to respect human rights, which was to hand a propaganda advantage to the West.
7. Hillel Ticktin, 'Towards a Political Economy of the USSR', *Critique*, no. 1, 1973. Further articles in nos 6 and 9 elaborate this thesis.
8. The East German Stasi were particularly notorious in this respect, giving the impression that one half of the population was spying on the other half.
9. Mary Buckley, 'Gender and reform', in Catherine Merridale and Chris Ward (eds), *Perestroika: The Historical Perspective*, Edward Arnold, 1991, p.67.
10. Ending in the execution of the ruler and his wife – on Christmas Day.
11. The communists who governed West Bengal were honest and popular, but could make little difference to polarised wealth and poverty.
12. In Bolivia, the government's collapse followed an attempt by the international company to which the water supply was privatised to stop citizens collecting the rainwater from their roofs.

CHAPTER 12

1. Francis Fukuyama, *The End of History and the Last Man,* Penguin, 1992.
2. Murray Friedman, *The Neoconservative Revolution: Jewish Intellectuals and the Shaping of Public Policy*, Cambridge University Press, 2005, p.101.
3. See Gore Vidal on John Updike, in *Selected Essays*, Abacus, 2007, ch. 11.
4. Perry Anderson, *Spectrum: From Right to Left in the World of Ideas*, Verso, 2005, p.9.
5. Catherine and Michael Zuckert, *The Truth about Leo Strauss*, Chicago University Press, 2006, lengthily excerpted at www.press.uchicago.edu/Misc/Chicago/993329.html (last accessed July 2010). The authors attempt to acquit Strauss of responsibility for the neo-conservatives; their argument is able, but rather disingenuous and not very convincing. Francis Boyle in 'My Alma Mater is a Moral Cesspool: Neo-Cons, Fundies, Feddies and the University of Chicago', *Counterpunch*, 2 August 2003, presents a damning if somewhat overheated indictment.
6. Ellen Meiksins Wood, *Citizens to Lords: A Social History of Western Political Thought from Antiquity to the Middle Ages*, Verso, 2008, p.5.
7. Anderson, *Spectrum*, p.9.
8. Scott Horton, 'Leo Strauss and the Iraq war', *Harper's Magazine*, July 2009, www.harpers.org/archive/2009/06/hbc-90005094 (published online 3 June 2009; last accessed July 2010).
9. Any reference to Indonesian massacres or the Khmer rouge is tactfully (and tactically) omitted.
10. Friedman, *The Neoconservative Revolution*, p.31.
11. Ibid., p.137.
12. Though not without opposition, as evinced in the movie *Wall Street*.
13. Friedman, *The Neoconservative Revolution*, p.179.
14. Ibid., p.37.
15. Glazer has since defected from neoconservatism.
16. Friedman, *The Neoconservative Revolution*, p.135.

17. Justin Raimondo, 21 September 2009, original.antiwar.com/justin/2009/09/20/irving-kristol-rip/ (last accessed July 2010). Raimondo is a most peculiar ideologue – although openly and proudly gay, he at one point supported Pat Buchanan, an aggressive homophobe.

18. Roger Scruton, *The Meaning of Conservatism*, 2nd edn, Macmillan, 1984, p.9.

19. Ibid, p.16.

20. Ibid, p.19.

21. Roger Scruton (ed.), *Conservative Thinkers: Essays from the Salisbury Review*, Claridge Press, 1988, from Scruton's 'Introduction' p.9. The essays, though including de Maistre and Bonald, avoid Maurras.

22. *Meaning*, p.58.

23. Ibid, pp.139–40.

24. Ibid, p.168.

25. Ibid, pp.170–4.

26. A comment by Andrew Gamble in *Marxism Today*, which *Conservative Thinkers* proudly displayed on its dust jacket.

27. Scruton, *The Meaning of Conservatism*, p.118.

28. Jim Wolfreys, 'The disposable heroes of hypocrisy', *International Socialism Journal*, Winter 2002, reproduced at www.pubs.socialistreviewindex.org.uk/isj96/wolfreys.htm (last accessed July 2010). A startling though not unsympathetic account of Lévy's domestic lifestyle is provided by Gaby Wood's profile, 'Je suis un superstar' in the *Observer* of 15 June 2003, available from www.guardian.co.uk/books/2003/jun/15/society (last accessed July 2010).

29. Thomas Sheehan, 'Paris: Moses and Polytheism', *New York Review of Books*, 24 January 1980.

30. Ibid.

31. G. Lardreau and C. Jambet, cited by Wolfreys, 'The disposable heroes of hypocrisy', *International Socialism Journal*, Winter 2002.

32. George Ross, 'Intellectuals against the Left: the Case of France', *Socialist Register*, 1990, p.207.

33. Wolfreys, 'The disposable heroes of hypocrisy', Winter 2002.

34. Ibid.

35. Ibid.

36. Ross, 'Intellectuals against the Left: the Case of France', 1990, p.201.

37. See Friedman, *The Neoconservative Revolution*, who is writing from a neoconservative viewpoint.

38. A satirical poster based on *Gone with the Wind* film publicity showed Reagan carrying Thatcher in place of Clark Gable and Vivien Leigh.

39. Adverts exhorting the public to 'Tell Sid!' featured in the campaign to sell shares.

40. This temporarily caused some of the neoconservatives to be annoyed with Reagan; they assumed that he would be outmanoeuvred.

41. Martin McCauley, *The Soviet Union 1917–1991*, 2nd edn, Longman, 1993, p.366.

42. Quoted in Catherine and Michael Zuckert, *The Truth about Leo Strauss*.

43. Margaret Thatcher, *Let our Children Grow Tall: Selected Speches 1975–1977*, Centre for Policy Studies, 1977.

44. Quoted in Friedman, *The Neoconservative Revolution*, p.185.

CHAPTER 13

1. The formal existence of other 'allied' parties was without significance.

2. The Indonesian CP was, however, in the Maoist camp. Brezhnev's expression of sympathy at the CPSU congress following the massacre was very perfunctory indeed.

3. Santiago Carrillo, *Euro-Communism and the State*, excerpted in Robert V. Daniels, *A Documentary History of Communism*, vol. 2, I. B. Tauris, 1985, p.375.

4. Carrillo's own authoritarian personality did not help.

5. *New Times* [CPSU international journal], 'Contrary to the Interests of Peace and Socialism in Europe', June 1977, in Bogdan Szajkowski, *Documents in Communist Affairs*, University College Cardiff Press, 1978, p.225.
6. Y. Sedov, 'Back to Eduard Berenstein? Ellenstein Discards the Mask', *New Times*, May 1978.
7. Ibid., pp.169–70.
8. *Our History Journal*, no. 18, November 1991.
9. Szajkowski, *Documents in Communist Affairs*, p.125
10. Sofia Kallistratova 'Comments on the Draft Constitution', in Szajkowski, *Documents in Communist Affairs*, p.152.
11. Ibid., p.160.
12. Mary Buckley, 'Gender and reform', in Catherine Merridale and Chris Ward (eds), *Perestroika: The Historical Perspective*, Edward Arnold, 1991, p.77.
13. Ibid., p.69.
14. Ibid., p.73.
15. Ibid., p.71.
16. Ibid., p.72.
17. Martin McCauley, *The Soviet Union 1917–1991*, 2nd edn, Longman, 1993.
18. Not only soviet-style economies are subject to this process. See Anthony Jay, *Management and Machiavelli*, Penguin, 1969.
19. McCauley, *The Soviet Union 1917–1991*, p.xvii.
20. Ibid, pp.376–7.
21. Even any mention of the Tiananmen Square events was forbidden.
22. Szajkowski, *Documents in Communist Affairs*, pp.174–85.
23. See Norman Cohn, *Cosmos, Chaos and the World to Come: The Ancient Roots of Apocalyptic Faith*, Yale University Press, 1993.
24. One of his key writings is titled *Socialism Utopian and Scientific*.
25. Marcel Liebman, *Leninism under Lenin*, Merlin, 1975.

CHAPTER 14

1. McCarthy found it expedient to have a Jewish attorney, Roy Cohen, at his service.
2. Around 80 people were killed on this occasion.
3. Testimony by Gladio agent Vincenzo Vinciguerra, in Chris Floyd, 'Sword Play: Attacking Civilians to Justify "Greater Security"', 29 February 2005, available from: www.prisonplanet.com/articles/february2005/290205swordplay.htm (last accessed July 2010). Even Sweden and Finland were not exempt; see Daniele Ganser, *NATO's Secret Armies: Operation Gladio and Terrorism in Western Europe*, Frank Cass, 2005.
4. Ibid.
5. Adolfo Morganti, 'The European Genius and the Rediscovery of the Sacred', 1983, in Roger Griffin, *Fascism*, Oxford University Press, 1995, pp.358–9.
6. Most syndicalists, however, joined the communist movement.
7. Alan Berger and Globe Staff, 'Russia's bad dream: Zhirinovsky's fascism is not an isolated phenomenon', *Boston Globe*, 19 December 1993.
8. Alain de Benoist and Charles Champetier, 'The French New Right in the Year 2000', available from: home.alphalink.com.au/~radnat/debenoist/alain9.html (last updated November 2005; last accessed July 2010).
9. Ibid.
10. Stewart Home, 'Danger! Neo-folk "musician" Tony Wakeford of Sol Invictus is still a fascist creep!', 28 July 2008. Available from: www.stewarthomesociety.org/wakeford.html (last accessed July 2010).
11. Roger Griffin, *Fascism*, p.348.
12. Ibid.
13. Endeavours to establish a Scottish or Welsh presence came to nothing.

14. Horacio Verbitsky, *The Silence*, excerpted by openDemocracy website at www. opendemocracy.net/democracy-protest/catholicchurch_2709.jsperbitsky as 'Breaking the silence: the Catholic Church in Argentina and the "dirty war"'.
15. Ibid.
16. Ibid.
17. Ibid.
18. Including in torture techniques.
19. Mike Reynolds, 'Faith-based fascists bridging the waters', *Searchlight*, June 2004.
20. ADL website, 'Extremism in America'.
21. Ken Adachi, 'The New World Order (NWO): An Overview', *Educate-Yourself*, last updated 2 June 2010, available from: http://educate-yourself.org/nwo/ (last accessed July 2010).
22. See Achin Vanaik, 'India's New Right', *New Left Review*, no. 9 Second Series, May/June 2001, pp.43–67

CHAPTER 15

1. See Giovanni Arrighi, *The Long Twentieth Century: Money, Power, and the Origins of Our Times*, Verso, 1994.
2. Francis Fukuyama, *The End of History and the Last Man*, Penguin, 1992, p.211.
3. Ibid., p.304.
4. The *Reader's Digest* in the 1950s speculated on the possibility of such an outcome. I forget what solution it proposed.
5. Fascist-minded nationalists in the former USSR have used a flag identical to that of Nazis, with a black hammer and sickle replacing the swastika.
6. The armed minority nationalist movements in Northern Ireland and the Basque country, though formidable, were contained.
7. Montenegro broke away some years later.
8. It has been suggested that the German government encouraged the breakup.
9. Such as attacks on plantations of genetically modified crops.
10. Likewise, the Reichstag Fire gave Hitler the opportunity to entrench his not-yet-consolidated regime.
11. Such as Fairfield Osborn's *Our Plundered Planet*, 1948, and Rachael Carson's *Silent Spring*, 1962. (A pulp science-fiction novel of 1953 envisaged an environmental movement called 'the Greens'.)
12. The author is currently a member.
13. Of late though, Die Grünen has entered coalitions with right-wing parties, as have the Irish Greens.
14. As any search of the Internet will reveal.
15. See Norman Cohn, *The Pursuit of the Millennium: Revolutionary Millenarians and Mystical Anarchists of the Middle Ages*, Oxford University Press, 1957.

Index

Printed in Great Britain
by Amazon

39668822R00169